[redacted]

Egypt and the Fertile Crescent 1516-1922

A Political History

P. M. HOLT

*Professor of Arab History in
the University of London*

Cornell Paperbacks

Cornell University Press

ITHACA AND LONDON

Published in the United Kingdom by Cornell University Press Ltd., 2-4 Brook Street, London W1Y 1AA.

First published in the United States of America 1966
by Cornell University Press
Second printing, 1967
First printing, Cornell Paperbacks, 1969
Second printing 1975

Library of Congress Catalog Card Number 66-18429
International Standard Book Number 0-8014-9079-0
Printed in the United States of America

Contents

Preface

The contemporary importance of Egypt and the countries of the Fertile Crescent is reflected in a large and constantly increasing body of publications, dealing with their history, their politics and ideologies, their social and economic development. Much of what has been written has naturally concentrated on the most recent times, or has viewed these lands from the outside, as pawns in the diplomatic and strategic designs of the great powers.

This book seeks to fill a gap in the available writing on the region. It lays emphasis on internal developments, rather than on external relations. By treating in more detail than has been done previously (except in specialist monographs) the important but neglected period which lies between the Ottoman conquests in the sixteenth century and the impact of Europe, three hundred years later, it aims at setting the recent history of these Arab lands in a wider perspective. Thus, my hope is that it will be of use to the reader who needs to know the outlines of the political history of the region as a framework for the understanding of the present day, or as an introduction to more intensive studies.

My thanks are due to my colleague, Professor Bernard Lewis, who read the book in draft and made many helpful suggestions, in particular clarifying certain matters of Ottoman history.

School of Oriental and African Studies P. M. HOLT
University of London
February 1966

Abbreviations

Antonius	George Antonius, *The Arab awakening*
BSOAS	*Bulletin of the School of Oriental and African Studies*
Hurewitz	J. C. Hurewitz, *Diplomacy in the Near and Middle East*
JAH	*Journal of African History*
JRAS	*Journal of the Royal Asiatic Society*
Zeine	Z. N. Zeine, *The struggle for Arab independence*

Acknowledgement

We are indebted to the Controller of Her Majesty's Stationery Office for permission to reproduce an extract from Command Paper *Cmd 5957—Palestine* (*Miscellaneous No. 3 1939*).

List of Maps

Egypt and the Fertile Crescent 1516–1922

Introduction: The Geographical, Social and Historical Background

The Geographical and Social Background

Egypt and the Fertile Crescent may be divided into three main areas of settlement, each with its distinct characteristics. The first of these is the lower valley of the Nile, north of the First Cataract, just above Aswān, which forms the gateway to Lower Nubia. The valley from Aswān to the Mediterranean has since ancient times been united under one administration, and has on recurrent occasions formed an independent state. Nevertheless, the geographical distinction between Upper Egypt, the narrow strip of fertile land watered by the annual flood, and Lower Egypt, the expanded and densely populated plain of the Delta, has been reflected in a tendency towards separation in periods of anarchy or weak government. At such times, Upper Egypt has been the refuge of enemies of the rulers seated in the Delta, an asylum both remote and secure until the nineteenth century.

Throughout history, Egypt has depended on the Nile flood, and this remains true today, even though dams and irrigation works have removed much of the old insecurity. Down to the nineteenth century, the provisioning of Egypt, and especially of Cairo, the capital, was precarious indeed. An excessively high Nile could cause severe damage, but more ominous and more usual was an insufficient flood. This set in motion a cycle of events frequently noted by the chroniclers: dearth and famine, the influx of starving people into Cairo, then epidemic disease, bringing high mortality.

The eastern Fertile Crescent, forming broadly the modern Iraq,[1] resembles Egypt in its dependence on flood-waters for the livelihood of its peoples. There are, however, certain differences. The floods of the

[1] In classical Arabic usage, al-ʿIrāq signified the Tigris–Euphrates valley from Takrīt to the Persian Gulf. From Takrīt northwards (i.e. ancient Mesopotamia) it was called al-Jazīra. The use of the term Iraq to cover both these regions dates from the establishment of the Iraqi kingdom after the First World War. As a matter of convenience, 'Iraq' or 'the Iraqi provinces' will be used in this work as a synonym of the eastern Fertile Crescent.

Tigris and the Euphrates are neither so regular nor so amenable to control as those of the Nile. Their exploitation depends on an elaborate system of canals, and this in turn on the maintenance of stable political conditions. Since the decline of ʿAbbasid power in the high Middle Ages, such conditions have rarely been present over long periods: Iraq has been much more liable than Egypt to administrative fragmentation, while, during the period studied in this book, it formed a border region between the mutually hostile Ottoman and Persian states. Moreover, the Iraqi provinces included also the mountainous country of the north-east, inhabited by the indocile Kurdish tribes, as well as the extensive marshlands of the lower Euphrates and Tigris, with an amphibious Arab population. Baṣra, at the head of the Shaṭṭ al-ʿArab, has tended to link its history with the Persian Gulf rather than with Mesopotamia.

The western Fertile Crescent[1] is in marked contrast to the eastern arc. It has neither great rivers nor wide plains, but is characteristically a region of broken highlands, dependent on Mediterranean rainfall rather than on irrigation for the greater part of its agriculture. The region can be subdivided into four parallel zones, running roughly from north to south. First comes the Mediterranean coastal strip, broadening in places to a plain, and punctuated by the sites of cities, from ancient Tyre and Sidon to modern Beirut and Tel Aviv. Pressing on this is the coastal range, rising from Jabal Anṣāriyya in the north to the heights of Mount Lebanon, and subsiding again to the highlands of Galilee, Samaria and Judaea. To the east lies a succession of river valleys: in the north the Orontes (Nahr al-ʿĀṣī), in the centre, the Leontes (al-Līṭānī), while the great southern depression contains the Jordan, the Dead Sea, and the Wādī al-ʿAraba, running down to the Gulf of ʿAqaba and the Red Sea. Eastwards again is another highland strip, most marked in the Anti-Lebanon range, which slopes gradually into the Syrian Desert (*Bādiat al-Shām*) between the two arms of the Fertile Crescent.

These areas of settlement have, throughout history, been linked together, and connected with the outside world, by great arterial routes. Over the centuries, the actual tracks followed by the caravans of traders, or by armies on the march, have fluctuated with changing physical and political conditions, but in general the routes have remained to serve the unchanging needs of the region. From the Persian Gulf, by water or by land, or a combination of both, commerce has, since ancient times,

[1] The terms 'Syria' and 'the Syrian provinces' will be used in this book as a synonym of the western Fertile Crescent, except where otherwise indicated. The region is approximately that of the modern Syrian Republic, together with Lebanon, Jordan and Israel.

been carried into the eastern Fertile Crescent, and thence across the desert to the towns of Syria and the ports of the Mediterranean. The western Fertile Crescent has always possessed both strategic and economic significance as the link between the great river-valley settlements of the Tigris–Euphrates and the Nile, which at various times have been competitors for hegemony in the Near East. Here the most critical area has been in the Palestinian lowlands, and particularly Lower Galilee, where the route from the north-east and the route from Egypt across Sinai and up the Palestinian coast meet at the Plain of Jezreel and the Pass of Megiddo. Here the battle of Armageddon has been fought, not once, but on many occasions, from the time of Thothmes III to that of Allenby.

The Mediterranean seaports on the coasts of Egypt and Syria are so many doors giving access to a wider world. The Red Sea also has its ports, less celebrated, but some of them of great antiquity. Although the Red Sea trade was threatened by the Portuguese discovery of the Cape route, it recovered during the sixteenth century. After a decline in the two hundred years that ensued, a revival took place in the nineteenth century, and the opening of the Suez Canal brought prosperity, especially to Suez. On the Shaṭṭ al-ʿArab, the link with the Persian Gulf, Baṣra remained, even in decline, a place of some economic and political importance.

Certain inland towns fulfilled a rôle similar to that of the seaports, since they gave access to the lines of land communication with territories outside the region. From Baghdād, a route ran north-eastwards by Khāniqīn into the Zagros Mountains and Persia. North-westwards from Aleppo was the way to Anatolia and the heart of the Ottoman dominions. Damascus was the gateway to the Ḥijāz and the Holy Cities of Mecca and Medina. In Upper Egypt, Asyūṭ was the starting-point of *Darb al-Arbaʿīn*, 'the Forty Days' Route' to the Sudanese Muslim sultanate of Darfur.

Nowadays Egypt and the Fertile Crescent are the centres of a nationalism which sharply differentiates the Arabs from their Near Eastern neighbours, the Persians, the Turks and the Israelis. This is a recent phenomenon, and most of its development lies outside the chronological scope of the present book. Until the nineteenth century in Egypt and the Fertile Crescent, political nationalism did not exist. Group loyalties were strong, but they were not rooted in either territory or language—the two bases of modern nationalist ideology. The strongest bonds were among the members of a family and its extensions into a clan and a tribe.

Although in the larger tribes there may be a fictitious element in the genealogical traditions, the fact that diverse groups were subsumed under the legend of a common ancestry is itself an indication of the primacy of kinship in the social structure. It follows that nepotism was neither uncommon nor disapproved: rather it was an obvious device to ensure the smooth working and continuity of society and the administration.

A noticeable feature in the history of the region during the Ottoman period is the tendency of society to polarize in two rival factions. In Egypt there were the two groups of Saʿd and Ḥarām, which subsequently merged into the Faqāriyya and the Qāsimiyya. In Syria the factions of Qays and Yaman may be traced back ultimately to tribal confederations of the Arab Empire. In Lebanon the extinction of this ancient feud was followed by the emergence of a new factionalism between Yazbakiyya and Janbalāṭiyya. Polarization of this kind seems to have been latent at all times, but to have become an important political phenomenon when the formal machinery of government was inadequate to its task. Thus, the seventeenth and eighteenth centuries, when the Ottoman sultanate and administration were at their weakest, were the heyday of factional strife. It subsided again in the nineteenth century, as administration was strengthened and centralized by the Ottoman sultans and the viceroys of Egypt.

The most enduring loyalty to a group larger than the family or the tribe was that which was felt towards the religious community. The great majority of the people of Egypt and the Fertile Crescent were, of course, Muslims, but there were also important and widespread minorities of Christians and Jews, as well as more localized religious communities—the Druzes and Nuṣayrīs of the western Fertile Crescent, and the Yazīdīs of Jabal Sinjar. The significance of Islamic sentiment throughout the whole of the Ottoman period can hardly be overestimated. For the most part it conduced to the strengthening of the empire. As the head of an extensive and durable Muslim state, the Ottoman sultan had a claim on the loyalty of his Muslim subjects, which was perhaps almost unconsciously rendered until the empire was threatened, by the Shiʿites in Persia, and later by European and Christian powers. It is worthy of remark that Muslim rebels and dissidents, however far they might go in usurping the powers of the sultan, rarely challenged his title to paramountcy. Down to the First World War, even the Arab nationalists accommodated their political demands within the traditional and sheltering framework of the Ottoman sultanate. Among the Muslims there was indeed a group which was in principle irreconcilable: the Shīʿa of the Iraqi provinces and the western Fertile Crescent. Practically, they were only dangerous when there was a strong Shīʿī monarchy in Persia, and this was a condition infrequently fulfilled after the sixteenth century.

Within Muslim society, there was a network of more limited but more intense and usually more conscious loyalties to the shaykhs of the Ṣūfī orders. Since the Middle Ages Sufism, reconciled with Islamic orthodoxy, had been strengthening its hold on the Muslims. Its ascetic and mystical disciplines, its emphasis on the authority of living and dead saints as channels of divine power and ecstatic illumination, its group rituals and devotions, were attractive to Muslims of every degree of standing and education. The Ṣūfī guides and teachers were, moreover, accessible to their followers, unlike the scholars and canon lawyers who formed the official *ʿulamāʾ*. The great orders flourished in the towns and villages of the Near East, and fresh ones arose as new teachers syncretized the teachings of their predecessors, or founded autonomous branches.

The Christians of Egypt and the Fertile Crescent did not form a united community, but retained mutual prejudices and animosities derived from the early sects of which they were the attenuated remains. Even in the Byzantine period, the Orthodox Church, supported by the power of the emperor, had failed to impose itself on the majority of the native populations. Under Muslim rule, its adherents continued to dwindle, while the existence of a Greek hierarchy dominating an Arabic-speaking lower clergy and laity weakened the homogeneity of the Orthodox community. The schismatic and heretical churches, which, before the Arab conquest, appear to have been the vehicles of protest against the Byzantine Empire and the Orthodox Church, still had local followings of some importance, notably the Coptic Church in Egypt, and the Nestorian (or Assyrian) Church, in the Iraqi provinces. A third group, the Maronites, chiefly to be found in northern Lebanon, entered into communion with the Roman Church. The Christians included both townsmen and country-dwellers, such as the Coptic villagers in Upper Egypt, the Maronite peasantry of Kisrawān, and the Nestorian herdsmen and cultivators in Kurdistan and the eastern fringes of Iraq.

The Jews, by contrast, were almost exclusively an urban population, although they formed village communities in Galilee, Kurdistan and even Egypt. Many of the Jewish communities in Egypt and the Fertile Crescent were very ancient indeed, although, like the more recent

Christian groups, they had suffered erosion over the centuries through conversions to Islam. Persecution of the Sephardim, the Jews of the Iberian peninsula and Italy, caused an influx of refugees, which was at its height in the last decade of the fifteenth century. The Sephardim were very different from the indigenous oriental Jews. They had played an important part in the social, economic and political life of the Iberian peninsula under both Muslim and Christian rule. They had, to a considerable extent, been assimilated to European society, and Spanish continued to be their mother-tongue. The Ottoman Empire was to profit from their talents.[1]

Besides the Christians and the Jews, there were several smaller religious groups. The only one of these which had any real political importance was the Druzes, who were mostly to be found in the southern part of Mount Lebanon. From the Sunnī Muslim point of view, their faith was a heresy of a heresy, being derived from Ismāʿīlī Shiʿism, but ascribing godhead to the Fatimid caliph, al-Ḥākim (d. 1021). The Mountain provided a refuge for these extremists, as it did for the Maronites, and the Druzes became a closed community, well able both to defend their independence and to raid their more orthodox neighbours in the plains.

The population of these lands consisted of three distinct but interconnected societies: the townspeople, the rural cultivators, and the nomads. The towns were of diverse origins. Some were on very ancient sites, such as Damascus in its great oasis, an outpost of civilization on the fringe of the desert. Others, such as Baghdād and Cairo, had grown up around the palaces and garrisons of former dynasties. Others again, such as Jerusalem, Najaf and Karbalāʾ, were holy cities. The most prosperous towns in the Ottoman period were those which were at the same time administrative centres, and in a favourable situation for trade. The two things, indeed, went together, since trade was most secure in the immediate vicinity of effective administration. Thus, Cairo, Damascus, Aleppo, Mosul, Baghdād and Baṣra were both provincial capitals and commercial centres. The economic revival of Beirut and Acre was closely connected with their utilization as residences by local dynasts, and it is significant that at a later stage first Acre, then Beirut, became a provincial capital.

Three main groups may be distinguished amongst the townspeople: the agents of government, the religious functionaries, and the merchants,

[1] There was also an internal migration of Spanish-speaking Jews from Istanbul to Syria and Egypt, as men of business of the Ottoman governors.

craftsmen and artisans. The agents of government included, as well as the governor (in the provincial capital) and subordinate administrative officials, the bureaucracy and the garrison with its officers. The line between this group and the men of religion was not easy to draw, since some of the latter fulfilled administrative functions. The *ʿulamāʾ* or men of religion did not form a priestly class, distinguished by sacerdotal functions from the laity, but were essentially scholars, doctors of the *Sharīʿa*, the holy law of Islam. Among them were the judges (*qāḍīs*) and the *muftīs*, who gave authoritative decisions on points of law. The *ʿulamāʾ* generally had prestige and influence with both the holders of political power and the mass of the people: hence they were able to mediate between the two, and performed a valuable service in maintaining stability in times of crisis. Closely associated with the *ʿulamāʾ* were the local heads of the Ṣūfī orders, who were also very influential. In the principal towns, an officer known as *naqīb al-Ashrāf* derived importance from his function as registrar of the *Ashrāf*, or reputed descendants of the Prophet.[1]

After the Ottoman conquest of Egypt and the Fertile Crescent, the higher agents of government, the garrison troops, and the principal judges at least were usually Turkish-speaking subjects of the sultan, drawn from the older provinces of the Empire. There was, thus, an alien ruling élite, although this was no new phenomenon in these Arab lands. We shall see that, as time went on, the original situation was modified by the passage of power into the hands of indigenous groups and individuals, by the assimilation of the Ottoman troops to civilian townspeople, and by the recruitment of local forces. Moreover, in spite of the Ottoman veneer to the administration, Arabic-speaking Egyptians, Syrians and Iraqis continued to staff the bureaucracy, and to fill the ranks of the *ʿulamāʾ*.[2]

The bulk of the townspeople, engaged in trade and crafts, were as Arab after the Ottoman conquest as they had been before. Although individuals and families from the Turkish provinces settled in the Arab lands, the sultans made no attempt to colonize their new possessions with Turks. The bourgeoisie of the Arab towns had no formal share in political power or executive authority. No town councils existed in any part of the Ottoman Empire until they were imitated from European

[1] There is evidence that, in the sixteenth century at least, the *Ashrāf* enjoyed certain fiscal privileges, which they are unlikely to have lost in the ensuing period of Ottoman decline.

[2] Arabic-speaking *ʿulamāʾ* had been important in the Ottoman Empire even before the conquest of the Arab provinces, and they retained this importance thereafter.

models in the nineteenth century.[1] Yet the townspeople were not wholly unorganized or defenceless. Their membership of craft-guilds, which were closely associated with the Ṣūfī orders, gave them a corporate strength and tenacity. As the Ottoman administration weakened, the bourgeoisie further strengthened their position by establishing close links with the powerful and privileged organizations of the Janissaries and the *Ashrāf*. The physical structure of the towns gave security to their inhabitants. Constructed on no regular plan, each was an agglomeration of separate quarters, often each quarter within its own containing-wall. A quarter would house families of a common kinship, a common occupation, or a common minority-faith. In these circumstances, systematic policing was almost impossible, and, until the nineteenth century, was not attempted. On the other hand, the fragmentation of the urban dwellers worked against their regular combination for political and social purposes. Riots were not infrequent, especially in times of dearth, but the passions of the mob were allayed with the stoning of a judge, or the removal of an unpopular governor. The political concepts of Western urban society were totally absent.

The villagers played even less part in history. They existed to serve the towns and the townspeople. Their crops fed the urban population. The taxes they paid, in cash or kind, were a principal source of revenue to the state. Since the sultans granted the villages in fiefs, or farmed out the taxes to agents known as *multazims*, they supported the military officers and administrative officials who were the principal recipients of these concessions. Unlike the feudal lords of Europe, the fief-holders and tax-farmers of the Ottoman Empire did not usually form a hereditary class—although there are exceptions to this in certain areas, such as Mount Lebanon, where special conditions obtained, and also in the eighteenth century, when a hereditary tendency appears. Neither did they reside on their estates, but in the great towns. This absentee landlordism, and the heavy drain of taxation, do much to explain the unprogressive and apathetic outlook of the cultivators. Not until the nineteenth century, when the traditional mould of society was being broken, and change was being imposed from outside and above, do we find the first outbreaks of rural revolt in Egypt, Lebanon and Iraq.

The areas of settlement in Egypt and the Fertile Crescent were fringed by vastly more extensive stretches of desert and semi-desert.

[1] In the Turkish provinces, the *a'yān*, or local notables, had functions in the towns partly analogous to those of town councillors, and their position had some degree of recognition from the government.

These were the home of the nomads, both the camel-rearing tribes, who penetrated the more remote and arid wastes, and the pastoralists, herding sheep and goats, who moved on the borders between the desert and the town. Most of these nomads were Arabs (or, in the Western Desert of Egypt, also arabized Berbers), but in the Fertile Crescent there were Turcoman tribes following a similar way of life.[1] The nomads had their part in the economy of the region. They supplied the villagers and townspeople with animals and animal products, while the camel-owning tribes provided transport and guides for traders and pilgrims. For their goods and services they required payment—not only the produce and manufactures of the villages and towns, but also tolls levied on travellers to ensure their safe conduct, and protection-money obtained from villagers to avert raiding. For, until the nineteenth century, the nomads had always the advantage over the settled population, since they were ultimately inaccessible to even the finest troops. Nevertheless, there was no hard-and-fast line between the smaller nomads and the cultivators. Drought, disorders and oppression could drive the marginal cultivator to pastoralism; while the semi-nomad, given favourable conditions, could settle down as a farmer. The sedentarization of the tribes, and the conversion of the chiefs into landowners, dependent on the government, were two factors which played an important part in the ending of the nomadic threat in the nineteenth century.

These were, in very broad outline, some of the aspects of geography and society which were significant in Egypt and the Fertile Crescent during the Ottoman period. We must now briefly review the past history of the region, to see how it had assumed its predominantly Islamic and Arab character.

The Historical Background

The great expansion of the Arabs in the seventh Christian century, associated with the rise of Islam, resulted in the formation of an empire which included territories in Asia, Africa and Europe. When the Prophet Muḥammad died in 632 in Medina, the oasis-settlement which had given him asylum ten years previously, his successor, the Caliph Abū Bakr, held a precarious domination over the capital, over the cult-centre at Mecca, and over the tribes of the Ḥijāz. Tribes elsewhere in Arabia, which had recognized the hegemony of the Prophet in the last years of

[1] The geographical range of the Turcomans, very extensive in the sixteenth century, seems to have become increasingly restricted to the north of the Fertile Crescent as time went on.

his life, considered their allegiance to have been dissolved by his death, and Abū Bakr's short reign (632–4) witnessed a series of campaigns, the so-called Wars of Apostasy, to establish the suzerainty of Medina throughout the Arabian peninsula.

The political domination of the Muslims, thus established, had as its natural consequence the islamization of the Arabs as a whole. United, albeit loosely, under the authority of the caliph at Medina, and led by former Companions of the Prophet, the Arab tribesmen found their energies directed into new channels. Their inveterate tribal warfare was for a time suspended; their continuing love of raids and hunger for booty, now sanctified by the consciousness that they were the chosen vehicles of a new and final divine revelation, led them to press into the settled lands of the Fertile Crescent, where the frontier districts were inhabited by sedentary tribes of their own kin. Thus within the space of three years from the Prophet's death, the great empires of Byzantium and Sasanid Persia found themselves threatened in Syria by an obscure and apparently insignificant foe, whose headquarters lay in the remote and impenetrable deserts of Arabia.

A series of victories, which the Muslims might well regard as miraculous proofs of divine support, destroyed Byzantine power in Syria, and Sasanid power in Iraq, during the reign of Abū Bakr's successor, the Caliph ʿUmar (634–44). The conquest of Syria was followed by the penetration and subjugation of Byzantine Egypt, by fighting in Christian Nubia (which however remained unconquered), and by the beginning of the Muslim advance through North Africa into Spain. These however were later conquests. In the east, after the conquest of Iraq, the Arabs struck up into the Iranian plateau, and finally overthrew the Sasanid Empire. The Byzantines were spared this utter catastrophe. Although the Arabs acquired Syria, Egypt and North Africa, they failed to establish themselves in Anatolia as they did in Iran, and Constantinople, although several times attacked, did not fall to a Muslim ruler until the time of Sultan Mehmed the Conqueror in 1453.

It was as a result of this expansion, beginning in the reign of ʿUmar and resumed at intervals throughout the seventh and early eighth centuries, that the Fertile Crescent and Egypt became the Arab lands that they are today. At the outset, however, they were Arab only in the sense that they formed part of an empire headed by an Arab ruler, the caliph. The political and military élite were Arabs. Garrisons of Arab tribesmen were established here and there in the conquered lands in camp-cities such as Kūfa and Baṣra in Iraq, al-Jābiya in Syria, and al-Fusṭāṭ in

Egypt. This ruling élite enjoyed preferential taxation, and was supported by the booty of conquest and the revenues levied from the subject-peoples. Ethnic pride and state policy combined at first to keep the Arabs in their camp-cities, apart from the artisans and merchants of the ancient towns and the peasantry of the country-side. Far from the Arabs seeking to impose Islam at the point of the sword on their Christian, Jewish and Zoroastrian subjects, they regarded it, in the early years of their empire, as an ethnic religion. The older faiths, however, received a degree of toleration which contrasted favourably with the treatment accorded to heretical sects by the former régimes.

This state of affairs did not last, for the conquerors began to merge into their subject-peoples. The Arab ruling and military élite quickly lost its unity. Under the fourth caliph, ʿAlī (656–61), civil war broke out among the Muslim Arabs themselves. The upshot was that the caliphate passed to the governor of Syria, Muʿāwiya, a scion of the Umayyad clan which had been one of the dominant members of the pre-Islamic oligarchy of Mecca. For ninety years the Umayyad dynasty held the caliphate. Their régime has been called 'the Arab kingdom', since it represented on the whole the domination of the Arab political and military élite in the Muslim Empire. This Arab domination was, however, weakened both by internal faction (the emergence in a new and aggravated form, and upon a wider scale, of those tribal hostilities which Islam seemed at first to have extinguished), and by the development of a numerous depressed class of Muslims, mostly non-Arabs, the *mawālī*, who were admitted into the master-religion as it were on sufferance, as clients of those Arab tribesmen who alone at this period were regarded as first-class Muslims.

The spread of Islam among the subject-peoples was facilitated by several factors. The boundaries between Islam and the older monotheistic faiths were not at this time as clear-cut as they were to become in later centuries, after generations of scholars had laboured to develop a subtle and comprehensive system of law and theology for the new religion. As in Negro Africa today, the few and precise basic demands of Islam, the simplicity of the cult, and the prestige attaching to it, would attract numerous converts. Furthermore, adherence to Islam promised relief in taxation, and entry into the governing élite. For these last reasons, the Umayyad régime was generally unsympathetic to converts, and the fiscal problem which they created was one which successive rulers failed to solve. Nevertheless, the process continued, and by the middle of the eighth century the *mawālī* constituted a serious social and political problem. The spread of Islam among the subject-peoples was inevitably accompanied by some measure of arabization, since Arabic was the language of the new revelation. The government also hastened the process of arabization, when the Caliph ʿAbd al-Malik (685–705) established Arabic as the language of administration in place of Greek and Persian, which had hitherto been used in the former Byzantine and Sasanid provinces respectively.

The Umayyad period (661–750), then, witnessed the beginning of the arabization and islamization of the empire. Although enfeebled by internal faction and menaced by the increase and discontent of the *mawālī*, the Muslim Arab élite still held on to political power. In the middle years of the eighth century, a revolution overthrew the last Umayyad caliph, Marwān II (744–50), and transferred the centre of gravity of the empire from Syria to Iraq, where a new capital was established at Baghdād. In consequence of this, the Arabs were forced to share, then to lose, their possession of power. The Umayyads were supplanted by another family, the ʿAbbasids, descended not merely from Quraysh of Mecca like their predecessors, but from the Prophet's own clan, Banū Hāshim. But in reality the revolution resulted in far more extensive political changes. It had been long prepared by a propaganda which played on the rivalries between Arab factions, and between the Arabs and the *mawālī*, and attained its first successes in the remote frontier-province of Khurāsān, in north-eastern Persia. The rebel forces, composed both of Arab colonists and *mawālī*, gained Khurāsān, advanced westwards, and, having defeated Marwān II, installed the first of the new dynasty as caliph.

With the coming to power of the ʿAbbasids, the star of Arab domination in the Muslim Empire began to set. To the end, the Umayyad caliphs had retained, although to a diminishing extent, something of the quality of Arab tribal shaykhs, gaining their ends by diplomacy rather than force, relying on their Syrian Arabs as the chief support of their rule, and exploiting, to maintain their hegemony, the factionalism which the tribesmen had carried from the Arabian peninsula on to the wider stage of the empire. The ʿAbbasids, on the other hand, had been brought to power by a movement in which the *mawālī*, especially the Persians, had played a large part, and the *mawālī* were the principal beneficiaries of the change of régime. Henceforward, except socially, Arab descent counted for little; the favour of the caliphs was bestowed on all those of their subjects, irrespective of ethnic origins or seniority in Islam, who could usefully serve them. The new capital, Baghdād, situated not far from the ruins of Sasanid Ctesiphon, symbolized the transformation of the caliphate into an oriental despotism, working through a numerous and efficient bureaucracy, and protected by a garrison of Khurāsānī guards. Meanwhile, the old camp-cities lost their *raison d'être*: they developed into great civilian towns, populated by merchants and artisans, while the descendants of the Arab tribal warriors fused with the mass of townspeople and peasants, or reverted to their former nomadism.

For about eighty years a succession of powerful 'Abbasid caliphs ruled from Baghdād. The greatest of them was the second, al-Manṣūr (754–75), the builder of the city and the real founder of the dynasty. Less able and less successful, but better known to modern Europeans, was the Caliph Hārūn al-Rashīd (786–809), the contemporary of Charlemagne. Already in his time symptoms of declining ʿAbbasid power began to show, and during the ninth century the caliphate shrank to a shadow of its former self.

A striking phenomenon of this period of decline in the ninth century was the revival of Iranian power and culture. Not only had the ʿAbbasid caliphate been deeply influenced by Persian political traditions, but this century saw the resurgence of autonomous dynasties on Iranian territory. In 945 one such family, the Buyids, intervened in the troubled politics of Iraq, and for over a century Buyid princes ruled in Baghdād as mayors of the palace to the ʿAbbasid puppet-caliphs. Ironically, the Buyids belonged to the Shīʿa, the minority group of Muslims who denied the legitimacy of the ʿAbbasid caliphate, and asserted that only the descendants of the Caliph ʿAlī had the right to the headship of the Muslim community.

The authority of the caliphs had crumbled also in the western provinces of the Muslim Empire. Henceforward Muslim Spain and North Africa had their own political histories, often closely linked together, but distinct from that of the ʿAbbasid caliphate. Two gubernatorial dynasties, each short-lived, the Tulunids and Ikhshidids, ruled Egypt for the greater part of the period from 868 to 969.

The first autonomous dynast in Egypt, Aḥmad ibn Ṭūlūn, represented a new ethnic element, which, for a millennium to come, would play a dominant part in the eastern and central lands of Islam. He was by origin a Turk, whose father had been sent in the tribute of slaves from Central Asia to the court of the ʿAbbasid caliph. Turkish slave-soldiers, converted to Islam, formed an increasingly important part of the caliphs' forces from the time of al-Muʿtaṣim (833–842), or even earlier. Within the course of a few decades they assumed the pretensions of a praetorian guard, dominating the capital and the court. In the tenth century their power was broken by the Buyid mayors of the palace, who substituted an Iranian for a Turkish military régime, but a century later the caliphate was to pass under a new Turkish domination with the coming of the Seljuks.

Unlike their predecessors of the ninth century, the Turks who entered the lands of Islam under the hegemony of the family of Seljuk were free tribal warriors. Coming from the steppes of Central Asia, they over-ran and dominated the Iranian plateau, and then, in 1055, extinguished the rule of the Buyids in Iraq itself. Their chief, Ṭughril Beg, did not seek to destroy the venerable and impotent ʿAbbasid caliphate, but was content to govern in its name, with the new title of *sulṭān*.[1] The dynasty of the Greak Seljuks, so established, ruled effectively from Baghdād until 1092, when the assassination of the great Persian minister, Niẓām al-Mulk, and the death of his sultan, Malik Shāh, in the same year, was followed by the fragmentation of the Seljuk empire.

Although the Great Seljuks had given the eastern Muslim lands a degree of political unity which had been lost since the eighth century, their power was neither effective nor recognized in the Muslim West. There, already in the previous century, two rival dynasties had disputed with the ʿAbbasids the title of caliph. In Spain, the Umayyad ʿAbd al-Raḥmān III declared himself caliph in 929. Muslim Spain, however, for all its attractive culture and intellectual brilliance, was politically a world in itself, somewhat peripheral to the affairs of the Islamic peoples as a whole. A far more serious rival to the ʿAbbasids, and to the soldier-statesmen who ruled in their name, was the Fatimid caliphate, which had been brought to power in North Africa early in the tenth century, by a highly organized conspiratorial organization, of extreme Shīʿī ideology. In 969 Egypt fell to the Fatimids, who transferred their capital to Cairo[2] and extended their authority over Syria and the coastal lands of the Red Sea. This was the most serious challenge from within Islam that the Sunnī majority of Muslims ever faced.

Although the Fatimid caliphate had passed its prime when the Great Seljuks ruled in Baghdād, its control of Syria led to conflicts between the two powers. The political rivalry was combined with, or masked by,

[1] The word is originally an Arabic abstract noun, meaning 'power'.

[2] Cairo (*al-Qāhira*) was founded in 969 by Jawhar, the Fatimid general who conquered Egypt from the last Ikhshidid ruler. The original city of Jawhar stood near the sites of two older capitals, al-Qaṭāʾiʿ, founded by Aḥmad ibn Ṭūlūn, and al-Fusṭāṭ, the camp-city of the Arab conquerors.

religious opposition, since the Seljuks were ardent Sunnīs, and vicegerents of the Sunnī ʿAbbasid caliphs. In the struggle, Syria played a rôle which had already been foreshadowed in the previous century, and was subsequently to be resumed on various occasions: that of a territory disputed between a power seated in the Nile valley and a rival established in the plains of Iraq.

The Syrian front was, however, less important to the Seljuks than the Anatolian front, where they encountered the military power of the Byzantine Empire. A victory won by the Seljuk sultan at Manzikert in Armenia (1071) was followed by the collapse of Byzantine resistance, and the inundation of the Anatolian plateau by Turkish tribesmen. In time the Byzantines succeeded in a partial stabilization of the front, and regained control of western Anatolia, but the centre and east, which had, for over four centuries, resisted the impact of Arab Islam, were forever lost, and began to assume the Muslim and Turkish character which is theirs to this day. The Turkish breakthrough had been an unplanned tribal movement, not a deliberate conquest, but the newly acquired territories were brought within the Seljuk political sphere by the establishment of a dynasty, the Seljuks of Rūm,[1] which had its capital at Konya, and long survived the parent family in Iraq.

While the extension of Seljuk rule deep into Anatolia was bringing Islam into territories that had long been Christian, elsewhere the Muslim tide was on the turn. The Norman conquest of Sicily, and the first major successes in the Christian *Reconquista* of Muslim Spain, both in the later eleventh century, were shortly followed by a still more audacious attack by Western Christendom on Islam—the Crusades. These wars, and the feudal states which they established on the Syrian littoral, bulk large in the histories of medieval Europe. To the Muslims, they appear in rather different proportions. The First Crusade (1097–9) assisted the Byzantines to re-establish their hold over western Anatolia against the Seljuks. It broke on Syria at a time of extreme political weakness, when both the Fatimid and the Great Seljuk régimes, which disputed its possession, were far gone in decay. It established a chain of petty feudal principalities, the head of which was the kingdom of Jerusalem. But these Crusader states were little more than garrison-outposts of feudal Europe, and their existence was in jeopardy from the moment that men of adequate military and organizing ability appeared in the

[1] *Rūm* (from *Rhomaioi*) meant in classical Arabic usage the (Byzantine) Greeks, as heirs of the Roman Empire. It was applied by extension to the lands they ruled, hence, particularly, to Anatolia.

neighbouring Muslim states, which developed out of the debris of the Seljuk Empire.

In 1144, the capital of the Crusader state of Edessa fell to Zengi, the Turkish regent[1] of Mosul. Later in the century, Saladin (Ṣalāḥ al-Dīn), a Kurdish general whose family rose to power as vassals of Zengi's son, made himself master of Muslim Syria and Egypt, where he extinguished the feeble Fatimid caliphate. He led the Muslim reconquest of the Crusader states. Jerusalem was retaken in 1187, and the Third Crusade failed to regain it for Christendom. Although when Saladin died in 1193 the Crusader states still retained the ports and considerable coastal areas of Syria, their power was on the wane, and during the course of the following century they were gradually liquidated.

Although the Crusades had been a troublesome and humiliating episode in Muslim history, they were far less important in their range and in their lasting effects than another invasion which fell upon the Islamic lands at the very time when the Crusader states were being reabsorbed. This was the coming of the Mongols, another steppe-people. United under the rule of Chingiz Khan in the opening years of the thirteenth century, the Mongol tribes were launched on a series of conquests from their Central Asian homeland which resembled in rapidity, and exceeded in extent, the Arab victories, six hundred years before. This is not the place to describe the campaigns which gave Chingiz Khan northern China and brought Mongol tribal armies into Russia and eastern Europe. Although Muslim Central Asia was conquered and Persia itself invaded during the reign of Chingiz Khan, the heartlands of Islam remained untouched until the great expedition of the Mongol prince, Hulagu. The campaign culminated in the siege and capture of Baghdād in 1258. When the ancient capital fell, the ʿAbbasid caliph was put to death.[2] So ended a dynasty which for over half a millennium had held at least the nominal headship of the greater part of the Muslim world. Nowadays, in popular historical writing, the fall of Baghdād is sometimes taken to mark the end of Arab greatness. This gives the date a spurious and artificial importance. Exclusive Arab control of the Muslim Empire had ended with the overthrow of the Umay-

[1] Zengi held the Turkish title of *atabeg*, which was originally given to guardians of Seljuk princes. As the minor Seljuk dynasties which resulted from the fragmentation of the Seljuk Empire became weaker, the *atabegs* gained power and became in effect regents of the petty states. Zengi, like some others, actually suppressed the nominal Seljuk ruler but continued to use the title of *atabeg*.

[2] A nominal ʿAbbasid caliphate, with its seat at Cairo, was restored by the Mamluk sultan, Baybars, and existed until the Ottoman conquest of Egypt. These 'caliphs' were, however, powerless functionaries at the Mamluk court.

yads, and by the thirteenth century the Arab and arabized inhabitants of the Muslim heartlands had lost control over their own political destinies. The real masters of the Muslim world from Egypt eastwards were the steppe-peoples.

This situation was dramatically illustrated in the years which followed the Mongol invasion of Iraq. Hulagu had intended to continue his conquests westwards, but the way was barred by a strong military power, centred in Cairo and ruling both Egypt and Syria. This was the Mamluk Empire. After the death of Saladin, his dominions split up into a loose dynastic empire, controlled by different members of his family, the Ayyubids. In this congeries of autonomous states, frequently divided by warfare amongst themselves, the paramountcy was often, but not always, held by the Ayyubid sultans of Egypt, whose control of a rich well-defined territory gave them a secure basis for their power. The Mamluks[1] had begun as a *corps d'élite* of Turkish slave-soldiers, recruited from the steppes of what is now southern Russia, for the service of the sultan of Egypt. After the death of the last effective Egyptian Ayyubid, in 1250, the political control of Egypt passed to the Mamluk guards, whose generals seized the sultanate. Thus it was the Turkish Mamluk, Quṭuz, who organized the military resistance to the Mongol advance.

The decisive battle was fought in 1260 at ʿAyn Jālūt in Palestine. Hulagu himself was not present, and the tide of the Mongol invasion may in any case have been on the turn. An important part in the fighting was played by a Mamluk officer named Baybars, who, shortly afterwards, assassinated Quṭuz, and made himself sultan. Baybars, who ruled from 1260 to 1277, was the real founder of the Mamluk Empire. He established his rule firmly in Syria, holding back the Mongols to their Iraqi territories, and penning up the Crusader states within their diminishing coastal enclaves. From their central dominions of Egypt and Syria, the Mamluk sultans also exercised suzerainty over the Ḥijāz and its holy cities, and reduced Christian Nubia to a puppet-state. The Mamluk sultanate lasted for two centuries and a half, until it was overthrown by the Ottoman conqueror, Sultan Selim I, but at the end of the fourteenth century power passed from the original Turkish élite to Circassians, whom the Turkish Mamluk sultans had in their turn recruited as slave-troops.

As a result of Hulagu's conquests, the eastern part of the Muslim world, including the Arabic-speaking territories of Iraq, was incorporated in the vast dynastic empire of the Mongols. Although all parts of this

[1] The Arabic word *mamlūk* means 'a possession', hence 'a slave'.

empire owed allegiance to the remote Great Khan, they were in practice ruled as separate, autonomous territorial blocks by various dynasties stemming from Chingiz Khan. Hulagu was the founder of one such dynasty, the Ilkhans. The Mongol conquests had been accompanied by considerable devastation and bloodshed, which, supervening on the deteriorating political and economic condition of the eastern Muslim lands in the later ʿAbbasid period, resulted in the decline of these ancient centres of Islamic civilization. Under the Ilkhans, political unity was indeed re-established, but the new rulers were at first neither Muslims themselves, nor sympathetic to their Muslim subjects, and the oriental Christian sects, especially the Nestorians (who had co-religionists among the Mongols), had a brief Indian summer of prosperity and influence in governing circles. Gradually however the Mongols were absorbed by the peoples they had subjugated, and a considerable cultural revival took place in the Persian and Turkish lands. These eastern lands had already, as we have seen, been largely turcicized, and as the fusion of the two steppe-peoples proceeded the Mongol language gave place to Turkish, and the Mongol tribesmen and Ilkhans adopted Islam. In the fourteenth century, the empire of the Ilkhans fell to pieces, and the eastern Muslim lands reverted to the situation they had been in before the Mongol invasions—fragmented territories ruled by petty, transient dynasties. At the end of the fourteenth century they were briefly swept under the suzerainty of the last great conqueror coming from the steppes, Timur Leng, the leader of a powerful Turco–Mongol horde. After his death in 1405 the old fragmentation returned.

Very different was the history of the western Islamic world, shielded by Mamluk power from the Mongol threat. Here Islam continued to flourish. The great cities, especially Cairo, the Mamluk capital, grew in prestige as centres of Muslim power and civilization when the light from Baghdād flickered into exinction. In spite of recurrent crises over the succession of sultans (particularly under the Circassian Mamluks, who did not recognize any dynastic principle), a ruling élite of Turkish-speaking soldiers and an Arabic-speaking bureaucracy kept the Mamluk Empire in being. Islam even made some gains in this region, not only through the continuing conversion of the Copts of Egypt (a process which had been going on since the Arab conquest) but in consequence of the penetration of Christian Nubia by Arab tribesmen from Upper Egypt, and the consequent arabization and islamization of what we now call the northern Sudan.

By the end of the fifteenth century the Arab lands as we know them today had come into existence: a great belt of territory comprising the Arabian peninsula, the Fertile Crescent, the lower and middle sectors of the Nile valley, and the southern littoral of the Mediterranean. These lands, the peninsula excepted, were not Arab in the sense that their populations were wholly (or even perhaps largely) descended from the conquering tribesmen of the seventh century; they were Arab in that their inhabitants mostly spoke and wrote the Arabic language[1] and practised the religion of Islam. These two elements formed the basis of a common culture. Persia and the lands of the east, once conquered by the Arabs, shared this culture but did not belong to the great block of Arabic-speaking populations. Neither did Anatolia, which had been islamized by Turks, deriving the Islamic elements of their culture from Persian rather than directly from Arab sources. The term 'the Arab lands' is therefore, at the beginning of our period, a geographical term only, a somewhat artificial delimitation of a portion of the Islamic oecumene. Historically, its artificiality is demonstrated by the political situation of the eastern arc of the Fertile Crescent which, from ʿAbbasid times down to the sixteenth century, was linked with Persia, and sometimes indeed (as under the Ilkhans) formed a subordinate portion of an empire whose centre of gravity lay further east. The preceding survey will also have made it clear that from the collapse of the Umayyad caliphate down to the end of the Middle Ages the Arab lands never possessed political unity. In the sixteenth century they were to be in large part reassembled, not, however, deliberately or as an autonomous political unit, but fortuitously, under the suzerainty of the Ottoman sultans.

[1] Colloquial Arabic developed a large range of regional dialects, whereas the written language maintained a high degree of standardization, the norms being set by the Qur'ān and the literature of the golden age.

Part I The Ottoman Heyday

I

The Rise and Zenith of the Ottoman Empire

From the early sixteenth to the early twentieth century, Egypt and the Fertile Crescent were parts of the Ottoman Empire. Their history during these four centuries can only be properly understood within this Ottoman context. Although, as we shall see, individual provinces and local dynasts obtained a high degree of autonomy, these very developments resulted from factors affecting the empire as a whole: one might say that the state of the Arab provinces was a barometer registering the external and internal pressures upon the Ottoman sultanate. But the integration of the Arab provinces in the empire took place at a comparatively late stage of Ottoman development, when the character of the empire was already formed, and when its institutions had attained maturity. This fact helps to explain certain anomalies in the history of the Arab provinces, as compared with the older Ottoman possessions in Anatolia and Rumelia, and imposes upon us the necessity of surveying the political and institutional development of the empire up to the early sixteenth century.

By the later thirteenth century, Anatolia was in a state of flux. The power of the sultanate of Rūm was in decline, and the sultans had indeed been reduced to vassals of the Mongols. At the same time, the Mongol conquests further east had set on foot a movement of Muslim (mainly Turkish) peoples and warriors, who made their way to the western territories beyond Mongol control. Some of these entered the service of the Mamluk sultanate: others settled on the Byzantine march which formed the western fringe of the sultanate of Rūm. Here they were easily assimilated to the older-established frontiersmen, and they adopted without difficulty the traditional ethos of the Byzantine march: the love of warfare against their Christian Byzantine neighbours, with the prizes it offered of booty, land and prestige in this world, and the reward bestowed on martyrs in the world to come.[1] Out of this chaotic situation, there crystallized in the second half of the thirteenth century

[1] Border-warfare of this kind was known as *ghazā*, and the warriors who waged it as *ghāzīs*: both these are Arabic terms which were adopted by the Turks. Since the *ghazā* was against Christian opponents, it was regarded as holy war, i.e. *jihād*, another Arabic noun which passed into Turkish.

a number of small militant dynastic states, each consisting of the territory controlled by an emir, a leader of *ghāzīs*, fighters in the holy war. For a time they succeeded in expanding their lands, both at the expense of the Byzantines, and into older Muslim territory in consequence of the final disintegration of the Seljuk sultanate of Rūm about the beginning of the fourteenth century.

One of these emirates, but not originally one of the first rank, was founded in the north-western sector of the Byzantine march by a war-leader named Osman,[1] whence is derived the term Ottoman, applied to his followers, and then to the subjects of his dynasty. Later Ottoman legend traced the descent of Osman from Oghuz Khan, the eponymous ancestor of the Oghuz Turks, whose migration into the Muslim world had been led by the House of Seljuk; and depicted the Ottomans as a nomadic tribe, extruded into Anatolia in the thirteenth century by Mongol pressure. Modern historical scholarship has demonstrated that the prestige of the House of Osman rested on its deeds rather than its ancestry; and its followers, it is clear, were not a tribe but a heterogeneous collection of march-warriors, united by community of aim and advantage, rather than by the bonds of kinship.

Historical and geographical factors combined to assist the development of the Ottoman emirate. It occupied that sector of the march where Byzantine resistance was most prolonged. After the other emirates had expanded to their fullest possible extent, there was still work for the *ghāzī* frontiersmen in the service of the House of Osman. Moreover, in the Ottomans' rear, and easily accessible from their territory, lay the ancient towns which had been the centres of Seljuk Islamic culture, with its strongly Persian inspiration. From the old Seljuk territories came the religious teachers and jurists, who brought to the emirate the traditions of Islamic orthodoxy and administration, and the merchants who assimilated the newly conquered towns to the economic and social patterns of Islam. Thus the unruly, unorthodox *ghāzī* element in the state came to be balanced, and ultimately controlled, by the representatives of the ancient Islamic urban civilization.

In the work of state-building, in the sense both of territorial expansion and of the creation of a strong and well-administered polity, the rulers played a leading part. Unlike many other dynasties, the House of Osman produced for over two centuries a succession of energetic and, for the most part, remarkably able rulers, who were able to call upon the best

[1] Osman is usually regarded as the Turkish form of the Arabic 'Uthmān, but it may be a Turkic name assimilated by learned tradition to 'Uthmān.

elements in the state for their service but did not fall under the control of their ministers. Moreover, the Ottoman state, as it grew, remained a political unity. Unlike its Seljuk predecessor, it was not fragmented among cadet branches of the dynasty.

The principal rulers (known first as beys or emirs, later as sultans) and the main stages in the expansion of the Ottoman state up to the beginning of the sixteenth century may now be briefly surveyed. Osman, the eponymous founder of the dynasty and the state, died in 1326. In the same year, his *ghāzīs* achieved their first major conquest, the capture of the important Byzantine city of Bursa (Brusa), which forthwith became the capital of the dynasty. The reign of Osman's son, Orhan (1326–1360) saw the taking of Iznik (Nicaea), and the absorption of almost all that remained of Byzantine Anatolia. From this firm foothold, the Ottomans crossed the straits into Europe, at first as allies of a claimant to the Byzantine throne. The Gallipoli peninsula became the base for fresh advances into south-eastern Europe, or Rumelia, as it is more conveniently called.[1] Their principal opponents were the Serbs and Bulgars not the Byzantines, who by this time had lost almost everything except the name of empire, and controlled only their great metropolis and its Thracian hinterland. Murad I (1360–89), son and successor of Orhan, conquered Edirne (Adrianople) and other territory which encircled Constantinople from the north, and thereby also confronted Serbia and Bulgaria. On the field of Kossovo (1389) the power of the Serbs was crushed, although Murad himself was assassinated during the battle. The new Muslim threat to Christendom was countered by a crusade, which advanced through central Europe, only to be overwhelmed at Nicopolis on the Danube in 1396.

The victor of Nicopolis, Sultan Bayezid I (1389–1402), whom the Turks called *Yıldırım*, 'the Thunderbolt', began his reign brilliantly. Besides the conquests in Rumelia, the Ottoman rulers had been steadily increasing their possessions in Anatolia, at the expense of the other Turkish emirates. In 1354, Orhan had taken Ankara (Angora), now the capital of the Republic of Turkey. Murad I had acquired further possessions by war, marriage and purchase. By the beginning of the fifteenth century, almost the whole of Anatolia had fallen to the Ottomans, including the great emirate of Karaman, which, with its capital at Konya, regarded itself as the heir to the Seljuks of Rūm. Although the Ottoman state was still inspired by the *ghāzī* spirit, it had now acquired the

[1] Rumelia is derived from the Turkish *Rum-ili*, the land of the Greeks. For the significance of *Rūm*, see above, p. 15, n. 1.

dimensions and multi-national composition of an empire. The later conquests, of Murad I and Bayezid I, were less the result of the spontaneous activity of the *ghāzīs* than of an imperial policy carried out by a highly organized war-machine. The military basis of the Ottoman state was shifting from the freeborn, Muslim *ghāzī* warriors, to islamized slave-troops, recruited at first from the captives of war, obtained in the Balkan campaigns. Among these slave-troops the infantry-corps of Janissaries[1] acquired the greatest renown.

The steady development of the Ottoman state from a march-emirate into a world empire was however sharply interrupted at this point. The reign of Bayezid Yıldırım coincided with the period when Timur Leng was building up his own empire in the centre and west of Asia. The existence of the powerful military monarchy of the Ottomans on his western flank was intolerable to Timur. Having failed to obtain a profession of submission from Bayezid, he marched against him, having first devastated Syria to prevent intervention by the Mamluk sultanate. Bayezid, preoccupied with plans for the capture of Constantinople, allowed him to march as far as Ankara before bringing him to battle. The subsequent fight was disastrous for the Ottomans; many of their troops went over to the enemy, while Bayezid himself was made a prisoner, and subsequently committed suicide. Timur restored the old emirates in Anatolia, and then withdrew. He might well feel that he had rescued his empire from the Ottoman threat, not only by establishing the barrier of buffer-states in Anatolia, but also by having deprived the dynasty of its head, since the sons of Bayezid began to fight amongst themselves for the remnants of the Ottoman state.

In fact there can be no more ironical contrast than that between the rapid fragmentation of Timur's empire after his death in 1405 and the tenacity with which the Ottoman ruling élite reasserted itself and reintegrated the dismembered state. The battle of Ankara was followed by ten years of dynastic struggles from which Sultan Mehmed I finally emerged as the acknowledged sole ruler. The Rumelian territories provided a firm base from which the work of reintegration could be undertaken, and Edirne, significantly, took the place of Bursa as the capital. The chief architect of the new empire was Murad II (1421–51), under whom the principalities of western and central Anatolia were gradually re-annexed, although Karaman retained its independence. Meanwhile the recruitment of Christian slaves from the Balkans for the service of

[1] 'Janissary' is a corruption of the Turkish term *yeni cheri*, i.e. 'new troops'. See below p. 30.

the sultan was systematized, or reintroduced, by a regular levy of youths from the Slav peoples. This levy was known as the *devshirme* (Turkish, 'collection'), and, as we shall see, the *devshirme*-recruits came to provide the Ottoman state with its administrators and its most reliable soldiers.

The task of rebuilding and extending the Ottoman state was continued by Murad's son and successor, Mehmed II, who is known in Turkish history as Sultan Mehmed the Conqueror, since he achieved the feat of which the rulers of Islam had dreamed from its earliest days, the conquest of Constantinople. Two previous Ottoman sultans, Bayezid I and Murad II, had attempted to capture the metropolis, and had been compelled to withdraw. But on this occasion no vision of the All-Holy Mother of God appeared on the walls to cheer the despondent citizens and their ruler, and on 29 May 1453 the city of the Emperors became the third and final capital of the House of Osman. The significance of the capture of Constantinople[1] has in some ways been misrepresented. The city which Mehmed took was no longer the prosperous capital of a great empire, but a depopulated stronghold, the rulers of which had long held their few remaining shreds of territory as vassals of the Ottoman sultans. But by the conquest of 1453, the metropolis was rejoined to its lost lands: it could regain the prosperity to which its site and its long imperial traditions entitled it. The lustre of its acquisition, shining upon the Turkish dynasty that now ruled it, raised Ottoman prestige throughout the whole of Islam. Henceforward the Ottoman ruler was the sultan *par excellence*, the foremost ruler in Islam, and an object of fear and reverence even to those Muslims who lived outside his dominions. Within the Ottoman state, the conquest of Constantinople marks the final step on the road which led from the comity of free warriors in the *ghāzī* emirate to the autocracy of the great sultans, guarded by their *devshirme* troops, and served by their *devshirme* administrators.

Mehmed II, in his reign of thirty years (1451–81) achieved much beside this notable exploit. The Ottoman Empire, as the state may now truly be called, was expanded in the Balkans and in Greece. The Black Sea became an Ottoman lake. In the heart of Anatolia, the emirate of Karaman was again absorbed into the empire. Then came a period of intermission in the course of Ottoman conquests.

On the death of Mehmed II in 1481, a struggle over the succession began between his two sons, Bayezid and Jem. The former obtained

[1] The name Istanbul, sometimes applied to Constantinople after the Ottoman conquest, is a much older Islamic usage. Constantinople (in the form Kustantiniye) remained in use as the official Ottoman term.

recognition in Istanbul, and defeated Jem in two brief campaigns in Anatolia. Jem, however, escaped from his brother's dominions, and sought asylum with the Knights of St John in Rhodes. By them he was sent to Europe, where he died in 1495. During the fourteen years when Jem was held as a hostage in Christian Europe, Bayezid II dared not commit himself to any major campaign, for fear that the Christian powers might invade the empire and seek to place his brother on the throne. During Jem's lifetime, however, a war occurred which, although in itself indecisive, foreshadowed a major conquest of the next reign.

This was the first Ottoman–Mamluk war, and was a consequence of the expansion and consolidation of Ottoman power in eastern Anatolia. The two great military sultanates of the Ottomans and the Mamluks now confronted each other across the ill-defined border-region of the Taurus. Two petty dynastic states occupied key positions in the marches: that of the Ramazanoghlu, controlling the plain of Cilicia at the foot of the Taurus, and the Dulgadir of Albistan, further east, in the vicinity of Malatya, on the upper course of the Euphrates. In addition, the Mamluks even claimed a protectorate over Karaman, now integrated into the Ottoman Empire.

The dynastic politics of Albistan played a large part in stimulating the mutual hostility of the Mamluks and the Ottomans. Various princes of the House of Dulgadir had sought help from one or other of the two great powers to gain the throne of Albistan. In 1480 Mehmed II had installed as ruler a certain ʿAlāʾ al-Dawla, thereby acquiring for the Ottomans a degree of influence in Albistan which the Mamluks resented. When Mehmed died in the following year, the Mamluk sultan, Qāʾit Bāy, supported Jem against Bayezid. Incessant friction on the frontier broke into open warfare with an Ottoman invasion of Cilicia in 1485. Hostilities continued until 1490. The major military successes fell to the Mamluks and their local allies, in consequence of which ʿAlāʾ al-Dawla abandoned his Ottoman protector. The Ottomans, for their part, preoccupied with the problem of Jem, were never able to exert their full military strength. The peace-settlement of 1491 in effect recognized the *status quo ante bellum*, the Mamluk suzerainty over Cilicia being confirmed, while Albistan retained its precarious independence, although now within the Mamluk rather than the Ottoman orbit.

In 1512 Bayezid II was compelled to abdicate by his dynamic son, Selim, usually known by the epithet of 'the Grim'.[1] Selim and his

[1] The Turkish adjective usually rendered as 'grim' is *yavuz*, meaning inflexible, inexorable, stern.

successor, Süleyman the Magnificent (1520–66), set on foot the last phase of the great Ottoman conquests, with consequences for the Arab lands which will be seen in the next chapter.

We now turn from the political history of the development of the Ottoman state to an examination of its structure and of the institutions in which its strength lay. At the centre of the military and administrative organization stood the sultan himself, and it is impossible to over-estimate the importance of the unparalleled succession of strong and able rulers, from Osman himself, the founder of the dynasty, to Süleyman the Magnificent, in the sixteenth century. Two customary practices contributed to the efficiency and the security of the ruler. It was usual for the sultan to appoint his sons as governors of provinces in the empire: thereby the princes gained invaluable knowledge and experience in preparation for the eventual succession of one of them to the throne. But another custom, promulgated in a formal edict by Mehmed II, required the new sultan, on his accession, to put his brothers to death. The protracted trouble which Bayezid II suffered from the continued existence of Jem was an object lesson in the political desirability of this regulation. Nevertheless, the Ottoman dynasty remained on the whole remarkably free from the succession-struggles which contributed so largely to the instability of other Muslim states.

The Ottoman sultan was the head of a polity which, although it numbered many Christians among its subjects, was conceived of as being essentially and typically an Islamic state. As such, he inherited the classical functions of a Muslim ruler: to maintain and extend the boundaries of Islam, both externally by waging the holy war, and internally by maintaining the *Sharīʿa* as the pattern of justice, and by promoting the true Faith. The execution of these duties was committed to functionaries of various types, who constituted broadly a dual hierarchy, which have been denoted respectively as the Ruling Institution and the Learned (or Muslim) Institution.[1] This twofold élite was sharply distinguished by function from the mass of subjects.

The Ruling Institution, or military-political élite, had undergone, as we have seen, a marked change during the fifteenth century. At its inception, and during its early growth, the Ottoman state had been

[1] The concept of the Ruling and Learned (or Muslim) Institutions was introduced by A. H. Lybyer, *The government of the Ottoman Empire in the time of Suleiman the Magnificent*, Cambridge (Mass.), 1913, and was adopted by H. A. R. Gibb and Harold Bowen, *Islamic society and the West*, I, 1, London, 1950. It has recently been criticized as an over-simplification, and its inadequacy to the conditions of the eighteenth century demonstrated by N. Itzkowitz, 'Eighteenth century Ottoman realities', *Studia Islamica*, xvi, 1962, 73–94.

dominated by freeborn Muslim warriors, who, if not all Turkish by their ethnic origins, had been effectively turcicized by their integration into this ruling group. On the pattern of earlier Islamic states, and indeed by a natural expedient in the prevailing circumstances, this élite had been organized on quasi-feudal lines, being rewarded for its services and maintained by grants of land (*timars*). The most numerous class of freeborn warriors were the cavalrymen (*sipahis*). While this freeborn élite, with its quasi-feudal structure, continued to exist, although latterly in a tenuous condition, until the great administrative reforms of the nineteenth century, it was overshadowed from the fifteenth century by a new-model élite, recruited by the *devshirme* from the Balkan Christian youths, which provided the standing forces, and occupied the great offices in the capital and the provinces.

The *devshirme*-recruits formed the greater part of the group known as *Kapı kulları*—'Slaves of the Gate', i.e. of the sultan. The conscripts were carefully graded, the most intelligent of them being trained in the palace schools, and then passing through a period of service as pages in the sultan's household. This completed, they were eligible for the highest posts in the central and provincial administration. The majority of the recruits were given a different type of training, in the households of *sipahis* and in Istanbul, and were drafted into various departments connected with the service of the Imperial Household. Subsequently they were enrolled in the standing army, particularly in the corps of Janissaries. Troops so recruited and trained played an indispensable part in the great Ottoman conquests of the fifteenth and sixteenth centuries.

The elaborate and complex hierarchy of the Ruling Institution cannot be described here. At its head stood the grand vezir, the sultan's general representative in matters of state. Until the time of the conquest of Constantinople, the grand vezirs had been freeborn Muslims, but thereafter, complying with the rising importance of the *devshirme* élite and the growing tendency of the sultans towards autocracy, the office was (with some exceptions) conferred on a *Kapı kul*. The grand vezir was absolutely dependent on the sultan for his maintenance in power, but while he enjoyed his master's favour he had absolute authority over the Ruling Institution, although not over the Learned Institution or the Imperial Household.

The provinces of the Ottoman Empire were originally administered by members of the feudal élite known as *sanjak beys*,[1] one of whose

[1] *Sanjak bey* means 'lord of a standard', from the distinctive insignia of these officers. The Arabic equivalent, sometimes used as an alternative, is *amīr liwā'*.

principal functions was to muster *sipahis* for campaigns. Subsequently the authority of the *sanjak beys* was diminished. The original small provinces were grouped together in great administrative units, which came to be known at a later date as *eyalets*. The first of these, Rumelia, was formed in the reign of Murad I from the Balkan possessions held at that time. A second *eyalet* was subsequently made in Anatolia, and others were added as the empire increased in size. The governors of these great provinces were entitled *beylerbeys*[1] and bore the personal honorific of *pasha*.

The Ottoman Empire was essentially conservative in its administrative policy, and a characteristic activity of the sultans was the codification of norms of practice, both generally and regionally in the various provinces of the empire. Codes of this kind were known as *qānūns*. Their issue was not a legislative act in the usual sense, since a *qānūn* did not, at least in appearance, make innovations but merely confirmed precedent and clarified usage.

In the heterogeneous frontier-society of the early Ottoman state, little attention was paid to rigid Islamic orthodoxy. Nevertheless, as the state grew in power, and became the standard-bearer of militant Islam, the sultans displayed themselves increasingly as the protectors and supporters of orthodox belief and practice, until they finally assumed the position of the paramount Sunnī rulers of the western Islamic world. In their quality of defenders of the Faith, the Ottoman sultans enriched Istanbul and other Muslim cities with splendid mosques and other religious foundations. They also developed throughout their empire a regular hierarchy of officials connected with the cult, which in its completeness has no precedent in any eastern Islamic state, although it was foreshadowed under the Seljuks.

This hierarchy of the *ʿulamāʾ*, the jurists and theologians of Islam composed the Learned Institution. It included, besides the staff of the mosques, and the teachers in the theological schools, the judges in the *Sharīʿa* courts throughout the empire. At the lowest level were the ordinary *qāḍīs*, appointed to districts in which they not only served as judges, but also exercised the main administrative functions. In each of the two great provinces of Rumelia and Anatolia there was a separate and elaborate system of promotion and grading. Rumelia and Anatolia each had its own chief judge, or *qāḍī ʿasker*, who nominated the subordinate judges of the province. Besides the judges, there was another class of

1 *Beylerbey* means 'lord of lords', and is the Turkish equivalent of the Arabic title *amīr al-umarāʾ*.

jurists, the *muftīs*, whose function was to give authoritative opinions on points of law submitted to them.[1] Pre-eminent amongst these was the *muftī* of Istanbul, who, with the title of *shaykh al-Islām*, was recognized during the reign of Süleyman the Magnificent as the head of the Learned Institution. The rôle of the *shaykh al-Islām* was of great importance, since it was to him the sultan had recourse in framing a *qānūn*, in order to ensure that its provisions did not contravene the *Sharīʿa*.

The Ottoman conquests, especially in the Balkans, had given the sultans a large number, even (before the acquisition of the Arab provinces) a majority, of non-Muslim subjects, both Christians and Jews. The sultans did not attempt to force Islam upon the mass of these people, although the *devshirme*-system involved the conversion of the recruits. This exception apart, a procedure of somewhat dubious legality, the non-Muslims were accorded the status of *dhimmīs*, a status recognized by the *Sharīʿa*, and one which had long been accorded to Christians and Jews in Islamic states. The *Sharīʿa* protected the lives of the *dhimmīs* and granted them certain rights, notably the practice of their religions. It excluded them from the body politic, placed them at a fiscal disadvantage, as compared with the Muslims, and, amongst other restrictions, imposed certain sumptuary regulations, which were not normally enforced. Under the Ottomans, with their tendency towards institutionalization and administrative precision, the non-Muslims were organized in definite groups, each known as a *millet* (Arabic, *milla*) which were in effect corporations with their own officers, their own systems of domestic law, and a large degree of internal autonomy. The Ottoman government communicated with the *millet* through a single channel, the *millet-bashı*, its responsible head. The chief of these in status was the Patriarch of Constantinople, as head of the Orthodox Christians, whose community, the *millet-i Rum*, was organized by Mehmed II immediately after the conquest of the metropolis. Although the Jews lacked the hierarchy found in the Christian churches, and were indeed deeply divided amongst themselves, they were given a *millet*-organization about the same time, and for a short period a responsible head was created for the community by the appointment of a chief rabbi, the *Ḥakham-bashı*. Other sects formed recognizable entities, which were treated in practice as *millets* by the Ottoman authorities.

[1] An authoritative opinion of this kind is known in Arabic as a *fatwā* (Turkish, *fetva*).

2

The Overthrow of the Mamluk Sultanate

During the reign of Bayezid II (1481–1512), the political situation in the lands bordering on the eastern frontier of the Ottoman Empire underwent an important change. When, early in the fifteenth century, the empire of Timur broke up on his death, the ultimate beneficiaries were two confederacies of Turcomans, known respectively as the Kara-Koyunlu (Black Sheep tribes) and Ak-Koyunlu (White Sheep tribes). The former of these rose into prominence in the first half of the century, and extended its control over western and southern Persia, and over Iraq. In 1466, the head of the Kara-Koyunlu was defeated and killed by Uzun Ḥasan, the chief of the rival Ak-Koyunlu, which thereupon became the dominant confederacy. Conflict between Uzun Ḥasan and Sultan Mehmed II, the master of the resurgent and expanding Ottoman state, was inevitable, and although Uzun Ḥasan sought to safeguard his position by an alliance with Venice, he was defeated in 1472 and 1473. A stalemate resulted. Uzun Ḥasan retreated to Āẕarbāyjān. Here he was safe from the Ottomans, while lacking power to renew his attack on them. The clash between Mehmed II and Uzun Ḥasan was the prototype of relations between the Ottomans and the rulers of Persia for three centuries to come.

Like the Kara-Koyunlu before them, the Ak-Koyunlu dynasty lacked the internal cohesion to form a stable empire. After Uzun Ḥasan's death in 1478 the state was rent by internal disorders, but the Ottomans were debarred from taking advantage of these because of their own dynastic troubles, arising from the contest between Bayezid II and Jem. In the event, the Ak-Koyunlu rulers were overthrown by another dynasty, the Safavids, stemming from Āẕarbāyjān, and linked to them by marriage.

The rise of the Safavids to power was a process unlike any that had hitherto been seen in the eastern Islamic lands, although it bore some resemblance to the development of the Almoravid and Almohad states in the Maghrib over four centuries before. The Safavids had first attained prominence as the head of a Ṣūfī religious order, the Ṣafawiyya (whence the term Safavid is derived), so called from its eponymous founder, Shaykh Ṣafī al-Dīn (d. 1334). The order had its headquarters at Ardabīl in Āẕarbāyjān; its members were devoted to the founder's family, and

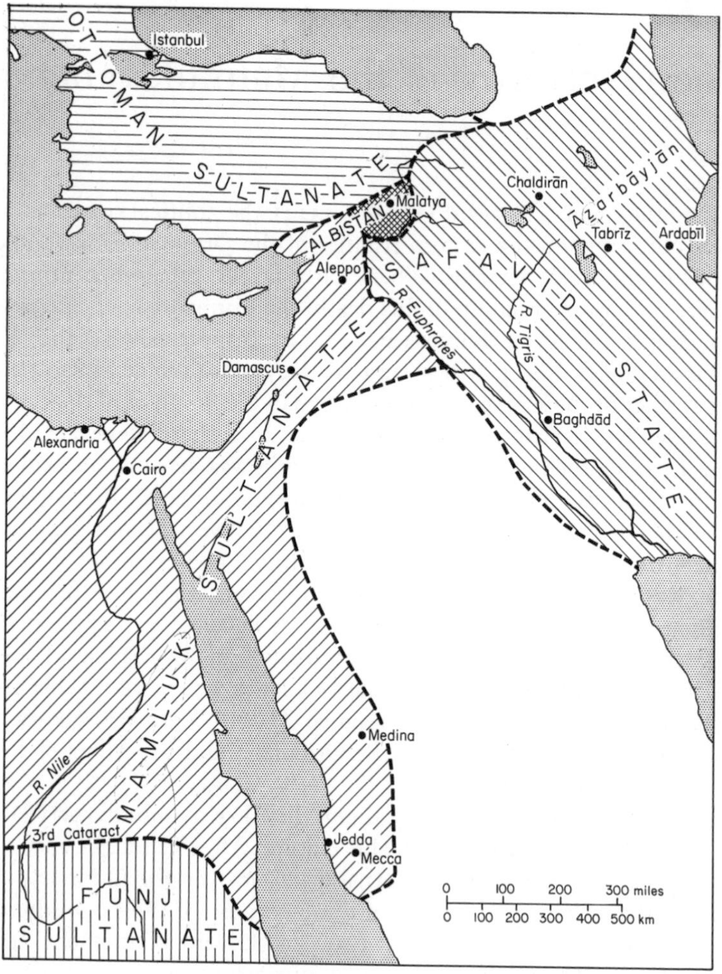

Map 1: The Near East in 1512

by about the middle of the fifteenth century it had become strongly Shiʿite. The then head of the order at that time, Shaykh Junayd, had political ambitions, and used his followers as a militant organization. He gained many adherents among the Turcoman tribes of southern and eastern Anatolia, in territories which were feeling the pressure of Ottoman expansion. He was protected by Uzun Ḥasan, whose sister he married, but fell in battle (1460) against the ruler of Shirvān, a territory lying to the north of Āẕarbāyjān. Under his son and successor, Shaykh Ḥaydar, the militant tendencies of the Ṣafawiyya continued. The propaganda in Anatolia did not cease to appeal to the Turcoman tribes of the marches, who came to constitute the major part of the Safavid forces. The distinctive uniform of the Ṣafawiyya was a red cap, whence they came to be known as Qizilbāsh (Turkish, *Kızıl bash*, i.e. 'Red heads'). Like his father, Shaykh Ḥaydar married an Ak-Koyunlu princess, a daughter of Uzun Ḥasan, and like him he died in battle against the ruler of Shirvān (1488).

At this juncture, the situation of the Safavid family, represented by the three infant sons of Shaykh Ḥaydar, was extremely precarious. They were saved by the devotion of their followers, and by the chaotic political situation in western Persia resulting from the collapse of Ak-Koyunlu power. This situation, indeed, enabled Ismāʿīl, one of the three brothers, to conquer a kingdom. Supported by the Shīʿī tribesmen, he combined the authority of the chief of a Turcoman confederacy with the spiritual influence of the head of a Ṣūfī order. A series of victories around the turn of the fifteenth century made him the master of Āẕarbāyjān, western Persia and Iraq. He assumed the title of shah in Tabrīz, and in the course of the next few years added eastern Persia also to his dominions. The Safavid Empire, which he thus erected on the ruins of the Ak-Koyunlu confederacy, was a theocratic state, strongly Shīʿī in ideology, ruled by Shah Ismāʿīl as the virtually absolute vicegerent of the Concealed *Imām*.[1] Ismāʿīl's accession to power was followed by a persecution of the Sunnī Muslims in his dominions, and a deliberate indoctrination with Shīʿī teaching. Thereby Shiʿism, which had had a foothold in Persia since its origin, became both the religion of the vast majority of the inhabitants of Persia (as it was of a large proportion of the Muslims of Iraq), and all

[1] According to Shīʿī doctrine, the headship of the Muslim community is inherent in the *imāms*, the descendants of ʿAlī, the cousin of the Prophet, and Fāṭima, the Prophet's daughter. The main group of the Shīʿa trace a succession of twelve *imāms*, the last of whom disappeared at Sāmarrā in 878. The doctrine teaches that he continues to exist as the Concealed *Imām*, and that, until his return as the Expected Mahdī, the Muslim community has no visible head.

the official cult of the Safavid state. It was also, at that time, widespread in Ottoman Anatolia, with consequences that will appear.

Shah Ismāʿīl's establishment of Shiʿism was to some extent a political measure, designed to distinguish his empire, with its Turcoman warriors and ruling élite, from its Sunnī Turkish neighbours, the Özbegs to the north-east and the Ottomans to the west. To the Ottomans, the rise of Safavid power represented a recurrence in a still more dangerous form of the situation which had existed under Uzun Ḥasan. The turbulent Turcoman tribes of the marches, which the Ottomans were seeking to bring under their control, found in the Safavid shah not merely a protector, but a charismatic leader, far more attractive to them than the Ottoman sultan, the embodiment of Sunnī orthodoxy. Already in Bayezid II's reign, the Ottoman government experienced difficulties from Safavid influence in Anatolia. In 1502, the sultan had deported sympathizers with Shah Ismāʿīl from Anatolia to the Morea, and in 1511 a very serious Shīʿī rising was only put down after military operations.

The coming of Selim the Grim to the throne precipitated a crisis in Ottoman–Safavid relations. Selim only secured his position by fighting and defeating an elder brother, one of whose sons sought refuge with Shah Ismāʿīl. At the same time the shah summoned his Anatolian adherents to join him in Persia—a summons which brought about fighting on the frontier. A Safavid embassy went to Egypt to seek the support of the Mamluk sultan, Qānṣawh al-Ghawrī, against the Ottomans.

At this juncture, Selim began to prepare for war. As a preliminary, he sent out punitive expeditions against the remaining Ṣafawiyya in Anatolia. Massacres ensued, in which forty thousand Shīʿa are said to have lost their lives. This act provided Ismāʿīl with a *casus belli*: he prepared to march in order to avenge his supporters, and to install the Ottoman prince, his protégé, as sultan. In April 1514 Selim began his advance across Anatolia towards Safavid territories. An important strategic rôle in the campaign would clearly be played by ʿAlāʾ al-Dawla, the prince of Albistan, who was Selim's maternal grandfather, and on whose assistance the Ottoman sultan was counting. But ʿAlāʾ al-Dawla continued to show the opportunist spirit of his house: he denied provisions and reinforcements to the Ottomans, and allowed his Turcomans to raid their forces.

The march across Anatolia was long and difficult, the more so since the Safavid ruler had devastated his western lands. The two armies finally met in August 1514 in the plain of Chaldirān, where Ismāʿīl prepared to defend the approaches to Tabrīz. In the hard-fought battle which ensued, their artillery and infantry gave the Ottomans the advantage. Ismāʿīl was driven from the field, and was unable to hold his capital, which Selim entered in September. But the Ottomans now were at the limit of their resources, and the Janissaries compelled the sultan to withdraw to winter quarters in central Anatolia.

To a large extent the Chaldirān campaign resulted in a stalemate. The Ottomans were strong enough to defeat the Safavids, but not to eliminate them; Ismāʿīl, for his part, no longer dared to assume an aggressive attitude towards the sultan. The Ottomans were unable to make a permanent conquest of Āẕarbāyjān: they did, however, make significant gains in the north-east of Anatolia. Furthermore, the unhelpful conduct of ʿAlāʾ al-Dawla brought an Ottoman army into Albistan during the winter of 1514–15. In June 1515 ʿAlāʾ al-Dawla was defeated and slain, while Albistan was incorporated as a vassal principality into the Ottoman Empire. Selim profited also from the resentment which the Kurdish chiefs felt at Safavid rule. Several of them had appealed to him for aid after Chaldirān. The fighting against the Safavids in this region centred around Diyār Bakr, which was finally taken by Ottoman forces in October 1515. During the following year, the greater part of Kurdistan, and also the important city of Mosul, fell to the Ottomans. The territory so acquired was largely left under the autonomous rule of the Kurdish chiefs: a policy which proved more effective than Shah Ismāʿīl's attempt to rule the Kurds by Turcoman governors.

The Chaldirān campaign had thus resulted in Ottoman power being brought to the fringe of the Fertile Crescent. More significantly, in the political situation of the time, it confronted both the Safavid and Mamluk rulers with a powerful military monarchy, which had eliminated the march territories that served as buffers to their mutual rivalries. In these circumstances the two threatened monarchs drew closer together, Qānṣawh al-Ghawrī entered into communication with Shah Ismāʿīl, and undertook, in the event of further hostilities, to move the Mamluk forces up to the northern frontier of Syria, thereby endangering the Ottoman flank.

The alliance was soon to be tested, for in the spring of 1516 Selim prepared a fresh expedition against Safavid territory. Qānṣawh promptly, although with some difficulty, mobilized his own forces and began to advance through Syria, leaving one of the great officers of state, Ṭūmān Bāy, as viceroy in Cairo during his absence. Early in July he reached Aleppo, which he made his advanced base. The news of the Mamluk movements had already reached the Ottoman commander, Sinan Pasha, who was stationed in Albistan, and he had informed Selim. To meet this perhaps unexpected threat, the Ottoman sultan sent envoys to offer terms of peace to Qānṣawh, but they were received with insults and abuse.

On 23 July Selim himself, accompanied by strong reinforcements, joined Sinan Pasha. He was now in a critical position, and had to decide whether to disregard the Mamluk threat to his flank and continue his advance on the Safavids, or whether to turn aside and try conclusions with the Mamluks. He decided on the latter course; partly for strategic reasons, partly perhaps from a realization that a defeat of the Mamluks might end the Ottoman–Safavid stalemate. Qānṣawh realized that an operation begun, it would seem, largely to bluff the Ottomans, was developing in a manner that might have serious consequences for him. He released the Ottoman envoys, and sent an embassy of his own to Selim, which in its turn found its terms contemptuously rejected.

Qānṣawh was indeed in a position of extreme danger. The local population was disaffected to Mamluk rule, and ready to listen to Ottoman propaganda promising a restoration of justice and good government. More serious still was the existence of a schism in the Mamluk ruling élite itself. The ancient and recurrent factionalism between the Mamluks of the reigning sultan and the veteran Mamluks of his predecessors was ready to reassert itself in a moment of crisis, while some of the high officers were fully prepared to see Qānṣawh overthrown and to recognize Selim as their ruler, if by so doing they could safeguard their own places and power. Chief of this collaborationist group was the governor of Aleppo, Khā'ir Bey.

Retreat was, however, impossible for Qānṣawh, and on 24 August 1516 the Mamluk and Ottoman armies met in battle on the plain of Marj Dābiq, near Aleppo. The military superiority of the Ottoman infantry and artillery was assisted by the divisions in the Mamluk high command. At a critical moment in the fighting, Khā'ir Bey withdrew the troops under his command. The battle turned to a rout, in which the aged Sultan Qānṣawh fell, stricken with apoplexy. The citizens of Aleppo shut their gates against the fugitive Mamluks, who made their way in a broken and distressed condition to Damascus, the chief town of southern Syria.

Selim entered Aleppo without striking another blow, and there seized the treasure and provisions that the Mamluks had been forced to abandon in the citadel. At the Friday prayer in the mosque the *khuṭba*[1] was read

[1] The *khuṭba*, or sermon delivered on the occasion of the congregational Friday prayer, includes a species of bidding-prayer for the ruler. The mention of the ruler's name in

in his name—the first Ottoman sultan to be recognized as sovereign in Arab territory.

Yet in reality he had taken only the first step to overthrowing the Mamluk sultanate. The refugee Mamluks in Damascus were struggling to re-establish their authority there, and for a few days in September it almost seemed as if southern Syria might be held. The illusion was dispelled as the Ottomans continued their southward march. The Mamluks slipped away, to resume their flight to Egypt. Within a week the notables of the city and the governor of the citadel agreed to surrender, and on 28 September Selim and the Ottoman army encamped outside Damascus.

With the acquisition of Damascus by Selim, who made his state entry into the city on 9 October, the whole of Syria as far as the frontier-town of Gaza passed under Ottoman control. The Mamluks, however, still retained Egypt, and the difficult desert territory of Sinai offered them protection against the Ottomans. On 10 October the Mamluk grandees compelled the unwilling Ṭūmān Bāy to accept election as sultan, and he was duly installed, but with diminished ceremonial, since part of the regalia had been lost with Qānṣawh. Selim, for his part, was not anxious to continue the war. He had achieved his objects. The Mamluk–Safavid alliance had been broken, while the conquest of Syria had interposed a block of territory between the old Empire and the Mamluks. Furthermore, his lines of communication were already dangerously prolonged. He therefore sent an embassy to Ṭūmān Bāy, offering to recognize him as a vassal-ruler.

This attempt to reach an agreement with the Mamluks did not succeed. Ṭūmān Bāy sent troops to retake Gaza, but they were defeated by Sinan Pasha on 21 December 1516. Some of Selim's own advisers, including the former Mamluk officer Khā'ir Bey, were urgent for an advance into Egypt. The Ottomans therefore set out, and passed the Sinai desert safely, although they were harassed by Arab tribes on their line of march. When the news of their approach reached Cairo, Ṭūmān Bāy wished to make a stand against them at al-Ṣāliḥiyya, where the desert-route entered the confines of the Delta. This was a sound strategic choice, but the Mamluk sultan was overruled by his own high officers, who insisted on making their stand at the fortified camp of al-Raydāniyya, immediately outside Cairo.

The defences of al-Raydāniyya were hastily improved. For the first

the *khuṭba*, and the striking of coinage, are the traditional prerogatives of Muslim sovereignty.

time, the Mamluk authorities, shaken by their defeat at Marj Dābiq, prepared to make a serious use of artillery in field-warfare. Cannon were mounted around the camp, while some troops, albeit of inferior status to the white Mamluks, were equipped with hand-guns. Ṭūmān Bāy was counting on a prolonged battle, or even a siege, but in fact the fate of Egypt was decided in a single hour on 23 January 1517. The Ottomans inflicted terrible havoc on the Mamluk forces, although among their own casualties was Sinan Pasha himself. For another eighty minutes Ṭūmān Bāy continued to fight deperately, supported by his own Mamluk guard, until at last he too was compelled to flee from the field.

On the following day, the last of the Muslim year, the congregations assembled in the mosques of Cairo for the Friday prayer. There they heard the *khuṭba* recited in the name of the Ottoman ruler:

'Give victory, O God, to the Sultan, the son of the Sultan, the Master of the Two Lands and the Two Seas, the Breaker of the Two Armies, the Sultan of the two Iraqs, the Servitor of the Two Holy Sanctuaries, the Victorious King, Selim Shah. Give him, O God, a glorious victory, and grant him a manifest conquest; O Master of this world and the world to come, O Lord of the worlds!'[1]

After the victory at al-Raydāniyya, Selim moved his camp to Būlāq, a port on the Nile, now incorporated in Cairo, but then lying outside the old walled city. Here he was attacked by Ṭūmān Bāy. The attack failed, but street-fighting continued in Cairo itself for three days, followed by a slaughter of Mamluks by the Ottoman troops. Ṭūmān Bāy made his way to al-Bahnasā in Middle Egypt. Here, while gathering a mixed force of Mamluks and Arabs, he entered into negotiations with Selim. He sought the intercession of the titular ʿAbbasid caliph, and announced his readiness to rule Egypt as a tributary vassal, if the Ottomans would evacuate the country. Selim took the proposal seriously, and despatched an embassy of high religious notables, including the four chief judges of Egypt and the caliph, to negotiate with Ṭūmān Bāy.

Once again, Ṭūmān Bāy was balked by his Mamluk colleagues, who attacked Selim's ambassadors and drove them away. Selim took this as a rupture of relations, and in revenge put to death a number of high Mamluk officers who had surrendered under an amnesty. Battle alone could now decide the issue between the Mamluk and the Ottoman sultans. Ṭūmān Bāy descended the Nile with his motley forces, and

1 Ibn Īyās, *Badāʾiʿ al-zuhūr* (ed. Muḥammad Muṣṭafā), v, Cairo 1380/1961, 148.

encountered the Ottomans at Giza, opposite Cairo, on 2 April 1517. Superiority in numbers and firearms gave the Ottomans the victory.

Ṭūmān Bāy fled to the province of the Buḥayra, lying between the Rosetta branch of the Nile and the Western Desert. Here he was betrayed to the Ottomans by two Arab chiefs whom he had sworn to loyalty. On 14 April the defeated sultan was hanged at the Zuwayla Gate of his former capital. It was said that his former colleague, Khā'ir Bey, was largely responsible for persuading Selim to put him to death.

Although Selim spent a further five months in Egypt, he did not attempt a detailed territorial conquest and military occupation of his new dominion. Apart from a short visit to Alexandria, he spent most of the rest of his time in a pavilion on an island of the Nile beside Cairo, relaxing after the arduous campaign. His invasion of Egypt had been forced on him by the course of events, rather than deliberately planned as an exercise in empire-building, and he was content to have destroyed, or reduced to impotence, his opponents in the Mamluk élite. Before he left Cairo, Selim received the son of Barakāt, the *sharīf* of Mecca, who had come to demonstrate his father's submission to the Ottoman, as formerly to the Mamluk sultan.[1]

On 10 September 1517 he began his return journey to Istanbul. He spent the winter months in Damascus, where there was some murmuring at the seizure of houses to billet the Ottoman troops. Ibn al-Ḥanash, the Arab chief of the Biqā', the great plain between the ranges of Lebanon and Anti-Lebanon, was causing trouble, so Selim led a punitive expedition, which put him to flight early in the new year. Then, after completing his final administrative arrangements, he left Damascus for ever on 21 February 1518. To commemorate his name in the Syrian capital, he selected a site on which a mosque was duly erected.

The arrangements which Selim made for the administration of his newly acquired Arab territories throw an interesting light on their relative importance to him. The old Mamluk Empire was broken up into three great provinces. The northernmost, with its centre at Aleppo, was strategically valuable as protecting the approaches to Anatolia across the Taurus—the territory which had been disputed between the Mamluks and the Ottomans a generation earlier, in the time of Bayezid II. This province of Aleppo was placed under an Ottoman governor, and, on the

[1] The dynasty of the Hashimite *sharīfs* of Mecca had been established about the year 1200 by Qatāda ibn Idrīs. The overlordship of Mecca by the Mamluk sultans had first been asserted by Baybars, later in the same century. In course of time, the *sharīfs* of Mecca established their supremacy throughout the Ḥijāz.

whole, had a markedly distinct history from that of southern Syria in the next four hundred years.

The southern part of Syria was not so strategically important to the Ottoman Empire at this time. Here the only essential administrative requirements were two: that internal order should be maintained; and that the great Pilgrimage caravan, which assembled annually at Damascus, should proceed in safety to the holy cities of the Ḥijāz, and return thence without suffering depredations from the Arab tribes. The maintenance of internal order (which of course affected the security of the Pilgrimage) was essentially a matter of restraining the predatory tribes and communities which abounded, especially in the highland regions such as Mount Lebanon, Ḥawrān and the Nābulus district. Here again the Ottomans never attempted a general territorial conquest, which would indeed have been beyond their powers. They were content to leave these territories under the control of their hereditary chiefs, granting recognition to those members of ruling houses who would accept the suzerainty of the sultan, and would undertake to transmit the tribute due from their people. Beyond this, the sultans and their governors had as their principal object the safeguarding of Damascus and the other great towns, and the protection of the network of routes.

The route from Damascus to the Ḥijāz, which ran through the territory later called Transjordan, was of particular importance, since it was normally the way of the Pilgrimage caravan. The Pilgrimage had both an economic and a religious significance. The pilgrims who came together in Mecca and Medina from all parts of the Muslim world found in their meeting an opportunity for trade. Damascus itself, as a commercial centre, depended largely on this trade, and on the provisioning of the Pilgrimage caravan. Furthermore, the Pilgrimage was a central institution of the Muslim faith. The Mamluk sultans, as rulers of Syria and Egypt, and overlords of the Ḥijāz, had borne a special responsibility for the maintenance and protection of the two great Pilgrimage caravans which assembled at Damascus and Cairo respectively. They had, furthermore, contributed to the prosperity of the Ḥijāz by the traditional assignment of certain revenues. These functions now devolved upon their Ottoman successors, to whom had passed their title of 'Servitor of the Two Holy Sanctuaries'. Thus upon the representative of the sultan at Damascus there lay a considerable responsibility for safeguarding his master's religious prestige.

While southern Syria was not a region of vital strategic importance, it did present complex administrative problems, so it is not surprising that Selim appointed a member of the old Mamluk ruling élite as governor of Damascus. This was Jānbardī al-Ghazālī, who had been governor of Ḥamāh under Qānṣawh, and had held the governorship of Damascus for a few days in September 1516, before the Ottoman advance on the city. He had commanded the Mamluk force which attacked Gaza in the following year, but obtained an amnesty from Selim after the battle of al-Raydāniyya. He was said to have been secretly in touch with the Ottoman sultan since before Marj Dābiq. On 16 February Selim appointed him governor of Damascus, with authority over the whole of southern Syria from Maʿarrat al-Nuʿmān to al-ʿArīsh. Until the end of Selim's reign he was principally occupied in repressing the tribes. Ibn al-Ḥanash, against whom Selim had made an expedition in February 1518, was hunted down and killed near Baʿalbakk in the following April. South of Damascus, the Arab chief of Ḥawrān endangered the safety of the Pilgrimage caravan, which in 1519 had been forced to go by way of Gaza. Jānbardī made two expeditions into the Ḥawrān region. The death of Selim in 1520 opened, as we shall see, tempting and disastrous prospects to the governor of Damascus.

Syria had long been accustomed to dependence on monarchies whose centres lay outside its borders. Not so Egypt, which from Fatimid times onwards had sustained independent dynasties, and had been the nucleus of imperial structures incorporating Syrian and Arabian territories. History and geography alike forbade the partition of Egypt, which, moreover, had in the sixteenth century an important part to play in Ottoman strategy. The Portuguese threat to the Red Sea, of which the later Mamluk sultans had been well aware, led to a curious collaboration between the Ottomans and Qānṣawh, almost on the eve of the conquest. Firearms and other military supplies for action against the Portuguese reached Cairo in 1511, and the expedition which set out for Gujarat in 1515 was commanded by an Ottoman captain, Selman Reis. With the overthrow of the Mamluk sultanate, it became incumbent on Selim to maintain Egypt as the bastion of his extended empire against the Portuguese.[1]

Egypt therefore was committed in its entirety to another survivor of the old régime, Selim's most trusted collaborator, Khāʾir Bey, who ruled the country for the remainder of his life, as the sultan's vassal rather than as a provincial governor of the usual Ottoman type. He retained his Mamluk title of *malik al-umarāʾ*, literally 'king of the commanders', and

[1] Ottoman interest in the Red Sea region should also be linked with the rise of Safavid power. The interposition of this hostile block of territory between the Ottoman Empire and the east rendered vitally important the maintenance of an open route through the Red Sea.

kept his court in the Citadel of Cairo, the ancient residence of the rulers of Egypt. Selim had hardly left Cairo before Khā'ir Bey began to act as if he were the successor of the Mamluk sultans. He continued the traditional custom of receiving the four chief judges at the beginning of every Muslim month. The defeated Mamluks, who had been dispersed and in concealment since the reign of terror which followed al-Raydāniyya, emerged from hiding, resumed their traditional costume, and were restored to favour by the viceroy. Before long, indeed, Mamluks were being used to arrest refractory Ottoman troops. The revenues of Egypt were held in farm by Khā'ir Bey, to his considerable profit.

Nevertheless, the viceroy was not permitted to rule unchecked. His tenure of office, although in effect for life, was subject to renewal at intervals which were perhaps annual. Furthermore, Selim, on his departure, had left some Ottoman troops to garrison Egypt and prevent the Mamluks from regaining a monopoly of military power. In the years immediately following the conquest, there were apparently four corps: the two infantry formations of garrison Janissaries (*Mustaḥfiẓan*) and *ʿAzeban*, and the two cavalry (*sipahi*) corps of *Gönülliyan* and *Tüfenkjiyan*, the latter being armed (as their name implies) with hand-guns. Later in the sixteenth century, three other corps were created locally: the *Mutafarriqa*, which formed the viceroy's bodyguard; the *Chavushan*, a small body of state envoiys and pursuivants; the *Cherakise*, a third cavalry corps, recruited from Circassian Mamluks—hence the name.[1]

The administraton of Egypt under Khā'ir Bey continued to follow the practice of the Mamluk sultanate. The agents of government in the provinces were known as *kāshifs*, a title they had held under the old régime, and one otherwise unknown in the Ottoman Empire. Where the names of these officials are known, they are men of Mamluk, not Ottoman, origin. Tribal areas were still, as in the past, governed by semi-autonomous Arab shaykhs. In Upper Egypt, tribal authority actually increased in the early Ottoman period. The appointment of a governor to this region lapsed, and the chief of the tribe of Hawwāra, belonging to the clan of Banū ʿUmar, was recognized as being responsible for the administration. The fiscal organization continued to function as it had done before the conquest, still dominated, as it had been for over a century, by the great bureaucratic family of the Awlād al-Jīʿān. In the

[1] See further S. J. Shaw, *The financial and administrative development of Ottoman Egypt*, 1517–1798, Princeton 1962, 189–97. The contemporary chronicler, Ibn Īyās, indicates three types of troops only: Janissaries, *Sipahis* and *Gönülliyan*—the last two apparently referring to distinct corps. Later legend ascribed to Selim the establishment of all the seven corps in Egypt.

year of the conquest, no Pilgrimage caravan had left Cairo, but it was resumed in the following season, and three years later a return to old custom took place with the conferment of the Command of the Pilgrimage on a high Mamluk officer.

Thus, although Selim had extinguished the Mamluk sultanate and annexed Egypt to his dominions, the degree of ottomanization which immediately followed was very limited indeed. The Mamluks were not extirpated, nor did their recruitment cease. A kind of symbiosis between the Mamluk and Ottoman elements in the ruling and military élite developed over the course of the years. It is therefore less of a paradox than it might seem that Selim, the destroyer of Qānṣawh and Ṭūmān Bāy, appears in later Mamluk legend as something of a folk-hero. Tales were told of his miraculous preservation in chidhood, while the great factions of the Faqāriyya and Qāsimiyya in the seventeenth and eighteenth centuries claimed as eponymous founders two legendary Mamluks who fought in the presence of Selim. Most striking of all, perhaps, is the story of how, when the sultan was about to leave Cairo, Khā'ir Bey interceded with him to receive the Circassians into his service, and to restore their wages. At this, the grand vezir reproached Selim for his favour to Khā'ir Bey and the Mamluks, saying, 'Our wealth and our troops are wasted, while you surrender their land to them!' Thereupon Selim summoned the executioner, who struck off the grand vezir's head. Later the sultan declared, 'We covenanted with them that if they gave us possession of their land, we should continue them in it, and make them its commanders. Could we break the covenant and prove false? What if we have put their children into our army: They are Muslims, the sons of Muslims, and will be jealous of their homes.'[1]

[1] This story appears in the chronicle of al-Isḥāqī, an early seventeenth-century source. It contains a memory of an authentic historical event, Selim's execution of his grand vezir, Yunus Pasha, when the latter complained of the trouble and expense of a campaign which had resulted in the handing over of Egypt into the hands of traitors. The legend dramatizes and telescopes the event, which actually took place on the Egyptian–Syrian border, at the spot henceforward known as Khān Yūnus.

3

Süleyman the Magnificent and the Arab Lands

Sultan Selim I died in October 1520. He was succeeded on the throne by his son, Süleyman, whose long reign (1520–66) marks the zenith of the Ottoman Empire. He is traditionally called 'the Magnificent' by European writers, but Turkish and Arab sources bestow on him the epithet of *Qānūnī*.[1]

In the newly acquired Arab provinces, Süleyman's reign began ominously with the revolt of Jānbardī al-Ghazālī, the Mamluk governor of Damascus. On receiving the news of Selim's death, Jānbardī removed the Ottoman governor of the Biqāʿ, who had been installed after the defeat and death of Ibn al-Ḥanash, and a member of the former chief's family was restored to power. He then returned to Damascus, where he besieged the citadel, which was under the command of an Ottoman officer. Having taken it by a ruse, he demonstrated his rejection of Ottoman suzerainty by forbidding the recitation of the *khuṭba* in the mosques in the name of Sultan Süleyman. He appointed two of his followers as governors of the towns of Ḥamāh and Tripoli, while their Ottoman predecessors fled to Aleppo.

Aleppo was indeed the key to Syria, and Jānbardī could not feel safe as long as it remained in Ottoman hands. Having set the defences of Damascus in order, therefore, he set out on 25 November 1520 to capture this northern fortress. The Ottoman governor of Aleppo prepared to defend the city, but was worsted in two clashes with Jānbardī's advanced forces. By 6 December Aleppo was besieged, and under bombardment from Jānbardī's artillery. The governor, however, continued to resist, and Jānbardī's position weakened with every day that passed. On the one hand, he rightly apprehended the approach of an Ottoman relieving force; on the other, he had failed to gain the support he had expected from Khāʾir Bey in his bid for independence. The viceroy of Egypt had been ostentatiously loyal to the Ottoman sultan, restraining the Mamluk hotheads from going off to join the rebels, and sending an army to Gaza, which killed the governor appointed by Jānbardī.

[1] i.e., the promulgator of *qānūns*. For the significance of this term, see above, p. 31.

On 20 December Jānbardī raised the siege, and began his retreat to Damascus. A few days later, the Ottoman reinforcements reached Aleppo. The fringes of Jānbardī's territory began to crumble: on 17 January 1521 the governor he had appointed to Tripoli arrived in Damascus, a fugitive before the Ottoman advance.

Jānbardī himself re-entered Damascus on the following day, and began to prepare for a desperate resistance. He put the citadel in a state of defence, and levied a militia from the local people. As he reviewed these troops, he urged them, 'Do not fight the Ottomans for me, but fight them to defend your women.' To strengthen their loyalty, they were brought before the chief judge of Damascus, one of Jānbardī's partisans, in the Umayyad Mosque, to swear that they would fight with their governor against the Ottomans. To legitimize Jānbardī's claim to be a sovereign ruler, on Friday 1 February the judge recited the *khuṭba* in his name. The title which he accorded to Jānbardī was, however, not 'sultan of Damascus', but 'sultan of the Two Holy Sanctuaries'.

The reign of the new sultan was to be of short duration. The Ottoman troops were already drawing near to Damascus, and on 5 February they encountered Jānbardī's followers outside the city. The Damascenes were routed at once; Jānbardī was killed in the fighting, and his capital was delivered over to massacre and pillage.

The destruction was stayed on the following day by the Ottoman commander, Farhad Pasha. The troops in the citadel made their submission, and Janissary officers were put in command of the citadel and each quarter of the town. Farhad installed a new governor, but this time he was an Ottoman, not a Mamluk, and his direct authority was limited to Damascus and its district. Subordinate governors were appointed to Gaza, Ṣafad and Jerusalem. Tripoli had already, in 1519, been raised to provincial status, ranking equally with Aleppo and Damascus. The revolt of Jānbardī thus resulted in the administrative partition of Syria being carried a stage further, and the Ottoman archives show that the regular fiscal system was applied throughout Syria, with only enclaves of indirect control, such as Mount Lebanon.[1]

On 5 October 1522 died Khā'ir Bey. As long as he lived, no revolt against Ottoman suzerainty had taken place in Egypt, but after his death the authority of the sultan was brought into question. His successor, significantly enough, was not another member of the Mamluk élite, but an Ottoman of high rank, Muṣṭafā Pasha, the brother-in-law of Sultan

[1] See further, Bernard Lewis, 'Studies in the Ottoman Archives—I', *BSOAS*, xvi, 1954, 469 ff.

Süleyman. After his arrival in Egypt, revolt flared out, headed by two Mamluk notables, Jānim al-Sayfī, the *kāshif* of al-Bahnasā and the Fayyūm (in effect, the governor of Middle Egypt), and Īnāl, the *kāshif* of the Gharbiyya, which lay in the western part of the Delta, on the right bank of the Rosetta branch of the Nile.

The speech which a chronicler ascribes to the rebel *kāshifs* well expresses the outlook of the old Mamluk military élite—their pride in their prowess, and their contempt for the new-fangled weapons with which the Ottomans had overthrown their sultanate: 'Sultan Selim is dead, and his son is a little boy. If he himself came to fight us, we should break him. We will not leave the kingdom to these Turcomans, who don't understand cavalry warfare.'

Jānim and Īnāl advanced to the Sharqiyya, the province lying to the east of the Delta, where they could cut communications between Cairo and Syria. Īnāl was the first to arrive. In the Sharqiyya he received an envoy from Muṣṭafā Pasha. This was al-Zaynī Barakāt, who was a prominent bureaucrat under both the Mamluk and the Ottoman régimes, and held the Command of the Pilgrimage in 1518. He had assured the viceroy that he would bring the rebel *kāshifs* in without a military expedition, and so, provided with a letter of amnesty for them, he made his way to the camp. His eloquence failed to beguile Īnāl, who had him beheaded as a traitor to the Mamluk cause.

On the following day Jānim joined his confederate, and the two *kāshifs* remained in the Sharqiyya, awaiting the arrival of other Mamluk notables. Some of these were privy to the conspiracy, and had undertaken to go over to the side of the rebels, when they went out on the pretext of fighting them.

Their promise, whether sincerely given or not, remained unfulfilled. When Muṣṭafā Pasha heard of al-Zaynī's death, he organized an expeditionary force consisting entirely of Ottoman troops. In the battle which ensued, Jānim was killed, while Īnāl fled towards Gaza, and disappeared from history. The credulous asserted that he had donned a cap of invisibility. It is interesting to note that, in spite of Jānim's treason, one of his *mamlūks* was *kāshif* of al-Bahnasā and the Fayyūm in the middle years of the sixteenth century.

Shortly afterwards a still more serious rebellion took place in Egypt, headed on this occasion by a viceroy. Aḥmad Pasha, the instigator of the revolt, was himself of Caucasian origin, and an ethnic bond thus linked him with the Mamluks. He had been disappointed of the grand vezirate, and the sultan had conferred on him the viceroyalty of Egypt as a consolation prize. The statement in some sources that Süleyman sent instructions to the commander of the Janissaries in Cairo to have him assassinated is unlikely.

Aḥmad Pasha is said to have intercepted the letter bearing the instructions. Be that as it may, soon after his installation as viceroy in August 1523 he displayed a harsh and masterful temperament, confiscating the wealth of notables, and putting high military officers to death. Among the objects of his anger was Jānim al-Ḥamzāwī, a man of Mamluk descent, who played an important part in the early years of the Ottoman régime, serving, it would seem, as a liaison officer between the sultans and the viceregal court. Aḥmad Pasha imprisoned Jānim, who had accompanied him from Istanbul. When the commander of the Janissaries sought to intercede on his behalf, he was arrested in his turn, and put to death. His execution may have been more than a tyrant's caprice: the sources which speak of Süleyman's plan to have Aḥmad killed, designate this Janissary officer as his intended successor. Furthermore, the Janissaries were the troops on whose loyalty the sultan could most implicitly rely, and Aḥmad Pasha may well have counted on breaking their morale by destroying their commander.

Aḥmad then passed into open rebellion by claiming the sultanate of Egypt, and asserting the royal prerogatives of having his name recited in the bidding-prayer and stamped on the coinage. Abraham Castro, the Jewish master of the mint in Cairo, horrified and alarmed at this manifest treason, fled to Istanbul to inform Süleyman. Aḥmad was meanwhile building up a private army, largely of Mamluks. The Janissaries, entrenched in the Citadel of Cairo, continued to defy him, and were put under siege. At last the rebels made their way, by a subterranean passage, into the garrison, and the Citadel fell to Aḥmad in February 1524. Having thus overcome his most dangerous opponents, Aḥmad sought to legitimize his position by demanding an oath of allegiance from the four chief judges of Egypt and from a scion of the ʿAbbasid house, the son of the last shadow-caliph, who seems to have been one of his advisers.

It is not clear how much support the pretender could count upon. One source suggests that his assumption of the sultanate was a popular move, since Egypt was more likely to be governed effectively by a sultan in Cairo than by one in distant Istanbul. On the other hand, the country-people refused to pay their taxes. This partly explains the abuses remembered in connection with his rule—the confiscations of property, and the extortions practised upon Jews and Christians. Aḥmad also conferred the farm of taxes of the Sharqiyya upon an Arab chief, ʿAbd al-Dāʾim ibn Baqar, thereby both obtaining ready money, and putting an ally on his exposed Syrian flank.

Another obscure aspect of Aḥmad's rebellion is its possible connection with the hostility existing between Shah Ismāʿīl and Sultan Süleyman. One of his principal advisers was a certain Qāḍīzāde Ẓāhir al-Dīn al-Ardabīlī, by origin a Shīʿī from Ardabīl, the headquarters of the Ṣafawiyya order. He had settled in Ottoman territory, and professed his adherence to Sunnī Islam. Al-Ardabīlī is said to have revealed himself in his true colours by converting Aḥmad Pasha to Shīʿism, and to have asserted that all the possessions of the Sunnīs had become lawful booty. Whether or not this report is literally true—it may have been a device of Ottoman propaganda to denigrate Aḥmad—it does at least suggest that the Ottoman authorities feared an alliance between the ruler of Egypt and Shah Ismāʿīl, like that which had led to Selim's campaign against Qānṣawh al-Ghawrī.

Aḥmad's power collapsed with dramatic suddenness. A counter-coup was planned by Jānim al-Ḥamzāwī, who had been released, with an Ottoman officer and a Mamluk grandee. On 23 February 1524 they surprised Aḥmad in a bathhouse. While their troops were struggling with his supporters, he fled across the roofs with his beard half-shaven, and managed to make his way to his Arab ally, Shaykh ʿAbd al-Dāʾim ibn Baqar. In the Sharqiyya he built up a following, mainly of Arabs and Circassians, but including some Ottomans. He promised them freedom to loot Cairo, and assured the Arabs of three years' relief of taxes.

Meanwhile the loyalist junta in Cairo had taken over the administration. A council of the military grandees appointed Jānim al-Ḥamzāwī to command the Janissaries, and his Mamluk associate to command the Circassian cavalry corps. The Ottoman officer was nominated governor of the Citadel. A general mobilization was proclaimed in Cairo against Aḥmad, who was stigmatized as an adherent of Shah Ismāʿīl and an infidel. Since a small force which had been sent out to arrest Aḥmad failed to do this, Jānim now led two thousand troops with eight cannon against the rebels. But Ahmad's following was already declining in strength because of a split between rival Arab factions. At this juncture came a report that a thousand Janissaries had landed at Alexandria. The father and brother of ʿAbd al-Dāʾim urged him to abandon Aḥmad, so as to save them from destruction by the Ottomans. He did so, and Ahmad's forces melted away. The rebel leader was captured in flight, and put to death on 6 March 1524. To the chroniclers, Ahmad Pasha, the first of several viceroys of that name, is invariably distinguished as *al-Khā'in*, 'the Traitor'.

The suppression of the revolt was followed by an energetic attempt to regulate the administration of Egypt. A year after Aḥmad's death, Süleyman's grand vezir, Ibrāhīm Pasha, reached Cairo to execute this commission. He remained in Egypt for only a few weeks, but left a durable memorial of his viceroyalty in the *Qānūn-name* of Egypt, the edict codifying administrative practice. This document falls into two main parts. The first deals with the military establishment of Egypt, and enumerates six corps of soldiers: the *Mutafarriqa* was not formed for another thirty years. The civil administration, as described in the second part of the *Qānūn-name*, inherited many features from the Mamluk sultanate. The local agents of government, as already mentioned, continued to be known by their old title of *kāshifs*; their principal duties were concerned with the maintenance of the irrigation-works on which the prosperity of the country depended, and the levying of the taxes paid by the peasantry. The *Qānūn-name* lists by name fourteen sub-provinces administered by *kāshifs*. Thirteen of these lay in Lower and Middle Egypt, one consisted of the remote Khārja oasis in the Western Desert. Upper Egypt, from Asyūṭ southwards, was still administered at this time by Arab shaykhs of the Banū ʿUmar, who are described in the *Qānūn-name* as performing functions similar to those of the *kāshifs*. Although there were occasionally clashes between the Ottoman administration and these tribal rulers, they were not deprived of their powers until 1576, when a bey was appointed as governor of Upper Egypt. There are frequent references in seventeenth- and eighteenth-century sources to his successors, who resided at Jirjā, and had under their control a considerable number of petty *kāshifs*.

At the head of the administration was the viceroy, whose position differed in some respects from that of other Ottoman provincial governors. The *Qānūn-name* assigned him the Citadel for his residence, although it did not confine him to it, as was asserted by later legend based on eighteenth-century usage. It also required him to hold regular meetings of a council of state (*Divan*) four times a week. A statutory institution of this kind was unique in Ottoman provincial administration: elsewhere the governor's *Divan* was an *ad hoc* body, summoned at will. There is, however, a striking resemblance between the viceroy's council of state and the Ottoman sultan's own *Divan*, which was also in the sixteenth century held four times weekly. The establishment of the *Mutafarriqa* corps (which bore the same name as the sultan's own bodyguard), and the rigid ceremonial which was followed at the reception of a new viceroy by the grandees of Cairo, were other indications of the special status held by the sultan's representative in Egypt.

After the transitional period of the rule of Khā'ir Bey, the troubles which followed his death, and the stabilization of Ottoman authority by Ibrāhīm Pasha, there ensued a time of quiescence, lasting about sixty years, during which Egypt had little recorded history. Viceroys came and went, their names and the impressions they made are briefly recorded by the chroniclers, but the political and social developments of these two generations lie in deep obscurity. Egypt, relegated to the status of an outlying province, lay passive under Ottoman rule. Nevertheless, it was not as fully integrated as the Syrian provinces into the Ottoman system. The land was not granted out in fiefs. The characteristic fiscal institution was the *iltizām*, or farm of taxes. As time went on, the *multazims* (tax-farmers) developed virtually into landlords, and their hold over the principal source of wealth in Egypt was broken only by Muḥammad ʿAlī Pasha, in the early nineteenth century.

The Ottoman sultans inherited from their Mamluk predecessors the function of guarding the Red Sea and its approaches against the Portuguese. The expedition which Qānṣawh sent to Gujarat in 1515 had, on its return, defeated the Arab ruler of the Yaman, and given the Mamluks a foothold in that region. In the following year, the Circassian governor, whose headquarters were at Zabīd, recognized the suzerainty of Selim, and was confirmed in office. He was followed by a succession of governors, some of Mamluk, others of Ottoman origin, whose intrigues and stormy relations with their troops frequently resulted in their violent deaths.

The seizure by the Portuguese of Diu led the ruler of Gujarat to send an embassy to Sultan Süleyman appealing for help. The sultan put Sulaymān Pasha, the viceroy of Egypt, in command of an expedition, which sailed in June 1538 from Suez. On its way, the expedition took Aden from its Arab prince, and an Ottoman governor was installed there. Early in October the fleet arrived off Diu, and the siege of the city began. But the ruler who had appealed for aid had been killed by the Portuguese, and his successor refused to help the Ottomans. Deprived of provisions, they were forced to raise the siege after twenty days, and made their way back to the Red Sea.

About the middle of the sixteenth century, the governor of the Yaman was a Circassian, related to the former Sultan Qānṣawh, and named Özdemir Pasha. On leaving the Yaman, he made his way to Egypt by an unusual route, crossing the Red Sea to the port of Suakin. Özdemir went on to Istanbul, where he proposed to Sultan Süleyman an expedition against Abyssinia. The conquest of the African coast around Bāb al-Mandab would further safeguard the Red Sea against the incursions of the Portuguese. Özdemir received permission from the sultan to enrol troops in Egypt. Having constituted his expeditionary force, he advanced by way of the Nile to Lower Nubia.

Nubia, the riverain territories of the Nile lying above the First Cataract, had remained under the rule of Christian kings long after the Arab conquest of Egypt in the seventh century. The valour of the Nubians, combined with the topographical difficulties and remoteness of their land, enabled them to maintain their independence throughout the great age of Arab expansion. Arab infiltration into the Aswān region, their northern march, began, however, in the ninth century, and in the eleventh century a dynasty of chiefs, the Banū Kanz, were ruling over people of mixed Arab and Nubian stock in these parts. The Arab element was supplied by immigrants of the tribe of Rabīʿa. The pressure of Arab immigration increased during the fourteenth century; the old Nubian kingdom of al-Maqurra broke up into a group of petty riverain principalities, ruled by dynasts who claimed Arab descent and professed Islam. The principal tribes of this mixed descent came to be known collectively as the Jaʿaliyyūn.

To the south of the Sixth Cataract, in the region of the confluence of the White and Blue Niles, lay another Christian Nubian kingdom, known as ʿAlwa, with its capital at Sūba, not far from modern Khartoum. This state continued to exist after the disintegration of al-Maqurra, but in the circumstances its downfall was only a matter of time. Unlike the northern kingdom, in which power seems to have passed peacefully through intermarriage from Nubian to Arab (or arabized) rulers, ʿAlwa perished in battle. The taking of Sūba is traditionally ascribed to an Arab chief named ʿAbdallāh Jammāʿ (the epithet, meaning 'Gatherer', perhaps indicating the mixed composition of his army) and probably took place in the later part of the fifteenth century. Thereafter the conqueror and his descendants, the ʿAbdallāb, exercised a loose hegemony over the Arab tribes of Nubia. Apart from Rabīʿa, settled in the far north, the immigrants belonged chiefly to the Arab tribe of Juhayna.

They were challenged by another immigrant group in the south, the Funj, a people of obscure origin, who make their first certain appearance on the upper Blue Nile.[1] The Funj clashed with the ʿAbdallāb, and

[1] The problem of Funj origins, one of the most difficult in Sudanese history, has given rise to several hypotheses, some of which are highly speculative. See further, P. M. Holt, 'Funj origins: a critique and new evidence', *JAH*, iv/1, 1963, 39–55.

defeated them in battle, but, while making them vassals, left them their hegemony over the northern Arabs and Nubians. In 1504–5 (if the traditional date may be accepted) the Funj established their capital at Sennar, on the Blue Nile, whence from ʿAmāra Dūnqas, the founder of the dynasty, to Bādī VI in 1822, a succession of rulers held at least titular sovereignty in what is now the northern Sudan. Although at first the Funj were neither Muslims nor Arabs, they were rapidly converted to Islam, while in due course, probably during the seventeenth century, they acquired a genealogy demonstrating their descent from the Umayyad caliphs.

At the time of Özdemir's expedition, two tribes were at war in the far north of Nubia, one of them being in alliance with the Funj. Özdemir's troops captured Ibrīm, the fortress dominating Lower Nubia, and the whole of the territory between the First and Third Cataracts was brought under Ottoman suzerainty. Garrisons of Bosniak troops were installed at Aswān, Ibrīm and Sāy, far to the south, and a Mamluk *kāshif* was appointed to administer the region. In Ottoman usage, the newly acquired territory was called Berberistan, the land of the Barābra, or Berberines.

After subduing Berberistan, Özdemir made his way to the Red Sea coast. He gained control of Suakin, which already in Mamluk times had had ties with Egypt. He took Massawa in 1557, and captured the port of Zayla. In alliance with a local ruler, at that time in rebellion against the Abyssinian king, he conquered a strip of the hinterland, but a complete conquest of Abyssinia was wholly beyond his powers. However, when he died in 1559 or 1560, he had given the Ottoman sultan a new province on the African Red Sea littoral. This was known as Ḥabesh (literally, 'Abyssinia'), and was governed from Massawa, where Özdemir himself was entombed.

Some years after Özdemir had left the Yaman, Ottoman power in that province crumbled. Led by a great Arab family of the interior, the Zaydī *imāms*, the tribes revolted against Ottoman rule. By 1567 almost the whole of the Yaman except Zabīd had been lost. Sultan Süleyman had died in the previous year, and had been succeeded by his son, Selim II, under whom a decline in the power of the empire manifested itself.[1] The new sultan, however, resolved to send a force to reconquer the Yaman. Its commander, Sinan Pasha, was the viceroy of Egypt, while the advance force was under ʿUthmān Pasha, the son of Özdemir.

ʿUthmān had already begun a successful campaign against the rebels, when Sinan arrived in the Yaman early in 1569. Before long, quarrels

[1] See below, Ch. 4.

broke out between the two men, and Sinan, relying on the plenary powers committed to him by the sultan, deposed ʿUthmān from his command. ʿUthmān and his followers fled by way of the Ḥijāz, and ultimately reached Istanbul, where he regained the sultan's favour. Meanwhile, Sinan advanced on Sanʿāʾ, while the admiral in command of the Egyptian fleet regained Aden for the Ottomans. Threatened by the military successes of Sinan, the Zaydī *imām* agreed, in May 1570, to negotiate peace. The sultan regained his lost province, and a new Ottoman governor was appointed, who suppressed the last flickers of rebellion.

During the reign of Sultan Süleyman, the remainder of the Fertile Crescent was brought under Ottoman rule. The Kurdish districts to the north of Iraq, and the important city of Mosul, had already been acquired after Selim's victory over Shah Ismāʿīl at Chaldirān, but central and southern Iraq, with the important cities of Baghdād and Baṣra, remained Safavid territory. Baghdād was administered by a Qizilbāsh governor, appointed by the shah, while the remote and impoverished port of Baṣra was ruled by an Arab tribal chief.

Shah Ismāʿīl died in 1524, and was succeeded by his son Ṭahmāsp, a boy ten years of age. This accession of a minor threatened the stability, and indeed the very existence, of the Safavid state. Within Persia, the Qizilbāsh tribal leaders regained their power, which Shah Ismāʿil had endeavoured in his later years to diminish, and for the first decade of his reign Ṭahmāsp was their puppet. Ṭahmāsp's accession had been greeted by a threatening letter from Sultan Süleyman, and an Ottoman attack on Persia seemed imminent. It was, however, delayed for ten years, during which Süleyman defeated the king of Hungary at Mohács, brought the central Danube valley under Ottoman rule, and in 1529 led his army to the walls of Vienna, which, however, he failed to capture.

In 1534 the long-delayed attack on Safavid Persia was delivered. Its immediate pretext was the unstable loyalty of some of the Kurdish chiefs, but the real motives behind Süleyman's campaign were similar to those which had brought his father to Chaldirān, twenty years before. During the interregnum, while Ṭahmāsp was dominated by the Qizilbāsh chiefs, Persia did not represent a serious military threat to the Ottomans, but by 1533 Ṭahmāsp had grown to manhood, and was in fact about to reassert his authority as shah. Süleyman's campaign seems to have been intended as a preventive war, to avert the revival of a strong military monarchy in Persia. Significantly, Süleyman is said by Persian sources to have tampered with the loyalty of the last Qizilbāsh regent, and to have intended to instal a younger brother of Ṭahmāsp as shah.

The Ottoman expeditionary force left its base at Aleppo in April 1534, crossed the Euphrates, and advanced through Kurdistan into Āẕarbāyjān. Tabrīz was taken without bloodshed. Here, in September, the sultan joined his army, and the second phase of the campaign began. The Ottoman army swept through north-western Persia, meeting no resistance from the Safavids, and then, passing by way of Hamadān, descended from the Iranian plateau into the plain of Iraq. The sultan's forces thus cut off Baghdād from the possibility of relief. At the last moment, the Qizilbāsh governor of the city made his escape, and the Ottomans entered Baghdād without resistance. Süleyman spent the winter in the former ʿAbbasid capital, restored the dilapidated tomb of Abū Ḥanīfa, the Muslim jurist whose legal doctrines were those officially followed in the Ottoman Empire, and visited the Shīʿī holy cities of Karbalā' and Najaf. In the spring the sultan left Baghdād, returning, again by way of Tabrīz, to Istanbul.

Süleyman's campaign completed the extension of Ottoman rule over the northern and central parts of Iraq. To the south, beyond the marshes of the lower Euphrates and Tigris, lay the port of Baṣra, under the rule of an Arab chief, Rāshid ibn Mughāmis. In 1538–9 Rāshid sent his son to Süleyman, to offer his submission to Ottoman suzerainty. He was confirmed in office as the sultan's representative, but did not long retain his position. In 1546–7 Iyas Pasha, the governor of Baghdād, was instructed to lead a force against him. The power of Rāshid crumbled at once, and Baṣra with its surrounding districts was within the next few years incorporated as a province into the Ottoman Empire.[1] Its acquisition brought the Ottomans to the head of the Persian Gulf, where, as in the Red Sea and Indian Ocean, they confronted the sea-power of Portugal

Baṣra was always a remote and difficult province to control, vulnerable to Persian attacks, and still more to those of the marsh and desert Arabs Only three years after its conquest, an expedition had to be sent against the marsh Arabs of Āl ʿUlayyān, who were defeated after bloody fighting. Beyond Baṣra, on the north-western coast of the Gulf, lay al-Aḥsā, over which Ottoman rule was still more tenuous. Although nominally a province of the Empire, al-Aḥsā was rather a tributary Arab state under autonomous rulers. Another fringe-territory was Shahrizor, in the Kurd

[1] See Bernard Lewis, 'The Ottoman archives as a source for the history of the Arab lands', *JRAS*, 1951, at p. 150.

[2] Also called al-Ḥasā and Laḥsā.

ish mountains of the north, lying on the Safavid–Ottoman march. Although its ruler had submitted to Süleyman at the time of the conquest of Baghdād, there was severe fighting, at first disastrous for the Ottomans, in the middle of the sixteenth century, and the Ottoman hold over Shahrizor does not seem to have been fully established until later.

The five provinces of Mosul, Baghdād, Baṣra, al-Aḥsā and Shahrizor were thus essentially a frontier region of the empire against Safavids and Portuguese. As we shall see, the most critical episodes in their history occurred when the Ottomans were confronted by a resurgence of military power in Persia, under Shah ʿAbbās in the early seventeenth century, and under Nādir Shāh in the middle of the eighteenth.[1] A second potential source of danger to the Iraqi provinces came from the Arab tribes on their western and southern flanks. Without the co-operation of these tribesmen, the trading caravans could not pass by the route which skirted the Syrian Desert from the head of the Persian Gulf to Aleppo. When the Ottoman governors were weak, or distracted by warfare with Persia, the tribes became insubordinate, and began to encroach on the settled lands: Baṣra in particular was exposed to their attacks, and occasionally subject to their domination. The Ottomans retorted with punitive expeditions, but although the Arab threat could be checked, the sultan's troops could not penetrate deep into the desert, and inflict a decisive defeat upon the tribesmen.

[1] See below, pp. 137–8 and 144–5.

Part II The Ottoman Decline

4

The Ottoman Empire in Decline

With Süleyman the Magnificent the long series of able and energetic Ottoman sultans comes to an end. With one exception, Murad IV (1623–40), there was no outstanding ruler from the House of Osman until, at the end of the eighteenth century and in the early part of the nineteenth, the first reforming sultans, Selim III (1789–1807) and Mahmud II (1808–39), strove to reorganize the military and administrative framework of their empire to meet the challenge of a new age.

To his son and successor, Selim II (1566–74), Süleyman left an empire that was to all outward appearance both well governed and strong in arms. Yet in fact ominous symptoms were already beginning to appear, and superstitious apprehensions about the approaching millenary of the Hijra (A.H. 1000/A.D. 1591–2) betrayed an underlying consciousness of incipient decay.[1] The beginnings of the decline first showed themselves conspicuously in the sultanate itself. The sultans had long ceased to be leaders of free *ghāzī* warriors, and had become oriental despots, withdrawn from their people, and dependent on the elaborate military and bureaucratic machines manned by *devshirme* recruits. Under rulers such as Selim I and Süleyman, the autocracy was an effective instrument of administration and warfare, but the degree to which its efficiency depended on the ruler's drive and control was demonstrated in the decades that followed. Selim II lacked the qualities of his predecessors: his succession had indeed been brought about by a harem conspiracy at the expense of his able elder brother. Selim's successors were no more capable than he of leading the state.

This decline in the quality of the sultans was accelerated by certain changes in the customs of the ruling house. The appointment of princes to provincial governorships ceased. At the same time the law of fratricide fell into disuse; the brothers of the reigning sultan were no longer put to death, but immured in palace-prisons, where lives of isolation and luxury sapped their abilities. This would have had no political significance, had

[1] Even during the reign of Süleyman, premonitions of decay were expressed by Lûtfi Pasha, a *devshirme* recruit, who married the sultan's sister, and ended a distinguished administrative career as grand vezir (1539–41).

it not been for a change in the law of succession in 1617, when Sultan Ahmed I died leaving only minor children. Henceforward the sultanate passed, not to a son, but to the eldest male relative of the late ruler. The inevitable result was that, almost without exception, the remaining sultans were men who not merely lacked training in administration, but had been deprived of following even normally active lives.

Even Süleyman the Magnificent had shown some signs of wishing to withdraw from the personal conduct of affairs of state: his successors for the most part displayed as little taste as ability for the more onerous duties of their office. This withdrawal of the titular head of the state has been a frequent phenomenon, in western as well as in oriental monarchies, and the powers and functions of the monarch have usually devolved in practice upon a minister or military chief. A frustrated development took place in the Ottoman Empire. As the powers of the sultan declined, those of the grand vezir grew. The old council of state, the Imperial *Divan*, declined into a formal assembly for ceremonial purposes.[1] In 1654, the grand vezir acquired an official residence, which for nearly two centuries remained the real centre of Ottoman administration.[2] During the later seventeenth century, a series of able grand vezirs from the family of Köprülü succeeded in arresting the administrative decay of the empire.

Yet the Grand Vezirate never completely succeeded in establishing its autonomy of the sultanate. From first to last, the grand vezir, however extensive his sway and however great his abilities, was the creature of the sultan, from whose will in making appointments or ordering dismissals there was no appeal. In the period of the shadow-sultanate, this meant that the grand vezir was at the mercy of harem factions, or intrigues of court favourites. It is, moreover, a recurrent feature of Islamic history that, as a kind of instinctive safety-device, the holders of power, in the absence of a strong ruler, tend to polarize into two opposing groups. This occurred with the institutionalization of the Grand Vezirate, which was confronted with the rival organization of the Imperial Household. In the seventeenth century the opposition of these two institutions was aggravated by ethnic rivalry; the Grand Vezirate being staffed by freeborn Turkish-speaking Muslims, mostly of Rumelian descent, while the

[1] The sultans down to Mehmed II used to preside in person over the sessions of the *Divan*. Mehmed introduced the practice of observing the proceedings concealed behind a grille. Süleyman ceased completely to attend the *Divan*.

[2] In the eighteenth century, the grand vezir's residence became known as *Bab-i ʿali*, i.e. the Sublime Porte—a term which does not (as is sometimes thought) signify the sultan's palace.

personnel of the Imperial Household was largely drawn from tribute-children from the Caucasus.

The last sentence indicates that during the seventeenth century profound changes took place in the recruitment of the imperial service. These were associated with the passing of the *devshirme*-system. The *devshirme* had provided the great sultans of the fifteenth and sixteenth centuries with admirable military and administrative instruments, but after the time of Süleyman, it came under attack from several sides. The essence of the system was that its vigour should be preserved by regular recruitment; that the privileges and dignities to which it opened the way should neither be heritable, nor available to the free-born Muslim peoples of the empire. The maintenance of the system thus meant that its very personnel were dissatisfied, since they could not hand on their status to their children; while its existence gave offence to a great body of people who, although Muslim subjects of a Muslim empire, were virtually excluded from the chief political and administrative positions. The acquisition of the Arab lands gave the Ottoman Empire, for the first time, a majority of Muslims, and this also may have contributed to the pressure on the *devshirme*-system later in the sixteenth century.

The *devshirme*-system was not only a method of recruitment, but also of selection, training and promotion. One of its products was, as we have seen, the corps of Janissaries, which, as time went on, began to threaten the authority of the sultans. There had indeed been dangerous symptoms at an earlier date, but as long as the sultans were the leaders of their armies in successful warfare, these had been only transient phenomena.[1] When the great age of imperial expansion came to an end, however, at the death of Süleyman, the political threat from the privileged corps of Janissaries became apparent.

Under Sultan Murad III (1574–95) a great expansion of the Janissaries by the admission of untrained recruits took place. This was partly, perhaps mainly, caused by the demands of war with Persia, but there seems to have been also an intention to weaken their dangerous *esprit de corps*. Their insubordination, however, increased, and in 1622 they brought about the deposition and death of Sultan Osman II. By the middle of the century the *devshirme* was obsolete. Janissaries still in service were allowed to marry, and to introduce their own children into the corps. Finally enrolment was thrown open to free-born Muslims

[1] The Janissaries had played a leading part in bringing about the accession of Selim I in 1512. They had occasionally been insubordinate under him and his successor, Süleyman.

generally. Not only in Istanbul, but also in the great towns of the empire, where bodies of garrison Janissaries were stationed, the Janissaries became essentially a stratum of the urban population, and engaged in civilian occupations. Their members intermarried with the local people, from whom also they drew recruits. The rank and file shared the outlook and desires of the artisan class, to which they were intimately allied; but their organization, their privileges, and their arms gave them an ascendancy ranging from petty local tyranny to the power of effective intervention in provincial, or even imperial, politics. By the eighteenth century the Janissaries existed less as a fighting force than as an entrenched privileged group.

The abandonment of the *devshirme*-recruitment, and consequently of the system of training and promotion dependent on it, had profound effects on the empire, since not the fighting forces only, but also the bureaucracy and administration—virtually the whole of the Ruling Institution, in fact—lapsed into disorder. The grand vezirs, lacking *devshirme* training and systematic promotion through a *cursus honorum*, show a marked decline in quality. Office became the reward of influence and favour, and was esteemed because of the material rewards, both legal and illicit, which it offered. Posts were purchased, and their holders used them to recoup their losses, and to amass private fortunes. As candidates for office increased, periods of tenure became even briefer, so that by the eighteenth century provincial governorships, for example, were frequently held for no more than a year.

Although the deterioration of the Ruling Institution, and the spread of corruption, are partly to be explained by the failure of the Ottomans to find a substitute for the *devshirme*-system, there were other, economic factors at work which contributed to the decline of the empire. In part, these were the result of the end of the long period of territorial expansion, which had gone on almost without interruption from the time of Osman to that of Süleyman. The conquests of the sixteenth century had brought the Ottomans up against two other great powers, the Safavids and the Habsburgs, as well as the unfamiliar geographical conditions of the Iranian plateau and the humid river-valleys of central Europe.[1] For a time the consequences of this confrontation were postponed. The Safavids were on the whole unable to meet the Ottomans on equal terms, while the Habsburgs during the first half of the seventeenth century were preoccupied with the Thirty Years War (1618–48).

[1] Thus, the camels, on which Ottoman military transport largely depended, suffered very heavy mortality in the European campaigns.

Thereafter the stalemate in Europe was broken. In 1683, for the second and last time, an Ottoman army besieged Vienna. The deliverance of the Habsburg capital by the Poles under John Sobieski marked the turning-point of Ottoman fortunes. In 1699 the Treaty of Carlowitz retroceded the greater part of Ottoman Hungary to the Habsburgs. The Austrian *Drang nach Osten*, which was to continue to the eve of the First World War, had begun.

The eighteenth century was to see the Ottoman Empire threatened from two other directions. On the ruins of the Safavid state, a Turcoman adventurer, generally known by his throne-name of Nādir Shāh, erected a military empire, which for a few years menaced the two older Muslim monarchies of the Ottomans and the Mughals of India. But this renewed danger from Persia ended with the death of Nādir Shāh in 1747. Slower to develop, but infinitely more portentous for the Ottoman Empire, was the threat from the rising power of Russia. Events in the reign of Peter the Great foreshadowed the future. The Tsar's determination to obtain a warm-water post led him to organize a great expedition in 1695–6 against Azov. Here he established a naval base, which however he lost after a further campaign against the Ottomans in 1711. Not until the reign of Catherine II, in the second half of the century, did the Russians regain a foothold on the shores of the Black Sea. The Russo–Ottoman War of 1769–74 was disastrous for the sultan. By the Treaty of Küchük Kaynarja which concluded it, the Ottoman claim to suzerainty over the Tatars of the Crimea was relinquished. Nine years later the Crimea was annexed by Russia. The Austrian push through Hungary to the Balkans had now a counterpart in the Russian push through the Black Sea to Istanbul and the Mediterranean. The conditions of the 'Eastern Question' of the nineteenth century were being created.

The phenomenon of the static and diminishing empire confronted the Ottomans with grave embarrassments. These were partly ideological. The old tradition of the *ghāzī* had survived the transformation of the Ottoman state from a polity of march-warriors to an autocratic monarchy. With the empire in decline, hard pressed by Christian rulers and Shīʿī heretics, the memory of the *ghāzī* past still lived on, ever more incongruously with current political realities. But the end of the period of expansion also brought serious financial and economic problems. The profitable booty of conquest ceased to flow in to sustain the magnificence of the ruling élite. Man-power and revenue diminished as rich provinces passed to the enemy. Thus, both morally and materially, the dwindling of the empire contributed to the corruption of the Ottoman Ruling Institution.

Besides these difficulties which were peculiar to the historical circumstances of the Ottomans, the empire shared a great economic problem with the other states of Europe. This was the price-revolution resulting from the influx of American silver into Europe. While the amount of silver in circulation increased, the Ottoman government failed to obtain an adequate share of it. Commerce was ineffectively taxed, and the customs-system was in any case evaded by large-scale smuggling—for example, of grain to Europe. Thus, on the one hand, the government was driven by its lack of silver to debasement of the currency (which had as its unit the silver *asper* or *akche*); while, on the other, large private fortunes were being built up, derived from speculation and money-lending, as well as from trade and the profits of office. Warfare against Persia in the last quarter of the sixteenth century was a factor of great importance in bringing about the Ottoman financial crisis. It is significant that the great initial debasement of the *akche* in 1584 followed by two years Murad III's expansion of the Janissary corps, and was accompanied by a similar devaluation of the Persian currency. The process of devaluation continued throughout the seventeenth century.

Since the salaries of the troops and bureaucracy remained fixed at their traditional levels, the great inflation of the sixteenth and seventeenth centuries bred corruption and other abuses throughout the whole framework of the Ruling Institution. Apart from increasing the avarice of administrative officials, and the rapacity and extortion practised by the soldiery on peasants and artisans, it may well have contributed to the transformation of the Janissaries from a genuine military force to a privileged order of lower middle-class society, dependent on its civilian earnings, and its illicit extortions, rather than its military pay. Another abuse resulted more indirectly from the financial stringency of this period. It became an increasingly common practice for the treasury to confiscate the accumulated wealth of high officials on their death or dismissal from office. To safeguard their property for themselves and their heirs, such men had recourse to the legal and recognized device of *waqf*. By transforming their possessions into *waqf ahlī*, they placed them under the protection of the *Sharīʿa*, as a species of family trust in perpetuity. Although this device was sound in law, and although the state endeavoured to discriminate between possessions which could, and could not, be placed in *waqf*, the process was pushed to a point that was socially harmful, and it had to be arrested abruptly by the reformers of the nineteenth century.

The great inflation which lay at the root of the financial and social evils of the Ottoman Empire would not in itself have had excessively deleterious effects if the general economy had been sound. This, unfortunately, was not the case. The Ottoman state depended essentially on its agriculture, and during this period the whole framework of agrarian society in the older provinces of Anatolia and Rumelia was being shaken. Traditionally, most of the land in these provinces was granted in fiefs to the *sipahis*, the feudal cavalry which represented the oldest part of the Ottoman armed forces. By the later sixteenth century, the rôle of the *sipahis* in warfare had become less important, and their decline as a class of landed gentry ensued. As *timars* fell vacant, they were resumed as imperial domain, and their revenues collected through tax-farmers (*multazims*). Nevertheless, the *sipahis* continued to exist, although as a dwindling element in rural society, until the reforms of the nineteenth century.

While agriculture declined, or at best remained stagnant, trade was in little better state. The great conquests, from the time of Mehmed II to that of Süleyman I, had placed in the hands of the sultans the entire coastline of the eastern Mediterranean, with its great historic ports—Istanbul, Smyrna, Alexandretta, Alexandria and the rest. Within their territories also lay the great inland emporia, such as Baghdād, Aleppo, Damascus and Cairo, and across them ran the ancient routes by which commerce passed between the Orient and the Mediterranean. The Ottomans succeeded to the trading inheritance of the Byzantines and the Mamluks, yet here as elsewhere the picture from the end of the sixteenth to the eighteenth century is one of general decline.

This was not wholly the fault of the sultans and their servants. As far as the trade of the Arab provinces was concerned, they were unfortunate in that they acquired possession of a region the eastern part of which had been an economic backwater since the Mongol conquest or even before, while the western part had lost much of its prosperity in the last century of Mamluk rule. They were unfortunate also in that the acquisition of the Arab provinces preceded by a comparatively brief period the general decline of the empire. Furthermore the whole current of commercial development was turning away from the lands under Ottoman rule to the great oceanic routes. Yet at the very worst the Ottomans profited by some trickles of the trade with Further Asia. By contrast, they were completely excluded from the other great fields of western European commercial enterprise—the Americas and West Africa.

One cause of the commercial backwardness of the empire must however be sought in the outlook of the Ottoman governing élite itself. Nourished on the *ghāzī*-tradition, the sultans and statesmen had little interest in or understanding of trade. The merchants, entrepreneurs and financiers of the empire were drawn, almost without exception, from groups outside the Ruling Institution. Many of them, indeed, were not even subjects of the sultan. Trade with Christian Europe was handled by merchants from the importing countries—at first particularly the Genoese, then in the sixteenth and seventeenth centuries the French and the English. Within the empire, many of the richest merchants and financiers were *dhimmīs*, Christians or Jews, who could at best exert a limited influence, rather than acquire power, in this Muslim state. Recent research has, however, demonstrated extensive activity by Muslim speculators and moneylenders in the late sixteenth and seventeenth centuries, in spite of the interdiction placed by the *Sharīʿa* on the taking of interest. Yet the Muslim traders and craftsmen remained on the whole petty bourgeoisie, lacking the incentive which stimulated the commercial expansion and the industrial development of western Europe.

To the Western observer, the Ottoman Empire in decline seemed an epitome of 'the unchanging East'. The traditional, grandiloquent formulae of politics and diplomacy, the religious and linguistic content of culture and education, the varied yet archaic costumes of its people, distinguishing their rank and function in society as well as their confessional or ethnic affiliations—all these seemed the hallmarks of a static and conservative polity, contrasting incongruously with a Europe emerging into the commercial, technical and industrial civilization of modern times. To some extent the Western view was justified. Like earlier Muslim states, the Ottoman Empire looked for its ideals and inspiration to a golden age in the past, was sceptical of the effectiveness of human endeavour, and found the idea of progress alien to its values. In this context the Ottoman concept of law was significant. Law was not an instrument for modifying the features of society under the pressure of historical events, for enunciating and safeguarding the right of individuals, or for realizing the ideals of political philosophers. Law was something given by God in the *Sharīʿa*, or sanctioned by custom in the *qānūns*. If properly understood, and rightly applied, the *Sharīʿa* would ensure the well-being of the Islamic community, and of the individual Muslim as a member of that community. Similarly, the *qānūns* would maintain the functioning of the Ottoman Empire in accordance with precedent and good usage.

But the Ottoman Empire had, by the eighteenth century, become conservative in a sinister sense. It had become a congeries of groups and organizations, the primary concern of which, in an age of diminishing military power, political instability and economic impoverishment, was to maintain their entrenched rights and privileges, many of which had been usurped, or extended by prescription, during the period of decline. One of these groups was the Janissaries, whose transformation we have already briefly reviewed. Another was composed of the *ʿulamāʾ*, the theologians and jurists, organized in a ramified corporation throughout the empire. Few of them, whether Turkish-speaking or Arabic-speaking, were notable in the eighteenth century for breadth of mind or depth of learning. Their training in the *madrasas* was the dried husk of a once-living curriculum. Nepotism and corruption flourished in the Learned no less than in the Ruling Institution. On occasion the two great reactionary corporations of the Janissaries and the *ʿulamāʾ* made common cause, as they did in 1807 to overthrow the reforming sultan, Selim III. The Janissaries and the *ʿulamāʾ* were, however, only the most outstanding of these groups, whose conservatism did not represent a survival of the traditional ethos of Ottoman society so much as a blind determination to retain the spoils of an empire in decline.

To a large extent the appearance of changelessness presented by the Ottoman state was misleading. Admittedly the façade of the classical empire remained. Sultans of the House of Osman followed each other in unbroken succession. The ancient offices and titles continued in use. The military and fiscal systems retained the forms that had been impressed upon them by the great rulers of the past. Yet in reality the distribution and exercise of power was far different: the fabric of social life—the more truly unchanging element in these lands—was maintained by new political structures, or by old structures which had acquired new functions. By the later eighteenth century this process was far advanced: the Ottoman Empire had ceased to be a unitary state, and had become an assemblage of petty authorities, some transient, others more permanently established, with the sultan as little more than a titular overlord.

Characteristic of this process was the emergence, beginning effectively in the seventeenth century, of a new rural aristocracy, the *aʿyān* or notables, composed of landowners, leaseholders of the great estates which were formed out of the old *sipahi* fiefs, and tax-farmers. Like the feudal nobility of medieval Europe, the *aʿyān* assumed administrative functions in the countryside. They flourished mainly in Anatolia and Rumelia, where the old fief-system had its deepest roots, although the term *aʿyān*, with a less precise significance, appears also in the Arab provinces. A specifically Anatolian class was that of the *derebeys* (literally, 'valley-lords'), local dynasts, who established petty principalities in the rural areas.

Within the Arab provinces, there was a similar fragmentation and localization of authority, differing however in details from the process in Anatolia. Broadly speaking, three main types may be distinguished. Some provincial governors endeavoured to make themselves practically autonomous of the central government, prolonging their periods of office over an exceptional number of years, and seeking to establish local dynasties. This was a parallel development to that followed by the *derebeys* in Anatolia. It was achieved in Baghdād during the eighteenth century, although after the second generation the succession went to the *mamlūks*, not the natural heirs, of the founders of the dynasty. Less successful was the ʿAẓm family, which, also in the eighteenth century, gained control of Damascus and other Syrian provinces, but failed to assert an unbroken hold over the region. But the most successful and famous of all the founders of provincial dynasties, Muḥammad ʿAlī Pasha of Egypt, established his power at the very end of the period of decline, and carried out in his viceroyalty reforms which paralleled (and sometimes even preceded) those of the Ottoman sultans themselves. In Egypt, at an earlier period, the Ottoman viceroys had been overshadowed by military grandees, the beys, who were in some respects the lineal successors of the military élite of the former Mamluk sultanate. Elsewhere rulers or dynasties arose from the Arabic-speaking inhabitants of the region, who obtained formal recognition usually as tax-farmers of the sultan, but whose power rested in reality on hereditary prestige, tribal or familial connections, or a shrewd exploitation of favouring circumstances. Such were the two successive dynasties who ruled in the Lebanon, the Maʿnids and the Shihābīs, while a more transitory domination was established in Upper Egypt by Shaykh Humām of Hawwāra, and in Galilee by Shaykh Ẓāhir al-ʿUmar.

By the end of the eighteenth century, the Ottoman Empire seemed about to break up, like the ʿAbbasid and other earlier Islamic empires, into a collection of petty dynastic states. But the pressure of Christian Europe, and the reaction which this provoked, produced a revival and transformation of Ottoman power, accompanied by technological developments, especially in communications, which postponed the catastrophe for another century.

5

Egypt in the Seventeenth Century

The general decline in the political condition of the Ottoman Empire, which set in during the last decades of the sixteenth century, is reflected in the course of events in Egypt. The great inflation, and the consequent depreciation of the salaries of the officials and soldiery, began to have political repercussions towards the end of the century. It is significant that a viceroy who ruled between 1580 and 1583 is described as avaricious, while bribery flourished openly in his time. The next viceroy carried out an inquisition into his predecessor's acts, and sent a report to the sultan, which was followed by the expropriation of the former viceroy's wealth. This procedure was later to become a matter of routine, but this occasion seems to have been its first occurrence in Egypt.

Meanwhile the power of the transient viceroys was visibly declining as it was challenged by the insubordination of the permanent garrison of Egypt. The first military revolt occurred in 1586, and was sparked off by an investigation held by the viceroy. For the first time, the troops suspended a viceroy from his functions, and brought him down from the Citadel to remain under house-arrest in Cairo. His successor turned his attention to the soldiery, only to provoke another revolt in 1589, in which members of his retinue and other notables were put to death, and his private quarters were pillaged. After several days of disorder, a conference of notables, headed by the chief judge and the *defterdar* (the chief financial official) of Egypt, assembled in the mosque of Sultan Ḥasan, and sought to restore order. The mutineers paid no attention, even though the viceroy sent the chief judge an order to grant them what they would. Two further revolts followed, in 1598 and 1601, the latter being precipitated by a grievance over the administration of the government grain-store.

During these revolts, two of the military corps remained loyal to the viceroys, their noble guard, the *Mutafarriqa*, and the *Chavushan*, or pursuivants. Neither of these was an effective military force, and the viceroys seem to have relied increasingly on the support and protection of a group of grandees known as the beys. The beys of Egypt are an anomaly in Ottoman administration. They had the same title (in Turkish,

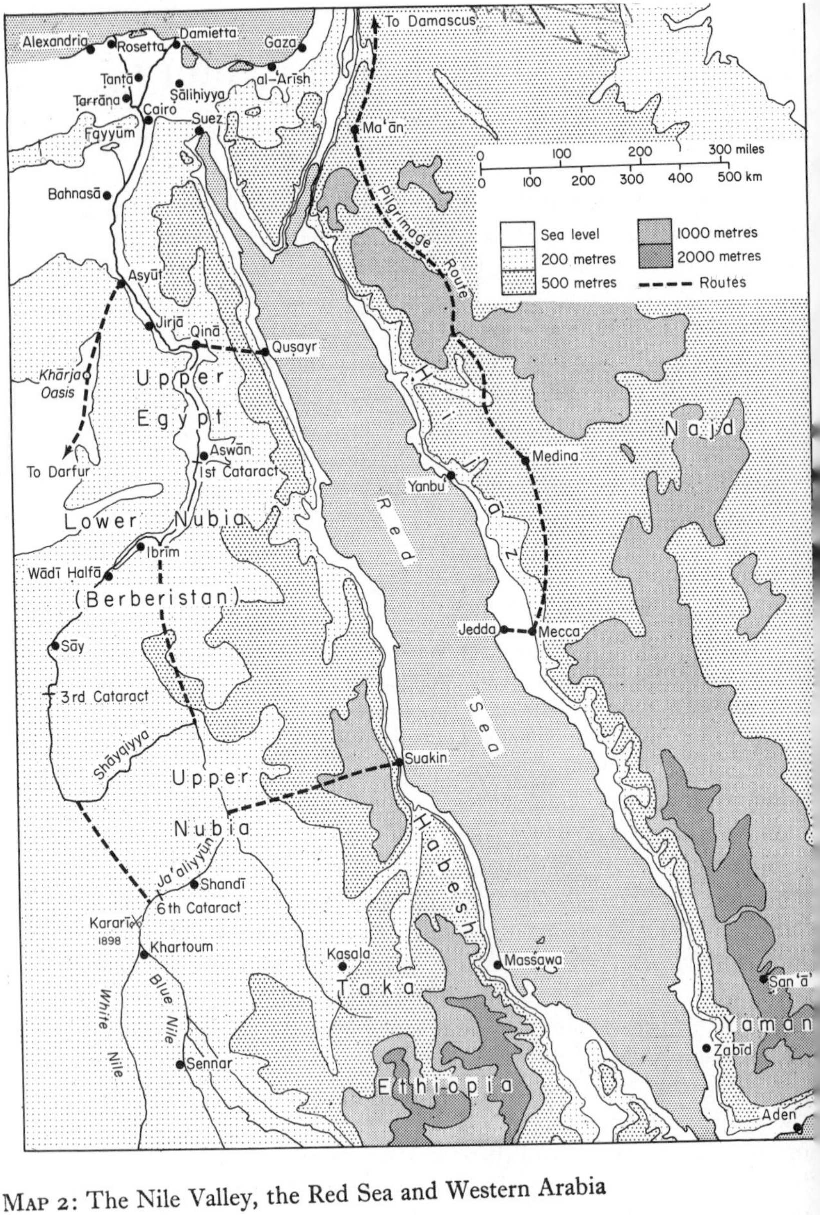

Map 2: The Nile Valley, the Red Sea and Western Arabia

sanjak bey) as the governors of the petty provinces in Anatolia, Rumelia and Syria. In Egypt, however, they were not at first governors of the sub-provinces, which were administered, as we have seen earlier, by officials bearing the old Mamluk title of *kāshif*. Neither were they fief-holders, but recipients of an annual salary (*saliyane*). The beys of Egypt, whose history in the sixteenth century is extremely obscure, seem to have been the institutional successors of the military grandees of the Mamluk sultanate, whose title of *amīr* is in fact rendered in Turkish by *bey*. An Egyptian bey was originally the holder of a rank, not of a specific office, and this absence of specialized functions was to assist them, in the seventeenth and eighteenth centuries, to establish their control over the whole administrative machine in Egypt. At first they seem to have been little more than *aides-de-camp*, attending on the viceroy's person, together with the *Mutafarriqa* and the *Chavushan*.

Not only were the beys the successors of the Mamluk *amīrs* in an institutional sense; they were also largely, although not exclusively, themselves Mamluks by origin. Evidence for the sixteenth century is almost completely lacking in the chronicles, but in the seventeenth century many of the beys were Circassians, and had passed an apprenticeship to arms, technically as slaves, in the households of beys of an earlier recruitment. There were some exceptions: occasionally an Arab chief or an Ottoman courtier would be promoted to the beylicate, while an important group of seventeenth-century beys originated from Bosnia. Nevertheless, the beylicate in the seventeenth century was, broadly speaking, an order of military grandees, standing outside the regimental cadres of the seven corps of the garrison,[1] largely recruited from Mamluks, and perpetuating itself through the formation of new Mamluk households.

When the viceroy Ibrāhīm Pasha (known as *al-Ḥājj* 'the Pilgrim', or, later, as *al-Maqtūl*, 'the Slain') came to Egypt in 1604, he began his administration with a show of determination. Confronted at Būlāq by troops demanding the customary donation bestowed by viceroys on taking up office, he answered them harshly. They thereupon pillaged his camp, and took the money by force. Once established in the Citadel, Ibrāhīm Pasha began to take his revenge on the soldiery. But this was an unpropitious time for stern measures. The previous two years had witnessed in turn dearth, famine and pestilence. The only result of the viceroy's severity was to induce the troops to plot his destruction.

[1] Regimental officers were sometimes promoted to the beylicate, as was the case with Koja Muṣṭafā, below, but seem to have lost their regimental appointments on promotion.

Their opportunity came in September 1605, at the time of the Nile flood, when Ibrāhīm Pasha left the security of the Citadel for Shubrā on the outskirts of Cairo. When his departure was known, the soldiery assembled and swore to kill him. They went to Būlāq, to find that he had already gone by boat to Shubrā, whither they made their way. When the news of their approach came in, some of the beys in the viceroy's retinue urged him to return to Būlāq, but he rejected this advice. The mutineers surrounded the house where he was, while fifteen *sipahis* with drawn swords broke in, and killed him. One of his courtiers protested against such an action by the sultan's troops against the sultan's minister, only to lose his own life. The rest of the company fled, and the assassins rejoined their comrades with the two heads, which were paraded through the streets of Cairo before being placed on the Zuwayla Gate, where criminals' remains were commonly exhibited.

This incident was too serious to be passed over, and the next viceroy brought an imperial order to carry out an investigation of the recent troubles. The beys and troops assembled in Kara Maydān, below the Citadel. Some of the senior beys were summoned to the viceroy's presence, and instructed to conduct the investigation. A long discussion ensued in Kara Maydān, which ended with the soldiery agreeing to surrender the ringleaders, in order to obtain pardon for the rest. A list of names was drawn up. The regimental commanders then arrested most of those implicated, and they were put to death in the audience-hall of the Citadel.

Further measures to reform the abuses of the soldiery were undertaken by the viceroy Muḥammad Pasha, who came to be known as *Kul Kıran*, 'the Breaker of the Mamluks'. To his first *Divan* in June 1607 he summoned the beys, the regimental commanders, the *Chavushan* and the *Mutafarriqa*. He began by enquiring into the death of Ibrāhīm Pasha. The officers of the *Chavushan* and *Mutafarriqa* accused the beys of complicity in the murder. Thirteen of them were deprived of their salary, and were banished from Cairo. The viceroy went on to forbid an illegal levy, the *ṭulba*, which was made by the *sipahis* in rural areas on the pretext of facilitating police duties. The *sipahis* were already perhaps the most disaffected part of the soldiery. They served in the sub-provinces and their financial situation was less favourable than that of the Janissaries and *ʿAzeban*, who were stationed in Cairo. They had played a prominent part in the risings in 1598 and 1605.

The abolition of the *ṭulba* produced a widespread revolt in January 1609, when the provincial soldiery mustered at Ṭanṭā, a town in the

Delta which contained the shrine of the saint Aḥmad al-Badawī. They swore not to give up the *ṭulba*, and also to kill the commanding officer of the *Chavushan*, Koja Muṣṭafā, and some of the beys. They appointed a sultan and ministers from amongst themselves. Setting out from Ṭanṭā, they provisioned themselves from the villages *en route*, and their numbers increased, since every soldier they met joined them, either freely or under compulsion. Thus they arrived in the sub-province of the Qalyūbiyya, north of Cairo, having on their way hunted down the fugitive *kāshif* of the Gharbiyya.

On hearing the news of the revolt, the viceroy summoned the commanding officers of the *sipahis*, and put to death a number of members of their regiments. This did not restore order, so Muḥammad Pasha assembled the beys, the *Chavushan* and the *Mutafarriqa*, and obtained a declaration of obedience to the sultan. He raised Koja Muṣṭafā[1] to the beylicate, and invested him with the command of a loyal force, which set out on 14 February to fight the rebels.

The rebels had now reached al-Khānqa, in the vicinity of Cairo. When they were confronted with Koja Muṣṭafā Bey's force, their courage and determination ebbed rapidly, and they declared themselves willing to surrender. Muṣṭafā Bey demanded the attendance of their chief officers, who were promptly put in irons. Those rebels who lacked the status and privileges of Ottoman soldiers, about fifty in number, were then brought forward, and beheaded on the spot. The rest, troops whose names were enrolled in the official registers, were brought in by companies, and disarmed. Two days after leaving Cairo, the triumphant loyalists re-entered the capital, and paraded through its streets from morning to mid-afternoon.

The rebel chiefs were put to death, as were also some fifty soldiers whose safe-conducts were revoked. At the news of this action, the remainder sought refuge in flight. The fugitives were plundered by the Arabs, while others who hid in Cairo were betrayed by the native Egyptians, who informed the authorities of them and thereby procured their deaths. On the Thursday after the victory, the chief judge interceded with the viceroy for the remnant of the rebels. At his request, they were exiled to the Yaman and, at the end of the month, about three hundred of the wretches, with shackled hands, were put on camels and sent to Suez on the first stage of their journey. The suppression of this

[1] For biographical details concerning Koja Muṣṭafā and other beys mentioned in this chapter, see the writer's article, 'The beylicate in Ottoman Egypt during the seventeenth century', *BSOAS*, xxiv/2, 1961, 214–48.

revolt was commemorated by an order from the viceroy instructing the people of Cairo to dig out a cubit's depth of earth before their houses and shops, to erase the foot-prints of the rebels from the ground they had trodden.

What was the significance of this episode? It was clearly a serious revolt, and one more extensive in its scope than the challenges to the earlier viceroys. But it may have been more than this. A contemporary chronicler speaks of Muḥammad Pasha's triumph as being 'in truth the second conquest of Egypt during the sacred Ottoman government'. The description seems absurdly exaggerated if one compares the pitiful capitulation of the rebels at al-Khānqa with the battles of Marj Dābiq and al-Raydāniyya, but this may not have been quite what the chronicler had in mind.

The episode had been preceded, as we have seen, by the removal from office of thirteen beys, a number representing just over half of the traditional establishment. Clearly an important proportion of these neo-Mamluk military grandees were disaffected to Ottoman rule, and were working behind the scenes to foment trouble for the viceroys. Furthermore, it must be remembered that one of the three *sipahi* corps, the *Cherakise*, had originally been formed from survivors of the old Mamluk cavalry, and was still recruited from Circassians.[1] These considerations, and the fact that the rebels of 1609 nominated a sultan and ministers, would seem to indicate that the revolt was not merely a military rebellion, but a separatist movement, such as Egypt had not known since the overthrow of Aḥmad Pasha al-Khā'in. The victory which Muḥammad Pasha achieved through the agency of Koja Muṣṭafā Bey (himself probably a member of the élite of neo-Mamluk grandees) was therefore a reaffirmation of Ottoman domination in Egypt, which was not again to be openly challenged until the time of Bulut Kapan ʿAlī Bey, over a century and a half later.

The rule of Muḥammad Pasha represented a serious endeavour to cope with the problems of Ottoman administration in Egypt. His severity in punishing the conspirators against Ibrāhīm Pasha, and the rebels of 1609, brought to an end the period of the *sipahi* revolts, and shattered the dream of a revived Mamluk sultanate in Egypt. His suppression of the *ṭulba*, and other attempts to enforce the land-law, were an endeavour to promote rural prosperity, while protecting the pro-

[1] In this connection, it may be noted that the chronicler mentioned above states that the *ṭulba* was practised by the Ghuzz—a term applied exclusively to the Mamluk element in Ottoman Egypt.

vincial and imperial treasuries against the encroachments of powerful local groups and individuals. Yet the limitations of his achievements were as important for the future as his successes. Like other Ottoman statesmen of his period, he totally failed to grasp the underlying economic factors which were affecting the condition of his province. His prescription for reform was the traditional one of abolishing innovations, and of seeking to restore, against the current of history, the institutions of Süleyman's time. Moreover, in spite of his obvious strength of personality and capacity for administration, he was granted no long tenure of office: in little over four years he left Egypt, although, an exceptional honour, he was not formally deposed by the sultan. With his departure, the succession of weak and transient viceroys begins once more.

Even Muḥammad Pasha's victory over the rebels demonstrates one of the chronic weaknesses of the viceroys of Egypt. To support their authority they had no independent and indisputably loyal forces. The seven corps of the Ottoman garrison were not a national Egyptian army in the modern sense, but they were groups which had vested local interests of their own: interests which could no longer be harmonized with those of the imperial government and its representatives. The viceroys were thus at a permanent disadvantage, having no reliable force to back their policies, and were forced to rely on those elements to whose temporary interest it was to support their authority. Some modern writers have seen in this painful and embarrassed search for props to sustain a failing power the application of a machiavellian policy of 'divide and rule', but this opinion ascribes too much of principle and intent to a matter of shifting expediency.

After the departure of Muḥammad Pasha, the beys rapidly come forward as the dominant political group in Egypt. Their lack of specific administrative functions (none are ascribed to them in the *Qānūn-name* of 1525, in which they are indeed hardly mentioned) left them free to establish prescriptive rights to a whole range of offices, and get a grip on the entire administrative and fiscal system of Egypt. Some of these offices were military: *ad hoc* forces, such as Koja Muṣṭafā's, expeditions against predatory Arabs within Egypt, or bodies of troops sent at the sultan's command to fight in the European or Persian wars, were placed under the command of a *serdar*, who was invariably a bey, not one of the regular regimental officers. Every year, when the tribute of Egypt had to be convoyed overland to Istanbul, it was placed in charge of a bey holding the title of *amīr al-Khazna*. The safe conduct of the annual

Pilgrimage caravan to Mecca and back was similarly committed to a bey who was entitled *amīr al-Ḥajj*, and who, as we shall see, became in the seventeenth century one of the great officers of state. Furthermore, the appointments of beys as sub-provincial governors became in the end so usual that the two terms came to be equated, while the *kāshifs* sank to a subordinate position. During the later sixteenth century, as we have seen, Upper Egypt was constituted into one immense governorate, with its capital at Jirjā, ruled by a bey with the title of 'governor of the South' (*ḥākim al-Ṣaʿīd*).[1]

All these offices were either purely military, or had military implications: the *amīr al-Khazna* and *amīr al-Ḥajj* were commanders of armed convoys, while the beys seem to have been appointed to the sub-provinces in the first place as military governors, to fend off the pressure of the nomad tribes on the settled lands. But the beylicate also controlled an important and lucrative civil appointment, that of the *defterdar*, who was the head of the fiscal administration in Egypt. A temporary appointment of great importance which came to be annexed to the beylicate during the seventeenth century was that of acting viceroy (*qāʾim maqām*). The *qāʾim maqām* exercised full viceregal powers between the death or removal from office of one viceroy and the installation of his successor. In earlier times this position was sometimes occupied by a judge, but after 1604 it seems to have been invariably held by a bey. We shall see the significance of this development in connection with the growing ascendancy of the beys in the seventeenth and eighteenth centuries.

The first signs of this ascendancy showed themselves only fourteen years after the masterful rule of Muḥammad Pasha. In 1623 orders were received from Istanbul recalling the viceroy Muṣṭafā Pasha and appointing a certain ʿAlī Pasha as his successor. Muṣṭafā Pasha accepted his supersession, but the troops were unwilling to receive the new viceroy, and demanded the continuance in office of Muṣṭafā Pasha, who awarded them a rise in pay. A formal petition for his retention was sent to Istanbul, and when ʿAlī Pasha actually arrived in Alexandria, the troops and the beys jointly informed him that he would not be received. He was attacked by the garrison of Alexandria, returned on board ship, and fled to Beirut. This high-handed treatment of a viceroy-designate was accepted by the imperial court. Muṣṭafā Pasha was permitted to resume his powers, which he retained until 1626.

In this episode it is not easy to see the extent to which the beys were

[1] See above, p. 51.

acting independently, since the initiative in the rejection of ʿAlī Pasha seems to have been taken by the regimental soldiery. Under Muṣṭafā Pasha's successor, Mūsā Pasha, however, the ascendancy of the beylicate is unmistakable. A clash developed between this viceroy and a leading grandee named Qayṭās Bey, whom Mūsā invested as the *serdar* of an expeditionary force to be sent to assist the sultan against Persia. But having made a special levy on the country, and mulcted Qayṭās himself of a considerable sum, Mūsā revoked his orders, declaring that the contingent could not be financed. The viceroy had thus created a dangerous enemy, of whom he sought to rid himself. On 9 July 1631 Qayṭās, who like the other beys had gone up to the Citadel to greet the viceroy on the occasion of a Muslim feast, was assassinated in Mūsā Pasha's presence.

The reaction of the beylicate was sharp and immediate. The beys refused to allow the viceroy's officer to proceed with the taxation of their dead colleague's estate, and forbade the troops to attend the viceregal banquet held in connection with the feast. The chief judge was sent to the viceroy to demand the reason for the assassination, and to require the production either of an imperial order or of the persons of the culprits. Mūsā Pasha refused to give any satisfaction, and was warned that if he continued in his refusal, the grandees would appoint a *qāʾim maqām* in his place. To this the viceroy replied, 'Let them do so—if they can do so lawfully.'

This they proceeded to do. Although some of the beys wished to kill Mūsā, while others were averse to suspending him from office without an order from the sultan, agreement was finally reached on the appointment of a *qāʾim maqām*. Mūsā Pasha deferred to the accomplished fact, and sent reports on the episode to the sultan and the grand vezir. The grandees took a similar course. Formal statements, in Turkish and Arabic respectively, were drawn up by the beys and regimental officers, and by the judges and the *ʿulamāʾ* of al-Azhar. These were sent off with a delegation, provided with funds from the estate of Qayṭās Bey, composed of representatives of the beylicate and the seven corps. The delegation met with success in its mission, and the grandees of Cairo thereby established a precedent for the deposition (or, more precisely, the suspension) of an obnoxious viceroy, and the installation of a complaisant *qāʾim maqām*, chosen from among themselves, pending a new appointment by the sultan.

During the twenty-five years which followed the overthrow of Mūsā Pasha, the most outstanding figure in Egypt was the greatest of the seventeenth-century grandees, Riḍwān Bey al-Faqārī. He was of Circassian origin, and was the leader of a faction of the beylicate and their dependents, known collectively as the Faqāriyya.[1] This group had allies among the artisans and nomad tribesmen who composed an older faction, called Niṣf Saʿd. Over against the alliance of the Faqāriyya and Saʿd stood a rival grouping, of the Qāsimiyya among the beys and their retainers in alliance with the artisan and nomad faction of Niṣf Ḥarām. By the end of the seventeenth century the old names of Saʿd and Ḥarām had been virtually superseded by the newer terms of Faqāriyya and Qāsimiyya, and Egyptian society was polarized into these factions. Between them existed a latent antagonism, which flared out on occasions, as we shall see, into a mutually destructive hostility.

In 1631 Riḍwān Bey al-Faqārī was *amīr al-Ḥajj*, and thus was absent from Cairo when the struggle between the beys and Mūsā Pasha took place, although a leading part in this was played by one of his close associates, ʿAlī Bey al-Faqārī. Although the Command of the Pilgrimage was technically an annual appointment, it was held by Riḍwān from 1631 almost uninterruptedly until his death a quarter of a century later. This was a situation of considerable prestige, which Riḍwān seems to have been anxious to enhance. A pedigree was drawn up, tracing his lineage from the Circassian Mamluk sultans, Barqūq and Barsbāy, and deriving the origin of the Circassians themselves from Quraysh of Mecca. The evident spuriousness of this genealogy does not conceal its serious political implications: it is tantamount to an assertion of Riḍwān's hereditary right to the throne of Egypt, with a further suggestion that he, by virtue of his alleged Qurashī descent, had a better claim than the Ottoman sultan to be 'the Servitor of the Two Holy Sanctuaries'.[2]

Had events developed differently, this almost-forgotten genealogy might have been adduced as the title-deed of a Mamluk sovereign in seventeenth-century Egypt. But Riḍwān, unlike Aḥmad al-Khā'in in the previous century, and Bulut Kapan ʿAlī Bey in the one which followed, never openly challenged the suzerain. His immense influence,

[1] It is usually asserted that the Faqāriyya obtained their name from an eponymous founder of a Mamluk household, Dhu'l-Faqār Bey. Dhu'l-Faqār is said by a Syrian biographer, al-Muḥibbī, to have been the master of Riḍwān Bey, but no information is given about him. The contemporary Egyptian chronicles mention no such person: the first Dhu'l-Faqār to be recorded appears *after* the death of Riḍwān. Dhu'l-Faqār may have been a sobriquet held by Riḍwān, and he himself may have been the founder of the Faqārī household, and hence of the faction. See further my article, 'Al-Jabartī's introduction to the history of Ottoman Egypt', *BSOAS*, xxv/1, 1962, 38–51.

[2] For further details, see the writer's article, 'The exalted lineage of Riḍwān Bey: some observations on a seventeenth-century Mamluk genealogy', *BSOAS*, xxii/2, 1959, 222–30.

and his undoubted popularity in Cairo, however, aroused on more than one occasion the jealousy of viceroys and the suspicions of the Ottoman court, who at these times exploited the inherent rivalry between the Faqāriyya and the Qāsimiyya.

In 1635, and again in 1637, Riḍwān was nominated as the *serdar* of an expeditionary force for a campaign against Persia, but on both occasions he succeeded in evading the appointment. Another dubious honour was bestowed on him in 1639, when he was appointed governor of the remote and dangerous province of Ḥabesh. The news of this reached him while he was on Pilgrimage. He fled to Istanbul, and sought the protection of influential mediators. Although for a time his life was in danger from the anger of Murad IV, he obtained an amnesty just before the sultan's death, and made a triumphal return to Egypt, where he resumed his former position and office as *amīr al-Ḥajj*.

Another attempt to oust him was made in 1647 by a viceroy who was under the influence of Qānṣawh Bey, a leader of the Qāsimiyya. Riḍwān went over his opponents' heads, to Sultan Ibrahim, and his accusations against Qānṣawh and his confederate Māmāy Bey were favourably received. To strengthen his position, Riḍwān summoned ʿAlī Bey al-Faqārī from Upper Egypt, where he ruled as governor. ʿAlī brought a considerable body of troops to Cairo, and the viceroy capitulated. The Faqāriyya now dominated Cairo, the Qāsimiyya were proscribed, and Qānṣawh and Māmāy died in prison. The crisis flared up again when ʿAlī obeyed the viceroy's command, and withdrew from Cairo, to return to Upper Egypt. The viceroy thereupon appointed another bey to the command of the Pilgrimage. Riḍwān fled to seek safety with ʿAlī, and the viceroy ordered an expeditionary force to march against them. But the troops refused to obey, and an imperial order arrived, conferring on both Riḍwān and ʿAlī the life-tenure of their offices.

A last attempt to weaken Riḍwān, by driving a wedge between him and ʿAlī Bey, was made by another viceroy after the deposition of Sultan Ibrahim, who had always been favourable to Riḍwān. In 1651, while Riḍwān was absent on Pilgrimage, ʿAlī was summoned to Cairo, and himself invested as *amīr al-Ḥajj*. But a fortnight later, the viceroy was deposed, and the appointment lapsed. Once again, Riḍwān made a triumphal return to Cairo where he was reconciled with ʿAlī Bey. But time was now running out for these two leaders of the Faqāriyya. ʿAlī died a year or so later, and Riḍwān survived him only until 1656.

With their passing, the Faqāriyya came to be directed by younger men, who exploited the ascendancy of their faction with an imprudent arrogance. Thereby they played into the hands of their opponents, the Qāsimiyya and the viceroys. On Riḍwān's death, the then viceroy tried to break the Faqārī monopoly of the command of the Pilgrimage by conferring it on a Qāsimī grandee, Aḥmad Bey the Bosniak, while Ḥasan Bey al-Faqārī, one of Riḍwān's *mamlūks*, who had expected to obtain the appointment, was fobbed off with the inferior command of the *Khazna*. The Faqāriyya made a tumultuous assembly, suspended the viceroy from office, and rusticated Aḥmad the Bosniak. Ḥasan Bey was appointed to the command of the Pilgrimage, and the Faqāriyya duly reported the incident to the sultan for his approval.

In the events of the next few years, Aḥmad Bey was to play a leading part. In 1658 an attempt was made to break the power of the Faqārī governor of Upper Egypt, Muḥammad Bey, a *mamlūk* of the late ʿAlī Bey, by appointing him to Ḥabesh, and giving Upper Egypt to Aḥmad Bey. Once again an army from Upper Egypt descended on Cairo. But the viceroy acted with resolution, and when Muḥammad Bey refused either to surrender Upper Egypt or to accept the investiture of Ḥabesh, he summoned a meeting of the grandees and religious notables, reported the disobedience of Muḥammad Bey, and obtained a *fatwā* authorizing warfare against him. An expeditionary force was constituted early in 1659, in which at least two of the five commanders belonged to the Faqāriyya. Muḥammad Bey's arrogance and hostility had alarmed the beylicate in general. He was pursued into Upper Egypt, where his followers were dispersed, and he himself captured and put to death.

Aḥmad Bey the Bosniak did not in fact take up the governorship of Upper Egypt, which went to yet another Faqārī. However, he was steadily strengthening his position, and in 1659 he was appointed *qāʾim maqām*. Meanwhile, with the removal of Muḥammad Bey, the Faqāriyya had regained their unity, but their ascendancy was seriously challenged by the rise of the Qāsimiyya under Aḥmad Bey the Bosniak. In 1660 it collapsed with dramatic suddenness.

'The Conflict of the Beys', as the incident is called by Egyptian chroniclers, began with a petty quarrel between two tax-farmers (*multazims*) in the Qalyūbiyya. An affray occurred in which the peasants of one attacked and killed some soldiers of the ʿ*Azeban* corps, sent to protect the rights of the other. But the offending party was none other than the chief of police in Cairo, who, on being summoned to appear before the viceroy's *Divan*, sought refuge with the Faqāriyya. Lachin Bey, the leading Faqārī grandee, took the culprit under his protection, and supported him in his contumacy. In due course the disobedience of the chief of police was legally established, and he was deprived of office, his post being given to a Qāsimī.

The Faqāriyya then took the fatal decision to resist the viceroy, another Muṣṭafā Pasha. They ignored his orders, and concerted a plan to bring him down from the Citadel, and reinstate his predecessor, who had been imprisoned in Cairo. They hoped to have the support of the Janissaries, while their adversaries could naturally count on the backing of the offended *ʿAzeban*. The hopes of the Faqāriyya were, however, disappointed: the *ʿAzeban* acted quickly, and the Janissaries did not rally to the Faqāriyya.

On hearing of this, the Faqāriyya rallied their forces to attempt a *coup de main*, but on meeting the fire of the *ʿAzeban*, they left Cairo and withdrew to the south. This was decisive for them. The initiative now passed from them to the viceroy, who ordered a general mobilization of the regimental troops in Cairo. He was working in co-operation with the Qāsimiyya: Shaʿbān Bey, the brother of Aḥmad Bey the Bosniak, was invested as governor of Upper Egypt; Aḥmad himself was appointed to the Manūfiyya, previously a Faqārī sub-province; Muḥarram, the son of the Qāsimī, Māmāy Bey, who had died in the proscription of 1647, was raised to the beylicate. The Qāsimiyya were now in control in Cairo, where they slew or exiled their opponents, and prepared to take their revenge on the fugitive Faqāriyya.

With the viceroy at its head, an expeditionary force, accompanied by a fleet of ships on the Nile, commanded by Shaʿbān Bey, set out for the south. In the meantime dissension had broken out among the Faqāriyya, some of whom wished to withdraw to Upper Egypt, others to go to the Buḥayra, whence (no doubt in alliance with Arab tribesmen) they could threaten the Delta and the capital from the west. Finally they broke up. One bey with his followers made his way into the remote Sudan, and disappeared from history. Muṣṭafā Bey, the proscribed Faqārī governor of Upper Egypt, went to his capital of Jirjā. Lachin Bey and two of his colleagues took Arab guides, who conducted them north-westwards to the Buḥayra.

The viceroy and his allies then proceeded to destroy the Faqāriyya piecemeal. Muṣṭafā Bey was captured, and sent a prisoner to Cairo. The viceroy and his *qāʾim maqām* in Cairo both sent troops against the rebels in the Buḥayra, who were soon surrounded and pinned down. They were offered a safe-conduct from the viceroy, which they accepted, and set out with their captors for Cairo. At al-Ṭarrāna, where a route from the Western Desert comes out on the Rosetta branch of the Nile, they were met by Aḥmad Bey the Bosniak, sent by the viceroy.

That night, 27 October 1660, while the captive beys were talking in their tent, a company of soldiers entered, loaded them with chains, and led them before Aḥmad Bey, in whose presence they were beheaded. Ahmad returned to Cairo, with their heads in his saddle-bag. As he rode up to the Citadel, Muṣṭafā Bey was decapitated before him. The viceroy celebrated his triumph, and that of the Qāsimiyya, by conferring over a hundred robes of honour on Aḥmad Bey's supporters.

Although the Faqāriyya were not completely extirpated, their political power was broken, and remained in abeyance for thirty years. Yet the ascendancy of Aḥmad Bey the Bosniak and the Qāsimiyya was to be of short duration. Aḥmad's very success in destroying his rivals, his apparent indispensability to the support of Ottoman authority in Egypt, was enough to render him obnoxious. So although the next viceroy entered Cairo accompanied by the Qāsimī grandee, he soon began to plot Aḥmad Bey's destruction. The story of Qayṭās Bey was repeated. On 26 July 1662 Aḥmad Bey went up to the Citadel to greet the viceroy on the occasion of a feast and was stabbed to death by the viceroy's retinue.

There, however, history ceased to repeat itself. The broken Faqāriyya and the leaderless Qāsimiyya were very different from the united and self-assertive beylicate which had confronted Mūsā Pasha in 1631. The viceroy remained in unquestioned control until his recall in 1664. The prestige of the beylicate had collapsed. In 1672 the *khidmat al-sanjaqiyya*, the sum paid by a prospective bey to obtain promotion, had dropped to a half or three-quarters of what it had been twenty years previously. At the same time there had been a reduction both in the *saliyane* of the beys, and in their total numbers. For some decades, the beys lost their pre-eminence in the political system of Egypt, until towards the end of the seventeenth century, a revival both of their self-confidence and of their factionalism took place.

6

The Ascendancy of the Beylicate in Eighteenth-Century Egypt

The overthrow, and almost complete extirpation, of the Faqāriyya in 1660, followed in 1662 by the assassination of the Qāsimī leader, Aḥmad Bey the Bosniak, seems to have checked the political ambitions of the beylicate, and to have arrested factional rivalry, for about a generation. During this time, the beys retained their hold on the great offices of state, and served as commanders of expeditions both abroad and against the Arab tribes of Egypt, but no longer sought to challenge the authority of the viceroys.

Nevertheless, the Faqārī and Qāsimī factions remained in being. Although the great household of Riḍwān Bey had been nearly eliminated, two of his retainers, Lachin Bey and Ḥasan Bey, had established Mamluk households of their own, and the successors of Ḥasan Bey in particular were to play an important part in events around the turn of the seventeenth century. The Faqāriyya were, moreover, allied, politically and by marriage, with another great Mamluk household founded by a regimental officer, Ḥasan Balfiyya, who finally rose to the position of *agha* (i.e. commanding officer) of the *Gönülliyan*. One of Hasan Agha's retainers, Muṣṭafā al-Qāzdughlī (like himself a regimental officer), in time established the powerful household of the Qāzdughliyya, who in the eighteenth century became the principal allies of the Faqāriyya. At the beginning of the eighteenth century the two leading members of the Qāsimiyya were Īwāẓ Bey and Ibrāhīm Bey Abū Shanab. The households founded by these two men formed the two branches of the Qāsimiyya clan in the decades that followed. Ibrāhīm Bey seems to have been, like Aḥmad Bey before him, of Bosniak origin.

When factional rivalry broke out again in Egypt, it was not at first among the beys, or between the Faqāriyya and Qāsimiyya, but within the seven corps of the Ottoman garrison. The first crimes are associated with the name of Küchük Muḥammad the *bashodabashı* of the Janissaries.[1] His origins are obscure, but he does not appear to have belonged

[1] See further, P. M. Holt, 'The career of Küçük Muḥammad (1676–94)', *BSOAS*, xxvi/2, 1963, 269–87.

to any of the great Mamluk households. Probably he came from the naturalized Janissaries of Cairo, perhaps a member of a Janissary family; or he may even have been of civilian origin and have bought his way into the corps because of the privileges and immunities which Janissary status conferred. It is significant that he never assumed the high regimental offices of *agha* or *kâhya*, which admitted their holders to membership of the *ikhtiyāriyya*, the order of veteran officers who theoretically directed the affairs of the corps and formed part of the ruling élite of Egypt.[1] On the contrary, his whole career was a running fight against the high command, and towards the end of his life he assumed the bearing of a tribune of the people.

Küchük Muḥammad was first appointed as *bashodabashı* of the Janissaries about 1674 or 1675. In 1676 he carried out his first *coup*, probably with the collusion of the viceroy, against two senior officers of the corps. These men were raised to the beylicate: an apparent promotion which was, in fact, a device for their destruction, since it withdrew them from the protection of their corps and made them immediately dependent on the viceroy's will. During the following months the viceroy connived at further measures against Küchük Muḥammad's opponents, but in 1680 a Janissary faction rose against the *bashodabashı*, who was banished from Egypt.

Six years later he returned and re-enrolled as a simple Janissary. In 1687 he carried out a second *coup*, regained his appointment as *bashodabashı*, and entered on a second struggle with his opponents. This time he enforced his will by turning the cannon of the Janissary headquarters on the *Divan*, where the grandees of Egypt were assembled to consider his case. His opponents were expelled from the corps, but Küchük Muḥammad's tenure of power was brief. A new *agha* of Janissaries arrived from the sultan, and compelled Küchük Muḥammad himself to leave the corps. He transferred himself to the *Gönülliyan*, then commanded by Ḥasan Agha Balfiyya. Clearly, an alliance between the *bashodabashı* and the Faqāriyya and their allies was in the making.

In 1692 the alliance bore fruit. At the head of the Faqāriyya was Ibrāhīm Bey, the son of a former *mamlūk* of Ḥasan Bey al-Faqārī. Ibrāhīm aimed at restoring in his own person the hegemony of the Faqāriyya in Egypt, and to do this he needed the support of the Janissaries. But the Janissary high command was at this time almost wholly Qāsimī in sympathy. Ibrāhīm therefore conspired with Küchük

[1] The *bashodabashı* was the chief of the *odabashıs*, junior officers, who headed the companies (*odas*) into which the Janissaries of Egypt were divided.

Muḥammad to bring about a *coup* in the Janissary headquarters, and restore the *bashodabashı* and his faction. This was accomplished, Küchük Muḥammad seized the headquarters, and his opponents were dispersed. One was killed, others were banished or expelled from the corps, two were reduced to impotence by being raised to the beylicate.

On regaining power, Küchük Muḥammad compelled the assembled *ikhtiyāriyya* of the seven corps to agree to the abolition of certain privileges, known as *ḥimāyāt* (literally, 'protections'), held by the Janissaries and the *ʿAzeban*. The *ḥimāyāt* are particularly mentioned in connection with the ports of Damietta, Rosetta and Būlāq, and seem to have been dues levied on the pretext of 'protection-money'. Since it is surprising for a Janissary to abolish privileges connected with his own corps, one must assume that the revenue from these dues accrued to Küchük Muḥammad's enemies, the senior officers, and one may also surmise that they were levied, at least in part, on those Janissaries who had become part of the urban artisan population. Recently introduced weighing-dues were abolished at the same time, and the whole programme of reforms was promulgated in a viceregal proclamation. Küchük Muḥammad's rôle as a popular tribune is depicted in another story. After his third seizure of power, a low Nile produced a rise in food prices. Thereupon Küchük Muḥammad went down to Būlāq, the port of Cairo for the produce of the Delta, and enforced the old price of corn, which remained stationary as long as he lived.

But his enjoyment of power was to be short. He had now acquired a new and dangerous rival, Muṣṭafā al-Qāzdughlī, the retainer of Ḥasan Balfiyya. Although Muṣṭafā held the high office of *kâhya* of Janissaries, he resented the obscurity into which the domination of the *bashodabashı* had thrown him, and Küchük Muḥammad obtained his virtual banishment to a post in Jedda. Two years later, on the intercession of Ḥasan Balfiyya, he was allowed to return. The rift between the senior officers, headed by al-Qāzdughlī, and the *odabashıs* and ordinary Janissaries led by Küchük Muḥammad, was openly recognized. The *bashodabashı* proved stronger than his opponents, and continued to hold his post, but in September 1694 he was assassinated by a gunman, hired by al-Qāzdughlī, as he rode through the streets of Cairo.

Küchük Muḥammad's power had been entirely personal, dependent upon his ability to build up a faction, and win the support of influential allies. Essentially, he was the boss of a Janissary gang, exercising unofficial authority from a position outside the established ruling élite of Egypt. The seizure of power by Ibrāhīm Bey ibn Dhi'l-Faqār, which he had facilitated, belonged to a different order of events; it marked the re-emergence of the beylicate as the dominant political group in Egypt, and the recrudescence of Faqārī–Qāsimī factional struggles.

For a time, however, the full implications of this were not plain. After Küchük Muḥammad's death Egypt was plunged into a severe economic crisis. The low Nile of 1694 was followed by dearth, famine and pestilence—a common sequence of calamities, but in this instance of unusual severity. The fiscal system was seriously dislocated, and conditions did not return to normal until the autumn of 1695. The death during the pestilence of Ibrāhīm Bey ibn Dhi'l Faqār, ended for the time being the ambitious project of a renewed Faqārī ascendancy in Egypt.

The turbulent corps of Janissaries continued to be a centre of trouble in Cairo. In 1698 and again in 1706 they were the source of serious incidents that disturbed public order. Then in 1707 a prolonged period of tension began, which culminated in the Great Insurrection of 1711, a minor civil war. As in the troubles at the end of the seventeenth century, a prominent part was played by a Janissary boss, on this occasion the *bashodabashı* Afranj Aḥmad. Nothing is known about his early life, although his name (*Afranj*, otherwise *Faranjī*, Aḥmad) may mean that he was of western European origin. His opportunity to acquire power in the Janissary corps came after the death of Muṣṭafā Kâhya al-Qāzdughlī in 1703 or 1704, but in 1707 he was ousted by his opponents. The crisis that followed saw a general mobilization of the seven corps, and was ultimately resolved by the compulsory elevation of Afranj Aḥmad to the beylicate.

From early 1709 it became increasingly clear that there was a rift between the Janissaries and the other six corps, who resented their privileges and arrogance. More than once, civil war seemed about to break out, but in June a reconciliation was effected between the Janissaries and the other corps, and between Afranj Aḥmad and his Janissary opponents. The viceroy withdrew Afranj Aḥmad's beylicate, and soon afterwards he was restored as *bashodabashı* of the Janissaries.

In March 1711 the concealed hostilities came into the open: faction linked with faction until a schism ran through the whole complex of the ruling and military groups of Egypt. As before, the trouble started within the corps of Janissaries, where the opponents of Afranj Aḥmad conspired with the Qāzdughliyya group to oust him. But this opposition party was further supported by the other six corps, especially the *ʿAzeban*, who most strongly resented the predominance of the Janissaries. The malcontents, occupying the headquarters of the *ʿAzeban*, attempted to blockade the Janissaries in the Citadel. The Janissaries, for their part, obtained permission from the viceroy who was virtually their hostage, to attack the *ʿAzeban* in their headquarters.

The beys and their Mamluk households now became involved. Ayyūb Bey, who was associated with the Faqāriyya, intervened on the side of Afranj Aḥmad, in spite of the links existing between the Faqāriyya and the Qāzdughliyya. The Qāsimiyya grandees threw the whole weight of their support behind the *ʿAzeban*, against Afranj Aḥmad, Ayyūb Bey and the viceroy. It was now early April, and seventy days of fighting, interspersed with negotiations, followed. During this period, Ayyūb Bey was reinforced by the arrival of the Faqārī governor of Upper Egypt, Muḥammad Bey, who arrived in Cairo with Arab tribal levies under their chiefs.

The Qāsimiyya grandees sought to legitimize their position, following the precedent set at the time of the clash with Mūsā Pasha in 1631, by declaring the viceroy suspended from office, and nominating one of their own faction as *qāʾim maqām*. On 1 June 1711 a battle took place outside Cairo, in which Īwāẓ Bey, one of the two Qāsimī leaders, was killed. When the news was brought to Ayyūb Bey, he was horrified, realizing that henceforward the Qāsimiyya would pursue a relentless vendetta against his faction. The death of Īwāẓ Bey marks the critical moment in the relations between the Faqāriyya and the Qāsimiyya, the point at which limited rivalries turned into a struggle for mutual extirpation.

The battle did not, however, decide the immediate issue, and the contest dragged on. At last, on 18 June, the council of war of the Qāsimiyya and their allies decided to call up the seven corps, all members of which were summoned to report to their commanding officers under threat of having their property plundered, and their families killed. Three days later, after further fighting, the resistance of their opponents began to crack. Ayyūb Bey fled to Syria, and thence to Istanbul, where he died in the following year. Muḥammad Bey made his way to Upper Egypt, but subsequently also escaped to Istanbul, where he was raised to the pashalic, surviving by ten years the collapse of his fortunes in Egypt.

Afranj Aḥmad was less fortunate. After the flight of the two beys, the Qāsimiyya bombarded the viceroy's residence and the Janissary headquarters into submission. The viceroy's person was spared, although the *qāʾim maqām* remained in office until a new viceroy arrived. Afranj

Aḥmad tried to escape in disguise, but was arrested and put to death, as were other notables of his faction.

The Great Insurrection of 1711 demonstrated the ascendancy of the beylicate in Egyptian politics. From this point, the squabbles of the seven corps sank into insignificance, compared with the bitter hostilities which characterized the relations of the Faqārī and Qāsimī beys, and their Mamluk households. The Ottoman viceroys became mere figure-heads, liable to deposition if they offended the dominant beylical faction. The object of an ambitious grandee was to attain the *riʾāsa*, the supremacy or effective authority in Egypt, as distinct from the constitutional lordship of the sultan or his viceroy. But the *riʾāsa* could be exercised in commission, as it were, by two or three beys, or other military grandees. During the eighty-seven years between the Great Insurrection and the landing of Bonaparte, two themes dominate the history of Egypt: the factional struggle, and, within each faction, the struggle of individuals for the *riʾāsa*.

The Great Insurrection prepared the way for the Qāsimiyya to establish their ascendancy in Egypt. When their leader, Īwāẓ Bey, was killed, their morale was temporarily shaken, but at this juncture their cause was saved by a retainer of the dead grandee, who induced the *qāʾim maqām* to confer a beylicate on his master's sixteen-year-old son, Ismāʿīl, who thereupon succeeded to the headship of his father's Mamluk household. But the Qāsimiyya were not yet in sole command, since they had to reckon with their Faqārī allies, headed by Qayṭās Bey. In 1714 Ismāʿīl Bey ibn Īwāẓ procured the assassination of Qayṭās at the hands of the viceroy's servants.

The Qāsimiyya were now the masters of Egypt. Nine of their faction were raised to the beylicate; four from the household of Īwāẓ, and five from that of Abū Shanab. As long as Abū Shanab lived, the faction remained united, but on his death in 1718 a dangerous schism developed. Ismāʿīl Bey now held the sole *riʾāsa*: he was the commander of Cairo (*amīr Miṣr*), but his authority was resented by the Mamluk household left by Abū Shanab, whose members intrigued and plotted against him. At first they failed. In 1722 Ismāʿīl Bey, backed by a friendly viceroy, was at the height of his power. The beylicate was brought up to its full establishment of twenty-four members, half of which belonged to the Īwāẓiyya group, while probably not more than three were Faqāriyya. The plots against Ismāʿīl continued, until he was assassinated in 1724. A proscription of his household followed.

The downfall of the Īwāẓiyya was followed by the ascendancy of their rivals, the household of Abū Shanab, in which Muḥammad Bey Charkas was the leading spirit. To obtain power, however, they had allied with the Faqāriyya, to which faction belonged Dhu'l-Faqār, the assassin of Ismāʿīl Bey. Immediately after the assassination, Dhu'l-Faqār was raised to the beylicate, and became the centre of a group of malcontent Faqāriyya. The brief alliance with Muḥammad Charkas dissolved, and the two factions rapidly became involved in a struggle for domination. After various intrigues, which culminated in fighting, Charkas fled, and Dhu'l-Faqār Bey assumed the *riʾāsa*. The Qāsimiyya, however, were not yet finished. Charkas rallied his supporters in Upper Egypt and defeated an expeditionary force sent by Dhu'l-Faqār. He moved down on Cairo, having secretly arranged that the Qāsimiyya within the city should rise in his support; but he was defeated in battle, and drowned in the Nile while fleeing from his enemies. Meanwhile the rising had taken place, and Dhu'l-Faqār was assassinated, not knowing of his rival's death. This rising, which took place in 1730, was the last attempt of the Qāsimiyya to reassert their supremacy. They were proscribed by the supporters of Dhu'l-Faqār.

Like the Qāsimiyya before them, the victorious Faqāriyya now split up into rival groups, of which the nuclei were the Mamluk households of contenders for the *riʾāsa*. At first the rivalry was between ʿUthmān Bey, the *mamlūk* and successor of Dhu'l-Faqār, and the powerful Qāzdughliyya household. The Qāzdughliyya were unusual in that, up to this date, they had not attempted to enter the beylicate, but had contented themselves with high regimental commands. This fact perhaps accounts for the greater stability and permanence of the household, since, as members of the privileged military corps, their chiefs had a measure of protection against the political vicissitudes which had befallen the brilliant but short-lived ascendancies of the beylical Mamluks. Only in the next generation did the Qāzdughliyya attain the beylicate, and then their history began to follow the same pattern of factional rivalry and mutual destruction that had characterized the Īwāẓiyya and the successors of Abū Shanab before them.

Hostility between ʿUthmān Bey and Ibrāhīm Kâhya, the head of the Qāzdughliyya, first developed in the year 1739. Ultimately, after an attempt had been made to assassinate him, ʿUthmān fled to Upper Egypt, where one of his *mamlūks* was governor, and where he had an ally in Shaykh Humām of Hawwāra, the power of which tribe had revived at this period. At Asyūṭ, ʿUthmān was joined by various malcontents, including some remnants of the Qāsimiyya, but he was defeated by an expedition sent from Cairo. In the end he made his way to Istanbul, where he died in 1776, never having returned to Egypt.

Ibrāhīm Kâhya owed his success partly to an alliance with another regimental officer who, like himself, was the head of a Mamluk household. This was Riḍwān Kâhya, the leader of the small Julfiyya group. By 1748 Ibrāhīm and Riḍwān had triumphed over all their opponents, and proceeded to hold the *riʾāsa* in association. Riḍwān was a sleeping partner in this duumvirate: he had no interest in the affairs of state, but occupied himself with building magnificent residences, with luxurious living, and with the patronage of poets. Although neither Ibrāhīm nor Riḍwān desired the beylicate for themselves, it was necessary for them to keep control of the order by appointing to it nominees of their own. Each duumvir appointed three of his *mamlūks* as beys, and the beylicate henceforward became practically a monopoly of the Qāzdughliyya until the end of the Mamluk régime in the early nineteenth century. Ibrāhīm further strengthened his position by laying his hands on the revenues of Egypt, and by building up a great Mamluk household. For about seven years he held unprecedented authority in Egypt, during which time Cairo was free from revolts, while security reigned throughout the land. He died in his bed towards the end of 1754. After his death, the Qāzdughliyya turned against Riḍwān Kâhya and brought about his assassination some six months later. This event marked the end of the Julfiyya as a political force, and set the seal on the ascendancy of the Qazdughliyya.

During the six years which followed the death of Ibrāhīm Kâhya, there was no political stability in Egypt, since the Qāzdughlī grandees were competing amongst themselves for the supremacy. This was held in rapid succession by three beys of Ibrāhīm Kâhya's household. The second of them was the holder of a title, *shaykh al-balad*, which was bestowed upon the premier bey.[1] The precise significance of the title is not clear: it seems to signify the senior grandee of Cairo. It was not an official Ottoman title, and did not imply a rank or position in the formal Ottoman hierarchy. Several other terms used in the eighteenth century appear to have been synonymous with *shaykh al-balad*: thus, about forty years earlier, Ismāʿīl Bey ibn Īwāẓ is spoken of as *amīr Miṣr*, 'the commander of Cairo', a title which reappears later, while the forms *kabīr al-qawm*, 'the senior of the people' (i.e., probably, of the Mamluks),

[1] Dr S. J. Shaw has noted that this title is first applied in the Ottoman archives to Muḥammad Bey Charkas (1724–6). Its usage by al-Jabartī, however, begins at the point indicated in the text. See Stanford J. Shaw, *Ottoman Egypt in the age of the French Revolution*, Cambridge, Mass., 1964, 11, n. 1.

and *kabīr al-balad* also appear. Until the end of the duumvirate of Ibrāhīm Kâhya and Riḍwān Kâhya, regimental officers of the seven corps might hold, or share in, the *ri'āsa*, but the title of *shaykh al-balad* was held only by beys.

A later grandee to hold the title of *shaykh al-balad* was ʿAlī Bey al-Ghazzāwī, also known as ʿAlī Bey al-Kabīr (i.e. the Elder), who achieved the supremacy after the assassination of his predecessor in November 1757. In 1760 al-Ghazzāwī left Cairo for the Ḥijāz as *amīr al-Ḥajj*. At this time the head of the Qāzdughliyya clan was the last of its great regimental officers, ʿAbd al-Raḥmān Kâhya. He had not hitherto played a conspicuous part in politics, but had devoted himself to building, pious works and magnificence of life. Before leaving Cairo, al-Ghazzāwī set on foot a conspiracy to kill ʿAbd al-Raḥmān Kâhya during his absence. The *kâhya* forestalled this by exerting his authority as head of the Qāzdughliyya, and requiring the grandees to accept as *shaykh al-balad* a nominee of his own. The new *shaykh al-balad* was a younger ʿAlī Bey, to whom his contemporaries gave the Turkish nickname of *Bulut Kapan*, 'The Cloud-Catcher', an implied comment on his lofty and unsubstantial ambitions. News of the *coup d'état* reached al-Ghazzāwī as he returned from the Ḥijāz. Recognizing that his cause was lost, he handed over the charge of the Pilgrimage, and fled to Gaza (*Ghazza*), whence the epithet by which he is generally known.

If ʿAbd al-Raḥmān Kâhya had hoped to find a puppet in Bulut Kapan ʿAlī Bey, he was gravely mistaken. From the outset the new *shaykh al-balad* showed his determination to rule, and laid a heavy hand on his colleagues. The numerous beys who, like himself, had been *mamlūks* of Ibrāhīm Kâhya, were all potential opponents, who might overthrow him as they had overthrown his immediate predecessors. To eliminate them and to fill the beylicate with his own *mamlūks* and allies became the primary object of his policy. The first to be promoted was a *mamlūk* of Ibrāhīm, Ismāʿīl Bey, whom ʿAlī married to the daughter of their late master. The marriage was the occasion of a sumptuous festival for the whole of Cairo, which lasted for a full month. This brilliant and extravagant display was a deliberate and successful attempt by ʿAlī Bey to impress all in the city and its vicinity with his magnificence and generosity. Other promotions to the beylicate followed, the most important being that of ʿAlī's *mamlūk*, Muḥammad Bey. It was customary for a new bey to be invested with a robe of honour by the viceroy, and, as he rode down from the Citadel, to throw silver coins among the crowd. Muḥammad Bey, however, scattered a largess of gold; an unprecedented act, which gained him the nickname of *Abu'l-Dhahab*, 'The Father of Gold'.

As ʿAlī's power increased, he proceeded to eliminate his colleagues. The first to go was the head of the Qāzdughliyya, his former patron and ally, ʿAbd al-Raḥmān Kâhya, who was banished to the Ḥijāz. At the same time, Ṣāliḥ Bey, the last surviving Qāsimī grandee, was banished to Gaza. Subsequently he went to Rosetta, and in 1765 he escaped to Upper Egypt, where he had extensive estates and enjoyed close and friendly relations with Shaykh Humām. When the power of the Qāsimiyya collapsed, the remnants of their faction had been given asylum by Humām, who was virtually autonomous in Upper Egypt. They entered his service as soldiers, intermarried with his people, and adopted Arabic as their language. Thus Ṣāliḥ Bey found himself amongst friends and allies. This powerful nucleus of opposition to ʿAlī Bey was augmented by other refugees from his rule. Their control of Upper Egypt could not be ignored, since they were able to cut off the revenues sent in grain to Cairo. ʿAlī Bey therefore sent out an expeditionary force, commanded by Ḥusayn Bey Kashkash, a former *mamlūk* of Ibrāhīm Kâhya, but Ḥusayn returned to Cairo and proceeded to build up a faction of his own.

Suddenly, ʿAlī found himself besieged in his house and abandoned by his comrades. He yielded to a show of force, and in March 1766 was banished to Syria. The supremacy was now held jointly by Kashkash and Khalīl Bey, a former *shaykh al-balad*, who immediately left Cairo on a new expedition against Ṣāliḥ Bey. In their absence ʿAlī and his retainers re-entered the city and took up residence in the houses of the absent grandees. Their object seems to have been to force a reconsideration of their treatment. In this they were successful. ʿAlī was rusticated to his estate in Lower Egypt, while Abu'l-Dhahab and others of his retinue were sent to Upper Egypt. Some months later, probably in March 1767, ʿAlī himself arrived at Asyūṭ. Through the mediation of Shaykh Humām, he was reconciled with Ṣāliḥ Bey. The two became sworn allies, and, assisted with men and money by Humām, their combined forces descended the Nile towards Cairo. Kashkash was defeated in battle, and his faction broke up, many of his followers deserting to ʿAlī. In October 1767 Khalīl and Kashkash fled from Cairo, which was entered on the same day by ʿAlī and Ṣāliḥ.

The restoration of ʿAlī Bey might seem nothing more than a shift of power among the unstable Mamluk factions, but to contemporaries the period of his rule that followed seemed something different in kind from the authority previously exercised by the grandees. In the unprecedented severity of his proscriptions, and in his conscious will to despotism, ʿAlī exhibited a sustained and ruthless determination that shocked and surprised Egyptian society. At the outset he was still threatened by Khalīl and Kashkash, who had fled to Gaza and were preparing to march on Cairo in their turn. In the spring of 1768 they reached the Delta and advanced to al-Manṣūra, where a force sent against them by ʿAlī Bey was defeated. In Cairo, all salaried members of the seven corps were summoned to render service in person, or to pay a contribution in lieu thereof. Reinforcements were sent out in May, under the command of Abu'l-Dhahab, who besieged Khalīl and Kashkash in Ṭanṭā. Here they defended themselves until their ammunition was exhausted. Relying upon a safe-conduct, Kashkash went to Abu'l-Dhahab's camp to negotiate terms. There he was murdered. For a while Khalīl sought sanctuary at the shrine of Aḥmad al-Badawī in Ṭantā, but he surrendered under a promise of amnesty, and was later put to death.

Having thus disposed of the last armed force of his opponents, ʿAlī went on to proscribe and exile his rivals, both great and small. The grandees of Cairo were banished to Upper Egypt, the Fayyūm and the Ḥijāz. Forces were sent out against the nomadic tribes, who had profited from the internecine warfare of the Mamluk factions. The allies who had brought ʿAlī Bey back to power were soon destroyed by him: Ṣāliḥ Bey was assassinated in September 1768; in the following year Shaykh Humām was overthrown and died. To serve his ends ʿAlī depended on the new grandees of his own creation, Ismāʿīl Bey, Abu'l-Dhahab, and, for a time, a Bosniak adventurer whom he raised to the beylicate, Aḥmad al-Jazzār. This last was subsequently to achieve notoriety in Syria, as governor of Sidon.

ʿAlī was rapidly assuming the position of a sovereign in Egypt—a situation which could not fail to produce tension with the Ottoman government and its viceroy in Cairo. At the time of ʿAlī's restoration the viceroy had formally confirmed him in office, and their relations were apparently friendly. At the end of November 1768, however, the viceroy attempted to instigate a rising in Cairo, and ʿAlī deposed him; assuming himself the post of *qāʾim maqām*. Thereby he combined the titular headship of the Egyptian administration, as acting viceroy, with his real supremacy as *shaykh al-balad*. A new viceroy arrived in Cairo in the summer of 1769, but a few weeks later he was deposed. ʿAlī Bey seemed about to proclaim himself an independent ruler. Men noted that he was interested in historical works, and he is reported to have said to his intimates, 'The kings of Egypt were Mamluks like us; these Ottomans took Egypt through superior force and the treachery of its people.' An incident at the end of 1769 showed the direction in which his ambitions were moving. One Friday, the preacher at the mosque recited the *khuṭba* in his presence, and inserted the *shaykh al-balad*'s name after that of the Ottoman sultan, thereby implying the sovereignty of ʿAlī Bey in Egypt. ʿAlī made a great display of anger, and had the preacher flogged for his temerity—but the next day he sent him a gift of money and a robe. Still more significant is the inscription which, in 1772, ʿAlī placed in the mausoleum of the great jurist, al-Shāfiʿī, which he repaired. In this, ʿAlī assumed the title of *ʿAzīz Miṣr*, 'The mighty one of Egypt', a term used in the Qur'ān of Joseph as the minister of Pharaoh, and sometimes applied in Ottoman texts to the Mamluk sultans.[1]

Nevertheless, ʿAlī hesitated to make an open break with the Ottoman Empire, and in 1770 an opportunity arose for him to perform a service for the sultan and at the same time to increase his own prestige. In consequence of one of the recurrent dynastic contests among members of the Hashimite family, which ruled Mecca,[2] a defeated claimant sought the sultan's assistance to regain his throne. The affairs of Mecca were traditionally handled by the sultan's representative in Egypt, and on this occasion ʿAlī Bey was empowered to act. He organized a great expeditionary force, commanded by Abu'l-Dhahab, which not only installed the refugee Hashimite as ruler of Mecca, but also substituted a Mamluk bey for the Ottoman governor of Jedda. ʿAlī Bey had now effectively excluded the sultan's authority both from Egypt and from the Ḥijāz: to the power he derived from the wealth of Egypt was added the prestige accruing from domination over the Holy Cities of Islam.

The old Mamluk Empire, as it had existed before the Ottoman conquest, consisted of three main territories: Egypt, Syria and the vassal-principality of the Ḥijāz. Now that ʿAlī controlled the first and third of these, it was natural that he should aim at a conquest of Syria, which rulers in Egypt have repeatedly sought to bring within their sphere of influence. Furthermore, the conquest of Syria would interpose a buffer between the Ottoman heartlands and the Egyptian core of ʿAlī Bey's dominions. There was also a personal motive. ʿAlī had gone to Mecca as *amīr al-Ḥajj* in 1764, and there had clashed with his Syrian counterpart, ʿUthmān Pasha al-Ṣādiq, the governor of Damascus, who still held

[1] The title was later to attract Khedive Ismāʿīl, see below, p. 196.

[2] See above, p. 41, n. 1.

office in 1770. Moreover, at this time, circumstances were particularly favourable to ʿAlī Bey's enterprise. In Syria, ʿUthmān Pasha's authority was threatened by the power of Shaykh Ẓāhir al-ʿUmar in the region of Galilee and Acre. More generally, the Ottoman Empire was desperately engaged in war with Russia. In July 1770 a Russian fleet annihilated the Ottoman navy, and thereafter remained in the eastern Mediterranean to assist potential opponents of the sultan.

In these circumstances, ʿAlī and Ẓāhir had no difficulty in concluding an alliance, while ʿAli got into communication with the Russians. In return for their assistance, he is said to have promised to give them possession of the towns in the Arab lands.[1] In November 1770 an expeditionary force under the command of Ismāʿīl Bey left Cairo for Syria. Combining with the troops of Shaykh Ẓāhir, it moved to a point south of Damascus. Ismāʿīl, however, failed to maintain the initiative, refused to attack Damascus, and withdrew to Jaffa, leaving ʿUthmān Pasha time and opportunity to strengthen his position. ʿAlī now sent out a second force commanded by Abu'l-Dhahab. In conjunction with Ẓāhir the Mamluk army overthrew Ottoman authority throughout Palestine in the summer of 1771, defeated ʿUthmān Pasha in a battle outside Damascus and captured the city.

At this juncture, when all seemed set fair for a conquest of Syria, ʿAlī Bey's power began to crumble from within. Members of his own household were now beginning to develop ambitions incompatible with those of their patron. Ismāʿīl's reluctance to attack Damascus had been a premonitory symptom. Now Abu'l-Dhahab suddenly, without warning Ẓāhir, decided to evacuate the city, and withdrew the Mamluk army to Egypt. Various explanations have been given of his action. The Mamluk grandees were war-weary, the Syrian campaign having followed so soon on the fighting in the Ḥijāz. Ismāʿīl and, perhaps, ʿUthmān Pasha also seem to have worked on Abu'l-Dhahab, warning him that the Ottoman Empire would take revenge upon its rebellious vassals in Egypt. Abu'l-Dhahab and Ismāʿīl assured the sultan that they were not rebels by choice, and by the late autumn of 1771 they were back with their troops in Cairo.

During the following weeks a concealed struggle for power developed between ʿAlī Bey and Abu'l-Dhahab, who fled from Cairo in January 1772 to Upper Egypt. There, as usual, the malcontents, including

[1] Ḥaydar Shihāb, *al-Ghurar al-ḥisān fī akhbār abnā' al-zamān*; edd. Asad Rustum and Fu'ād Afrām al-Bustānī, *Lubnān fī ʿahd al-umarā' al-Shihābiyyīn*, Beirut 1933, i, 79; cf. p. 91.

Hawwāra and the remnants of the Qāsimiyya, rallied to his standard. ʿAlī Bey sent out a force against him, but most of the troops, as well as Ismāʿīl Bey, the commander, deserted to Abu'l-Dhahab. To fill the gaps in the beylicate, ʿAlī promoted seven young Mamluks, whom the people of Cairo promptly nicknamed 'the seven girls'. The rebels descended the Nile towards Cairo, and defeated ʿAlī Bey's forces in April 1772. The *shaykh al-balad* hastily loaded up his possessions, and, with a retinue of loyal followers, fled to seek asylum with Ẓāhir in Palestine. Abu'l-Dhahab entered Cairo and assumed the supremacy.

For twelve months ʿAlī remained with Ẓāhir. Early in 1773 he received letters from the grandees in Cairo, urging him to return and promising him assistance against Abu'l-Dhahab. Shaykh Ẓāhir's minister, Ibrāhīm al-Ṣabbāgh, urged him not to heed the letters; the similarity of their phrasing suggested that they were framed by Abu'l-Dhahab to deceive him. But ʿAlī rejected his advice with the fatuous comment, 'These are the suspicions of a clever fellow, but I know my sons and my household better than you!' At al-Ṣāliḥiyya, on the eastern fringe of the Delta, his little force found its way barred by Abu'l-Dhahab and his army. There, on 1 May 1773, a battle was fought in which ʿAlī was wounded and captured. Abu'l-Dhahab received him with honour and respect, and had him conveyed to Cairo. There, a week later, he died. In the circumstances it was inevitable that suspicions of foul play should arise.

The career of ʿAlī Bey looks back to the Mamluk sultanate, and forwards to the viceroyalty of Muḥammad ʿAlī Pasha. In several respects his policy foreshadows that of Muḥammad ʿAlī, notably in his ruthless elimination of his Mamluk opponents, his reduction of the authority of the sultan to a nominal suzerainty, and his attempt to re-establish the traditional Egyptian control over the Ḥijāz and Syria. Why, then, did his achievements prove so much more transitory than those of the great viceroy? Broadly, the answer would seem to lie in two sets of circumstances. Unlike ʿAlī Bey, Muḥammad ʿAlī Pasha seized power at a time when the Mamluk ascendancy had been severely shaken by the French invasion of 1798 and its consequences. Secondly, Muḥammad ʿAlī was not himself a member of the Mamluk organization, and in establishing his power he could employ a military force (the Albanian contingent) which was independent of Mamluk loyalties and rivalries. ʿAlī, by contrast, could only supersede his Mamluk colleagues by his own Mamluk household: an expedient which ultimately proved suicidal.

After ʿAlī Bey's death the ascendancy of the beylicate continued in the Qāzdughliyya clan. Abu'l-Dhahab abandoned his master's attitude of insubordination to the Ottoman sultanate and professed a demonstrative loyalty. In pursuance of this he invaded Palestine in 1775 to suppress Shaykh Ẓāhir al-ʿUmar. The Mamluk forces swept northwards up the Palestinian coast, capturing Jaffa on the way, as far as Ẓāhir's capital of Acre. There Abu'l-Dhahab suddenly died. The Mamluk grandees lost the drive which he had imparted to them and retreated with their army to Egypt. Never again was the Mamluk ascendancy to show any ambition to conquer Syria.

The decade which followed Abu'l-Dhahab's death was a time of prolonged struggles for the supremacy among the Qāzdughlī grandees. The principal rivals were Ismāʿīl Bey and two of Abu'l-Dhahab's *mamlūks*, Ibrāhīm Bey and Murād Bey. The latter two succeeded in ousting Ismāʿīl and their other opponents, and Ibrāhīm, the elder partner, was recognized as *shaykh al-balad.* Subsequently they quarrelled, but, after various vicissitudes, they composed their differences in 1784 and shared authority in Egypt.

In 1786 the duumvirate of Ibrāhīm and Murād was seriously challenged by an Ottoman attempt to break their power and reassert direct control over Egypt. In May of that year letters were received from the sultan demanding long neglected financial dues. Hard on these orders came the news that an Ottoman fleet, commanded by the admiral, Ḥasan Pasha, was approaching Alexandria. The duumvirs and the grandees attempted to procrastinate, but in July Ḥasan Pasha landed at Alexandria and received the submission of the local people. Thence he moved to Rosetta, distributing Arabic proclamations directed against the beys, promising that taxes should be reduced and that the administration should conform to the *Qānūn* of Süleyman.

The grandees now determined on resistance, and Murād Bey led an expeditionary force down the Rosetta branch of the Nile against the Ottomans. It was defeated at al-Raḥmāniyya. The viceroy, emboldened by this, asserted his authority in Cairo, called all loyal garrison-troops to the colours, and produced an imperial edict granting an amnesty to all the grandees except Ibrāhīm and Murād. Ibrāhīm fled from Cairo and on 6 August joined forces with Murād south of the city. Two days later Ḥasan Pasha arrived at Būlāq.

On 10 August the *Divan* assembled to promulgate the reforms intended by Ḥasan Pasha. New appointments were made to the regimental offices and the beylicate—the new beys being chosen from various Mamluk households in order to prevent them from combining against the Ottomans. The goods of the evicted grandees were sequestrated. A series of proclamations over the next few days emphasized the Islamic character of the new régime:[1] the traditional sumptuary regulations were enforced against Christians, who were also forbidden to employ Muslims or to buy slaves; the *Ashrāf* were to be treated with respect; the public activities of women were restricted; Christians and Jews bearing the names of the prophets were ordered to change them.

Ḥasan Pasha and the Ottomans held Cairo and Lower Egypt, but the fugitive duumvirs were the masters of the south. Between the two parties a military deadlock developed and remained unbroken as long as Ḥasan Pasha remained in Egypt. The tide of war moved up and down the Nile valley, but it proved as impossible for Ḥasan to dislodge the rebels from Upper Egypt as for them to retake Cairo. An attempt was made in November 1786 to solve the matter by negotiation. Ibrāhīm and Murād were offered an amnesty, and estates for themselves wherever they wished—outside Egypt. But Ibrāhīm and Murād refused to be expatriated, and the struggle continued. It was no longer a simple conflict between Ottomans and Mamluks, since a party of the duumvirs' Mamluk opponents was anxious to co-operate with Ḥasan Pasha. At the head of the collaborators was Ismāʿīl Bey, who was appointed as *shaykh al-balad*. By the end of November the rebels were established near the Pyramids, threatening Cairo: but early in December they were driven off and pushed back to Upper Egypt.

An expeditionary force occupied Upper Egypt as far as Aswān, while the rebels withdrew into Nubia. But the army could not remain permanently in the south. In March 1787 it began to fall back on Cairo. Garrisons of Ottoman and regimental troops were left in Upper Egypt, as well as loyalist beys. In April the rebels began to return from Nubia and advance northwards, while Ḥasan Pasha again attempted to negotiate a settlement. He was working against time, since the Ottoman Empire was on the brink of war with Russia, and his services were urgently required. In September he made his final arrangements. To support the authority of Ismāʿīl Bey after his departure, Ḥasan Pasha left him a supply of armaments and a garrison of five hundred Ottoman troops. Ibrāhīm and Murād were to live in Upper Egypt, and not to enter Cairo. His dispositions hardly survived his withdrawal. Ismāʿīl died in 1791, and the duumvirs resumed their rule over Egypt until the coming of Bonaparte in 1798.

[1] This feature may perhaps be associated with the recent assertion of the Ottoman caliphate in the Treaty of Küchük Kaynarja (1774).

Although the Ottoman expedition to Egypt failed to procure any lasting results, it presents some interesting features. In the first place, it anticipates the policy of destroying local autonomies and re-integrating the provinces in a centralized empire, which was to be followed by the Ottoman sultans of the nineteenth century. Secondly, it provides a prototype for Bonaparte's invasion of Egypt, both in respect of the course of the campaign and of the measures employed to win Egyptian support against the Mamluks. The use of Arabic proclamations as a vehicle of propaganda, the conciliation of the *Ashrāf* and *ʿulamāʾ* and the ostentatious deference to Islam of the new régime, were all expedients later to be adopted by Bonaparte. Finally, the difficulty of evicting the Mamluks from Upper Egypt by the power controlling Cairo was to be experienced, not only by the French, but, for many years, by Muḥammad ʿAlī himself. In conclusion, the involvement of ʿAlī Bey and Abu'l-Dhahab in the politics of Syria, the contacts between ʿAlī and Russia, and the Ottoman expedition, all indicate the end of Egyptian isolation from imperial and international affairs, and foreshadow developments in the nineteenth and twentieth centuries.

7

Ottoman Decline and the Syrian Provinces

The weakening of Ottoman power and the deterioration of the Ottoman administrative system produced in Syria effects very broadly similar to those we have observed in Egypt. These were aggravated by the lack of political unity of the region, by its geographical divisions, and by the absence of an established and powerful group, like the Egyptian Mamluks, who were able to resume authority behind the façade of Ottoman provincial government. Only in Mount Lebanon, where the geographical circumstances and historical background were unique, did a local autonomous government emerge and succeed in maintaining itself throughout this period. It must also be borne in mind that the history of the Syrian provinces (and of the Fertile Crescent as a whole) was deeply influenced by relations between the settled peoples and the nomadic tribesmen. The period of Ottoman decline was also a time when changes were taking place in the tribal composition of *Bādiat al-Shām*, the Syrian desert. Two great tribal migrations from Najd took place in the seventeenth and eighteenth centuries. The first brought the ʿAnaza northwards into *Bādiat al-Shām*, where they were challenged by a second wave of immigrants, the Shammar. This rival group was, about the middle of the eighteenth century, forced eastwards across the Euphrates, and tribes of the ʿAnaza have since retained their predominance in the Syrian Desert.

The two great cities of Syria, Aleppo and Damascus, suffered in different ways from the Ottoman decline. The environment of Aleppo was more varied than that of Damascus. Situated on the northern fringe of the Arab lands, and lying at the junction of routes from Syria, from the Iraqi provinces, and from Anatolia, it was sensitive to developments in the debatable land where the Ottoman Empire confronted Persia. The tribes, over whom its governors attempted to exercise control, were not only Arabs, but also nomadic Turcomans and semi-sedentary Kurds. Aleppo was an important centre of trade with Europe: it contained a factory of merchants of the English Levant Company.[1] Damascus was

[1] The Levant Company's factory at Aleppo carried on a great trade in raw Persian

a more purely Arab city in its population, interests and surroundings. Its governors and garrison had the primary function of maintaining security along the great routes which fanned out from the city: northwards by Ḥimṣ and Ḥamāh to Aleppo; southwards to the Ḥijāz and its holy cities; westwards, across the Biqāʿ to the ports of Beirut and Tripoli, or through Galilee and the Palestinian coastal plain to Egypt. In particular, for religious, political and commercial considerations alike, the safety of the annual Pilgrimage caravan had to be ensured.

Both in Aleppo and in Damascus the governors were hampered in exercising control by their brief tenure of office: thus, in the seventeenth century, over eighty pashas were appointed to Damascus. As the hold of the governors weakened, the Ottoman garrison-troops grew in strength. During the later sixteenth century, the Janissaries became a permanent element of the town-populations. In Damascus, patronage-groups formed around Janissary bosses in the later sixteenth and early seventeenth centuries. At the same time, with the lapse of the *devshirme*, the way was opened for local people to buy themselves into the corps, and thereby acquire the privileges of the Janissaries: an imperial edict reprehending this practice was issued to the governor of Damascus in 1577.[1]

By the end of the sixteenth century, the Janissaries of Damascus had come to dominate Aleppo also. On the pretext of collecting the imperial taxes, they had imposed themselves on the townspeople and had acquired wives and property. After a struggle, the governor of Aleppo managed to oust them in 1599. His successor obtained a detachment of imperial troops, to be stationed in Aleppo, but this did not prevent the Damascenes from regaining their position in the city and the countryside. Once again they were ejected, but they returned in force, and, after fighting and a siege, established their power in Aleppo more strongly than ever.

The ascendancy of the Damascenes was broken by a combination between Naṣūḥ Pasha, who was appointed governor of Aleppo in 1602, and Ḥusayn Pasha Jānbulād, a member of a Kurdish clan which had for

silk. This declined in the late seventeenth and the eighteenth centuries, partly because of competition from the East India Company, which diverted the sources of supply through the Persian Gulf, and partly because of the wars and political changes which followed the collapse of the Safavid dynasty in 1722 and lasted throughout the century. In its earlier and more prosperous days, the Aleppo factory had indirectly assisted the development of Arabic studies in England. Edward Pococke, as chaplain to the merchants from 1630 to 1636, had there acquired the immense erudition which he subsequently displayed as the first Laudian Professor of Arabic at Oxford, while manuscripts obtained by himself and a later chaplain, Robert Huntington (1671–81), form an important part of the Arabic collection in the Bodleian.

[1] See U. Heyd, *Ottoman documents on Palestine*, 1552–1615, Oxford 1960, 68–9.

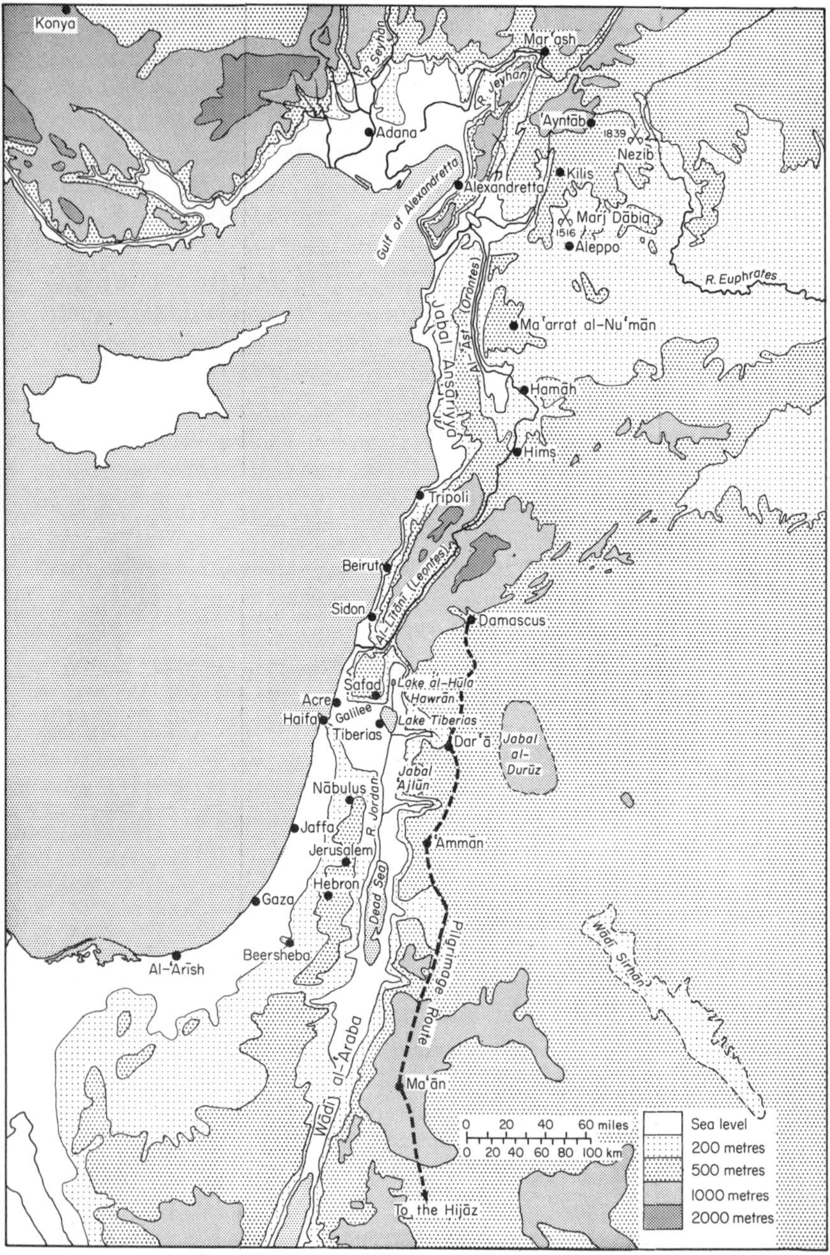

MAP 3: The Western Fertile Crescent

a generation dominated the district of Kilis to the north.[1] After further fighting, the Damascenes were cleared out of the vicinity of Aleppo, and by the summer of 1604 they had been pushed back to Damascus.

The alliance of Naṣūḥ and Ḥusayn Jānbulād had a curious sequel. The Ottoman government was suspicious of the dynastic governorship of the Jānbulāds in Kilis, and connived with Naṣūḥ to secure Ḥusayn's overthrow. Hostilities were in progress between the two governors, when, with a reversal of policy not unusual in this period, the Ottoman authorities nominated Ḥusayn as governor of Aleppo. Naṣūḥ protested at this appointment of a tribal chief to a governorship, and resisted Ḥusayn's forces. Once again, in 1603-4, Aleppo was laid under siege. After four months a reconciliation was effected by a newly appointed judge; Naṣūḥ withdrew from the city, and Ḥusayn Jānbulād entered upon his governorship.

His period of office was short. He failed to answer a summons from the Ottoman commander, Chighalazade Sinan Pasha, to join in a campaign against the Persians. Sinan was defeated and on his return in 1605 accused Ḥusayn of treason, and had him put to death. The news of this provoked a revolt of the Jānbulād clan in Aleppo, headed by ʿAlī Pasha, the nephew of the dead governor. ʿAlī conspired with another rebel, the governor of Adana, to procure the assassination of the sultan's nominee to Aleppo. The governor of Tripoli, Yūsuf Pasha Sayfā,[2] failed to defeat ʿAlī Jānbulād, who went on to defeat the troops of Damascus, and to lay a heavy fine on the city. For a short time he was the dominant ruler in Syria, and was in alliance with Fakhr al-Dīn II, the paramount *amīr* of Lebanon.[3] His ascendancy came to an end when he was defeated by the grand vezir in October 1607.

During the middle years of the seventeenth century recurrent troubles associated with the Janissaries in both Aleppo and Damascus are evidence of the continuing weakness of the Ottoman administration. Then, in 1657, Aleppo became the base of another of the great rebels against the sultan, Abaza Ḥasan Pasha, who was appointed governor in that year. Abaza Ḥasan had already had a turbulent career, and his revolt on this occasion was against the new and competent grand vezir, Mehmed Köprülü. He was supported by a number of other malcontents, including the governor of Damascus. In the end he and his leading supporters were treacherously killed in ʿAynṭāb (February 1659).

One consequence of this revolt was momentous for Damascus. Since the local Janissaries had been implicated, a considerable new force of

[1] See Appendix 2 (p. 311). [2] See below, p. 115. [3] See below, pp. 115–20.

imperial troops was sent to garrison that city. This did not mean the end of the older force, which were becoming assimilated to the local population. On the contrary, the two groups continued to exist as rivals for power. The old Janissaries were designated as *Yarliyya* (from the Turkish, *yerli*, local), while the new contingent, which was augmented from time to time, was known by various corruptions of the Turkish term *Kapı kulları*, 'slaves of the gate'. This was the name originally applied to *devshirme* recruits: here it signifies merely troops that were not of local origin. There was a division of function between the two groups: while the *Kapı kuls* guarded the citadel of Damascus, the *Yarliyya* were supposed to man the fortresses along the Pilgrimage-route to the Ḥijāz.

The safe conduct of the Pilgrimage was a growing preoccupation of the authorities in Damascus during the seventeenth century, and this is reflected in changes in the office of *amīr al-Ḥajj*, the commander of the Pilgrimage.[1] There is little evidence available for the first few decades of Ottoman rule, but between 1573 and 1635 the usual procedure seems to have been to appoint the *sanjak bey*, or governor, of one of the sub-provinces under Damascus. At this time these *sanjak beys* were members of local notable families. During the middle decades of the seventeenth century the command of the Pilgrimage was frequently held by Damascene Janissary officers, who at the same time were appointed governors of sub-provinces. Local notables, however, still commanded the Pilgrimage from time to time. As the century drew to its close, members of a new group began to be appointed: these were Ottoman administrative officials, including governors of Damascus. This process perhaps reflects two developments: the need for greater financial and military resources than were available to local notables or Janissary officers (the two categories were not wholly distinct), and a revival in the authority of the governor.

The governorship of another Naṣūḥ Pasha from 1708 to 1714 was a turning-point in the political history of Ottoman Damascus. His appointment was the first of the longer governorships, which were to give the province a degree of stability which it had lacked in the previous century. Each year he held the command of the Pilgrimage, and from his time the two offices of governor of Damascus and commander of the Pilgrimage were invariably held together. This association generally led to greater

[1] In the following account of Damascus in the seventeenth and eighteenth centuries, I have drawn upon the research of my former student, Dr Abdul Karim Rafeq of the University of Damascus, and wish to record my obligations to him.

security for the pilgrims; it also enhanced the prestige of the governor. Naṣūḥ's successful administration, however, aroused the suspicions of the Ottoman government. An army was sent against him on his return from his last Pilgrimage and he was captured and killed.

Although the strong rule of Naṣūḥ Pasha had been only a transitory episode, it foreshadowed later developments in the governorship of Damascus. The traditional system of Ottoman provincial administration was weakened and had become a mere façade for anarchy and extortion. Security and prosperity could not only be restored by governors holding office for long periods and depending on sources of strength outside the degenerate military establishment to maintain that authority.

In Damascus the forces of anarchy were checked by the emergence of a powerful family, the ʿAẓms, who acquired a quasi-dynastic hold over Damascus and extended their power to Tripoli, Sidon[1] and even, at times, Aleppo. Their origins are obscure, but they seem to have come from the rural population of Maʿarrat al-Nuʿmān, and they were of Arab (or arabized) stock. The founder of the family fortunes was a soldier in Maʿarra about the middle of the seventeenth century, and was killed in a local clash with the Turcomans. His son, Ismāʿīl, became governor of the region of Maʿarra and Ḥamāh and then of Tripoli, during the first quarter of the eighteenth century.

As governor of Tripoli, Ismāʿīl Pasha al-ʿAẓm performed an important function connected with the Pilgrimage: the command of the *Jarda*, a military escort which was sent out with provisions to relieve and convoy the returning pilgrims in the last stages of their journey out of the Ḥijāz to Damascus. Like the commander of the Pilgrimage, the commander of the *Jarda* was chosen, in the sixteenth and seventeenth centuries, from various categories of notables and officials; but just as the command of the Pilgrimage came to be annexed to the governorship of Damascus, so, in the eighteenth century, the command of the *Jarda* fell to one of the other Syrian governors. The acquisition of the Syrian governorships by members of the ʿAẓm family had thus, as its natural consequences, the assumption of both of these important commands.

In 1725 Ismāʿīl al-ʿAẓm exchanged the governorship of Tripoli for that of Damascus. The misgovernment of his predecessor had produced complaints and ultimately provoked a revolt in which the leading part

[1] A province of Sidon, including the territories of Beirut and Ṣafad, had been created on 1614, presumably in order to limit the power of the Maʿnids after the first defeat of Fakhr al-Dīn II: see Heyd, *Ottoman documents*, pp. 47–8. It seems to have had no long continuance. It was revived in 1660, and remained in existence until the nineteenth century.

was taken by the *muftī*, who was important not only because of his office but also because he belonged to the venerated Syro-Egyptian clan of al-Bakrī al-Ṣiddīqī. This traced its descent from the Caliph Abū Bakr al-Ṣiddīq and enjoyed great prestige in the Ottoman Empire. It had, furthermore, very close links with the Ṣūfī orders. The installation of Ismāʿīl in Damascus in consequence of the action of the *muftī* of Damascus represented a triumph for Syrian localism. Nevertheless, the old difficulties continued. Although Ismāʿīl was a successful commander of the Pilgrimage he was unable to stop the quarrels of armed factions in Damascus itself: thus, in 1726 a particularly serious riot broke out between the *Yarliyya* and the *Kapı kuls.* He himself used his position to monopolize the meat market in Damascus, which produced some outcry, and may have contributed to the disorders in the city during his governorship.

The rise of Ismāʿīl was accompanied by the rise of his kinsmen. He was succeeded at Tripoli first by a brother, Sulaymān, then by a son, Ibrāhīm. Sulaymān subsequently became the governor of Sidon. So, by 1728, the whole of southern Syria was administered, at least in name, by members of the ʿAẓm family. Moreover, they had vast estates in their original homeland, the region of Ḥimṣ, Ḥamāh and Maʿarra, which they held as *malikanes*, i.e. tax-farms for life. Yet in 1730 a sudden check came to their prosperity. In consequence of a palace revolution in Istanbul, the sultan was deposed, and the ʿAẓms lost their protector and advocate at court. A clean sweep was made of their governorships.

A year later, however, they had begun to creep back with favour and power. Ismāʿīl never returned to Syria, but died in Crete. His brother, Sulaymān, however, was appointed to govern Tripoli and command the *Jarda.* Two of Ismāʿīl's sons, Ibrāhīm and Asʿad, were at various times governors of Sidon. Then in 1733 Sulaymān Pasha al-ʿAẓm, like his brother before him, was transferred from Tripoli to Damascus, which he ruled on this occasion for five years. He was not wholly successful in suppressing disorder within the city; on one occasion the *Kapı kuls* rose against their commanding officer and killed him. When Sulaymān was transferred to Egypt in 1738, he left an unstable political situation in Damascus. His successor had to endure two popular insurrections and was compelled ultimately to flee from the city. The next governor fared little better. A factional struggle between the *Yarliyya* and the *Kapı kuls* broke out in 1740. Two new regiments of *Kapı kuls* arrived from Istanbul and added to the confusion by oppressing the artisans of the town. The *ʿulamā* joined with the governor and notables to protest to the sultan against them and demand their expulsion. This was sanctioned, and measures were taken against the whole *Kapı kul* faction: some were killed, others expelled, while the remainder were permitted to adopt civilian dress and remain in Damascus.

Alien governors were no more successful than the ʿAẓms, and in 1741 Sulaymān Pasha returned to Damascus. The eclipse of the *Kapı kuls* had destroyed the local balance of factional power, such as it was, to the advantage of the *Yarliyya*, but Sulaymān trod carefully, and avoided an open clash with them. Meanwhile, the rise of two other local notables was threatening the power of the ʿAẓms. One of these was an Arab potentate, Shaykh Ẓāhir al-ʿUmar, the master of Galilee.[1] The other was a Damascene bureaucrat, Fatḥallāh Efendi al-Falāqinsī, whose family originated from a village near Ḥimṣ. Fatḥallāh himself had been appointed *defterdar* of Damascus about 1735—whence he is usually called Fatḥī al-Daftarī. He had acquired great wealth, some of which he expended judiciously in pious works, thereby acquiring the praises of the religious poets. He had also a close connection with the *Yarliyya*, and a powerful patron at Istanbul in the *kızlar agha*, the chief black eunuch who was the head of the Imperial Household. During Sulaymān's second short governorship of Damascus the two did not come into open conflict. Sulaymān died suddenly in 1743, while on campaign against Shaykh Ẓāhir.

At this juncture the ascendancy of the ʿAẓms might have seemed unchallenged. Sulaymān was immediately succeeded by his nephew, Asʿad, who held the petty governorship of Ḥamāh. Asʿad's rule in Damascus lasted from 1743 to 1757—an unprecedentedly long period. Nevertheless, Asʿad was challenged at the outset by Fatḥī al-Daftarī. As soon as the news of Sulaymān Pasha's death reached Damascus, Fatḥī placed the late governor's possessions under seal, appointed an acting governor, and informed Istanbul of the occurrence. On the very day that Sulaymān's corpse was brought to Damascus for burial, the *Yarliyya* attacked and killed some of his private troops. Fatḥī then proceeded to arrest and imprison members of Sulaymān's household and family.

When Asʿad arrived to assume the government of Damascus, he was in a very precarious position, and acted with great circumspection. A treasury official from Istanbul carried out a vigorous investigation into his uncle's estate, ill-treating the women and servants of the family, but in spite of the general expectation Asʿad made no move against him or Fatḥī. For over two years he quietly made his preparations until, after

[1] See below, pp. 124–8.

returning from Pilgrimage in February 1746, he was ready to strike. His first act was to summon his private troops. This provoked the *Yarliyya*, who donned their weapons and robbed the townspeople. Then, early in the afternoon of 16 March, the sound of gunfire was heard. The governor's private army had captured the citadel and were bombarding the quarter of the town where the *Yarliyya* lived. Next they fired on the residence of the factional leader, who called himself the 'sultan of Damascus', and drove him to flight. The governor ordered the shaykhs of the various quarters and the *imāms* of the mosques to arrest other insubordinates, who were put to death. Order was restored, with the governor's force of about 400 men controlling the city. Those of his opponents who escaped with their lives fled—some to Shaykh Ẓāhir, others to Lebanon, or to the Arab tribes.

The *Yarliyya* had become so powerful because, since the expulsion of the *Kapı kuls*, some five years earlier, there had been no effective military force in Damascus to counterbalance them. Having broken their strength, Asʿad decided to re-establish the *Kapı kuls*. A new regiment of imperial troops arrived in the city in May 1746, and Asʿad stringently warned its commanding officer against admitting Damascenes on his strength. The way was now open for him to destroy Fatḥī. Not only had the *Yarliyya*, Fatḥī's local supporters, been deprived of power, but also the *kızlar agha*, his protector at court, had died. Asʿad, for his part, had acquired two powerful allies, the Ottoman grand vezir and a member of the family of al-Bakrī al-Ṣiddīqī resident at Istanbul. It was thus not difficult for him to obtain an imperial warrant for Fatḥī's execution. Fatḥī was arrested in July 1746 at a meeting of notables and beheaded. Some of his household shared his fate, and his estate in its turn was confiscated by the government. Having thus overcome his rivals, Asʿad, in August, took steps to safeguard his own possessions by constituting a family *waqf*, a species of trust which was regarded as a pious endowment, and was protected by the *Sharīʿa*. Part of his wealth went on building a magnificent residence, which remains in Damascus to this day.

The governorship of Asʿad Pasha was remembered as a period of just and peaceful rule, while the fourteen safe Pilgrimages which he commanded were public evidence of his piety. At the same time other members of the family held governorships. One of Asʿad's brothers died as governor of Sidon; another held at various times, amongst other governorships, Tripoli, Aleppo and Sidon; a third was appointed in turn to Sidon, Adana and Mosul. Yet the family's tenure of power was inherently precarious and rested on delicate relations with factions at the sultan's court. Having incurred the enmity of another influential *kizlar agha*, Asʿad Pasha was constrained in 1757 to accept transfer to Aleppo. In the following year he was disgraced and put to death.

The ʿAẓms were now for a time in eclipse, and indeed never regained the ascendancy which they had possessed in Asʿad's prime. The next two governors of Damascus were chosen from outside the ʿAẓm household. The first of them, Ḥusayn Pasha ibn Makkī, the protégé of the *kizlar agha*, was another man of local origin, coming from Gaza. During his governorship, the *Yarliyya* resumed their factional rivalry with the *Kapi kuls*, who were driven into the citadel and blockaded there. Ibn Makkī's single Pilgrimage was disastrous. The first *Jarda* was attacked and broken up by Arabs. The quarrels of the *Yarliyya* and *Kapi kuls* hindered the formation of a second *Jarda*, and, when one was constituted, it failed to contact the Pilgrimage caravan, because of reports that the Arabs were massing. Ibn Makkī waited in vain for the relieving force; provisions ran short, and when at last in desperation the pilgrims resumed their march, the Arabs fell on them and looted the caravan. The governor managed to escape, and fled to Gaza. His successor at Damascus brought fresh troops, with which he routed the *Yarliyya*, and ended the blockade of the citadel. When he was removed from office early in 1760, the governorship of Damascus was conferred upon ʿUthmān Pasha al-Ṣādiq, a Georgian, who had formerly been a *mamlūk* of Asʿad Pasha. ʿUthmān had risen to power at the expense of his patron's family, and his governorship did not in any real sense indicate an ʿAẓm revival.

8

The Amirate of the Maʿnids and Shihābs in Lebanon

Throughout the Middle Ages Mount Lebanon formed an almost impregnable natural fortress. Over its inhabitants, the rulers of Damascus and the Syrian plains asserted their suzerainty, but they were never able for long to control the turbulent and bellicose highland peasantry. At most they could hope to receive tribute and to contain the hillmen within their mountain bastion, away from the lowlands and the routes which linked the great cities. But while geographical conditions gave a high degree of security to the inhabitants of the Mountain, they did not promote internal political unity. Furthermore, the very security itself had throughout the centuries attracted ethnic and religious minority groups, as well as individual refugees. Thus, history as well as geography contributed to the disunity of Lebanon.

The general pattern of Lebanese society was thus one of fairly small groups of cultivators, living under the authority of hereditary dynasties of chiefs. From the point of view of the suzerain, these chiefs were the channels by which his power was mediated to the Lebanese and through which he obtained the tribute of the region. But it must be emphasized that the authority of the chiefs sprang from local roots, although it might be recognized and confirmed by the suzerain. There was thus a complex interplay of relationships between the factions and dynastic ambitions of the Lebanese chiefs, and between these and the suzerain power. From time to time a Lebanese dynasty would obtain a degree of paramountcy over some of the other chiefly families, and this development in the Ottoman period inevitably produced a tension with the sultan and his local representatives, in particular the governors of Damascus, whose power was openly or implicitly threatened.

At the time of Selim I's conquest of Syria from the Mamluk sultanate there was a broad religious distinction between Kisrawān, the most northerly part of the Mountain, inhabited by a Christian, Maronite peasantry under chiefs of their own faith, and the southern districts of the Gharb and the Shūf, where the peasantry and their chiefs were for the most part Druze. Running across this confessional division there was however, a purely political polarization, remotely descended from the antagonism between northern and southern Arabs in the early days of Muslim rule in Syria. The genuinely tribal significance of this polarization had long been lost, but the chiefly families, and hence their peasantry, continued to attach themselves to one or other of the traditional factions of Qays and Yaman.

Under the later Mamluk sultans the paramount family in the Mountain had been the Buhturids, a Qaysī dynasty of the Gharb. The active support which this clan gave to Qānṣawh al-Ghawrī led to their decline under Ottoman rule, and their paramountcy came to be shared by two other dynasties. In the Shūf were the Druze Maʿnids, whose eponymous founder had settled with his tribe in that district early in the twelfth century. Like the Buhturids they belonged to the Qaysī faction. In Kisrawān were the Muslim ʿAssafids—Turcomans who had been settled there since the fourteenth century. It is said that the Maʿnid chief, Fakhr al-Dīn I, made his submission to Selim at Damascus and received the title of *sulṭān al-barr*,[1] but this may well be a later tradition, reflecting the unquestioned hegemony of his grandson.

Selim's object in the campaign of 1516–17 was, as we have seen, to end the threat from the independent Mamluk sultanate, not to effect a detailed territorial conquest of Syria and Egypt. Thus the chiefs of Mount Lebanon retained under the Ottomans the virtual autonomy which they had known under the Mamluks, and were free to pursue their dynastic policies and factional feuds so long as these did not threaten Ottoman control over the routes and cities of Syria. From the sultan's point of view they were farmers of the taxes of their peasantry. If this function were fulfilled, the sultans, and the governors of Damascus, who were their immediate agents, required little of the Lebanese chiefs besides their good behaviour.

The peaceful relations between the chiefs and the Ottomans were rudely shattered in 1584, when the decline of the empire was just beginning to be felt in the provinces, by the raiding and pillage of the tribute-convoy from Egypt at Jūn ʿAkkār on Lebanese territory. A punitive expedition under the viceroy of Egypt penetrated the Mountain and dealt particularly harshly with the Druzes of the Shūf. Korkmaz, the reigning *amīr*, son of Fakhr al-Dīn I, perished as a fugitive, and for a time Maʿnid power was in eclipse.

[1] *Sulṭān al-barr* was apparently a title bestowed on powerful tribal chiefs. The same title was applied in the mid-seventeenth century to the Arab chief who at that time dominated the vicinity of Aleppo.

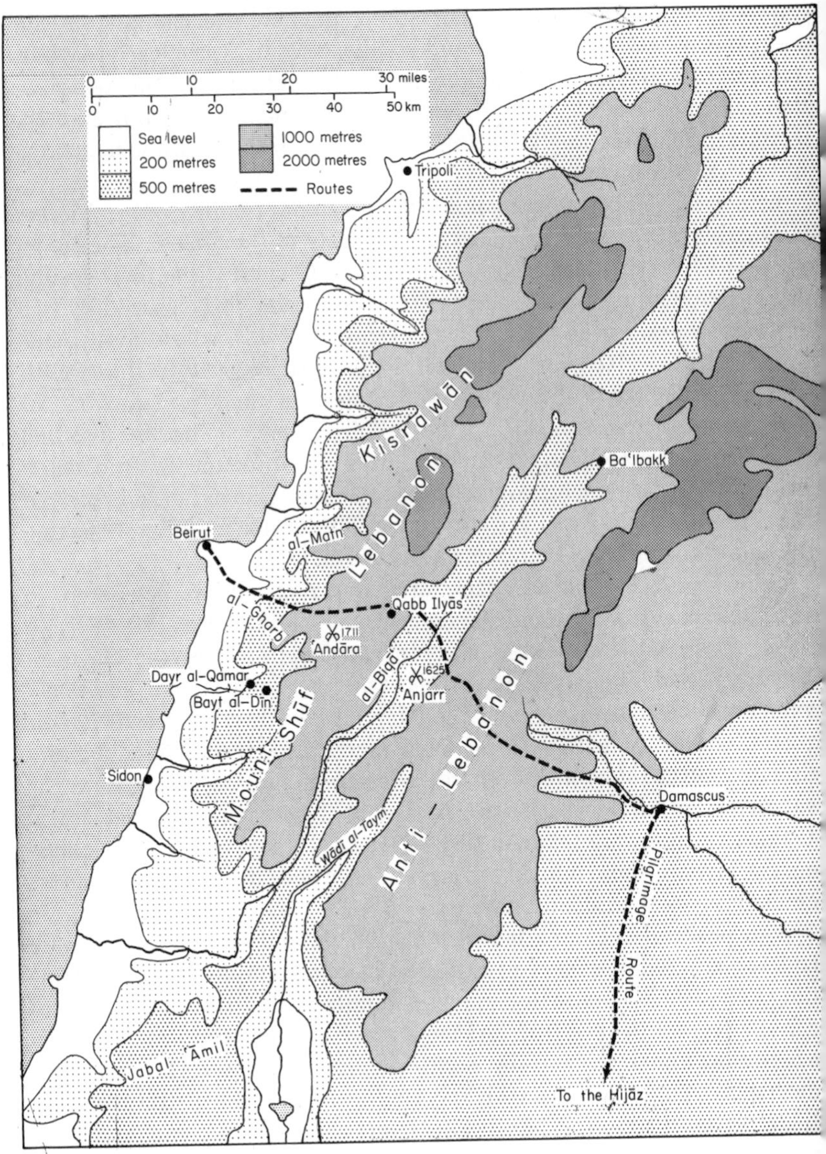

MAP 4: Lebanon

The overthrow of Korkmaz worked to the advantage of a northern chief, Yūsuf Sayfā, a Muslim of Kurdish origin, who had been appointed governor of Tripoli by the sultan in 1579 in order to counterbalance the great power of the ʿAssafids in that region. Although Yūsuf was himself under a cloud after the Jūn ʿAkkār episode, he succeeded in regaining Ottoman favour. In 1590 he ambushed and killed the last ʿAssafid *amīr*, took his possessions, and married his wife; thereby establishing himself as the new paramount dynast in northern Lebanon.

The fortunes of the Maʿnids were to be restored by the son of Korkmaz, Fakhr al-Dīn II, who had been preserved as an infant with his brother, Yūnus, from the vengeance of the viceroy. From 1590, when he was about eighteen years old, Fakhr al-Dīn II worked steadily to rebuild the position of his family in the Shūf and thence to obtain an undisputed hegemony over Mount Lebanon and the neighbouring territories. In his endeavours his most constant allies were another chiefly family, the Muslim Shihābs of Wādī al-Taym. Nowadays Fakhr al-Dīn is often presented as a precursor of modern Lebanese nationalism, who sought to create a progressive, united state, independent of Ottoman rule. This is an anachronism. Fakhr al-Dīn aimed at a dynastic hegemony over Lebanon, and the realization of this aim involved conflict with rival powers within Lebanon, with the Ottoman governors of Damascus, and ultimately with the sultan himself. The unity which he sought and temporarily achieved was dynastic not national. His measures for the economic development of his possessions, and the toleration which characterized his rule, while admittedly good in themselves, were political means to his dynastic ends.

Examined in detail, the career of Fakhr al-Dīn consists of a confused and repetitive series of local struggles. To follow these through from year to year is an unprofitable exercise: in this account we shall consider first the broad aspects of his policy, which remained constant throughout his lifetime, and secondly, the three great crises in which the tension between Fakhr al-Dīn and his opponents was at its height.

Fakhr al-Dīn's primary aim was the extension of his hegemony, based on the Shūf, over Kisrawān and the northern Lebanese littoral. This involved him in a long struggle with Yūsuf Sayfā. Their personal antagonism had also a factional significance, since the Sayfā family were Yamanīs. Fakhr al-Dīn won his first victory at the battle of Nahr al-Kalb in 1598, but did not succeed in holding the northern region for more than a year. Generally speaking, Yūsuf Sayfā had the moral backing of the Ottoman government, but on some occasions, when the Ottomans wished to check Yūsuf's power by installing new nominees to the governorship of Tripoli, their aims and those of Fakhr al-Dīn temporarily coincided.

A second aim of Fakhr al-Dīn's policy was to extend his sphere of influence beyond the Mountain to include other highland areas, especially Ḥawrān, ʿAjlūn and Nābulus. Like Lebanon itself, these were districts inhabited by turbulent hillmen, only loosely controlled by the Ottomans. Fakhr al-Dīn had clients among their chiefs and notables, whom he supported against their rivals. The extension of his power outside Lebanon constituted an immediate challenge to the Ottoman governors of Damascus; in particular, by controlling Ḥawrān and ʿAjlūn, he could threaten the vital Pilgrimage route to the Ḥijāz, which ran between them. Hence, while Fakhr al-Dīn could generally pursue his northern policy without making himself obnoxious to the Ottomans, he could hardly move in the south without producing serious repercussions.

Over many years, Fakhr al-Dīn secured his position by playing adroitly on the avarice and dissensions of the Ottoman ruling élite; the maxim of 'divide and rule' was one which he practised more skilfully and more consistently than they. His agent at Istanbul was prompt to forestall or avert the opposition of imperial officials by heavy bribes. The frequent changes and personal animosities of the Ottoman officials and provincial governors further served his purposes. Only rarely did the concurrence of Fakhr al-Dīn's local opponents, the Ottoman governor of Damascus, and the central government, make possible concerted and effective action against him.

One such crisis came to a head in 1613. Some years earlier Fakhr al-Dīn had allied himself with ʿAlī Pasha Jānbulād, the Kurdish triba dynast of Kilis, who had usurped the governorship of Aleppo, anc against whom Yusūf Pasha Sayfā, Fakhr al-Dīn's rival, had marchec with the approval of the Ottoman government.[1] When ʿAli Pasha wa defeated (by another army under the grand vezir), Fakhr al-Dīn effecte a hasty reconciliation with the Ottomans; but it was clear that the loca antagonism of Maʿn and Sayfā was liable to involve Fakhr al-Dī in dangerous collusion with declared rebels against the sultan. A another level Fakhr al-Dīn was provoking Ḥāfiẓ Aḥmad Pasha, governo of Damascus, by the support he gave to local malcontents. Then in 161 a new grand vezir was appointed, Naṣūḥ Pasha, who was no friend t Fakhr al-Dīn.

It was now only a matter of time before a clash occurred. Ḥāfi

[1] See above, p. 105.

Aḥmad built up a party of Fakhr al-Dīn's local opponents. In 1613 he removed from office the notable who held the district of ʿAjlūn and the Arab shaykh of Ḥawrān, both of whom promptly sought the aid of Fakhr al-Dīn. The Lebanese *amīr* tried to arrange the matter by sending his agent to Istanbul, but finally yielded to pressure, and put his son, ʿAlī, in command of a force which defeated the Damascenes. The party of Ḥāfiẓ Aḥmad thereupon complained to the sultan that Fakhr al-Dīn had become paramount in Ḥawrān and ʿAjlūn, and was threatening Damascus. Ḥāfiẓ Aḥmad was put in command of an imperial army, a fleet was sent to the Lebanese coast, and Fakhr al-Dīn, overwhelmed by Ottoman power, slipped on board a European ship with his family and retinue, and made his way to Leghorn, the port of the grand-duchy of Tuscany.

By doing this, he had saved the amirate for his family. His son, ʿAlī, was recognized as *amīr*, and his brother, Yūnus, also remained in Lebanon, to watch over the dynastic interests. For five years Fakhr al-Dīn remained in Europe, at first as a guest of the Grand-duke Cosimo II of Tuscany, then at Messina, under the protection of the king of Spain. Gradually the situation in the east changed in his favour. Naṣūḥ Pasha fell from office, Ḥāfiẓ Aḥmad left Damascus, and in 1615 Fakhr al-Dīn paid a brief visit to his homeland. Three years later, his old opponents out of the way, he obtained a letter of amnesty from the Ottoman government and returned to Lebanon.

On returning to power in 1618, Fakhr al-Dīn set to work to achieve his old aims in the old way. The intermittent hostilities with Yūsuf Pasha Sayfā were resumed, while he continued to intervene on behalf of his clients in the south. Here he achieved a marked success in 1622, when Ṣafad, ʿAjlūn and Nābulus were granted by the imperial government to his nominees. So extensive was his power at this time, that the governor of Damascus begged him to subsidize the Pilgrimage. In return, Fakhr al-Dīn stipulated that the Syrian commander of the Pilgrimage should be either one of his sons or his agent. That the direction of the Pilgrimage should depend on the will of a Druze chief was a curious situation, and one that cannot have been welcome to the Ottomans.

Events were now moving to another crisis. Hostilities broke out between Fakhr al-Dīn and the Amīr Yūnus al-Ḥarfūsh, the paramount chief of the Biqāʿ. Yūnus was worsted, and Fakhr al-Dīn obtained possession of Qabb Ilyās, a position from which he could control the important road from Damascus to Beirut. His growing power alarmed Muṣṭafā

Pasha, the governor of Damascus, who made an alliance with Yūnus al-Ḥarfūsh and Yūsuf Pasha Sayfā to overthrow him. On this occasion, however, Fakhr al-Dīn, thanks to lavish bribes, was able to prevent the intervention of the central government, which indeed confirmed his possession of Ṣafad, Nābulus and ʿAjlūn. The combat was thus between local forces only. At the battle of ʿAnjarr (1625), Muṣṭafā Pasha was defeated and made a prisoner, while his allies were completely routed. The governor recognized Fakhr al-Dīn's existing possessions, and even appointed him the tax-farmer of remote Gaza, although Fakhr al-Dīn's attempt to lead an expedition there was unsuccessful. In 1624 his old antagonist, Yūsuf Pasha Sayfā, died; and in the same year Fakhr al-Dīn's paramountcy in Lebanon and the adjoining districts was officially recognized by an imperial edict, purchased at a high price. He was to have the title of *sulṭān al-barr* (which, as we have seen, tradition had conferred on his grandfather) and to rule over *ʿArabistan* from the boundaries of Aleppo to the boundaries of Jerusalem. In this context, the term *ʿArabistan* probably signifies the tribal areas, outside the territories administered by Ottoman officials.[1] During the years that followed, Fakhr al-Dīn strengthened his grasp over his territories, and prepared against the eventuality of a reckoning with the Ottomans by building and restoring castles at the approaches to the highlands.

The years of Fakhr al-Dīn's final and most complete ascendancy, the decade which followed ʿAnjarr, were a time of weakness for the Ottoman government. Not until Sultan Murad IV (who had ascended the throne as a child in 1623) took control of the state did the Ottoman Empire show some signs of renewed vitality. The flourishing condition of Fakhr al-Dīn's affairs in these years was due to the more serious preoccupations of the suzerain power, no less than to his own able management.

The downfall of Fakhr al-Dīn, like the overthrow of the Mamluk sultanate, was a by-product of Ottoman–Safavid hostility. The treachery of Bakr Ṣūbāshī had enabled Shah ʿAbbās to take Baghdād in 1623, and Ottoman attempts to recover it had been in vain.[2] In 1633 Murad IV reopened the Persian war. But in any campaign designed to reconquer Baghdād, Fakhr al-Dīn represented a threat to the Ottoman flank, as the Mamluks had done over a century earlier. His mountain-bastion, protected by castles (the most northerly of which menaced Antioch and Aleppo), and his dubious loyalty to the Ottoman sultanate made him

[1] In sixteenth-century Ottoman documents, *ʿArabistan* usually means the Arab provinces of Asia.

[2] See below, pp. 137–8.

too dangerous a ruler to be left alone. There were even rumours, which may not have lacked substance, that he was aiming at complete independence; undoubtedly he had long used each new accession of power as a means to further acquisitions.

At the order of the grand vezir, an expeditionary force was organized under the governor of Damascus, Küchük Aḥmad Pasha, who had formerly been a tax-gatherer in the service of Fakhr al-Dīn, and, after quarrelling with his master, had entered Ottoman service. Thus in 1634 as in 1613 there was a combination of Ottoman authority at both central and local levels against Fakhr al-Dīn. Once again it proved irresistible. ʿAlī, Fakhr al-Dīn's eldest son, was killed in battle. The Maʿnid hegemony crumbled as the Ottomans pressed on. Fakhr al-Dīn fled to seek refuge in a mountain cave, but was captured early in 1635 and sent to Istanbul. There he and his sons, who were made prisoners with him, were well treated by the sultan. For some weeks they lived in honourable captivity as hostages.

The extensive, if transitory, hegemony of Fakhr al-Dīn II rested on on a more solid military basis than the armed peasantry of the Mountain. He built up a professional army of mercenaries, which is said to have attained the number of forty thousand. To maintain these and the castles which fringed his domain, as well as to provide the money needed for bribes at the imperial court, a large and steady revenue was necessary. This was obtained partly through territorial expansion, partly through the better exploitation of economic resources and the development of the commerce of the lands he ruled. He encouraged the cultivation of the mulberry and the olive, and developed the decayed ports of Beirut and Sidon for overseas trade. His principal trading ally was the grand-duchy of Tuscany, with which he signed a commercial treaty in 1608, but French and Venetian merchants were also welcome in his ports. Tuscany sent him not only traders but also architects, engineers and agricultural experts, who assisted him in the construction of public works and the development of cultivation.

The prosperity of his dominions rested also upon religious toleration. The Druzes of southern Lebanon and the Maronites of Kisrawān were both minority-groups in the orthodox Muslim Ottoman Empire. In his time these two religious groups began to enter into closer association. Maronite peasants were encouraged to emigrate into the southern districts, where they contributed to the development of agriculture and served a political purpose in diluting the power of the Druze chiefly families. Maronite nobles, particularly the Khāzin family (the Khawāzin), rose high in his service. At the same time, the Mountain, as in past centuries, remained as an asylum for refugees from outside. In 1630 Fakhr al-Dīn welcomed Jānbulād, the great-nephew (or grandson) of his old ally, ʿAlī Pasha Jānbulād, who brought his people from the Aleppo district to settle under Fakhr al-Dīn's rule. They took their place among the Lebanese aristocracy, and their descendants, the clan of Janbalāṭ (Junblāṭ), are still prominent in the Lebanon of today.

Another aspect of Fakhr al-Dīn's tolerant policy appears in his attitude towards European Christian missionaries. No obstacle was placed in the way of their entry and settlement, while he permitted, and even subsidized, the building of Christian churches and convents. His political ambition was devoid of fanaticism, and he left it to his subjects and allies to argue whether he was in reality a Druze, a Muslim, or a Christian, while drawing what profit he could from their uncertaintie and from the pleasing belief of the Europeans that the Druzes wer descended from a Crusader Count de Dreux.

With the overthrow of Fakhr al-Dīn, the Maʿnid hegemony ove Lebanon collapsed. Even over his original homeland in the Shūf, th Ottomans tried to instal a paramount chief from the Yamanī family o ʿAlam al-Dīn. There remained, however, the Amīr Mulḥim, son c Yūnus and nephew of Fakhr al-Dīn, to continue the struggle. Th disorder and fighting that ensued rapidly assumed the character of factional struggle between Qaysīs and Yamanīs. Küchük Aḥmad Pash blamed the troubles on the intrigues of the exiled Fakhr al-Dīn, wh was accordingly put to death in Istanbul in April 1635. One of his son named Ḥusayn, was spared, and rose in due course high in the imperi service. Ultimately Mulḥim gained the upper hand in the Shūf, an handed on the paramountcy to his son Aḥmad, who died leaving n children in 1697.

At an assembly held at al-Samqāniyya, near the Maʿnid capital Dayr al-Qamar, the vassals of the Maʿnids elected as their new paramou chief Bashīr ibn Ḥusayn, a member of the Shihāb clan from the oth side of the Biqāʿ. There had long been an alliance between the Maʿni and the Shihābs, and Bashīr I was the maternal nephew of the la Aḥmad Maʿn. The choice of the electors was duly reported to t Ottoman governor of Sidon. When the sultan's confirmation was r quested, however, an objection was raised by Ḥusayn, the surviving s of Fakhr al-Dīn II, now an influential personage at the Ottoman cou On his advice the paramountcy was conferred on Ḥaydar Shihāb, t maternal grandson of Aḥmad Maʿn, and a cousin of Bashīr. Sin

Ḥaydar was at the time only twelve years of age, Bashīr continued to rule in his name as regent. Ten years later, Bashīr died, allegedly poisoned at the instigation of Ḥaydar, who thereupon began his personal rule.

The Shihābs had inherited from the last Maʿnids only a precarious hegemony in the Mountain. The Sayfā dynasty, which had been Fakhr al-Dīn's principal opponent, had lost its importance with the death of Yūsuf Pasha and was expelled from Tripoli in 1637, but the family of ʿAlam al-Dīn remained as a constant centre of opposition, attracting in particular the support of the Yamanī faction. In Ḥaydar's time, however, the power of the ʿAlam al-Dīn and of the Yamaniyya was finally broken.

At the beginning of his personal reign, Ḥaydar had extended his authority over the Shīʿī district of Bilād Bishāra, to the south of the Mountain proper. He appointed as his agent and tax-gatherer a Druze shaykh from the Shūf named Maḥmūd Abū Harmūsh. Three years later, on receiving reports that Maḥmūd was oppressing the people and appropriating their taxes, Ḥaydar called him to account. But Maḥmūd fled to Sidon and sought the protection of its governor, who obtained for him the rank of pasha and appointed him as governor of the Shūf. Provided with a military force, Maḥmūd Pasha defeated Ḥaydar. The new governor of the Shūf allied himself closely with the Yamaniyya and married a daughter of the family of ʿAlam al-Dīn. The Qaysiyya thereupon turned increasingly to Ḥaydar and assured him of their support in any trial of strength.

In 1710 or 1711 Ḥaydar emerged from concealment and established his headquarters in the Matn, the central district of the Mountain between Kisrawān and the Shūf. His hosts and chief supporters were a family of petty chiefs known as Abu'l-Lamʿ (Ballamʿ). As the Qaysiyya of the Shūf and Kisrawān gathered at his call, the Yamaniyya came in to support Maḥmūd Pasha, who begged the Ottoman governors of Sidon and Damascus for aid. They brought up their forces to Beirut and Qabb Ilyās respectively, while he himself advanced northwards to ʿAndārā (ʿAyn Dārā).

On receiving the news of Maḥmūd Pasha's advance, Ḥaydar mustered his troops, divided his army into three parts, and made a night-march to take Maḥmūd by surprise, before the governors of Sidon and Damascus could intervene. He was completely successful. The Yamaniyya were overwhelmingly defeated. Three of the ʿAlam al-Dīn *amīrs* were killed in battle, and four captured, together with Maḥmūd Pasha himself. The four *amīrs* were subsequently put to death. Mahmūd's life was spared, since he was a shaykh of the Shūf, but he was rendered innocuous b mutilation. Seeing that the matter was decided, the two Ottoma governors went back to their provincial capitals without striking a blow while Ḥaydar entered Dayr al-Qamar in triumph.

The victory of ʿAndārā overthrew for all time the Yamanī faction i Lebanon, and established the Shihāb hegemony on a firm foundation. I was followed by a migration of Yamanī Druzes from the Mountain t Ḥawrān, which came to be known by the name formerly given t Lebanon itself, *Jabal al-Durūz*, 'the Mountain of the Druzes'. Mean while the migration of the Maronites from Kisrawān to souther Lebanon, which had begun under Fakhr al-Dīn II, was continuing This erosion of the regional distribution of the religious communitie contributed to the development of a sense of Lebanese nationality rooted in a common soil and transcending confessional differences. A awareness of this becomes apparent as the eighteenth century moves or and it was to assert itself vigorously after the fall of the fostering dynast in the mid-nineteenth century.

The defeat of his opponents and the absence of Ottoman interventio at this critical juncture, enabled Ḥaydar to reward his followers an place the various districts of the Mountain under vassals linked to th Shihābs by interest and marriage. The greatest profit was reaped b the Abu'l-Lamʿ, who were raised from the rank of petty chiefs to becom *amīrs* and social peers of their paramount chief. The alliance of th Shihābs and the Abu'l-Lamʿ was cemented by repeated intermarriag between the two clans. While the Abu'l-Lamʿ were given the Matn a a species of fief, other districts were allotted to other loyal follower 'Alī Janbalāṭ, the descendant of the Kurdish immigrant, Jānbulā acquired the Shūf through marriage. Kisrawān remained under th Khāzin dynasty who had been the faithful friends of Fakhr al-Dīn, an whose chief had been the spokesman of the Qaysiyya, summonin Ḥaydar to lead the faction against Maḥmūd Pasha. The composition c the new Lebanese aristocracy strikingly illustrates the religious diversit of the Shihābī state. A nucleus of great families was still Druze, such a the Abuʿl-Lamʿ and the Janbalāṭ, and a number of others. But th Khawāzin of Kisrawān headed the Maronite aristocrats, while th Shihābs themselves at this time were neither Druzes nor Christians bu Sunnī Muslims.

The history of Lebanon after ʿAndārā is no less turbulent than in th preceding period, but in spite of internal troubles, clashes with Ottoma authority, and even fratricidal strife within the dynasty itself, a gradu strengthening and extension of Shihābī power is evident. As in Fakhr al-Dīn's time, the Lebanese rulers asserted their authority, not always permanently, over the districts and coastlands fringing the Mountain, such as the Biqāʿ and the port of Beirut. The growing influence of the Christians in political and social life was demonstrated by the conversion of some members of the ruling dynasty, as well as the Abu'l-Lamʿ, to Catholicism—perhaps a unique occurrence in the predominantly Muslim Near East. Less unusual was a revival of factionalism between two groups known as the Janbalāṭiyya (centring round the Janbalāṭ family) and the Yazbakiyya, linked with another great vassal family, the ʿImād al-Dīn. This polarization, like the earlier Qaysī-Yamanī rivalry, divided Druzes, Christians and Muslims: but by contrast it did not entail partisanship for or against the Shihāb dynasty, although it might involve support for one member of the dynasty against another.

The dynastic history of Lebanon in the middle decades of the eighteenth century may be briefly summarized. Ḥaydar abdicated in 1732 in favour of his son Mulḥim. After a successful reign Mulḥim also abdicated, stricken by an incurable disease, and retired to Beirut in 1754. The paramountcy was then contested by two of his brothers, Manṣūr and Aḥmad, supported by the Janbalāṭiyya and Yazbakiyya respectively. A time of troubles ensued, until Mulḥim's son, Yūsuf, a child at the time of his father's abdication, succeeded to the undivided amirate in 1770. Under Yūsuf, Christian predominance increased. His guardian, Saʿd al-Khūrī, was a Maronite who founded a family of considerable importance down to the present day. Yūsuf himself was a Christian, although he was not publicly known as such. His reign coincided, as we shall see, with the zenith of Shaykh Ẓāhir al-ʿUmar's power, and his last years ended miserably in a struggle with the despot of Sidon, Aḥmad Pasha al-Jazzār.

9

The Ascendancy of Ẓāhir al-ʿUmar and al-Jazzār in Syria

During the middle decades of the eighteenth century it had seemed possible that the ʿAẓm family would establish a lasting ascendancy in southern Syria. This they had failed to do, and with the removal of Asʿad Pasha from Damascus in 1757 a new phase of political history may be said to begin. This had two characteristics: first, the centre of importance shifted from Damascus to Galilee and the coast; and secondly, the isolation of Syria was ended and, as in the past, the western Fertile Crescent was invaded by powers based in Egypt. The shift of importance is exemplified in the two ascendancies of Shaykh Ẓāhir al-ʿUmar al-Zaydānī and Aḥmad Pasha al-Jazzār; the powers which invaded Syria were the Egyptian Mamluks and the French troops of Napoleon Bonaparte.

Ẓāhir's clan, the Zayādina, were Arab peasants living to the west of Lake Tiberias. This was territory which fell within the Ottoman province of Sidon, but its immediate overlord was the *amīr* of Lebanon. By the end of the seventeenth century the Zayādina were people of some consequence. They held the tax-farm of their district, and Ẓāhir's father was appointed shaykh of the hill-town of Ṣafad by the Shihābī ruler. Ẓāhir was born about the year 1690. When he was still a boy, his father died and his elder brother arranged for the tax-farm to be transferred to him. At the same time Ẓāhir assumed the nominal responsibility for another farm of taxes held by the family on the sea-coast near Acre. The intention of the brothers was no doubt to use Ẓāhir as a figurehead, but in fact they had enabled him to obtain the two limits between which he was to build up his shaykhdom.

During the years which preceded the rise of ʿAẓm power in Damascus and southern Syria, Ẓāhir steadily increased his territorial possessions in Galilee. He fought the neighbouring shaykhs, and took their lands; the Ottoman governor of Sidon acquiesced, since Ẓāhir assured the regular payment of taxes, while the people welcomed his rule, which protected them from the nomads and secured their roads. Finally he cast off his feudal subordination to the Shihābī *amīr*.

When the coming of the ʿAẓms injected new life into the Ottoman provincial system, a clash was almost inevitable. Its roots lay in the conflict over the control of southern Syria. In 1737 an expedition by Sulaymān Pasha al-ʿAẓm succeeded in capturing one of Ẓāhir's brothers, who was put to death. Sulaymān resumed hostilities against Ẓāhir during his second governorship of Damascus. He led two more unsuccessful expeditions against Tiberias, during the second of which, in 1743, he died.[1]

Meanwhile Ẓāhir had been entering into friendly trading relations with the French merchants in Acre, whom he supplied with cotton and grain. Acre was at this time a decayed port dependent on the governor of Sidon and administered by an Ottoman tax-farmer. In 1746 the tax-farm was granted to Ẓāhir, who fortified Acre and turned it into his capital. This action was followed by an extension of his power in the coastal districts: Haifa was also taken and fortified. This growth of Ẓāhir's shaykhdom was not checked by Asʿad Pasha al-ʿAẓm, who maintained peaceful relations with Ẓāhir during the fourteen years of his governorship from 1743 to 1757.

Ẓāhir was now in an entrenched position in Galilee and the coastal districts of Palestine. He obtained the formal approval of the Ottoman government for his recent acquisitions. In 1768 the outbreak of war between the Ottomans and the Russians worked in his favour. A request by ʿUthmān Pasha al-Ṣādiq, the governor of Damascus, that he should be allowed to start military operations against Ẓāhir was rejected. Ẓāhir at this juncture had the powerful protection of a high official at the sultan's court, through whom he obtained an imperial edict restraining ʿUthmān Pasha from action and referring to the *Sharīʿa* court at Acre the dispute between ʿUthmān and Ẓāhir over Haifa and the other newly acquired territories. Since the court was in a city controlled by Ẓāhir, and since the shaykh's case was argued by his able and wealthy minister, the Christian Ibrāhīm al-Ṣabbāgh, it is not surprising that the judge found for Ẓāhir. For the time being ʿUthmān was foiled.

Soon afterwards, however, Ẓāhir's sponsor at Istanbul died and his situation became less favourable. ʿUthmān bought the appointment of two of his sons to the governorships of Sidon and Tripoli. The balance of power in southern Syria shifted against Ẓāhir, and he began to look elsewhere for an ally. He found one in Bulut Kapan ʿAlī Bey, who then dominated Egypt.[2] ʿAlī had, moreover, an old grudge against ʿUthmān Pasha, and an alliance with Ẓāhir against him was quickly forged. While

[1] See above, p. 109. [2] See above, Ch. 6.

Ẓāhir supplied ʿAlī with munitions of war, ʿAlī enabled Ẓāhir to recruit necessary troops in Egypt. Meanwhile ʿAlī established contact with the Russian fleet in the eastern Mediterranean, which had destroyed the Ottoman navy in July 1770 and was now cruising in Levantine waters.

The first Mamluk expeditionary force, under the command of Ismāʿīl Bey, left for Syria in December 1770. It effected a combination with Ẓāhir's troops, and put to flight ʿUthmān Pasha, who had advanced to Jaffa. Then the allied effort languished. Ẓāhir fell seriously ill and retired to Acre. The Mamluks failed to press home their offensive against Damascus and the winter season broke off the campaign. In the spring of 1771 ʿAlī Bey sent out a second force, under Muḥammad Bey Abu'l-Dhahab, which joined with troops led by Ẓāhir's sons. ʿUthmān Pasha was defeated outside Damascus and fled to Ḥimṣ. The city of Damascus surrendered, but the citadel still held out and was laid under siege. Then came Abu'l-Dhahab's sudden and unexpected withdrawal with his army to Egypt, and Ẓāhir was left to maintain his position in Syria as best he could.

ʿUthmān Pasha, again in possession of Damascus, summoned the assistance of the Amīr Yūsuf Shihāb and his Druze forces. Ẓāhir encountered ʿUthmān near Lake al-Ḥūla and routed him before the Druze levies could join him. When Yūsuf himself advanced to try conclusions, most of the subordinate Druze chiefs favoured Ẓāhir, and Yūsuf was routed in his turn. ʿUthmān Pasha's son, dangerously exposed at Sidon, fled to his father in Damascus. Ẓāhir promptly annexed Sidon and placed it under the command of his mercenary, the Algerian, Aḥmad al-Dinkizlī. ʿUthmān Pasha al-Ṣādiq was deposed, and the command of Ottoman forces in Syria was given to his namesake, ʿUthmān Pasha al-Miṣrī.

In March 1772 ʿAlī Bey fled from Egypt, expelled by Abu'l-Dhahab. He joined Ẓāhir in Syria, and four Russian ships shortly afterwards arrived to support their efforts. Ẓāhir was now openly in rebellion against the Ottoman government, which, distracted by the war with Russia, could do little to oppose him. Such resistance as there was in southern Syria came from ʿUthmān Pasha al-Miṣrī, working in conjunction with Yūsuf Shihāb. An attempt by Yūsuf to recapture Sidon failed, and Ẓāhir went on to press an offensive against Beirut. The acquisition of this port would seriously discomfit the Shihābīs and would strengthen Ẓāhir's hold on the coast. The Russians bombarded the town from the sea and pillaged it, but did not permanently occupy it. At Yūsuf's request ʿUthmān Pasha al-Miṣrī sent troops to reinforce its garrison, under the command of Aḥmad Bey al-Jazzār, the Bosniak soldier of fortune who had formerly been a retainer of ʿAlī Bey in Egypt.[1]

Having failed to acquire Beirut, Ẓāhir and ʿAlī Bey moved southwards down the Palestinian coast to besiege Jaffa, which had revolted against them. Soon afterwards ʿAlī returned to Egypt, lured by the prospect of overthrowing Abu'l-Dhahab and restoring his own hegemony. There he was defeated and died in 1773, leaving Ẓāhir once again to face his Syrian opponents alone. For a while he was saved by the continuance of the Russo-Turkish War and the development of a breach between ʿUthmān Pasha and Yūsuf Shihāb. The prolonged occupation of Beirut by the masterful Jazzār roused Yūsuf's resentment. Through the mediation of his uncle, Manṣūr, he effected a reconciliation with Ẓāhir and sought his aid to evict al-Jazzār. The arrival of Russian ships, originally intended to support ʿAlī Bey, provided them with the instrument they needed. The Russians were paid 300,000 piastres by Yūsuf and Manṣūr to assist in the blockade of Beirut, which in due course surrendered. Ẓāhir tried to persuade al-Jazzār to enter his service as commander of his forces, but al-Jazzār managed to elude him and made his way to Damascus, where he was raised to the rank of pasha. The Ottoman authorities now acquiesced in the hegemony which Ẓāhir had acquired; the sultan, who had recently come to the throne, granted him an amnesty and confirmed him in his possessions.

This favourable situation did not last long. In July 1774 the conclusion of the Treaty of Küchük Kaynarja ended the Russo-Turkish War. ʿUthmān Pasha al-Miṣrī, who had taken the lead in the policy of conciliating Ẓāhir, was removed from his command. Confronted by two autonomous rulers, Muḥammad Bey Abu'l-Dhahab in Egypt, and Shaykh Ẓāhir al-ʿUmar in Galilee, the Ottomans proceeded to use one against the other. Abu'l-Dhahab was induced to invade Syria and to attack Ẓāhir. He found a secret collaborator in Ẓāhir's own son, ʿAlī, who no doubt resented his father's prolonged tenure of power. In March 1775 Abu'l-Dhahab left Egypt and advanced up the coast. Jaffa was captured and its inhabitants massacred. ʿAlī evicted his father from Acre, which was taken over by Abu'l-Dhahab. Ẓāhir fled to Sidon but soon had to leave, as the town was surrendered by al-Dinkizlī to Abu'l-Dhahab's envoys.

The Ottoman government had no wish that Ẓāhir's Syrian possessions should fall intact into the hands of the powerful Mamluk chief of

[1] See above, p. 95.

Egypt, and sent an expedition under the admiral, Ḥasan Pasha,[1] to occupy Acre and the rest of the region. A clash between Ẓāhir's opponents might have developed, but Abu'l-Dhahab suddenly fell ill and died, and the Mamluk army evacuated Syria. Al-Dinkizlī recaptured Acre, and urged Ẓāhir to return thither without delay, since a faction of the mercenaries would have preferred to hand it over to ʿAlī. Ẓāhir did so, but al-Dinkizlī's loyalty to him had already been corrupted. He was secretly in touch with Ḥasan Pasha, to whom he promised to surrender the city and the head of Ẓāhir. Acre was laid under siege, by the troops of Muḥammad Pasha al-ʿAẓm, the governor of Damascus, by land, and the Ottoman fleet by sea. When Ẓāhir realized that he had been betrayed by al-Dinkizlī he sought safety in flight. Overcome by his great age, he fell from his horse and was beheaded by his own mercenaries. His death, in 1775, marked the end of the autonomous state he had created: none of his sons profited from his overthrow, and his territories reverted to the provinces of Damascus and Sidon.

Ẓāhir's shaykhdom did not possess the elements of permanence. It emerged to fill the power-vacuum resulting from the breakdown of the traditional Ottoman provincial system. It was established at a time when neither of the two principal traditional centres of authority in southern Syria, the pashalic of Damascus and the Lebanese amirate, was in a position to exert strong and sustained control over Galilee. The revival of the pashalic threatened its continued existence: while the period of Asʿad Pasha's governorship was abnormal in this respect, Sulaymān and ʿUthmān al-Ṣādiq exhibited the instinctive reactions of governors of Damascus to a quasi-autonomous ruler within their sphere of authority. The last phase of Ẓāhir's rule, when his dominions were most extensive and his ambition for independence most clearly proclaimed, showed its innate instability. He was protected by no natural features (as were the Lebanese *amīrs*), and supported by no cohesive group-loyalties, whether religious, linguistic or ethnic. The foundations of his power were his own family and his mercenaries, and their unsoundness was demonstrated by the treachery of his son, ʿAlī, and his lieutenant, al-Dinkizlī. His chosen allies were the enemies of the sultanate, ʿAlī Bey and the Russians, and this was, in the long run, a fatal flaw in his policy. Even at this time of military weakness and political imbecility the prestige of the sultanate was an impalpable yet powerful weapon in the hands of the House of Osman, which assured it ultimate victory over Muslim rebels and separatists.

[1] For Ḥasan Pasha's subsequent expedition to Egypt, see above, pp. 99–101.

Yet in spite of its inherent weakness, the rule of Shaykh Ẓāhir was of significance for the development of southern Syria. Within the territories he controlled he maintained order and security. His peasants were not crushed under excessive taxation, and trade flourished in his towns. Above all, he brought new life to Acre, turned it into a flourishing centre of foreign commerce, and repopulated its wasted hinterland with a thriving peasantry. When he himself had been swept away, Acre remained the most prosperous and best fortified town on that sector of the coast. It superseded Sidon as the administrative centre of the province of that name, under the new governor, Aḥmad Pasha al-Jazzār—a despot who totally lacked the benevolence of Shaykh Ẓāhir.

Aḥmad, a Bosniak by origin, had gone as a young man to Istanbul, where he entered the service of a high Ottoman official. In 1756 he went to Egypt, where his master had been appointed viceroy, and two years later he made the Pilgrimage in the service of the *amīr al-Ḥajj*. When he returned to Cairo, he found that his master had left the country, whereupon he attached himself to the Mamluk military system. His Mamluk patron was killed fighting the Arabs of the Buḥayra, but he himself was appointed *kāshif* of that sub-province by Bulut Kapan ʿAlī Bey, who had become *shaykh al-balad*. The slaughter which he inflicted on the Arabs, in revenge for his patron's death, won him the cognomen of *al-Jazzār*, 'the Butcher', by which he was to become notorious. He was raised to the beylicate, and accompanied ʿAlī when he was first ousted from power in 1766. When ʿAlī, in alliance with Ṣāliḥ Bey al-Qāsimī, regained Cairo, Aḥmad returned with them. Shortly afterwards, ʿAlī decided to have Ṣāliḥ assassinated, but Aḥmad warned him of the plot. When Ṣāliḥ was ultimately killed, Aḥmad fled from Egypt in 1768 and ultimately settled in Syria. There he began to form a Mamluk household of his own, which was to be the basis of his later power.

On Ẓāhir's downfall, al-Jazzār received, with the pashalic of Sidon, the prosperous and fortified city of Acre, which he made his residence. Here, like the ʿAẓms in Damascus, he set to work to transform the decadent Ottoman provincial system into a personal territorial dominion. Under his rule, the remnants of Zaydānī power were liquidated. Ẓāhir's son, ʿAlī, was killed, and extortionate taxes were laid on the territories over which the Zayādina had ruled. The fortifications of Acre were strengthened, a *corvée* being placed on the local villagers for this purpose.

Before the time of al-Jazzār, the governors of Sidon had played a subordinate rôle to their colleagues of Damascus, and in the period of ʿAẓm ascendancy Sidon was usually held by a junior member of the family. The old relationship was completely transformed during al-Jazzār's governorship. It so happened that the early years of this coincided with a temporary revival of ʿAẓm power in Damascus. Muḥammad Pasha al-ʿAẓm, who belonged to a cadet branch of the family but was a maternal grandson of Ismāʿīl, was appointed governor of Damascus in 1771, and held this position (with a short break in 1772–3) until his death in 1783. His period of office was quiet, the old factional struggles had subsided during these years, while on the whole he tended to avoid a clash with al-Jazzār.

This was not always easy. Al-Jazzār was anxious to extend his authority over Damascus. Furthermore, the governor of Sidon was repeatedly and actively intervening in the politics of Lebanon in order to establish control over the Mountain. On the overthrow of Ẓāhir, Ḥasan Pasha had recognized Yūsuf Shihāb as the paramount ruler over Mount Lebanon, the Biqāʿ, and the coastal regions of Beirut and Jubayl, and had conceded him autonomy of the governor of Sidon, except in fiscal matters. The existence of so independent a neighbour was intolerable to al-Jazzār, and as soon as Ḥasan Pasha left Syria he began his efforts to bring the Mountain under his direct control.

A complex situation thus developed. Al-Jazzār was seeking to diminish the power both of the ʿAẓms and the Shihābs, and Muḥammad Pasha al-ʿAẓm could therefore usually be counted on to help al-Jazzār's Shihābī opponent. But towards Yūsuf, al-Jazzār's policy was strictly opportunist: his aim was not merely to weaken the *amīr* but the Shihāb dynasty as a whole. Hence he would back Yūsuf's rivals within his family, encourage their pretensions to the amirate, and then swing over to support Yūsuf. This policy promoted factional warfare in the Mountain and undermined the prestige of the Shihābs. No claimant could long support himself without the concurrence and assistance of al-Jazzār, but al-Jazzār's help had to be bought. The rivals were led on to outbid each other in promising tribute, and the price of their vain ambitions was paid by the Lebanese peasantry, who were subjected to extortionate taxation.

In 1783, however, Muḥammad Pasha died, and his governorship was held in rapid succession by the two sons of ʿUthmān Pasha al-Ṣādiq, who in Ẓāhir's time, had been governors of Tripoli and Sidon. The latter was supplanted in 1785 by al-Jazzār, who appointed two of his own *mamlūks*, Salīm and Sulaymān Pashas to Sidon and Tripoli. Al-Jazzār held Damascus for nearly two years, and when he was deposed the governorship did not revert to an ʿAẓm.[1]

[1] This was, however, not quite the end of ʿAẓm rule in Damascus. ʿAbdallāh Pasha, a

Acre remained the firm base of al-Jazzār's power, and the attempt to dominate the Mountain his principal preoccupation. In 1789 the struggle was interrupted by an episode which seemed for a time to threaten al-Jazzār's fall. Like Ẓāhir and ʿAlī Bey, al-Jazzār was vulnerable to attacks from his own household and personal followers, and it was a domestic revolt which almost undid him. Al-Jazzār recruited his retinue from two principal sources: from his own Bosniak and Albanian compatriots, who formed the free element in his household, and from *mamlūks* and domestic slaves. At the head of his Mamluk forces were Salīm Pasha and Sulaymān Pasha, whom, at this time, he had sent off with an expeditionary force against Yūsuf Shihāb. During their absence, al-Jazzār used his Bosniak servants to punish his Mamluk and slave household. This led to fighting, and the Mamluks threatened to fire on al-Jazzār's residence and the town. Finally, al-Jazzār agreed to allow them to leave and they joined the expeditionary force.

Salīm Pasha attempted to intercede for the rebels, but his mediation was refused, and al-Jazzār found himself confronted with a mutinous Mamluk army, headed by Salīm and Sulaymān. The two pashas made a truce with Yūsuf Shihāb, and marched on Acre. Al-Jazzār, with a handful of Albanian troops, augmented by armed artisans from his workshops, prepared for a siege. The cause of the rebels was popular with the townspeople and with the notables and tax-farmers of the region. Al-Jazzār contemplated flight by sea, but a surprise night-attack by his supporters dispersed the rebel forces, and abruptly ended the danger.

After this threat to his power, al-Jazzār became even more ferocious and despotic than he had been before. He turned his anger first against Yūsuf Shihāb, whom he regarded as an accomplice of the rebels. Yūsuf was defeated in a battle in the Biqāʿ, and abdicated. The Lebanese chiefs chose as his successor his young cousin, Bashīr II, who was to hold the paramountcy until 1841. At the beginning of his reign, however, he was very weak. Al-Jazzār saw in him a puppet through whom he could exert control over Lebanon; while Bashīr, for his part, displayed a servile submission to the governor of Sidon. On al-Jazzār's orders, he expelled Yūsuf from his territory, but soon al-Jazzār returned to his old tactics of playing off one party against the other. He promised to

---

son of Muḥammad al-ʿAẓm, held the governorship three times for quite extended periods between 1205/1790–1 and 1222/1807–8. He also served as governor of Tripoli and of Aleppo. His brother, Yūsuf Pasha, also held the governorship of Tripoli and Aleppo.

restore Yūsuf to the amirate in 1790, but Bashīr succeeded in outbidding his rival and secured his own position. Bashīr's extortions to fulfil his promises to al-Jazzār stirred up a revolt in Lebanon, and al-Jazzār seized the opportunity to impute the responsibility to Yūsuf, whom he put to death.

For eight years al-Jazzār continued to play his game of cat-and-mouse in Lebanon, supporting sometimes Bashīr, sometimes the party formed around the young sons of Yūsuf Shihāb. Then in 1798 Bonaparte and his French troops landed in Egypt: an occurrence which was to have important repercussions in Syria and on the career of al-Jazzār.

While these developments were taking place in southern Syria, Aleppo stood apart, a prey to factional rivalry. Here, the growing power of the Janissaries was checked in the last decades of the eighteenth century by the emergence of the *Ashrāf* as an armed political faction, consisting, it would seem, mainly of the notables of the city with their clients and retainers. Although the *Ashrāf* elsewhere occasionally played a part in the turbulent politics of the period of Ottoman decline, it was only in Aleppo that they made a sustained bid for dominance. The reasons for this phenomenon are obscure, but the emergence of the *Ashrāf* seems to be associated with the leadership of a rich and influential *naqīb*, Muḥammad ibn Aḥmad Ṭāhāzāde, known as Chelebi Efendi, who formed a faction including the notables and chief men of Aleppo. Although twice exiled, Chelebi Efendi remained a powerful figure until his death. Subsequently, much of his influence appears to have passed to his former servant, Ibrāhīm Qaṭārāghāsī, who became the chief financial official (*muḥaṣṣil*) of Aleppo, and ultimately rose to the rank of pasha.

Rivalry between the *Ashrāf* and the Janissaries was at its height between 1768 and 1798. There were numerous armed conflicts between the two factions, and, on occasions, the *Ashrāf* even revolted against the Ottoman governors. To recount their clashes in detail would be tedious and repetitive, but an incident which occurred in the early part of 1798 seems to mark the end of the ascendancy of the *Ashrāf*. After a scuffle in the streets, a party of *Ashrāf* took refuge in a mosque, where they were blockaded by the Janissaries. Reduced by thirst and hunger, they made terms with their opponents. When the doors of the mosque were opened, however, the Janissaries made a treacherous attack and slaughtered the *Ashrāf*. Although this was a landmark in the conflicts between the two parties, the *Ashrāf* were not eliminated.

The rivalry of the Janissaries and the *Ashrāf* was one instance of the factionalism which, as we have seen, was endemic in the socio-political structure of the region, and which became virulent at times when the official administrative organism was enfeebled. It is paralleled by the rivalry of Faqāriyya and Qāsimiyya, when the Ottoman viceroys of Egypt lost power; and by the Qaysī-Yamanī, and later the Janbalāṭī-Yazbakī, polarization in Lebanon during the weakness of the Maʿnid and Shihābī amirates. In northern Syria the hostility of Janissaries and *Ashrāf* appeared in the later eighteenth century also in ʿAynṭāb, while a similar schism has been noted in Marʿash.

10

The Iraqi Provinces in the Period of Ottoman Decline

In the late sixteenth and early seventeenth centuries, the symptoms of the breakdown of the established system of Ottoman government appeared in the Iraqi provinces, as elsewhere. The history of Baṣra is a case in point. We have already seen something of the geographic isolation and strategic vulnerability of this province. After the punitive expedition against Āl ʿUlayyān in 1549, there was a period of nearly twenty years during which Baṣra had little recorded history.[1] The hold of the Ottomans over the tribes nevertheless remained precarious, and in the summer of 1567 a punitive expedition was again sent out against Āl ʿUlayyān. The commander was the governor of Baghdād, and his force comprised, as well as regular troops, Kurds from Shahrizor, and Arabs, and a fleet of river-boats commanded by Jānbulād Bey, the dynast of Kilis.[2] The Arabs were defeated, and Ottoman rule over the marshlands was re-established.

Thirty years later, however, the decay of Ottoman administration within Baṣra itself had gone so far that the governor found his position untenable. By an obscure and remarkable transaction, he sold the city to a local magnate named Afrāsiyāb, the clerk of the garrison, who thereupon, while continuing to recognize the nominal suzerainty of the sultan, proceeded to administer the province as his private domain. Neither from the governor of Baghdād, nor from the sultan, was there any hostile reaction, while the local population quietly accepted the authority of the new ruler. Afrāsiyāb's origins are not clear, although he was partially at least of local Arab descent, but it is significant that, like Riḍwān Bey in Egypt, he sought to legitimize his rule by deriving his pedigree from a former dynasty, and the legend of Afrāsiyāb's Seljuk descent was duly propagated. On his death he was peacefully succeeded by his son ʿAlī.[3]

[1] See above, p. 56.

[2] Jānbulād was the father of Ḥusayn Pasha and the grandfather of ʿAlī Pasha Jānbulād the ally of Fakhr al-Dīn II; see above, p. 116.

[3] Like many other events in Iraqi history at this period, the reign of Afrāsiyāb cannot be precisely dated. Al-ʿAzzāwī (*Al-ʿIrāq bayn iḥtilālayn*, iv, Baghdād 1369/1949, 139) dates Afrāsiyāb's assumption of power in 1005/1596, and his death (*ibid.*, 47) 1012/1603;

The drift of Baṣra from Ottoman control was accompanied by the breakdown of the administrative system in Baghdād itself. Here, as elsewhere, the fundamental political cause of decline was the weakness of the transient Ottoman governors in face of the garrison-troops. These had developed into an entrenched social class permanently established in the city, probably largely composed of local recruits and dominated by their own leaders, whose interests were by no means synonymous with those of the Ottoman government.

One such leader, who emerged in 1603–4,[1] was Muḥammad ibn Aḥmad al-Ṭawīl, a regimental commander in Baghdād, who had inherited his command from his father. An army was sent against him under the command of Naṣūḥ Pasha,[2] the governor of Diyār Bakr. It is significant that an important part of Naṣūḥ Pasha's army was composed of mercenaries, who, on reaching the environs of Baghdād, were induced to desert, so that Naṣūḥ was defeated. Muḥammad al-Ṭawīl, however, soon fell a victim to the treachery of his own supporters. He was assassinated, probably in 1607, at the instigation of his chief secretary, who installed the late ruler's brother, Muṣṭafā Bey, in his place. Meanwhile the Ottoman government was making another attempt to defeat the rebels. Chighalazade Mahmud Pasha, the son of Chighalazade Sinan Pasha,[3] was appointed governor and sent with an army to reduce the city. He set out in January 1608, and entered into secret negotiations with the military grandees of Baghdād, who swung over to his side. Ultimately, through the intervention of mediators, Muṣṭafā Bey capitulated and was granted a petty governorship within the province of Baghdād.

The revolt of Muḥammad al-Ṭawīl was followed by a much more complex sedition, associated with the name of Bakr Ṣūbāshī. Bakr, whose origins are completely obscure, was an officer of the Janissaries in Baghdād. For a time he held the office of *subashı*, chief of police, hence the epithet which is always linked with his name. Subsequently he rose to be the commanding officer of the regiment. He built up a large following among the local troops, and from about 1619 onwards he became the most powerful man in Baghdād, far exceeding the Ottoman governor in influence. Inevitably, he had created enemies as well as friends among

---

Longrigg (*Four centuries of modern Iraq*, Oxford 1925, 104, n. 1) states that 'Afrasiyab himself did not assume the government of Basrah till about 1612' and places his death in 1624.

[1] Other sources would place the revolt five years later: cf. al-ʿAzzāwī, *op. cit.*, pp. 147–8; Huart, *Histoire de Bagdad*, Paris 1901, 46. The dating of the whole episode is very confused.

[2] See above, pp. 103, 105. [3] See above, p. 105.

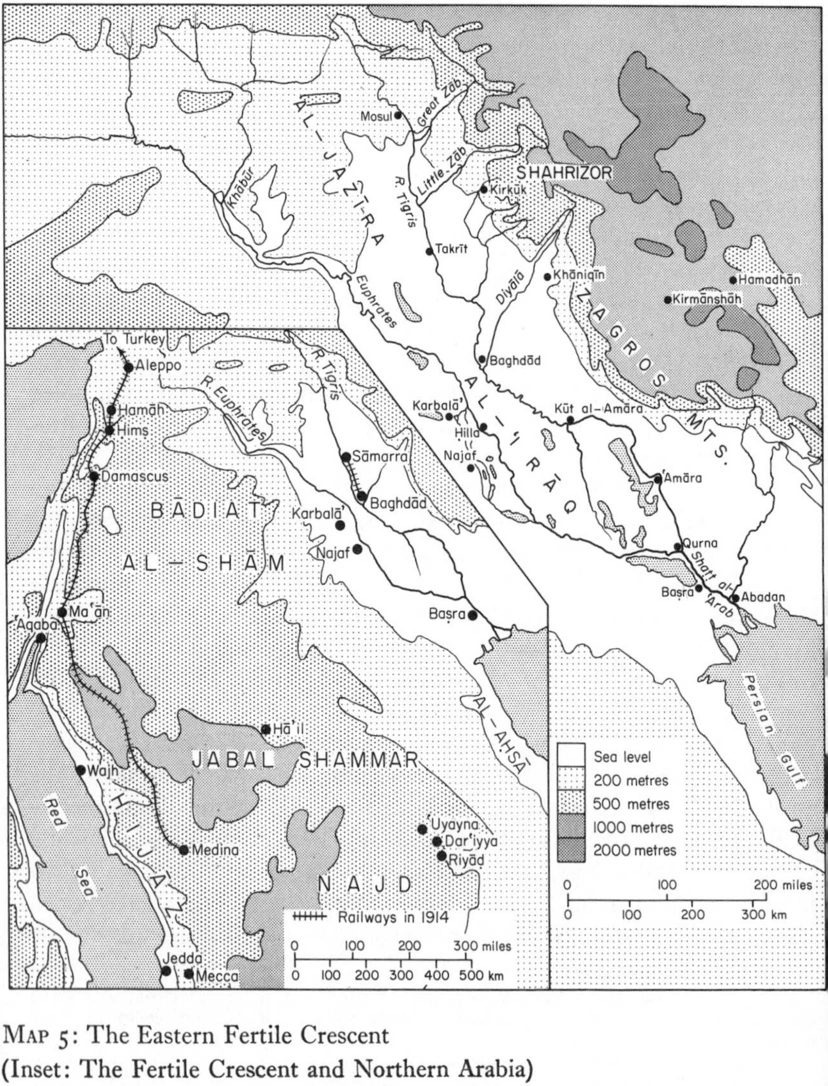

MAP 5: The Eastern Fertile Crescent
(Inset: The Fertile Crescent and Northern Arabia)

the local notables, especially Muḥammad Qanbar, the commanding officer of the rival infantry regiment of *ʿAzeban*.

In 1621 the governor, Yūsuf Pasha, and Bakr's opponents saw an opportunity of breaking his power. Bakr had left Baghdād in command of a punitive force sent against some troublesome tribesmen, and the opposition faction took advantage of his absence to prepare to resist his return. Unfortunately the plot was disclosed prematurely, and came to the ears of Muḥammad, Bakr's son, and ʿUmar, his steward, both of whom had been left in Baghdād. Muḥammad fled, while ʿUmar saved his own life by a feigned compliance with the conspirators, after which he set to work to build up Bakr's faction in the city. Muḥammad Qanbar's son, ʿAbdallāh, and a party of *ʿAzeban*, had accompanied Bakr on the expedition. A letter from Qanbar to ʿAbdallāh, giving particulars of the plot, fell into Bakr's hands, enabling him to put ʿAbdallāh to death and disperse his followers before he himself returned to besiege Baghdād.

After heavy fighting, in which Yūsuf Pasha was killed, Bakr and his party were victorious. The citadel was looted, while Muḥammad Qanbar was brutally done to death. Having made himself the master of the city, Bakr sought to obtain recognition from the Ottoman government through Ḥāfiẓ Aḥmad Pasha, the governor of Diyār Bakr.[1] But for reasons both of strategy and prestige, Baghdād was too important a city to be allowed to slip into the hands of a usurper as Baṣra had done. A new governor was appointed, and his *mutasallim*, or personal representative, went to Baghdād to take over the administration. Bakr refused to allow the *mutasallim* to function, and prepared to fight. An army commanded by Ḥāfiẓ Aḥmad Pasha descended on Baghdād and laid the city under siege.

Bakr therefore turned for aid to the Safavid ruler, Shah ʿAbbās I (1587–1629), the greatest of his dynasty. Shah ʿAbbās snatched at the prospect of regaining the lost Iraqi provinces, and sent an advance force to the relief of Baghdād. Ḥāfiẓ Aḥmad, now in a dangerous strait, tried to gain time by acceding to Bakr's former demands and nominating him, on behalf of the sultan, governor of Baghdād. Thereupon the Ottoman besieging army withdrew. Bakr now tried to revoke his submission to the shah, only to find the city again besieged, this time by the Persians. After a desperate resistance Baghdād was finally betrayed to Shah ʿAbbās by Bakr's own son, Muḥammad, who hoped thereby to obtain the reversion of the governorship. Bakr was arrested and put to death. Baghdād was devastated and a fierce persecution of the Sunnīs took place.

[1] See above, p. 116.

The rise of Afrāsiyāb and the revolt of Bakr had lost the centre and south of Iraq to the Ottomans. The northern provinces of Mosul and Shahrizor also passed for a time under Safavid rule, but they were soon regained. The reconquest of Baghdād was a more difficult exploit, which was to preoccupy the Ottoman government for some years to come. In 1625 Ḥāfiẓ Aḥmad, who had become grand vezir, endeavoured to recapture the city which he had been forced to abandon two years previously. Once again Ottoman forces besieged Baghdād, which was relieved by an army personally commanded by Shah ʿAbbās. After bloody fighting Ḥāfiẓ Aḥmad was compelled by mutiny in his own camp to withdraw to Mosul.

The death of Shah ʿAbbās seemed to promise better success to the expedition commanded by a later grand vezir, Khusraw (Husrev) Pasha, in 1629. Severe floods in central Iraq made transport impossible, and the Ottoman forces were diverted to an unnecessary campaign against Safavid vassals in the Shahrizor marches. Hamadān was reached and devastated before the Ottoman army began its descent on Baghdād, which, in the autumn of 1630, was again laid under siege. On this occasion the Safavid garrison by its own efforts wore out the patience of the besiegers, and after an unsuccessful assault in November 1630 the Ottomans once again withdrew to Mosul.

The reconquest of Baghdād was to be the achievement of Sultan Murad IV, who had come to the throne as a child during the revolt of Bakr. Murad was the last of the great fighting sultans, the belated successor of Selim and Süleyman, and under his rule the old military vigour of the Ottoman Empire temporarily revived. His preparations for the Baghdād campaign involved, as we have seen, the elimination of Maʿnid power in Lebanon,[1] and in the spring of 1638 the great expedition set out. The Ottoman forces advanced according to a preconceived plan, and took up their siege positions around Baghdād in November. Although the shah set out with a relieving force, he dared not advance as far as Baghdād, which fell to Murad in December. Thereafter for two hundred and eighty years Baghdād remained an Ottoman city.

In 1639 the Treaty of Zuhāb, dictated to the representatives of the shah, brought to a close the long period of Ottoman–Safavid hostilities which had been going on since the time of Selim I and Shah Ismāʿīl.[2] Baghdād was confirmed as an Ottoman possession, and a rough boundary

[1] See above, pp. 118–19.

[2] Text in J. C. Hurewitz, *Diplomacy in the Near and Middle East*, Princeton 1956 i, 21–3. This work will subsequently be referred to as Hurewitz.

was established between the two monarchies. Until the final collapse of Safavid power, nearly a century later, no fresh threat was to arise from Persia to Ottoman control in Iraq. So the period following the reconquest of Baghdād is one of comparative tranquillity, during which local problems engross the attention of the Ottoman administration.

As in the past, the soldiery of Baghdād remained a source of disturbance, challenging on occasion the authority of the governors. In one respect the situation was better after 1638; never again did a military boss arise to emulate Muḥammad al-Ṭawīl or Bakr and seek to make himself the independent ruler of the province. The rivalry between Janissaries and *ʿAzeban* seems also to have come to an end with the Safavid occupation, but it was succeeded by a new factionalism between the army of Baghdād, composed of infantry and cavalry who were locally recruited and paid, and the imperial Janissaries, whose salaries came from the sultan's treasury and who seem to have been appointed to temporary garrison duty in Baghdād.

A serious incident took place in 1647. Death had removed the strong hand of Murad IV seven years previously, and the weaknesses of the empire were again beginning to show themselves. The governor of Baghdād, Ibrāhīm Pasha, had been appointed by a grand vezir who was put to death in September 1647. His successor appointed a new governor, Semiz Mūsā Pasha. Ibrāhīm thereupon organized a faction of notables and local soldiery, who refused to allow the *mutasallim* of Semiz Mūsā to take over the administration and demanded the confirmation of Ibrāhīm in office. This action was however opposed by the Janissaries, who, by a stratagem, induced Ibrāhīm Pasha to place himself in their power. A prolonged struggle lasting for three months took place between the two factions of soldiery, from which the Janissaries emerged triumphant. Ibrāhīm Pasha was put to death, and Semiz Mūsā was at last installed as governor. He took strong measures against his opponents, and troops were drafted to Baghdād from Diyār Bakr and elsewhere to reinforce the depleted garrison.

The condition of the soldiery remained, however, a problem and a danger for the administration. The short tenure of office permitted to the governors, and their lack of a force under their own control, left them almost powerless in their own capital. Another serious crisis developed in 1657, under Khāṣṣakī Muḥammad Pasha, the eighth governor of Baghdād in the decade which had elapsed since the fall of Ibrāhīm Pasha. In the autumn of that year a punitive force was sent against some Arab tribesmen of the marshes, but after leaving Baghdād the local troops, who formed part of the expedition, mutinied, killed some of their loyal comrades, and proceeded to make their way back to the capital. The governor, in agreement with the Janissaries of the garrison, closed the gates in their faces, but some nights later sympathizers within the city admitted the mutinous troops. The governor was overpowered, and the mutineers set to work to hunt down the principal objects of their hatred. These were the head of the merchants' corporation, the chief accountant, and the commissioner of the state granaries, of whom only the first escaped death. The choice of victims is significant since it suggests that the grievances of the local groups were financial and economic: there is a close parallel between this sedition and the risings of the *sipahis* in Egypt, rather earlier in the century.[1]

In the disorder, Khāṣṣakī Muḥammad Pasha fled from the city. But the violence of the revolt had now spent itself. The mutineers, lacking leadership and any definite political aims, sent to invite him to return. In this juncture, control was assumed by the Janissaries, who dispersed the local mutinous troops, and compelled them to surrender the officers who had been their ringleaders. They were brought before the governor, who exiled one and sentenced the rest to death. Three hundred of the local soldiery were struck off the pay-roll. After this revolt there were no further major risings of the troops in Baghdād, although they continued to be a potential danger until the end of the century.

The principal external preoccupation of the governors of Baghdād in this period was with Baṣra, under its local dynasty, the House of Afrāsiyāb. Throughout the period of the Ottoman–Safavid struggle over Baghdād, ʿAlī Pasha had followed his own independent line of policy. On two occasions, in 1625 and 1629, he had beaten off expeditions intended to bring him under Safavid control. He maintained trading-relations with the Portuguese. He brought under his control the turbulent marsh-Arabs, who interposed themselves between the areas effectively ruled from Baṣra and Baghdād respectively. The fortress of Qurna, at the junction of the Tigris and Euphrates, was the key to his dominions in this direction.

The Ottoman reconquest of Baghdād was followed by a certain amount of friction on the frontier between the two provinces, but serious hostilities did not begin until after the death of ʿAlī and the succession of his son, Ḥusayn Pasha, in or about the year 1650. Then, as so often in the Arab lands, a dynastic quarrel gave the Ottomans an opportunity to interfere and restore direct control over Baṣra. Two brothers of the late

[1] See above, Ch. 5.

ʿAlī Pasha, named Aḥmad and Fatḥī, had obtained from the sultan, as nominal overlord of Baṣra, letters appointing them *sanjak beys* of two sub-provinces. Ḥusayn Pasha, naturally suspicious of this, had sought to kill them, but they had succeeded in escaping to al-Aḥsā, where the governor, Muḥammad Pasha, had advised them to lay their complaints before Murtaḍā Pasha, then governor of Baghdād. This was in 1654. Murtaḍā forthwith decided to send an army against Ḥusayn, and to capture Baṣra. In this he was successful. The tribesmen of the marshes, ever eager to throw off the government which pressed upon them at the moment, lent him their support. Qurna was captured, the town of Baṣra fell, and Ḥusayn Pasha fled. Aḥmad Bey was installed as vassal-ruler of the province.

Unfortunately Murtaḍā Pasha chose to follow up this easy conquest by seizing the accumulated treasures of Baṣra, and by establishing a reign of terror in which Aḥmad and Fatḥī were themselves put to death. The province turned against him, the marsh-Arabs attacked the garrison he had left at Qurna, and the local soldiery of Baghdād, who had accompanied the governor to Baṣra, now deserted *en masse* and set out for home. In these circumstances Murtaḍā was compelled to flee to Baghdād, and Ḥusayn Pasha re-entered Baṣra. His position was now stronger than ever. Murtaḍā's actions had rendered Ottoman government odious, while his execution of Aḥmad and Fatḥī had eliminated Ḥusayn Pasha's dynastic rivals. Although Murtaḍā wished to make another attack on Baṣra, he was overruled by the Ottoman government.

Ten years were to pass before the Ottomans found another opportunity of intervening in the affairs of Baṣra. The next pretext was provided by developments in al-Aḥsā. In this remote province of the Ottoman Empire, there was a long-standing struggle for power between the chiefs of the Arab tribe of Banū Khālid and the family of Ottoman governors who had ruled al-Aḥsā since the late sixteenth century. Between the governor in office, Muḥammad Pasha, and Ḥusayn Pasha of Baṣra, there was already hostility, as the incident of Aḥmad and Fatḥī had shown. Some years later, Ḥusayn incited Barrāk, chief of the Banū Khālid, to evict Muḥammad Pasha from al-Aḥsā. This was accomplished (although Barrāk himself was shortly afterwards expelled by Ḥusayn's forces), and Muḥammad Pasha implored the assistance of the Ottomans to regain his province.

The governor of Baghdād, Uzun Ibrāhīm Pasha, took command of an army composed of troops from his own and neighbouring provinces. With these he marched out in November 1665 and invested the fortress of Qurna, the possession of which was essential to his further advance. Ḥusayn Pasha was himself at Qurna, and during his absence from Baṣra the merchants and notables of that city staged a coup against him. They wrote to Uzun Ibrāhīm, tendering their submission and asking him to send them a *mutasallim*, which he did. This situation did not last. A counter-coup by one of Ḥusayn's supporters was overcome by the city oligarchy, but they ineptly left open the gates of the city, which was pillaged by Arab tribesmen loyal to Ḥusayn. Meanwhile the siege of Qurna continued, to the detriment of the Ottomans. Ultimately negotiations were undertaken. It was agreed that the House of Afrāsiyāb should continue to rule in Baṣra, although the pashalic was nominally transferred to Ḥusayn's son. Muḥammad Pasha was to be restored to al-Aḥsā. Baṣra was to pay a regular annual tribute to the sultan. On these terms the siege was raised, and Uzun Ibrāhīm Pasha returned to Baghdād.

After the conclusion of peace, Ḥusayn Pasha returned to Baṣra as its effective ruler, but his days of power were numbered. A deputation of merchants from Baṣra went to the sultan to complain of Ḥusayn's exactions, and on this pretext the governorship was transferred to Yaḥyā Agha, Ḥusayn's steward. The governor of Baghdād, now Kara Muṣṭafā Pasha, was commissioned to evict Ḥusayn and install his successor. Once again, an expeditionary force was levied in Baghdād and the neighbouring provinces; once again, in February 1668, Qurna was laid under siege. But this time the event had a different outcome. After a month the defenders could no longer resist the Ottoman forces. Ḥusayn Pasha fled from Qurna to seek the shah's protection, and finally disappeared from history. Baṣra surrendered to Kara Muṣṭafā and accepted Yaḥyā as its governor. The dynasty of Afrāsiyāb had come to an end.

The reintegration of Baṣra in the empire was no easy task. Yaḥyā Pasha, in his turn, asserted his independence by expelling the Ottoman troops and bureaucrats, and attempted in vain to take Qurna from its Ottoman garrison. In the summer of 1669 Kara Muṣṭafā Pasha was victorious in his second campaign against Baṣra. Yaḥyā fled to India and an Ottoman official replaced him as governor. Kara Muṣṭafā intervened again in the following year, to carry out the tax-assessment of the province. When he was removed from the government of Baghdād in 1671 he was given the province of Baṣra, where he died a few months later.

The last years of the seventeenth century saw an increase in the power of the tribal chiefs as the strength of the Ottoman administration declined. In southern Iraq the great confederacy of the Muntafiq united both marsh-Arabs and desert-Arabs in a loose political bond. The chief of the Muntafiq, Māniʿ ibn Mughāmis, extended his power over Lower Iraq and in 1694 captured Baṣra itself. The governor of Baghdād was powerless to intervene effectively. Baṣra was saved for the Ottomans, ironically enough, by the Safavid governor of the neighbouring province of Ḥuwayza. This official had his own troubles with the Muntafiq, and obtained the authorization of Baghdād to expel Māniʿ from Baṣra. He succeeded in capturing both Baṣra and Qurna, and sent their keys to his own master. The shah obligingly surrendered the keys and his acquired rights in southern Iraq to the Ottoman sultan.

During the eighteenth century the administration of Baghdād required greater force. From 1704 to 1831 the province was ruled by a quasi-hereditary dynasty of pashas. The founder of the dynasty, Ḥasan Pasha (1704–23), was born about 1657, and had held several provincial governments before he was appointed to Baghdād. The early years of his unprecedentedly long governorate were occupied with a series of campaigns against the Kurdish and Arab tribesmen. Perhaps the most serious tribal danger came from the Muntafiq, who continued to menace the Ottoman governors of Baṣra. A considerable army was assembled, under Ḥasan Pasha's command, from Baghdād and the neighbouring provinces. It advanced towards Baṣra in 1708 and inflicted a defeat on Shaykh Mughāmis of the Muntafiq and his Arab confederates. Further operations were, however, necessary before the power of Mughāmis was finally broken. Baṣra was clearly not strong enough to stand on its own, and the Ottoman government conceded to Ḥasan Pasha the right of nominating its governor. He appointed his steward, who was also his son-in-law, and henceforward Baṣra was administered as a dependency of the dynasty in Baghdād.

The last years of Ḥasan Pasha's rule were marked by an event of major importance in Ottoman history—an event moreover which was perhaps the principal factor in establishing the dynastic pashalic of Baghdād. The conclusion of the treaty of 1639 was followed by a long period of peace on the Ottoman–Persian frontier. The declining power of both the Safavid and the Ottoman states in the later seventeenth century contributed largely to this quiet interlude, which ended abruptly with the collapse of the Safavid dynasty in 1722. A rebellious Afghan vassal, Mīr Maḥmūd, led his tribal forces into the heart of Persia, and overthrew the Safavids at the battle of Gulnābād. Maḥmūd, a Sunnī Muslim, took over the rule of the Shīʿī Safavid state. At this time of turmoil the Ottoman government and Peter the Great of Russia saw an opportunity to increase their territories. Baghdād, and the Iraqi provinces generally, were the obvious base for an Ottoman advance into western Persia.

In this way there opened a period of hostilities which lasted nearly a quarter of a century. The details of the campaigns need not be given here, but the war falls into five main phases, punctuated by short periods of peace. In the first phase, from 1723 to 1727, the Ottomans at first took the initiative. While one Ottoman army mustered at Erzurum, another gathered around Ḥasan Pasha in Baghdād to invade western Persia by way of Khāniqīn and Kirmānshāh. After the surrender of Kirmānshāh, while the Ottoman troops were wintering there, Ḥasan Pasha died. His only son, Aḥmad Pasha, had long been his principal lieutenant and was at this time governor of Baṣra. On the recommendation of the military chiefs, the Ottoman government appointed Aḥmad to succeed his father, both as governor of Baghdād and as commander of the expeditionary force. Aḥmad was to hold Baghdād for even longer than his father had done, from 1723 (with an interval of two years) until his own death in 1747.

In 1724 Aḥmad pressed on with the invasion of Persia and captured Hamadān. Other regions of western Persia were brought under Ottoman control. By 1726, however, the Ottoman initiative had weakened and the morale of the troops was declining. In the old days of warfare against the Safavid shahs, the enemy could be represented as impious schismatics, and the campaigns as holy wars, but the Afghans were as orthodox Sunnīs as the Ottoman sultans, and their propaganda did not fail to press this point home. The campaign of 1726, which had as its objective Iṣfahān, then the capital of Persia, ended in a heavy defeat for the Ottomans. Aḥmad Pasha set out on a further campaign in the following year, but peace negotiations ensued and the first phase of the war ended.

The brief Afghan domination of Persia was already drawing to a close. A *condottiere* of the Turcoman Afshār tribe, best known under the name of Nādir Shāh (which he took when he ascended the throne of Persia some years later),[1] lent his support to the Safavid pretender. The Afghans were defeated in a series of battles, and their ruler, the successor of Mīr Maḥmūd, was killed. The Safavid restoration in 1729 was followed by a demand that the Ottomans should surrender the territories they had annexed in western Persia. After initial losses in 1730 the Ottoman forces under Aḥmad Pasha regained Kirmānshāh and inflicted a heavy defeat on the Safavid army in the following year. Once again

[1] He had earlier been known as, successively, Nādir Qulī and Ṭahmāsp Qulī.

negotiations for peace took place, and a treaty made in January 1732 ended the second phase of the war.

Meanwhile Nādir was playing the part of king-maker. He deposed his nominal sovereign, and installed himself as regent for a child of the Safavid family. Early in 1733 he brought his army up to Baghdād and laid Aḥmad Pasha's capital under siege. As the months passed, the situation in the city became increasingly critical, and it seemed as if Nādir would repeat the exploits of Shah ʿAbbās. A relieving force under Topal Osman Pasha, a former grand vezir, approached Baghdād in July 1733 just in time to save the city. Nādir's army was defeated in the field, while Aḥmad Pasha's troops annihilated the force left to maintain the siege. As Nādir withdrew to Persian territory, Topal Osman moved into northern Iraq. His army dwindled, while Nādir reconstructed his own forces. In October 1733 the two clashed again, near to Kirkūk, but on this occasion the Ottomans were crushingly defeated, and Topal Osman himself was killed. The Iraqi provinces were again in jeopardy, but fortunately for the Ottomans Nādir was distracted from a fresh invasion by a rising within Persia itself. For a third time Aḥmad Pasha undertook peace negotiations, thereby bringing the third phase of the war to a close.

The treaty was, however, rejected by the sultan's government, and Aḥmad Pasha himself was transferred from Baghdād to another province. The war re-opened, but did not at first touch the Iraqi sector of the front. In March 1736 Nādir openly assumed sovereignty over Persia, and the Safavid dynasty passed from the scene. At this time Nādir Shāh was pursuing a conciliatory policy towards the Ottomans. He proposed a reconciliation between the Sunnīs and the moderate Shīʿa. The Ottomans responded to his overtures, and the fourth phase of the war ended with a treaty which recognized the validity of the frontiers of 1639.

But Nādir Shāh had not finally abandoned his hopes of territorial gains in the west. In 1741, after a victorious campaign in India, he began to prepare fresh hostilities against the Ottomans. Once again the Iraqi provinces bore the brunt of his attack, which was delivered in 1743. His chief opponent was Aḥmad Pasha, who in 1736 had returned to Baghdād after a two-year interval. Mosul was besieged, and courageously defended by its governor, Ḥusayn Pasha al-Jalīlī, and garrison, but Nādir Shāh withdrew his forces when the city was on the brink of falling into his hands. Inconclusive fighting and protracted negotiations dragged on until 1746, when a final peace-treaty was arranged between the two parties. The assassination of Nādir Shāh in June 1747 marked the virtual end of his short-lived dynasty. Never again was a ruler of Persia to offer a serious threat to the Ottoman Empire.

Some two months after Nādir Shāh, Aḥmad Pasha himself died suddenly in Baghdād. He left no son. For over forty years he and his father had ruled almost continuously over central and southern Iraq. The Ottoman government was naturally averse to such a prolonged concentration of power in the hands of a single family, and with the ending of the Persian war the circumstances which had made it desirable were no longer operative. But Ḥasan and Aḥmad had created in Baghdād an institution which was to perpetuate the virtual autonomy that they had established. They had recruited and trained for their personal service a household of *mamlūks*, mostly obtained from Georgia. The existence of this Mamluk organization, together with the long periods during which Ḥasan and Aḥmad held office, enabled them to extricate themselves from that dependence on the Ottoman garrison which had impeded the action of their predecessors. The Mamluks, in Baghdād as in Egypt, formed not only a military but an administrative élite. Their chief men, as stewards of the pashas, were fully experienced in government, and Aḥmad Pasha did not hesitate to marry his daughters to them.

Thus, when the Ottoman government attempted to introduce its own nominees as governors of Baghdād, it came up against the opposition of a determined body of men who had already a strong vested interest in the province. From 1747 to 1749 the situation deteriorated. In the latter year, Sulaymān Pasha, a son-in-law and former steward of Aḥmad Pasha, who had obtained the governorship of Baṣra, marched on Baghdād, expelled the governor, and reunited the territories formerly ruled by his master. The sultan acquiesced in his assumption of power, which he retained until his death in 1762. A powerful influence in his government was that of his wife, ʿĀdila, the elder daughter of Aḥmad Pasha. He continued to recruit Georgian Mamluks, and developed the system of training which they received.

So, when Sulaymān Pasha died, the Mamluks had acquired an impregnable position in the administration of Baghdād. But, as in Egypt, their organization failed to develop any adequate procedure for the transfer of power on the death of its holder. The death of Sulaymān left two principal contestants for the pashalic, both of whom had held the high office of steward. One of these, ʿAlī Pasha, actually succeeded in obtaining the sultan's commission for the two provinces. The other, ʿUmar, had more impressive local support, since he was backed by ʿĀdila, and was the husband of her younger sister, ʿĀʾisha. In 1764

ʿUmar's faction was strong enough to oust ʿAlī from the government and to put him to death. ʿUmar's seizure of power was in due course formally ratified by the commission of the sultan.

In the time of ʿUmar Pasha there was another outbreak of war with Persia, on a much smaller scale than the conflicts in the first half of the century, but sufficiently serious in its consequences. The death of Nādir Shāh had been followed by a time of troubles, out of which emerged, as the most powerful ruler in Persia, Karīm Khān-i Zand, nominally the regent of a shadowy Safavid shah. Persian and Ottoman interests clashed, as always, in the frontier-districts of Shahrizor, where local dynastic quarrels provided the suzerain powers with pretexts for intervention. These remote Kurdish valleys were of less importance, however, than the port of Baṣra, which by this time had become a flourishing centre for trade with the Persian Gulf and India. As such it was naturally tempting to Karīm Khān. The Persian ruler had also grievances over the treatment of Shīʿī pilgrims to Karbalāʾ, and in 1775 he despatched his army against Baṣra. The governor of Baṣra was at this time another of the Mamluks of Baghdād, named Sulaymān. After a long defence, he was forced to surrender the city in April 1776, and went into captivity at Shīrāz, the capital of Karīm Khān.

ʿUmar Pasha made no attempt to meet the Persian threat as it developed, and the feebleness of his rule encouraged the Ottoman government to attempt his removal. His successor-designate, chosen from outside the Mamluk élite, was sent with an army to oust him, but ʿUmar surrendered without a blow and left the city. He was attacked by order of the new governor, and died in flight. The removal of a Mamluk pasha did not, however, ensure the establishment of effective government in Baghdād. The overthrow of ʿUmar Pasha early in 1776 was followed by three years of political confusion.

The death of Karīm Khān early in 1779 had repercussions upon Iraq. Another struggle for power took place in Persia. Baṣra was evacuated, and Sulaymān, its former governor, was released from captivity in Shīrāz. For a short time he resumed his old position in Baṣra, but soon, with the backing of the British agent there, he received the sultan's commission to take over the government of Baghdād, Baṣra and Shahrizor. After defeating his local opponents, he entered Baghdād in July 1780.

Büyük Sulaymān Pasha, 'Sulaymān Pasha the Great', ruled in Baghdād until his death in 1802. His period of office marks the zenith of the Mamluk pashalic. The danger from Persia was at an end, and until the last years of the eighteenth century no major threat appeared to the established order in the Iraqi provinces. The tribes, of course, were a constant source of unrest. As in the past, the Muntafiq were troublesome neighbours to Baṣra. In 1786 their chief, Shaykh Thuwaynī ibn ʿAbdallāh, captured the deputy-governor of the city, and set up a tribal government there. It was overthrown by Büyük Sulaymān in the following year, and Thuwaynī was deposed from the chieftaincy of the Muntafiq. A year later there was a dangerous conspiracy between the Kurdish deputy-governor of Baṣra, the Kurdish dynast of Shahrizor, and Thuwaynī, which was, however, discovered and rendered harmless by Büyük Sulaymān. Like the Muntafiq in the south, the Kurdish tribesmen were always difficult to control.

The campaigns of the governors of Baghdād against the tribes of the marshes, the deserts and the hills, are monotonously frequent in the history of Ottoman Iraq. At this very time, however, a new movement was developing in the heart of Arabia which was to impart a religious sanction to the old tribal love of raiding and warfare, and was to confront Büyük Sulaymān with a challenge that was beyond his power to meet. The Wahhābīs of Najd were beginning to press on the frontiers of Iraq.

The tendency towards dynasticism in provincial government, which we have seen in Damascus, Baṣra and Baghdād, appeared also in Mosul during the eighteenth century. The founder of the dynasty was a certain ʿAbd al-Jalīl, a Christian servant in the household of a governor of Mosul. His descendants, the Jalīlīs, became Muslims, and held the governorship, although not continuously, for over a hundred years. The first of them, Ismāʿīl Pasha ibn ʿAbd al-Jalīl, assumed office in 1726. He was succeeded by his son, Ḥusayn, who was governor eight times between 1730 and 1759, and conducted the gallant defence of Mosul against Nādir Shāh in 1743. Ḥusayn's period of power overlapped with that of his son, Amīn Pasha, who was governor six times. Amīn was in turn succeeded by his own son, Muḥammad, whose governorship lasted for eighteen years, from 1789 to 1807. The history of Mosul was not of great importance during their ascendancy: they were overshadowed by the holders of Baghdād, with whose vicissitudes their own fate was closely associated.

11

Two Challenges: The Wahhābīs and Bonaparte

The Wahhābī Movement and the Saʿūdī Empire

About the end of the eighteenth century, a movement which originated on the Arab fringe of the Ottoman Empire was to threaten the maintenance of the sultan's rule in the Fertile Crescent, and was to play an important part in the development of modern Islamic thought. This was the Wahhābī movement, which developed in the remote plateau of Najd, in central Arabia. The region lay outside the sphere of effective Ottoman power, which by the eighteenth century was felt only in the Arabian coastal regions of the Ḥijāz and al-Aḥsā. Sandy deserts largely isolated the hill-country of Najd from neighbouring areas of settlement, but its remoteness was mitigated by two major routes which converged upon it. One of these ran south-eastwards from Syria, by the Wādī Sirḥān, to Jabal Shammar, the northern outpost of Najd: the other, a Pilgrimage-route, lay across the peninsula, from the coastlands of the Persian Gulf to the Ḥijāz.

In the eighteenth century Najd had a comparatively large settled population in the small towns and villages of the mountain areas, where there was sufficient water for irrigation. The passage of pilgrims and merchants through the country stimulated trade. Politically, the region was divided among powerful local families, who were virtually sovereigns of greater or smaller amirates. Amongst these was one, the family of Saʿūd, which had originally come from al-Aḥsā in the middle of the fifteenth century, and established itself on the Wādī Ḥanīfa, a fertile valley in the hill-country of Jabal Ṭuwayq. Here the Saʿūd family ruled a small amirate, centring upon the town of Darʿiyya. Besides the settled townsmen and villagers, Najd also had its nomad tribes, a more primitive element in the population.

Like Islam itself, the Wahhābī movement originated and developed among the Arab townsmen rather than the nomads. Its founder, Muḥammad ibn ʿAbd al-Wahhāb, came from a family of *ʿulamāʾ*. They were the hereditary *qāḍīs* of ʿUyayna, the capital of another petty amirate of the Wādī Ḥanīfa, which was ruled by the family of Ibn Muʿammar.

Muḥammad ibn ʿAbd al-Wahhāb was born in 1703, and, as a youth, he followed the usual practice of Muslim students in travelling widely to study at different *madrasas*. He made the Pilgrimage, and subsequently read under teachers at Medina and Baṣra. He was already noted for his strict outlook. He was a Ḥanbalī, a follower of the most rigorous of the four Sunnī Muslim law-schools. In addition, he had been deeply influenced by the teaching of Ibn Taymiyya. A theologian and a jurist, Ibn Taymiyya, who passed his career in Mamluk Damascus in the late thirteenth and early fourteenth centuries, had endeavoured to recall his contemporaries to the practices of primitive Islam, and had opposed the innovations connected with Ṣūfī mysticism. His austere interpretation of Islam won him few followers, but in Damascus and elsewhere Ḥanbalī students cherished his ideas. Not until the eighteenth century, however, and in a society lacking the organization and rigidity of the Mamluk and Ottoman states, did a disciple of Ibn Taymiyya find an opportunity tc put those ideas into practice.

This was the achievement of Ibn ʿAbd al-Wahhāb, but it was some time before he was able to found his ideal Muslim community. After his years of study, he returned to Najd. Ibn ʿAbd al-Wahhāb's puritanica teaching made him unpopular, so after his father's death he sought the protection of ʿUthmān ibn Muʿammar, the chief of ʿUyayna. But his rigorism rapidly produced a reaction, and a crisis finally developed wher Ibn ʿAbd al-Wahhāb sentenced to death a woman who had confessed t adultery. Banū Khālid, the chiefly family of al-Aḥsā, intervened t demand the death of Ibn ʿAbd al-Wahhāb, and threatened to withhol the annual subsidy of goods and money sent from the coast to th amirates of the interior. The reformer was not put to death, but wa expelled in 1745 from ʿUyayna. He made his way to Darʿiyya, where h received the protection of the reigning *amīr*, Muḥammad ibn Saʿūd. I was the co-operation of these two men which made possible the founda tion of the Wahhābī state, the predecessor of the present-day kingdom o Saʿūdī Arabia.

As a theologian and a jurist, Muḥammad ibn ʿAbd al-Wahhāb sough to do away with all innovations in Islam. Chief among these were th popular Ṣūfī practices of the veneration of saints, and the making c pilgrimages to their tombs. He sought to restore the conception of transcendent God, totally distinct in kind from the creation, and ur approachable through human intercessors. Pilgrimages to the tombs c saints were in some respects the islamized equivalent of the ancient Ara practice of visits to sacred trees and other holy places; and, in fac primitive cults connected with trees still survived in Najd: hence, the destruction of sacred trees was a prominent activity of the early Wahhābīs. A practice of much more recent introduction was that of smoking: this was forbidden as being equivalent to the drinking of alcohol, and abstention from tobacco became a touchstone of Wahhābī observance. Ibn ʿAbd al-Wahhāb's assertion that smoking was *ḥarām*, forbidden by the law of God, was characteristic of his reaction against the lax practices of his time, which in turn had been nourished by the Ṣūfī tendency to antinomianism, and indifference to distinctions between licit and illicit acts.[1]

Wahhabism was, therefore, a way of life which sought to conform to the practices of primitive Islam—or, it would be truer to say, to the traditional image of primitive Islam—and which accepted as its only and sufficient law the *Sharīʿa*, as formulated during the first three centuries. Its emphatic assertion of God's unity, and emphasis on the divine transcendence, was not merely a theological abstraction, but a declaration of war on the Ṣūfī practices and beliefs which had become closely associated with the Islamic establishment. Thus, in principle, the Wahhābīs challenged the authority of the Ottoman sultanate as the protector of Islamic orthodoxy; and this ideological challenge was soon followed by a physical threat to Ottoman suzerainty in the Ḥijāz, and Ottoman rule in the Fertile Crescent. Against the established system of authority, represented by the hierarchy of the Ottoman *ʿulamāʾ*, it set up its own authoritarianism, founded on a rigorous adherence to the Qurʾān and the Sunna. It was a restatement of the fundamental values of Islam, and its effect was revolutionary.

With the establishment of the alliance between Muḥammad ibn Saʿūd and Ibn ʿAbd al-Wahhāb, a process of political development and expansion was initiated which was to continue for nearly seventy years, and was to result in the formation of the first Saʿūdī empire in Arabia. Three main periods may be distinguished. The first of them was a time of tribal warfare, sanctified by taking place under the auspices of the new religious movement, between the Saʿūdī amirate and its neighbours. The principal hostilities were with Riyāḍ, and lasted from 1746 to 1773, with two periods during which the town was temporarily submissive to the Wahhābīs. When Riyāḍ finally fell, it was almost deserted by its inhabitants, most of whom had fled with the *amīr*. ʿUyayna had long since been incorporated in the Saʿūdī state. Its chief, the Amīr ʿUthmān

[1] Ottoman jurists had, in fact, tried to ban both tobacco and coffee, but had finally given way, as their prohibitions were flouted by public opinion.

ibn Muʿammar, had been a confederate of Ibn Saʿūd, but doubts had arisen about his loyalty. In 1750 he was assassinated in the mosque of ʿUyayna, and his amirate passed under Saʿūdī control.

The repercussions of these struggles in central Arabia began to be felt more and more widely. During the last year of Muḥammad ibn Saʿūd's life, tribal forces from Najrān marched to the Wādī Ḥanīfa, to avenge victims of the Wahhābīs. The Saʿūdī forces suffered a serious defeat, and were glad to negotiate a settlement with the Najrānī chief Hardly had he withdrawn, before the chief of Banū Khālid appeared in the vicinity of Darʿiyya. Lacking Najrānī support, however, he achieved little, and shortly afterwards took his warriors back to al-Aḥsā.

This was in 1765, and shortly afterwards Muḥammad ibn Saʿūd died to be succeeded as *amīr* by his son, ʿAbd al-ʿAzīz I. He had for some years been the commander of the Wahhābī forces in the field, and the first period of his rule saw the consolidation of Saʿūdī control over the tribes and districts of Najd. Riyāḍ, as we have seen, was finally annexed in 1773. In the north, the submission of Ḥāʾil in 1787 gave the Wahhābī control over Jabal Shammar. Saʿūdī territory now marched with three older polities: in the east, the Banū Khālid tribal territory of al-Aḥsā in the west, the Hashimite hegemony in the Ḥijāz; in the north-east, on the desert fringe of Iraq, the powerful tribal confederacy of the Muntafiq, at this time under one of its greatest chiefs, Thuwaynī ibn ʿAbdallāh. Raids on al-Aḥsā and the Muntafiq resulted in the defeat of Banū Khālid and the installation of a Saʿūdī nominee as *amīr* in 1789. This however, had to be followed by another campaign in 1792–3. At its close al-Aḥsā passed fully into Saʿūdī control. The tombs of holy men were destroyed, and provision was made for the teaching of Wahhābī doctrine. The conquest of al-Aḥsā was followed by an increase in Wahhābī militancy. Raids were made on the desert-fringe of Syria, as well as on the frontiers of the Ḥijāz and Iraq. The *amīr* of Mecca, Ghālib ibn Musāʿid, had already taken alarm, and made a fruitless raid into Saʿūdī territory. Another was made in 1795, and hostilities between the two parties were to continue until the Saʿūdī occupation of the Ḥijāz.

Meanwhile, the dynastic character of the new Arabian state was secured in 1788, when ʿAbd al-ʿAzīz I obtained an oath of allegiance from the provinces under his rule, to his son and future successor, the Amīr Saʿūd. This was accomplished through the powerful influence of the old religious teacher, Muḥammad ibn ʿAbd al-Wahhāb, who died four

[1] See above, p. 148. Thuwaynī was deposed from the chieftancy by Büyük Sulaymān Pasha in 1787, but restored before the clash with the Wahhābīs, ten years later.

ears later, in the summer of 1792. In the space of nearly half a century which had passed since he left ʿUyayna, Ibn ʿAbd al-Wahhāb had seen the realization of an Arab theocracy.

The movement which had developed in remote Najd was now beginning to appear as a threat to the outposts of Ottoman power. The first action taken by an Ottoman governor was in 1797, when Büyük Sulaymān Pasha of Baghdād provided forces as a stiffening to the Muntafiq and other tribal levies led by Shaykh Thuwaynī. But as the expedition advanced, Thuwaynī was assassinated. Banū Khālid, who had supported him, in hopes of regaining their lost supremacy in al-Aḥsā, abandoned the expedition, which broke up in disarray. Wahhābī raids on the Syrian and Iraqi frontiers followed, while an offensive launched by the Amīr Ghālib from the Ḥijāz was heavily defeated in 1798.

A second expedition against the Wahhābīs was organized by Büyük Sulaymān Pasha, and made its rendezvous in Baṣra at the end of 1798. Under the *kâhya* (deputy-governor) ʿAlī Pasha, combined Ottoman and tribal forces, said to number over 10,000, advanced into al-Aḥsā. Here they stuck, in an unsuccessful siege of two forts. After two months ʿAlī Kâhya was compelled to withdraw, and was allowed by the Amīr Saʿūd, who had brought up a relieving force, to extricate his troops and return to Baṣra. A lull followed, marked by a truce with Baghdād and another with Mecca, to which, in 1800, Saʿūd went on Pilgrimage.

This period of quiescence ended abruptly in 1802, when Saʿūd, who was now deputizing for his octagenarian father, led a great raid into Iraq. The object of his attack was the city of Karbalāʾ, the burial place of the Imām Ḥusayn ibn ʿAlī and a centre of pilgrimage for all Shīʿī Islam. The town was captured and pillaged, and the shrine around the tomb of Ḥusayn was robbed and ruined. Fanaticism stimulated the looting proclivities of the tribesmen, and the barbarous desecration that ensued shocked the Sunnīs as well as the Shīʿa. Muḥammad ibn ʿAbd al-Wahhāb's teaching had, in effect, declared all Muslims except his own followers to be in schism; the sack of Karbalāʾ was a practical expression of this doctrine. The reaction of the outraged Muslim majority was thenceforward inevitable.

Meanwhile, hostilities between the Saʿūdī state and Mecca broke out again, and at the time of the Pilgrimage in 1803 Saʿūd and the Wahhābī army entered the holy city. The Amīr Ghālib had already fled to Jedda, where he was able to hold out. The acquisition of Mecca was the last achievement of the reign of ʿAbd al-ʿAzīz I. In October 1803 he was assassinated in the mosque of Darʿiyya, apparently by a Shīʿī who wished to avenge the sack of Karbalā'. The succession in the amirate passe smoothly to Saʿūd, who continued his father's militant policy. Raids wer made on the Iraqi provinces: in 1803 and again in 1806 Najaf, the othe Shīʿī holy city, withstood Saʿūdī attacks. The forces of Najd were neve strong enough to capture and hold the towns of Iraq, although the remained a constant threat to security on the fringes of Ottoman terri tory. In the Ḥijāz, Medina surrendered to the Wahhābīs in 1805, an peace was patched up with the Amīr Ghālib.

The Saʿūdī occupation of the two holy cities meant that a direct clas with the Ottoman sultanate was certain to occur. As Servitor of the Tw Holy Sanctuaries, the sultan had to be in a position to secure the safet of the Pilgrimage, and could not tolerate the tenure of Mecca an Medina by a militant schismatic. Saʿūd, for his part, feared an alliance o Ghālib and the Ottomans to expel him from the Ḥijāz. At this juncture the most likely agent of Ottoman intervention was the Syrian com mander of the Pilgrimage, the governor of Damascus, ʿAbdallāh Pash al-ʿAẓm.[1] In 1807, therefore, Saʿūd concentrated his tribal levies a Medina, and forbade the Syrian Pilgrimage caravan to proceed. Thi prohibition was repeated in the next three years, and Yūsuf Pasha, wh succeeded ʿAbdallāh al-ʿAẓm in Damascus, showed himself no mor capable of dealing with the Wahhābīs. Indeed, in 1810 Saʿūd brough an expedition into the frontier-districts of Syria, which caused alarm i Damascus and led to the deposition of Yūsuf Pasha. The breaking o Wahhābī power was not to be accomplished by the governors either o Baghdād or of Damascus, but by Muḥammad ʿAlī Pasha, the successfu soldier, who had made himself viceroy of Egypt, and who, in 1811, wa to launch his first expedition against the Amīr Saʿūd.

The overthrow of the first Saʿūdī empire will be described in a late chapter,[2] but it is convenient here to summarize the significance of th Wahhābī movement in the history of the Arab lands. Its importanc is twofold. In the first place, it was as champions of this religious refor that the Saʿūdī family have twice acquired predominance, in Najd an in Arabia as a whole. Yet it is possible to wonder whether Wahhabis did not lose more than it gained by this close association with Saʿūd dynastic ambitions. It is significant that during the nineteenth century after the power of the Saʿūdī dynasty had been broken, many of the idea and attitudes of Wahhabism quietly passed into the body of orthodo Islam, and profoundly altered the outlook both of the *ʿulamā'* and o

[1] See above, p. 130, n. 1. This was his third governorship of Damascus.

[2] See below, pp. 179–80.

educated Muslims generally. This is seen in various phenomena. The Ṣūfī orders have declined in prestige, and retain their appeal mainly to the unsophisticated and fringe-elements of the Muslim community. Certain new religious groups which arose in the nineteenth century, and which institutionally are closely akin to the older Ṣūfī orders, originated not so much as vehicles of mystical enlightenment as communities seeking a purer faith and practice: examples of this kind are the Sanūsiyya and Khatmiyya orders in Cyrenaica and the Sudan, and the Anṣār of the Sudanese Mahdī. The Wahhābī influence can also be traced in a still more recent movement, that of the Muslim Brethren. A different temper and appeal characterizes the work of Shaykh Muḥammad ʿAbduh and of the group of Muslim thinkers known as the Salafiyya, who were also influenced by the principles of Wahhabism. Seeking to reformulate Islam to meet the challenges of the nineteenth and twentieth centuries, these men found the answer in a nucleus of revealed truth, purged of the accretions of centuries of custom and tradition. In these diverse ways, the spirit of Wahhābī reform, divorced from its political incarnation in the first Saʿūdī state, has affected profoundly the modern development of Islam.

Bonaparte and the French Occupation of Egypt

On 1 July 1798 a French expeditionary force under the command of Napoleon Bonaparte disembarked near Alexandria. This event was to mark a turning-point in Egyptian history, and was to inaugurate a phase in the relations between western Europe and the Arab East which ended only with the Suez campaign in the winter of 1956. The French had long been perceptive of the strategic significance and commercial potential of Egypt. The last of the great Crusades was Louis IX's unsuccessful invasion of Egypt in the middle of the thirteenth century. More recently, schemes for the conquest and occupation of the country had been considered by French statesmen at intervals from the time of Louis XIV onward. During the eighteenth century the principal share of the European trade of Egypt was held by French merchants and, indeed, the complaints of these against the extortions of Ibrāhīm Bey and Murād Bey, the ruling duumvirs, served as the pretext for Bonaparte's expedition.

The real cause of the expedition is, however, to be sought in the strategy employed by France against Britain in that period of the French Revolutionary War. The young General Bonaparte, who had defeated the Austrians in Italy and negotiated the Treaty of Campoformio in October 1797, was summoned to take command of a projected scheme for the invasion of England. This he quickly dismissed as not feasible, and instead advocated the occupation of Egypt, whence he could threaten the British hold over India, and disrupt the trade on which British prosperity rested. But the scheme envisaged more than an immediate strategic advantage. The French hoped to occupy Egypt permanently, and to profit from its agriculture and trade, while liberating the Egyptians from Mamluk rule, and communicating to them the enlightenment of revolutionary France.[1] The invasion forces, which sailed from Toulon on 19 May 1798, were accompanied by a commission of scholars and scientists, whose function was to investigate every aspect of the life of Egypt in ancient and in modern times.

At the outset, the course of events in Egypt bore a curious similarity to what had happened at the time of Ḥasan Pasha's expedition twelve years before. Alexandria was taken without difficulty, and Bonaparte began to spread his propaganda, in the form of a proclamation announcing to the Egyptians that the French were come, as friends of the Ottoman sultan, to overthrow the Mamluks.[2] Advancing towards Cairo, the French met and defeated a Mamluk force under Murād Bey at Shubrākhīt. He was again defeated in the decisive battle of Imbāba, opposite the capital (the so-called Battle of the Pyramids) on 21 July. Murād fled to Upper Egypt. Ibrāhīm, who, cautious as ever, had remained in Cairo to see the outcome of his colleague's expedition, made his way towards Syria, accompanied by the Ottoman viceroy. The collapse of the Mamluk régime was followed by rioting and pillage in Cairo, but on 25 July Bonaparte entered the city and the reorganization of Egypt began.

Although Bonaparte, with the advantages of surprise and superiority of troops and armament, had won the first round, his position in Egypt was precarious. He held the vital strip linking Alexandria with Cairo but the Mamluks were still the masters of much of the country, and Murad's withdrawal to Upper Egypt was an ancient tactic, which had proved its use in the struggle with Ḥasan Pasha. Furthermore, the true attitude of the Egyptians remained unknown to Bonaparte. Although in his propaganda he depicted the French as liberators, 'true Mussulmen who had overthrown the Papacy and the Knights of Malta; this made little impression on the Egyptians, ignorant of the nuances of latter-day European thought. This persistence of misunderstanding was to render abortive French efforts to reform the administration of Egypt, and to regenerate its people.

Within a few weeks of Bonaparte's landing, two events were to demon

[1] For Bonaparte's instructions, see Hurewitz, i, 61–2.

[2] Text in Hurewitz, i, 63–4.

strate the precariousness of his tenure of Egypt. On 1 August 1798 a British fleet under Lord Nelson, who had narrowly failed to intercept the French invasion-force while at sea, annihilated the French ships as they lay at anchor off Abū Qīr, thus isolating Bonaparte's land-forces in Egypt. On 11 September Sultan Selim III declared war on France, and the news of this, assiduously passed into Egypt from Syria by Aḥmad Pasha al-Jazzār, gave the lie to Bonaparte's claim that he had come as the friend of the sultan to punish the enemies of the Ottomans. Thus, although the military hold of the French over Egypt was strengthened in these weeks, their moral authority was steadily undermined.

Events in Cairo were, as always, of critical importance. Although Bonaparte had made a serious effort to conciliate the people of the capital, and especially the *ʿulamāʾ*, whom he rightly diagnosed as being the key figures for the management of public opinion, his professions of sympathy for Islam were regarded as unconvincing. In any case, they were outweighed by material grievances. Military occupation had produced its inevitable incidents of sporadic clashes and resistance in the provinces. To promote security in the capital, Bonaparte had ordered the destruction of the gates which turned each quarter of Cairo into a separate little urban community. Similarly the houses which had been built in the vicinity of the Citadel were expropriated and demolished. A mildly terrorist policy had been shown in the public executions of persons threatening security. Other grievances arose from French taxation. Although the French claimed to be liberators, they maintained, and even increased, the financial burdens of Ottoman–Mamluk rule. Under an alien administrator-general, there was, indeed, a more rigorous and uniform levy of taxes, while special demands were made from time to time.

One such demand was a property-tax, which was not only odious in itself but also in its method of assessment, since this was to be made by the actual inspection of houses. The privacy of the Muslim household, which had been respected even under oppressive Muslim régimes, was threatened by the new European rulers. This was the final factor in exacerbating the resentment and frustration of the people of Cairo, and on 21 October an insurrection broke out, centring, significantly, around the mosque of al-Azhar. Although the French were taken completely by surprise, the insurgents had no hope of a successful rising. An artillery bombardment finally broke their resistance, and after two days of struggle the city returned to submission. The insurrection was, however, decisive for relations between the French and the Egyptians: the new régime was henceforward undisguisedly a military occupation; while the French showed themselves to be more incompatible with the Egyptians than their Ottoman and Mamluk predecessors had been.

For the time being, however, Cairo and Lower Egypt were quiet, while French forces in Upper Egypt were waging a successful campaign against Murād. The greatest immediate danger came from Syria, where al-Jazzār had given asylum to Ibrāhīm Bey, and whence an Ottoman attack on the French in Egypt might be expected. To forestall this threat Bonaparte decided to take the initiative by a campaign into Syria. The strategic rôle of Syria, as a buffer-zone to protect the ruler of Egypt from an Ottoman invasion, was clearly appreciated by Bonaparte, as formerly by ʿAlī Bey, and as subsequently by Muḥammad ʿAlī Pasha. His subsequent claim, that he intended to capture Istanbul, was a romantic afterthought.

On 20 February 1799 the Syrian frontier-fort of al-ʿArīsh surrendered to the French, who continued their advance up the Palestinian coast. The first serious obstacle was Jaffa, which fell, after a refusal to capitulate, on 7 March. Two ominous incidents accompanied the capture of Jaffa. Two thousand survivors of the garrison were shot in cold blood, an act detrimental to Bonaparte's prestige; and plague, which had been dogging the French, now began to cause numerous casualties. Bonaparte, however, pushed on to Acre, the residence of al-Jazzār. The governor was co-operating with a small British naval force under Sir Sidney Smith, which intercepted French ships, and captured Bonaparte's siege-train. On 19 March the siege of Acre began. Against all expectation, the town did not fall, and Bonaparte found himself pinned down on the coast, with plague making daily ravages in his army. He wrote to Bashīr II Shihāb and to the son of Ẓāhir al-ʿUmar, seeking to gain their support, but Bashīr prudently temporized, while the authority of the Zayādina was a thing of the past. Although French troops succeeded near Nazareth in defeating relieving forces sent from Damascus, and at the foot of Mount Tabor, these victories were nullified by the continuing resistance of Acre, to which an Ottoman fleet brought reinforcements. On 20 May the French began their long retreat to Egypt, in which they incurred heavy losses from fighting and plague.

Although Bonaparte staged his return to Cairo as a triumphal entry, the future of the French occupation of Egypt was now more uncertain than ever. On 11 July Ottoman troops began to disembark at Abū Qīr but Bonaparte concentrated his forces and practically annihilated his opponents. He had, for the time being, secured the French position, but his own days in Egypt were numbered. During the occupation he had been practically cut off from news of France. Early in August he received a packet of newspapers from Sir Sidney Smith, with whom he was arranging an exchange of prisoners. The information he obtained of the political situation in France determined him to leave without delay. He made his plans in great secrecy and, on 22 August, embarked with a very small company, reaching France on 9 October. On leaving, he nominated General Kléber as his successor in the chief command.

The remaining history of the French occupation of Egypt can be briefly told. Kléber found himself the unwilling commander of a dispirited army with a bankrupt treasury. His main anxiety was to secure the evacuation of his troops to France, and this he thought he had obtained when, on 24 January 1800, he signed with the Ottomans the Convention of al-ʿArīsh. Since the fulfilment of the evacuation depended on British sea-power, the convention was guaranteed by Sir Sidney Smith. In doing this, however, Smith had contravened his instructions, and the convention was disavowed by his superiors. An Ottoman army had meanwhile occupied Lower Egypt, and the two principal French garrisons, at Cairo and Alexandria, were preparing for evacuation. When Kléber heard that the British government required the surrender of the French, he determined to resist, and, in spite of his very unfavourable position, inflicted a serious defeat on the Ottomans at Heliopolis (ʿAyn Shams), outside Cairo, on 20 March. Some of the Ottomans entered Cairo and stirred up a second insurrection, which was suppressed after lasting for over a month. Kléber's efforts had thus sufficiently restored the situation in Egypt to enable the French to hold out, when he himself was assassinated by a Syrian Muslim, and the command devolved upon General ʿAbdallāh Jacques Menou, a French convert to Islam.

The occupation was finally terminated by a combined British and Ottoman invasion of Egypt. British forces landed at Abū Qīr in March 1801, and subsequently joined with Ottoman troops at Rosetta to march on Cairo. A British Indian force advanced from the Red Sea coast to the Nile valley. Another Ottoman army, commanded by the grand vezir, Yusuf Ziya Pasha, was advancing from Syria. The French were pent up in Cairo and Alexandria. The former surrendered on 18 June; the latter, with Menou himself, on 3 September. Ironically, they were evacuated on the terms which had been granted in the Convention of al-ʿArīsh.

Brief and unsuccessful though the French occupation had been, it was an episode fraught with consequences for Egypt. Hitherto the Arab provinces of the Ottoman Empire had lain outside the political spheres of interest of the European powers. Apart from commercial dealings, only isolated occurrences, such as the diplomatic relations between Fakhr al-Dīn and Tuscany, or the dealings of ʿAlī Bey and Ẓāhir al-ʿUmar with the Russian fleet, indicated transitory and fortuitous links of interest. For over two centuries the provinces in Rumelia had felt the impact of Austrian and Russian military power; while the Arab lands, however disturbed by internal struggles, had remained unthreatened by any enemy from the west. With Bonaparte's expedition, this isolation from the great world conflicts came abruptly to an end. The Near East, Egypt in particular, was revealed as an area of immense strategic importance to the great powers, and its rulers, however extensive their internal autonomy, became in the last resort dependent on the policies and rivalries of the European states. In particular, successive British governments held it as a maxim that Egypt must be held by a friendly ruler, and at all costs denied to the French.

Within Egypt, the French occupation prepared the way for changes which, in the course of a century, were to transform the country. It is not correct to ascribe directly to the occupation that powerfully Francophile strain in Egyptian culture, which, in spite of political vicissitudes, is still so marked today. The scholars and scientists who accompanied Bonaparte came to Egypt to learn rather than to teach, and their investigations, published in the monumental *Description de l'Égypte*, have been the foundation of modern research into the history, society and economics of Egypt. Their nearest counterparts in Egypt, the *ʿulamāʾ*, complacent representatives of the traditional learning of Islam, were ill-fitted by training and habit of mind to appreciate the inquisitive humanism of the Enlightenment. Moreover, the culture of the Europeans came in the baggage-train of a conquering, infidel army. One may surmise that the shocks of military defeat and alien rule, by shattering the assumption of Muslim superiority, at least on the material plane, may have prepared the way for the reception of European ideas at a later date, but this was a long-term effect. The true implanting of French culture in Egypt can better be ascribed to the reign of Muḥammad ʿAlī. The Bonapartist occupation confirmed French interest in Egypt, rather than Egyptian interest in France.

Foreign conquest undoubtedly administered a severe shock to the social system of Egypt. Ottoman Egypt in the eighteenth century constituted (in spite of factional struggles) an essentially stable society, dominated by the military élite and the *ʿulamāʾ* in tacit alliance, with an urban artisan and trading class safeguarding its privileges through its guilds and links with the military corps, and based on a large rural population of peasants, whose apparent weakness before oppression was to some degree offset by their age-old customs and prescriptive rights. The non-Muslim communities, the Copts and the Jews, lacked formal political power, but had considerable influence in the bureaucracy. Custom, which assigned them an inferior place in society, at the same time protected them from tyrannous innovations.

This organic structure of functions, interests and prescriptive rights was damaged by Bonaparte's conquest. The old military élite, largely Mamluk in composition, forfeited its place to the soldiers of the Republic. With its passing, the other element in the traditional partnership, the *ʿulamāʾ*, increased in prestige and influence. Not only were the *ʿulamāʾ* the natural leaders and spokesmen of the Muslim community in times of crisis, but their status was recognized and indeed enhanced by Bonaparte. By cultivating their acquaintance and flattering them he sought to win their support, but his tactics must have seemed crude and childish enough to men grown old in the politics of Ottoman Egypt. With the habitual deference to authority of their order, they accepted his decorations and subscribed the documents drafted for them, while remaining totally uncommitted in their hearts to republicanism, France or Napoleon Bonaparte.

Bonaparte's attempt to establish a new symbiosis of the French and the *ʿulamāʾ* for the old one of *ʿulamāʾ* and Mamluks was institutionalized in the *divans* he set up. These are less important for what they achieved than for the ideas they represented. The first *divan* was that of Cairo, constituted by an order of 25 July 1798. It was composed of nine or ten members, almost all of whom belonged to the great *ʿulamāʾ*. It was responsible primarily for the local government of Cairo, and in this respect it was an innovation in Egypt, where municipal councils were at that time unknown.[1] The *Divan* of Cairo worked under close French control and supervision; nevertheless, in spite of its limited functions it was an interesting experiment in conferring actual political power on men whose role in the state had previously been to act as mediators and conciliators, possessors of influence rather than of executive authority. In his other *divans*, Bonaparte gave a less exclusive share to the *ʿulamāʾ*. The General *Divan*, which sat from 5 to 20 October 1798, and served as a kind of advisory council, was formed of delegations drawn from all parts of Egypt. Each delegation consisted of three *ʿulamāʾ*, three merchants, and three village headmen or tribal chiefs. Cairo sent three

[1] See above, pp. 7–8.

delegations, two of the provinces sent two delegations each, the rest one each. Four specific questions were submitted to the General *Divan*, and its answers to two of them epitomize the difference in outlook between the Egyptians and the French. Asked what system of civil and criminal justice should be established, the *Divan* declared itself opposed to any change either in the system of justice or the organization of the law-courts. Asked its opinion on legislation concerning inheritance, the *Divan*, as behoved a Muslim body, affirmed the maintenance of the *Sharīʿa* rules on this matter. The strength of custom had been the chief security of all classes in Egypt under centuries of foreign rule, and the notables of the General *Divan* instinctively mistrusted the reformist policy so suddenly thrust upon them.

The most important internal political consequence of the French occupation was the rapid decline in the power of the Mamluks. This decline resulted not only from the defeats inflicted on them by the French, but also from the circumstances in which the occupation terminated. When the French finally evacuated the country, the Mamluk grandees were, as so often, divided into factions among themselves. Murād Bey, after composing his differences with the French, had died in Upper Egypt in April 1801. Ibrāhīm Bey, who had returned to Egypt with the grand vezir, had many years of life still before him, but at the time the chief contenders for the leadership were two of Murād's *mamlūks*, ʿUthmān Bey al-Bardīsī and Muḥammad Bey al-Alfī.

The Mamluk beys, however, had no longer an open field in which to struggle for the domination of Egypt. An Ottoman army, as well as British forces, were in occupation of the country, and the Ottoman government was resolved to prevent any revival of Mamluk autonomy, and to bring Egypt under the control of an Ottoman viceroy. Their British allies were less enthusiastic about this; tardily awakened to the strategic importance of Egypt, the British government would have preferred a restoration of the Mamluk régime, which might be more susceptible to influence than would a viceroy, acting for the sultan. The interest of Britain in the Mamluks was shown by a visit which Muḥammad Bey al-Alfī paid to London in 1803–4. The permanent control of Egypt was, however, not yet a British aim, and in March 1803 the troops withdrew, in accordance with the Treaty of Amiens.

The withdrawal of the British left the Ottomans and the Mamluks contending for power in Egypt. A viceroy, Khusraw (Husrev) Pasha, had already been installed, and hostilities were taking place between his forces and the Mamluks, who had established themselves in Upper

Egypt. Shortly after the British withdrawal, a third party emerged in the struggle for power: the Albanian contingent, which had originally come to Egypt to fight the French, and by this time was in effect a private army, fighting for its own hand. In May 1803 it mutinied in Cairo over arrears of pay, and Khusraw Pasha fled to Damietta. The Albanian commander was installed as *qā'im maqām*, only to be assassinated a few days later. His successor in the command was an officer in his thirties, Muḥammad ʿAlī Bey, who was in the course of the next few years to make himself viceroy of Egypt.

Part III The Last Phase of Ottoman Rule

12

The Revival of the Ottoman Empire

Although the decline of the Ottoman Empire began in the later part of the sixteenth century, the empire's military weakness did not for some time become indisputably apparent. The disastrous Treaty of Carlowitz in 1699 was the first of a series of instruments by which large cessions of Ottoman territory were made to European powers after a clear defeat. Gradually Ottoman statesmen realized that military superiority had unquestionably passed to the Christian states of Europe, and understood that only by a programme of westernization could the future of the empire be secured.

It was easier to diagnose the sickness and state the remedy than to carry out the necessary treatment. The Ottoman westernizers of the eighteenth century achieved only limited and sporadic successes, and much of their work was very transient. Thus, the first Turkish printing press was set up by a Hungarian renegade, Ibrahim Müteferrika, in 1727. It printed seventeen books and was closed in 1742. Not until its reopening in 1784 did the continuous history of printing in Turkish begin. Of more immediate relevance to Ottoman military requirements was the establishment in 1734 of a school of geometry. This was connected with an attempted reform of the Bombardier corps, then being carried out by a French renegade. The school was soon closed, under pressure from the Janissaries, and further measures for the improvement of military education were delayed until 1773.

Effective impetus to carry out even the most necessary reforms could only be derived from the sultan's initiative, and not until 1789 did a sultan come to the throne with sufficient determination and energy to attempt the essential westernization of the army. This was Selim III, who endeavoured, at first with French assistance, to train a new officer corps for his army and navy, and to supersede the archaic, turbulent and inefficient Janissaries by a newly raised body of infantry. In the short run, his attempt failed. The establishment of Selim's new model army, the *Nizam-i jedid*, naturally antagonized the Janissaries, and in 1807 the sultan was confronted with a mutiny. Although he abolished the *Nizam-i jedid*, the Janissaries brought about his deposition. He was put to death in 1808, by order of his successor, who himself reigned for barely a year.

During the months of his confinement before his death, Selim discussed his frustrated schemes with the prince who, as Sultan Mahmud II (1808–39), was to continue his work. It was many years before Mahmud was able to resume Selim's programme of westernization and reform. His two immediate predecessors had been deposed, and his own position was at first precarious. Nevertheless, the pressure on the empire continued. In 1821 a new phase in the disintegration of the empire in Europe opened with the Greek insurrection in the Morea. In the meantime the viceroy in Egypt, Muḥammad ʿAlī Pasha, was dealing with a local situation which closely resembled that confronting the sultan, and, after eliminating all rivals for power, was reorganizing the country and consolidating his own position. The situation in Greece enabled Mahmud to follow the example of Muḥammad ʿAlī. In 1826 the old-style Ottoman forces were doing badly against the Greek insurgents, while Muḥammad ʿAlī's new model army of Egyptian conscripts had gained notable successes in the Morea. At this juncture, Mahmud authorized the creation of a new, western-style army. The Janissaries of Istanbul rose in their last mutiny, but the sultan was ready for them, and they were annihilated by artillery fire. 'The Auspicious Event', as this episode is called, freed Mahmud and his successors to carry out more far-reaching reforms.

While the Janissaries had been consistent and fanatical opponents of reform, the attitude of the *ʿulamāʾ* was more ambiguous. At times they had combined with the Janissaries; and the lower *ʿulamāʾ*, together with the students at the *madrasas*, were easily incited into opposition to the government. The higher *ʿulamāʾ* were, however, usually more cautious and circumspect in their attitude, and were prepared to co-operate with the reforming sultans, or at least to acquiesce in innovations which they could not conscientiously approve. The economic independence of the *ʿulamāʾ* (resting on their position as beneficiaries of *waqf* endowments), rather than their open opposition, was obnoxious to Mahmud II. Under the pretext of introducing order into the administration of the *waqfs*, the sultan brought them under the centralized control of a ministry, responsible to himself, which collected the revenues and made disbursements for the purposes envisaged by the pious founders. This unprecedented measure would in itself have ended the financial independence of the *ʿulamāʾ*: in addition, Mahmud and his successors increasingly diverted *waqf* funds to the general purposes of the state.

The status and traditional rôle of the *ʿulamāʾ* were more insidiously menaced by another development: the establishment of new types of education, maintained directly by the state, and based on western models. The purpose of the new educational system was to provide the cadres of military officers and government officials needed by the reorganized state. Although schools for Ottoman military and naval officers had been set up in the eighteenth century, these were short-lived: bold educational experiments could not be undertaken until after the destruction of the Janissaries. As in other respects, parallel developments may be observed in Cairo and Istanbul. Specialized schools were founded in both capitals. Of these, perhaps the most important were the two schools of medicine, both set up in 1827. They were intended for training army doctors, and both had French instructors. In addition to the specialist schools, which were ancillary to the military reorganization being carried out by both sultan and viceroy, a number of civilian schools were established, giving a general education. These had, however, a strictly utilitarian purpose: they were intended to feed the civil service or the specialist schools, and their pupils were salaried and maintained like government employees. The extension of civilian education did not take place until later in the nineteenth century. The problem of staffing the new educational institutions was overcome by the recruitment of European teachers, and by the sending of educational missions abroad. The supply of renegades, who made notable contributions to the Ottoman Empire as late as the eighteenth century, virtually ceased in the nineteenth. Mahmud II and Muḥammad ʿAlī were fortunate in that the termination of the Napoleonic wars made available the services of many Frenchmen and Italians whose careers had been prematurely terminated. Both Turkish and Egyptian educational missions were sent to Europe, and especially to Paris, London and Vienna, from the 1820s onwards, and included a number of students who subsequently had distinguished careers.

Increasing diplomatic, military and cultural contact with Europe made necessary the study of European languages (especially French and Italian) and the translation of European works into the two principal languages of the Ottoman Empire. Once again, the same pattern of events recurs: the first tentative experiments are made in eighteenth-century Istanbul but continuous development starts concurrently under Mahmud II and Muḥammad ʿAlī. In 1821 the last Greek dragoman of the Sublime Porte, the imperial interpreter, was put to death, and his post conferred on a Turkish-speaking Muslim. From 1833 onwards, bureaux of translation were established in all the chief government departments in Istanbul. Meanwhile, translations of European text-books, especially of medicine and the sciences, were being made by individual Turks, although literary translations did not appear until the second half of the century.

These developments all diminished the status of the *ʿulamāʾ*. They lost their monopoly of education. Beside the traditional system which they controlled, classical and religious in its curriculum and outlook, was this new and developing network of schools, Western in inspiration, secular in approach, utilitarian in aim. The highest offices in the government and the armed forces went to the graduates of the new schools. Between the *ʿulamāʾ* and the old ruling élite, a symbiosis had been possible, because they shared a common background of traditional culture, a common, if limited, world-view. This was far less easy to attain when the two groups were the products of different educational systems, each bearing the imprint of a distinctive culture.

One aspect of Mahmud II's reforming programme was, as we have just seen, the reorganization and westernization of the army and the administration. Another was the reintegration of the provinces, involving the destruction of the power-groups and local autonomies which had grown up in them during the period of Ottoman decline. He had set to work on this task even before the annihilation of the Janissaries, and by the end of his reign had attained a fair measure of success. The obsolescent fief-system, which had long ceased to serve a useful military purpose, was finally abolished in 1831, and the estates were resumed as crown domain. The elimination of the *derebeys* of Anatolia had begun earlier, and went on until after the middle of the century. Some of the provincial autonomies were ended. The last of the long line of Mamluk pashas of Baghdād was displaced in 1831. In Syria, the sultan's work was done for him, albeit inadvertently, by Muḥammad ʿAlī Pasha, who occupied and administered the territory from 1831 to 1840. Elsewhere, the sultan was less successful. Under Muḥammad ʿAlī, Egypt became even more openly autonomous than she had been in the previous century. Tripoli in North Africa was recovered from the Qaramānlī dynasty of pashas, but the virtual independence of the beys of Tunis remained unimpaired. The capture of Algiers by the French in 1830 meant only the loss of a peripheral province, which had long been autonomous, but the emergence of an independent Greek state in the same year indicated the crumbling of Ottoman power in Rumelia—its chief seat for over four hundred years.

The reign of Mahmud II was followed by the period of reforms known as the *Tanzimat*. These were formulated in a long series of laws and regulations between the death of Mahmud in 1839 and the suspension of the Ottoman Constitution by Abdülhamid II in 1878. Three of the reforming ordinances are outstanding, and caught the attention of Europe, as they were intended to do. These are: the *Hatt-i Sherif* of Gülhane, promulgated on the accession of Sultan Abdülmejid, Mahmud's son and successor in 1839; the *Hatt-i Hümayun* of the same sultan, promulgated in 1856; and the Constitution of 1876, granted by Sultan Abdülhamid II.[1]

The *Hatt-i Sherif* was the basic charter of reform. It specified as necessary 'to give to the provinces composing the Ottoman Empire the benefit of a good administration', the following:

'1. The guarantees insuring to [Ottoman] subjects perfect security for life, honour, and fortune.
'2. A regular system of assessing and levying taxes.
'3. An equally regular system for the levying of troops and the duration of their service.'

The *Hatt-i Hümayun* of 1856 was specifically concerned with the problems arising from the religious heterogeneity of the empire. It confirmed the traditional privileges of the non-Muslims, and, somewhat illogically, affirmed the equal status and duties of all Ottoman subjects without distinction. The Constitution of 1876 was based on the Belgian Constitution of 1831, and its more authoritarian derivative, the Prussian constitutional edict of 1850, and provided for a bicameral parliament to share, within limits, the legislative powers of the sultan.

All three documents have been denounced by western writers as empty verbiage, intended to conceal from a progressive Europe the oriental conservatism and corruption of the Ottoman Empire. It is indeed true that each was promulgated with great publicity on an occasion of critical relations with Europe. The *Hatt-i Sherif* of 1839 was proclaimed when Muḥammad ʿAlī Pasha seemed to be on the verge of overthrowing the Ottoman Empire, and the power of Britain was the principal security for its continuance. From one point of view the *Hatt-i Sherif* is an affirmation of the Ottoman government's loyalty to the liberal principles sponsored by Britain. The *Hatt-i Hümayun* of 1856 was issued at the end of the Crimean War, when France and Britain had been the sultan's allies against Russia. The Constitution of 1876 was promulgated on the eve of an international conference, convened to impose a settlement in the Balkans.

Nevertheless, these three edicts were not simply window-dressing. In

[1] For the *Hatt-i Sherif* and *Hatt-i Hümayun*, see Hurewitz, i, 113–16 and 149–53.

assessing their timing and contents, two considerations should be borne in mind. In the first place, the need to conciliate Western Europe on each of these three occasions gave the Ottoman reformers precisely the opportunities they needed to commit the government to the policies they advocated. The three edicts should (like the *Sharīʿa* itself) be regarded rather as statements of purpose and programmes for action, than as explicit legislation. In the second place, it is possible to regard the *Hatt-i Sherif* and the *Hatt-i Hümayun* in two very different ways. The general phraseology of these two decrees is liberal, but the specific reforms projected in them were fully consonant with the development of a powerful centralizing autocracy. This was true also of the Constitution of 1876, which was in form a concession by the sultan: it did not rest on any theory of political contract, still less on an agreement of the people. Its authoritarian character was demonstrated, for example, by an article enumerating, but not exhausting, the sultan's prerogatives, and another reserving to the government wide powers in the proclamation of martial law, and giving the sultan an extensive right to deport obnoxious persons.

Some Ottoman statesmen sincerely desired reform, and did a good deal to bring into effect the kind of reforms they desired, but the spirit which infused the new developments was only briefly and exceptionally liberal; it was more usually despotic and centralizing. The cumulative effect of the changes from 1826 down to 1876, when Abdülhamid II succeeded to the throne, was to make the sultan far more of an absolute monarch than he had been even in the heyday of the traditional Ottoman Empire. The annihilation of the Janissaries symbolized the overthrow of the entrenched power-groups which had in practice circumscribed his despotism; the weakening of the *ʿulamāʾ* typified the abolition of the limitations imposed by the *Sharīʿa*. European administrative and military methods had armed the sultan with new powers; European techniques of transport and communications had placed him in close and speedy touch with every part of his dominions.

By the 1860s the fruits of authoritarian reform were ripening, and some of the rising generation realized that a new problem had arisen—that of curbing the sultan's despotism. Like their predecessors, they sought an answer to their problem in the theory and practice of Europe, and found it in the ideas of limited monarchy and parliamentary government. The Constitution of 1876 marked a temporary but still restricted deference to this mood and these ideas. The spirit which brought it into being did not last. Midhat Pasha, the grand vezir who was the principal architect of the Constitution, was dismissed by Sultan Abdülhamid II even before the parliament for which it provided had met. The parliament itself was dissolved, and the Constitution suspended, in 1878. For the next thirty years the sultan enjoyed the plenitude of autocratic power over the empire which his predecessors had saved from imminent destruction. The reign of Abdülhamid II is a measure of both the success and the failure of the *Tanzimat*.

The strengthening of the sultan's power within the empire synchronized with the further shrinking of its boundaries. Losses of territory in the Balkans, the establishment of a French protectorate over Tunisia in 1881, the British occupation of Egypt in 1882, were all developments which left the Ottoman Empire predominantly an Asian state, and one, moreover, in which the Arabs formed an increasingly large proportion of the inhabitants. Nevertheless, as the largest and (in spite of its evident weaknesses) the most powerful of the remaining independent Muslim states, the empire was still the bulwark of Sunnī Islam, and the sultan enjoyed and deliberately cultivated, prestige and influence far outside the territories he ruled. In reaction both to European pressure from without and westernizing reform within, there developed in the later decades of the nineteenth century a tendency to emphasize the concept of the Ottoman Empire as potentially the universal Islamic state, with the sultan laying claim to the title of caliph.

There had been an early and sporadic manifestation of this tendency in 1774, when, in the Treaty of Küchük Kaynarja with Russia, the sultan had claimed to be 'Grand Caliph of Mahometanism', with a species of spiritual authority over Muslims outside his political control.[1] The pretension was taken up and developed in the 1860s under Sultan Abdülaziz. In 1876 the title of caliph, and its universal significance as 'protector of the Muslim religion', were written into the Ottoman Constitution. Although Abdülhamid II quickly suspended the Constitution, he cherished the title and emphasized its implications. It gave him an overriding claim to the loyalty of the non-Turkish Muslims within his own dominions, as well as that of Muslims outside the empire. Many of these were under British rule in India, as later in Egypt and the Sudan; others were under French rule in North Africa, Russian rule in Central Asia, and Dutch rule in the East Indies. Nearly forty years later the British were still apprehensive of the hold of the Ottoman caliphate over their Muslim subjects, when the sultan joined Germany and Austria in the First World War. Although their fears proved largely illusory, they

[1] See Hurewitz, i, 56, column 1.

had important consequences in shaping Britain's Arab policy in the war years.

Resentment at both the despotism of Abdülhamid II and the continuing erosion of the empire's periphery, stimulated the development of opposition movements, which are known collectively as the Young Turks, and which began to organize themselves from 1889 onwards. Although their primary purpose was the overthrow of the sultan's régime, the Young Turks were inevitably led on to consider the means of preserving the empire after his downfall. During 1902, two rival groups, propounding alternative and mutually incompatible schemes, had come into being among the exiled leaders of the Young Turks. One, organized in the Committee of Union and Progress (C.U.P.), asserted the existence of an Ottoman nation, uniting diverse ethnic, religious and linguistic groups around the dynasty. This was a political fantasy, as events were to show. The other group of Young Turks sought the panacea for maladministration in the empire in decentralization: the construction of a federal state under a constitutional sultanate. Their sector of the movement was known by the cumbrous title of 'League of Administrative Decentralization and Private Initiative'. Whether their solution would have been feasible is highly dubious: in any case, it was never tried.

The overthrow of the Hamidian despotism was brought about by a military revolt, inspired by the C.U.P. In July 1908 Sultan Abdülhamid yielded to the revolutionaries and proclaimed the restoration of the Constitution of 1876. After a further clash in the following year, he was deposed, and his successors, the last two Ottoman sultans, were powerless figureheads. The C.U.P. steadily increased its control over the government until, in 1913, the reality of power passed into the hands of a military triumvirate, who ruled until the collapse of the empire at the end of the First World War. During the years immediately before the war, the C.U.P. had an almost free hand to govern as seemed best to them. They attempted to reinforce the administrative centralization of the *Tanzimat* reforms by ottomanizing the peoples of the empire. This was, in effect, an attempt to create a Turkish nation-state out of a polity which was largely non-Turkish. It was unlikely to have been a successful policy in the circumstances of the early twentieth century, but its failure need not in itself have entailed the collapse of the Ottoman Empire as such. As with contemporary Austria-Hungary, the fall of the imperial régime and the disintegration of the state were brought about by defeat in the First World War.

As a result of the British victories in the Fertile Crescent, the Ottomans lost the Arab provinces which they had acquired four centuries earlier. As a result of the defeat of Germany, the ally and defender of the Ottoman Empire in its last phase, the existence of even a Turkish successor-state was for a time in jeopardy. The fragmentation of the Turkish heartland in Anatolia was averted by an unexpected resurgence of energy, directed by an army officer, Mustafa Kemal, to the creation and then the salvation of a Turkish nation-state. The Ottoman tradition had outlived its usefulness. When Mustafa Kemal (later known as Atatürk) had finally established his authority in Anatolia and Thrace against foreign foes and domestic opponents, had evicted the last sultan in 1922, abolished the caliphate in 1924, and established the Republic of Turkey, the secular ottomanism of the Young Turks passed into the museum of obsolete political theories. The westernization of Turkey entered a new phase, under the most dynamic and thoroughgoing of Turkish reformers.

13

Muḥammad ʻAlī Pasha

The career of Muḥammad ʻAlī

When Muḥammad ʻAlī succeeded to the command of the Albanian contingent in May 1803, he took the first step towards acquiring supreme power in Egypt. The hereditary pashalic which he founded became the Egyptian monarchy in the twentieth century, and his dynasty came to an end only in 1953 after the army revolution of the previous year. Seen from one point of view, therefore, Muḥammad ʻAlī belongs to a type which had not been uncommon in the eighteenth century—the Ottoman governor who sought to establish an hereditary, autonomous rule in his province. Muḥammad ʻAlī's success is, however, remarkable in that he ultimately acquired autonomy and established his dynasty at the very period when the Ottoman central power was being effectively re-asserted in the Turkish-speaking provinces and the Fertile Crescent. The reasons for this success will be considered later: here we must give an outline of his career.

Muḥammad ʻAlī was born in 1769 in the Macedonian town of Kavalla. His father, presumably of Albanian stock, was a commander of irregulars, and died while his son was young. In 1801 Muḥammad ʻAlī came to Egypt with a small force of local levies from Kavalla. Promotion came rapidly, so that two years later he found himself in command of the most homogeneous fighting force in the country. From this point his career may be divided into four main stages. Between 1803 and 1805 he was one among several contenders for power in Egypt. With the acquisition of the viceroyalty in the latter year, he attained nominal supremacy, but had yet to establish his power on a firm basis by eliminating his rivals and creating an efficient and reliable military force. This was the work of the next two decades, and his achievements were rigorously tested by the Greek war and its aftermath. The third phase of his career begins in 1831, with his conquest of Syria. The clash of the viceroy and his suzerain, with its repercussions in international diplomacy, was formally terminated in 1840, and was followed by the last few years of relaxed effort and growing senility, until Muḥammad ʻAlī's death in 1849.

Between 1803 and 1805 Egypt was in a state of anarchy. At first

Muḥammad ʿAlī worked in alliance with ʿUthmān Bey al-Bardīsī to exclude from power a new Ottoman viceroy-designate and the rival Mamluk chief, Muḥammad Bey al-Alfī, who returned from England in February 1804.[1] A month later Muḥammad ʿAlī broke with al-Bardīsī and expelled the Mamluks from Cairo. He then succeeded in obtaining the appointment of Khūrshīd Pasha, the Ottoman governor of Alexandria, as viceroy of Egypt. Military operations next took place against the Mamluks, who were blockading Cairo. After they had been thrown back into Upper Egypt, the alliance between Khūrshīd and Muḥammad ʿAlī broke down. An attempt to get Muḥammad ʿAlī out of Egypt, by appointing him to the governorship of Jedda with the title of pasha, was unsuccessful. Muḥammad ʿAlī now sought the support of the *ʿulamāʾ*, and especially of the *naqīb al-Ashrāf*, ʿUmar Makram, against Khūrshīd Pasha. On 12 May 1805 the *ʿulamāʾ* raised complaints to the judge against the extortions of Khūrshīd and the misbehaviour of his troops. Two days later ʿUmar Makram and his colleagues invested Muḥammad ʿAlī with viceregal powers, while Khūrshīd shut himself up in the Citadel of Cairo and tried to obtain help from the Mamluks.

A prolonged period of instability then ensued. Even when, in July 1805, the sultan's firman arrived, formally appointing Muḥammad ʿAlī as viceroy, Khūrshīd refused to accept it. It was reinforced by the arrival of the Ottoman admiral at Abū Qīr, to confirm the appointment of Muḥammad ʿAlī, and the deposition of Khūrshīd. On 3 August Khūrshīd gave in and evacuated the Citadel.

The events of May 1805 have been represented as a species of popular election, conferring on Muḥammad ʿAlī the right to rule Egypt. This is a misrepresentation. ʿUmar Makram and the *ʿulamāʾ* were acting, as the *ʿulamāʾ* traditionally acted in times of political crisis, to safeguard the interests of the Muslim community by supporting the authority of the strongest contender for power. They were not in any real sense king-makers, still less spokesmen of the national will. Their action was valuable to Muḥammad Alī, since it afforded an interim legitimation of the power he had gained by force and intrigue, but he did not delay to obtain the more effective validation of the sultan's firman, nor, as we shall see, did he forget for a moment that armed strength was the true basis of his authority. Like the *ʿulamāʾ* of Cairo, the Ottoman government followed its traditional policy of recognizing effective power, without prejudice to future action. Since the expulsion of the French, the

[1] See above, p. 162.

sultan had nominated three viceroys of Egypt, and Muḥammad ʿAlī had played a large part in the downfall of each of them. By nominating him in his turn, the sultan in no way committed himself to the maintenance of Muḥammad ʿAlī's position in Egypt.

At the outset, there was indeed no reason to think that Muḥammad ʿAlī's viceroyalty would be of long duration. Inside the country he was confronted by the Mamluks, who were masters of Upper Egypt. His principal military support consisted of the turbulent and insubordinate Albanians. The Ottoman government, although frustrated, had by no means abandoned its aim of resuming full control over the administration of Egypt. And, in the background, the struggle between Britain and France had been renewed after the short-lived Treaty of Amiens: Egypt might again become a strategic necessity to either of the contestants.

Gradually these obstacles were overcome. The Ottoman danger was perhaps the least pressing. In May 1807 the vigorous reforming Sultan Selim III was deposed. With his fall, the reorganization of the empire virtually ceased for nearly twenty years, except for the restoration of the central authority in the provinces in much of Rumelia and Anatolia. When, in 1826, Sultan Mahmud II opened a new period of reform and centralization, Muḥammad ʿAlī had had ample time to entrench himself in his viceroyalty and to reorganize the institutions of Egypt to enhance his own power. The threat from the Anglo-French war was more acute and immediate. In 1806, Napoleon, whose prestige and power were at their highest point, succeeded in breaking the Anglo-Ottoman alliance. In order to secure a British base in Egypt, a body of troops was thereupon sent to occupy Alexandria, which they did in March 1807. They then made a disastrously unsuccessful attempt to capture Rosetta, and were pent up in Alexandria, from which they were released only after the conclusion of a convention with Muḥammad ʿAlī. This was the last appearance of British troops in Egypt for seventy-five years, during which period the British endeavoured with considerable success to build up their influence and secure their interests by diplomatic means.

The Mamluks were altogether a tougher problem. Their long experience of Egypt, their tactics of retiring up the Nile to recruit their strength, and their grip on the revenues of Egypt through their tenure of *iltizāms* (tax-farms which had come to approximate to landed estates), made them a formidable and tenacious enemy. During the early years of his viceroyalty, Muḥammad ʿAlī moved carefully to avoid a direct clash. He was helped by the feud between the two main houses, which continued after the deaths of their chiefs, ʿUthmān Bey al-Bardīsī in

November 1806, and Muḥammad Bey al-Alfī in January 1807. Ultimately he disposed of the leading grandees by a treacherous coup, which, rather surprisingly, they failed to anticipate. Invited on 1 March 1811 to the Citadel to assist at the investment of Aḥmad Tusun Pasha, Muḥammad ʿAlī's son, as commander of an expedition against the Wahhābīs, the beys and their followers were shot down as they passed in procession down a rocky passage. Simultaneously their houses were sacked and those Mamluks who had not attended the ceremony were hunted down. The last body of Mamluk forces in Upper Egypt was almost entirely destroyed during the following months by Ibrāhīm Pasha, Muḥammad ʿAlī's eldest son. A small group escaped beyond the limits of Egyptian territory, south of the Third Cataract, and established their camp on the west bank of the Nile, where now stands the town of new Dongola.[1] Here they competed with the Shāyqiyya horsemen for the domination of that reach of the Nile, and recruited their failing numbers with black slaves. In this remote place of refuge, the aged Ibrāhīm Bey, who had once been the master of Egypt, ended his life early in 1816.

The investiture of Tusun, which had been the occasion of the massacre in the Citadel, was the preliminary to the despatch of an expedition against the Wahhābīs who were then under the Amīr Saʿūd ibn ʿAbd al-Azīz.[2] The Wahhābī occupation of Mecca and Medina, the power of Saʿūd to close at will the Ḥijāz to the Pilgrimage caravans, represented an insulting defiance of the claim of the Ottoman sultan to be caliph and Servitor of the Two Holy Sanctuaries. Ever since the extension of Ottoman suzerainty over the Arab lands, however, the affairs of the Ḥijāz had normally been delegated to the ruler of Egypt, as successor of the Mamluk sultans. Thus the sultan's appointment of Muḥammad ʿAlī to organize an expedition against the Wahhābīs was made as much in accordance with established precedent as in virtue of the viceroy's personal capacities. The idea that it was a machiavellian stroke designed to exhaust his resources and use up his troops'[3] is probably rather far-fetched. What is less unlikely is that the viceroy himself saw in the expedition a means of employing his soldiers, who, having now secured his position in Egypt, might grow disorderly and troublesome.

The Arabian war falls into two main phases. In the first, the forces from Egypt under Tusun's command secured the port of Yanbuʿ in

[1] The Sudanese name for the place is *al-ʿUrḍī*, from the Turkish, *ordu*, meaning 'camp'.

[2] See above, p. 154.

[3] H. Dodwell, *The founder of modern Egypt*, Cambridge 1931, 43.

1811, captured Medina in 1812, and Mecca in 1813. The Hashimite dynasty was restored, and Muḥammad ʿAlī made the Pilgrimage. In 1814 Saʿūd died, and was succeeded by his son ʿAbdallāh. Tusun, in 1815, concluded a truce with the new *amīr*. This, in effect, secured the *status quo*; the Wahhābīs retained the Saʿūdī homeland of Najd, and some parts of the Ḥijāz, while the viceroy's men controlled the holy cities, and assured the safety of the Pilgrimage. Tusun returned to Egypt to die, and in 1816 the war was resumed. Under the much more capable command of Ibrāhīm Pasha, the viceroy's forces advanced steadily into Najd from their base at Medina. One after another the Wahhābī fortresses were besieged and fell. Finally, in 1818, after a siege of several months, the Saʿūdī capital of Darʿiyya was taken. The Amīr ʿAbdallāh was sent to Istanbul, where he was put to death.

Although the object of the Arabian war was to break the power of the Wahhābīs and to restore the suzerainty of the Ottoman sultan, its practical result was to establish the power of the viceroy of Egypt on the eastern coast of the Red Sea. For a short time, indeed, it seemed as if much more of Arabia would be held: a force even occupied al-Aḥsā on the Persian Gulf. But these far-flung conquests were untenable, and in 1824 even Najd was evacuated, when Turkī, the son of ʿAbdallāh ibn Saʿūd, regained power. The viceroy's protectorate over the Ḥijāz and the coast-lands of the Yaman lasted until the collapse of Muḥammad ʿAlī's power vis-à-vis the Ottomans in 1840.

The Arabian war was followed by another campaign, undertake by Muḥammad ʿAlī on his own account and not as the representative o the sultan, although he subsequently obtained Ottoman recognition o his conquests. This was the campaign in Nubia, Sennar and Kordofa which laid the foundations of what came to be known as the Egyptia Sudan. We have already seen how, in the time of Süleyman the Mag nificent, Özdemir Pasha extended Ottoman suzerainty south of Egyp proper, into the region between the First and Third Cataracts, know to the Turks as Berberistan.[1] By Muḥammad ʿAlī's time this was autono mous under hereditary *kāshifs*. The Funj sultanate, which, from it capital at Sennar, had established in the sixteenth century a hegemon over the tribes northwards as far as the Third Cataract, was far gone i decline, and a chain of tribal kingdoms dominated the banks of the mai Nile. These included the predatory confederacy of the Shāyqiyya, an the kingdom of the Jaʿaliyyūn around the commercial metropolis Shandī. Far to the west of the Nile lay the still vigorous Muslim sultana

[1] See above, p. 54.

of Darfur, with its dependency, Kordofan, taken from the Funj in the previous century.[1]

Muḥammad ʿAlī's motives in attempting the conquest of these remote regions, which had never been under Ottoman control, were primarily military. The campaign would rid him of his turbulent soldiery. The remnant of the Mamluks in Dongola menaced his rule in Egypt: their immediate threat might appear to be slight, but the history of Ottoman Egypt bore abundant witness to Mamluk tenacity. Already in 1812 the viceroy had sent an embassy to urge the Funj sultan to expel the Mamluks. The sultan was far too feeble to comply, but at least the embassy brought back useful information of the situation in the Nilotic regions. Muḥammad ʿAlī's chief motive in the conquest was probably to obtain slaves for his army. His Albanians were undependable. Furthermore, to assure his superiority over all internal rivals (and possibly over external enemies as well), Muḥammad ʿAlī wanted an army on the European model. Attempts at army reform had been the cause of the downfall of Sultan Selim III, and the news that Muḥammad ʿAlī was contemplating innovations produced a military revolt in Cairo during the Arabian war. To recruit a loyal army of slaves was a traditional device of Muslim rulers when threatened by the soldiery that had brought them to power. By conquering the lands which lay to the south of Egypt the viceroy did not, of course, mean to enslave the free Muslim peoples there but to tap the reservoir of slaves which they held and to gain direct access to the pagan areas, still further south, which were the traditional fields for slave-raiding.[2] Another incentive to conquest was an exaggerated report of the alluvial gold to be found in the Sudan.

The command of the principal expeditionary force was committed to another of the viceroy's sons, Ismāʿīl Kāmil Pasha. The army left Aswān in the summer of 1820, and in June of the following year it reached Sennar, where Ismāʿīl received the submission of the last Funj sultan. The Mamluks of Dongola had fled before his advance, and the only resistance encountered was from the Shāyqiyya, who were defeated in battle. Meanwhile, in 1821, a second expeditionary force, under the command of the Defterdar, Muḥammad Bey Khusraw, the viceroy's son-in-law, struck across the desert to Kordofan, which was conquered in

While in Egypt, Bonaparte had corresponded with the then sultan of Darfur, ʿAbd al-Raḥmān al-Rashīd.

The supply of African slaves was increasing in importance during this period, since the Russian conquest of the Caucasus (finally recognized in the Russo-Persian Treaty of Turkmanchay in 1828) ended *mamlūk* recruitment from this region.

a couple of engagements. This force had been intended to conquer Darfur also, but the project was too difficult to be accomplished.

Although the initial conquests had been made easily, the resentment of the Sudanese at the new, alien rulers and their taxes flared out in a sudden revolt which began with the massacre of Ismāʿīl Pasha and his retinue at Shandī, in October or November 1822. For a time, the continuance of the new régime was seriously threatened, but the rising was harshly suppressed by the Defterdar, hastily brought from Kordofan. Thereafter, for sixty years, until the outbreak of the Mahdia, the Sudanese territories remained submissive to Turco-Egyptian rule.

The conquest of the Sudan was followed immediately by the organization of Muḥammad ʿAlī's new slave army. The first necessity was the training of a cadre of officers. For this purpose, about a thousand young *mamlūks*, belonging to the viceroy and notables of Egypt, were placed in newly constructed barracks at Aswān, and given a European-style military training by former French and Italian officers of Napoleon's army whose career had been abruptly terminated by the Vienna settlement. The most outstanding of them was a certain Colonel Sèves, who became a Muslim, and is known in Egyptian history as Sulaymān Pasha. The rank-and-file of the new army, which was known as *Nizam-i jedi*[d] (Arabic, *al-Niẓām al-jadīd*) were recruited from black slaves, originating from the Sudan, where they were taken from their former masters i[n] payment of taxes, or obtained in raids on the pagan tribes of the souther[n] fringe. By 1823 thirty thousand slaves are said to have been brought t[o] a training-camp near Manfalūṭ, where six regiments were formed, commanded by the *mamlūk* officers.

This experiment was, however, far from successful. The negro slave soldiers died in their thousands, and it rapidly became clear to Muḥammad ʿAlī that he must look elsewhere for the main body of his recruit[s]. Acting, it is said, on the advice of the French consul-general, he decide[d] to conscript the Egyptian peasantry. This was indeed an innovation. F[or] centuries, even millennia, the armed forces in Egypt had been of alie[n] origin; at most, the nomad Arabs had provided auxiliary irregul[ar] troops. The peasantry had no desire for military service, and, indee[d], their conscription was carried out by barbarous methods. Many of t[he] young men fled from their villages, thereby placing agriculture [in] jeopardy. The conscription was undoubtedly one factor in the ru[ral] revolts, which were so common a feature of Muhammad ʿAlī's vic[e]royalty that measures for their repression were specified in the Agrari[an] Law of 1830.

Hateful as it was, the conscription of the peasantry had come to stay, and it was to have portentous consequences for the country and the dynasty. Muḥammad ʿAlī thereby established a dichotomy in the army between officers of Ottoman or Circassian (i.e. *mamlūk*) origin, speaking Turkish, and soldiers who were Arabic-speaking native Egyptians. This in later years was to be a source of tension. Even after Egyptians had made their way into the cadre of officers, they were conscious of inferior esteem and treatment. This situation, complicated by external factors, was to give rise to the ʿUrābī movement, the first outburst of Egyptian nationalism.[1]

This lay half a century in the future. For the present, Muḥammad ʿAlī had created an army which, whatever its deficiencies by European standards, was the most up-to-date of any in the Near East. By so doing he had secured his own position and the continuation of his rule in Egypt. There was no comparable force within Egypt, and the Ottoman sultan could not hope to displace it with the obsolete army nominally under his command. Mahmud II was indeed to have recourse to the viceroy of Egypt when he needed aid in suppressing the Greek insurrection.

The revolt of the Greeks against Ottoman rule began in 1821. Muḥammad ʿAlī was not at first involved: unlike western Arabia, Greece formed no part of the traditional Egyptian sphere of control. In 1822, however, the sultan offered him the pashalic of Crete, on condition of reducing it to order. This he did by 1824, and Mahmud II then granted him the pashalic of the Morea on similar terms. Participation in the Greek war gave Muḥammad ʿAlī the opportunity of testing out his *Nizam-i jedid*, as well as the navy, which for some years past he had been assembling. The expeditionary force left Alexandria in July 1824 under the command of Ibrāhīm Pasha, whose powers were, however, limited. The sultan had appointed as admiral the same Khusraw Pasha who had been viceroy of Egypt in 1803, and had been the first rival for power evicted by Muḥammad ʿAlī.

In spite of the divided command and the feud between Ibrāhīm and Khusraw, the tide began to turn against the Greeks. In 1825 Ibrāhīm landed in the Morea, and the success of the Egyptian troops contrasted with the previous failures of the sultan's traditional forces. Ibrāhīm was, in fact, too successful. Lacking the political intuition of his father, he sought a purely military solution by violent action against the mainland Greeks. This was intolerable to the European powers. Unilateral

[1] See below, pp. 212–16.

intervention by Russia was narrowly averted; and in July 1827 Russia, Great Britain and France agreed to impose an armistice by a naval blockade of the Morea. The confrontation of the European squadrons and the Egyptian and Ottoman fleets in the Bay of Navarino resulted in a battle on 20 October 1827. The Muslim navy was annihilated, and the land-forces of Ibrāhīm were cut off in the Morea.

The settlement which in due course followed is no part of Egyptian history. Muḥammad ʿAlī had lost his fleet, and was not minded to continue a land campaign in which his army also might be destroyed. Ibrāhīm took no further action until, in August 1828, a convention was signed which enabled him to withdraw his forces from the Morea.

The intervention in the Greek war had been an anomalous phase in Muḥammad ʿAlī's policy, from which he gained little. His next exploit was in Syria, a region traditionally within the sphere of interest of Egyptian rulers. His determination to acquire Syria may be ascribed quite simply to the demands of strategy: the necessity for a buffer-zone between his heartland in the Nile valley and the ancient centres of Ottoman power in Anatolia. His interest in the region went back at least to 1821, when he had interceded with the Ottoman government on behalf of ʿAbdallāh Pasha, the governor of Acre, and Bashīr II, the Shihābī *amīr* of Lebanon, who had fled to Egypt for refuge.[1] In Bashīr and ʿAbdallāh, Muḥammad ʿAlī obtained two clients who were bound to him at least by gratitude and possibly by more specific undertakings.

For the time being, Muḥammad ʿAlī went no further. At the end of the decade, however, the desirability of occupying Syria became more urgent. Sultan Mahmud II had profited from the discreditable performance of the Ottoman troops in Greece to destroy the Janissaries (1826) and organize his own reformed army. The Greek *débâcle* had been followed by war with Russia in 1828, but with the signing of the Treaty of Adrianople in September 1829 the sultan was free once more to continue his military and administrative reforms. Muḥammad ʿAlī's military superiority was in jeopardy, and Mahmud's centralizing policy, which destroyed the *derebeys* of Anatolia and the Mamluk pashalic of Baghdad, increased his autonomy in Egypt. There were also personal considerations. His old enemy, Khusraw Pasha, was high in the sultan's favour and held from 1827 to 1836 the new office of *serasker* of the Ottoman forces.[2]

[1] For details of this incident, see below, p. 234.

[2] The title of *serasker* (or *serdar-i ekrem*) had in earlier times been used for field commanders. Under Mahmud II it was given to a high officer who combined the duties of commander-in-chief and war minister.

Muḥammad ʿAlī at first attempted to gain Syria by peaceful means. A request made to Istanbul as early as 1827 had been rejected. He therefore sought an excuse for intervention in Syrian affairs, and found one in the conduct of ʿAbdallāh Pasha. ʿAbdallāh was no longer anxious to maintain his entente with the viceroy, and had given offence by harbouring Egyptian peasants who had fled from the conscription. This was the actual *casus belli*, and in October 1831 Egyptian forces, commanded by Ibrāhīm Pasha, crossed the frontier and moved on Acre. The interval which had elapsed since the evacuation of the Morea had allowed Muḥammad ʿAlī to build up his army, while the nucleus of a new navy had been constructed to replace that destroyed at Navarino. In Bashīr II he had a cautious but ultimately faithful ally, whose followers rendered valuable service in the campaign.

At first, the war was, in appearance, no more than a squabble between neighbouring provincial governors, such as had often occurred in the last two centuries. It is significant of the new spirit which was developing at Istanbul that the Ottoman government did not hesitate to declare Muḥammad ʿAlī a rebel. The news came early in 1832, when Ibrāhīm was besieging Acre. The struggle now took on a more serious aspect: the viceroy of Egypt was openly flouting his suzerain. Acre surrendered in May. In the following month, the governor of Damascus fled, and Ibrāhīm entered the city without opposition. Advancing northwards in the month of July he defeated a Turkish force near Ḥimṣ, took Aleppo, and won a victory at the pass of Baylān, near Alexandretta, over an Ottoman army coming to the defence of Syria. Continuing his advance on to the plateau of Anatolia, Ibrāhīm defeated in December 1832 an Ottoman army commanded by the grand vezir himself, near the town of Konya.

At this point Ibrāhīm would have pressed on to Istanbul or have declared his father an independent sovereign. Muḥammad ʿAlī was more cautious. He was anxious above all to avoid an intervention of the European powers, such as had nullified his military successes in Greece. Turning the tables on Mahmud II, who had proclaimed him a rebel, he presented himself as the saviour of the Ottoman Empire from the perverse sultan, who had abandoned Muslim customs and adopted the ways of the Europeans. This was an ironical role for Muḥammad ʿAlī, whose programme of westernization had begun before that of Mahmud II. There were also indications that the viceroy might press for Mahmud's deposition. In January 1833, however, rumours of a Russo-Turkish alliance began to circulate. These were premature, but a Russian naval squadron anchored off Istanbul in February, and was followed in April by land forces. This move alarmed Britain and France, who were anxious to end hostilities before the Russians intervened actively. Pressure was brought to bear on both the sultan and Muḥammad ʿAlī. After negotiations, the sultan ceded to Muḥammad ʿAlī the Syrian provinces and the district of Adana, at the foot of the Taurus passes. When these arrangements had been set down in the Convention of Kütahya (April–May 1833), Ibrāhīm withdrew his forces from Anatolia.

Once again, as in the days of the Mamluk sultanate, the ruler of Egypt governed the whole of geographical Syria. Muḥammad ʿAlī was, however, denied the full fruition of his gains. The Syrian provinces were his only for life, tribute had to be paid for them, and his position still remained that of a vassal. For the next six years, Ibrāhīm Pasha governed the new territories as his father's personal representative, while Bashīr II was granted an almost autonomous status in Lebanon. Ibrāhīm's rule, with its concomitants of heavier taxation, forced labour, disarmament of the population, and military conscription, soon became unpopular, and encountered serious insurrections from 1834 onwards.

By 1839 matters had moved to a crisis. Within Syria the situation was explosive; externally, even more so. In the previous year Muḥammad ʿAlī had informed the consuls-general of Britain, France, Austria and Russia that he intended to declare his independence. Their replies were discouraging, but he did not renounce the project. Meanwhile Mahmud II was preparing for war, and in April 1839 Ottoman forces crossed the Euphrates into Syria. No immediate encounter followed, but on 7 June Muḥammad ʿAlī was proclaimed a traitor. Seventeen days later Ibrāhīm overwhelmed the Ottomans at the battle of Nezib, north-east of Aleppo. Two other catastrophes followed hard on this defeat. On 1 July Mahmud II died, leaving as his heir an inexperienced boy, Abdülmejid His first grand vezir was Khusraw Pasha—an appointment which implie the continuation of the struggle with Muḥammad ʿAlī. Its immediat effect, however, was to cause the Ottoman admiral, an old enemy o Khusraw, to surrender his fleet to the viceroy in the harbour o Alexandria.

As in Greece, Muḥammad ʿAlī had been too successful. The Britis government was opposed to the disintegration of the Ottoman Empire and, in spite of French support for Muḥammad ʿAlī, it succeeded o 15 July 1840 in concluding the Convention of London with Russia Austria and Prussia. In effect, this Convention imposed a settlemen on the sultan and the viceroy alike. The sultan agreed to make the viceroyalty of Egypt hereditary, and to give Muḥammad ʿAlī the pashalic of Acre for life. These concessions were, however, made contingent on the evacuation of the other conquered territories. To enforce the settlement, a British and Austrian naval squadron appeared off Beirut, which was captured on 9 October. Acre fell on 3 November. Meanwhile a revolt, fomented by British and Ottoman agents, had broken out in Lebanon. Ibrāhīm's position was becoming untenable, and on his father's orders he evacuated the whole of Syria. A British naval force, anchored off Alexandria, had extorted this last submission from Muḥammad ʿAlī on 27 November. In return, the British government secured from the unwilling Abdülmejid the grant to Muḥammad ʿAlī of the hereditary viceroyalty of Egypt in the firman of 1 June 1841.[1]

This was the end of Muḥammad ʿAlī's empire-building. In both Greece and Syria his larger schemes had failed, since they were incompatible with the policies of the great powers, which since 1798 had interested themselves in the eastern Mediterranean. Yet he had achieved certain very definite successes. In 1805 he had obtained the precarious title of viceroy of Egypt. He was the first viceroy for two centuries to exercise real power; he constructed a military force by which he secured his position not only against potential rivals in Egypt but against the sultan himself. In the interior of Africa, a region as yet undisturbed by the rivalries of the European powers, he had built up an empire outside the traditional limits of Ottoman authority; and pioneering expeditions up the White Nile prepared the way for the Turco-Egyptian advance to the Equator in the following generation.

Nevertheless, with the loss of Syria, Muḥammad ʿAlī's dynamic energy seemed to leave him. He lived for nine more years, but towards the end of his life became incapable of government. On 2 August 1849 the old viceroy died in Alexandria. His body was taken for burial to the great mosque he had built in the Citadel of Cairo.

The Reorganization of Egypt

Muḥammad ʿAlī's innovations were all ancillary to his primary purpose of securing his own position. To do this, he relied chiefly on his new model army, but long before it came into being he had begun to reorganize the fiscal and agrarian systems in order to concentrate power in his own hands. The first necessity was the destruction of the *iltizām* system, where the bulk of the landed revenue of Egypt went to the

[1] Text in Hurewitz, i, 121–3.

multazims (tax-farmers), pre-eminent amongst whom were the Mamluk grandees. The *ʿulamāʾ* also had a vested interest in the traditional system, since they profited from landed endowments (*rizaq aḥbāsiyya*), which were assigned in perpetuity to pious objects. During the early years of his rule, Muḥammad ʿAlī could make tentative experiments only in Lower Egypt, since Upper Egypt was still under Mamluk control. In 1809 a crisis arose when he set on foot a pilot-scheme in the Buḥayra. A new land-register was compiled for this province, and taxes were imposed on the private land of the *multazims*, as well as on the *rizaq aḥbāsiyya*. The *multazims* and the *ʿulamāʾ* combined to resist these demands. They were headed by the formidable *naqīb al-Ashrāf*, ʿUmar Makram. In the trial of strength which followed, ʿUmar Makram was defeated, dismissed from office, and rusticated. Thereafter the *ʿulamāʾ* no longer sought to act as an organized political force.

With the elimination of the Mamluks in 1811–12, a general attack on the *iltizām*-system became possible. First, the *iltizāms* in Upper Egypt were confiscated, then (in 1814) those in Lower Egypt. Life pensions were paid by the treasury to the former *multazims* of Lower Egypt. Land belonging to *rizaq aḥbāsiyya* was similarly confiscated, Muḥammad ʿAlī undertaking to compensate its former holders. These measures, which brought a great part of the cultivated land of Egypt back into state ownership (i.e. into the hands of the viceroy), prevented the development of a landed class which might challenge his authority, and undermined the independence of the *ʿulamāʾ*.

That these changes were brought about primarily as a political measure is clear from later developments in Muḥammad ʿAlī's time. A new landed class was permitted to develop, constituted from persons who would be helpful, or at least innocuous, to the viceroy. Among the principal beneficiaries were members of his own family. Even before the general resumption of the *iltizāms*, some *multazims* had been expropriated and their estates transferred to his relatives and supporters. During the last two decades of his reign, enormous grants of land were made to the viceregal family as *jifliks* (Turkish: *chiftlik*, meaning, in Ottoman usage, an estate), which consisted mostly of abandoned and insolvent villages. Other large estates, known as *ibʿādiyyāt*, were formed by the reclamation of uncultivated land, and were granted, free of taxes, to notables and high officials. Even the farm of taxes, which had been the original nature of *iltizām*, reappeared towards the end of Muḥammad ʿAlī's reign. In March 1840, wealthy officials, officers and others were compelled to receive villages as *ʿuhda*: they were required to pay the tax-arrears of these villages, and to meet their future liabilities. Muḥammad ʿAlī's agrarian changes, therefore, were not true reforms. No new principle was involved. He was, in fact, repeating a traditional process which has frequently accompanied a change of régime in Egypt; namely, the resumption of lands from a former proprietorial group, and their re-granting to the supporters of the new ruler. The effect of his measures was to create a new landed class.

The administrative history of Muḥammad ʿAlī's reign is complex and in many respects obscure. This is because he achieved power after a period of anarchy. During the seven years which had elapsed since Bonaparte's landing, the old Ottoman and Mamluk ruling élite had been dispersed and proscribed. The governmental institutions, as they had existed before the French occupation, had been totally subverted. Muḥammad ʿAlī was, no doubt, a centralizing despot by instinct, but the circumstances in which he came to power meant that he had to evolve a new administrative machine and produce from the narrow circle of his own relatives and close associates the new men needed to fill the key posts. The period was therefore one of experiment.

The fluidity of the administrative institutions is reflected in changing terminology. Old titles and names of offices become obsolete and disappear, or else assume a new meaning. Neologisms appear, and establish themselves in the language. Thus, with the disappearance of the old ruling group of the Mamluk beys, the title reverted to being a mere honorific, as it had been in the earliest period of Ottoman Egypt, and became debased by being too lavishly bestowed. The titles and offices of the *defterdar* and the *kāshifs* survived well into the reign, but fell into disuse in consequence of financial and provincial reorganization. The developments in provincial administration were marked by the emergence of two new titles, *mudīr* and *maʾmūr*, which acquired respectively the significance of provincial governor and district officer. Another neologism was the word for province, *müdürlük* in its Turkish, and *mudīriyya* in its Arabic form, which completely superseded the designations used under the old régime of *iqlīm* or *kashiflik*. The acquisition of territory outside Egypt proper led to the adoption of another new title, that of *hükümdar*,[1] bestowed in 1832 on the civil governor of Syria, and in 1835 on the governor-general of the Egyptian Sudan. The latter usage survived down to the Mahdī's capture of Khartoum and the death of General Gordon, the last *hükümdar* of the Sudan, in 1885.

[1] This was an old Perso-Turkish word originally signifying 'sovereign'. In the limited sense given to it by Muḥammad ʿAlī, it was, in effect, a neologism.

Under Muḥammad ʿAlī the functions of government became more complex and diverse than they had been under the old régime. The resumption of the alienated lands, with the implications of this for the territorial revenue, necessitated changes in the government financial system. The creation of the *Nizam-i jedid* demanded the organization of a system of military administration such as Egypt had not previously possessed. The building of a navy, the development of state schools, the promotion of trade and industry were all new concerns, which required the establishment of government machinery. Naturally, therefore, the trend of administration in Muḥammad ʿAlī's reign was towards the departmentalization of government business. The division of functions never assumed a completely logical form, nor did the heads of the departments ever acquire the full duties and responsibilities of ministers. An elaborate and, it seems, to some extent theoretical, description of the departmental system in its mature form was given by the ordinance called the *Siyasetname* of 1837. This established seven departments (sing. *dīwān*), dealing respectively with the Interior, Finance, War, the Navy, Education and Public Works, Commerce and Foreign Affairs, and Industry. The new title of *mudīr* was bestowed on the heads of these departments.[1]

The disappearance of the old ruling élite caused problems of staffing in the army (as we have seen), the civil administration and the ancillary services. In the administration, the highest positions were held by Ottomans of heterogeneous origin. A particularly important role was played by the sons of the viceroy, especially Ibrāhīm, and by the eldest grandson, ʿAbbās Ḥilmī. The technicians needed for both civil and military development were, in the first place, Europeans, particularly French and Italians. The native Egyptians had, however, a place, if a subordinate one, in the new political order. By 1840 the *maʾmūrs* were almost all Egyptians.

The need for trained staff led the viceroy to develop, albeit in a rudimentary form, the first system of secular state education in a Muslim country. It developed in a haphazard fashion, to meet the needs of the new army and bureaucracy. A number of schools providing technical instruction of various kinds appeared sporadically. The first of them, significantly, was a school of surveying, established in 1816. The relevance of this to Muḥammad ʿAlī's agrarian reorganization is obvious.

[1] Like Bonaparte, Muḥammad ʿAlī experimented briefly with a consultative body. This was the Advisory Council (*Majlis al-mashwara*), which met in 1829, under the presidency of Ibrāhīm Pasha. It was composed of 156 members, including officials, *ʿulamāʾ* and notables.

The medical needs of the new army led to the foundation, in 1827, of a school of medicine, the director of which, Clot Bey, was one of Muḥammad ʿAlī's best-known French advisers. A vital part was played, in the system of teaching, by the translators, who rendered the French lectures of the instructors into the Arabic of the students. In 1836 a school of languages was set up, under the direction of Rifāʿa Rāfiʿ al-Ṭahṭāwī, the first of a succession of Egyptians who have sought to interpret European culture to Muslim readers. The cultural significance of the school was greater than its name might suggest. The curriculum comprised the study of Arabic, French, Turkish and Persian, as well as some Italian and English: it also included some literature, history, geography and law. In 1841 al-Ṭahṭāwī also took charge of a bureau of translation attached to the school, and he himself translated about a score of works.

This activity in translation would have had but a limited effect had it not been for the establishment of a government printing press at Būlāq, about the year 1822. This was not strictly the first press in Egypt: there had been a Hebrew press as early as the sixteenth century. The first Arabic press had been brought to the country by Bonaparte in 1798, and was taken away by the French when they evacuated. Only with the opening of the Būlāq press, however, did printing begin to make a contribution to the cultural life of Egypt.

The training of technicians and experts of various kinds was also fostered by the sending of educational missions to Europe. The earliest of these were sent to Italy in about 1813, but on a larger and more systematic scale they began in 1826. Between that date and 1847, nine missions, composed of 219 members, were sent, almost entirely to France, although some students visited Britain and Austria. Among the Egyptians who first made personal contact with Europe in this way was al-Ṭahṭāwī, who spent five years in Paris as the *imām* of the students of the first mission there.

The administrative reorganization of 1837 resulted in the setting up of a Department of Schools (*Dīwān al-Madāris*). Under its auspices, the range of the educational system was widened by the foundation of 'preparatory' schools in Cairo, Alexandria and the provinces, to feed the specialist higher schools. Many of these projected schools failed to survive: the difficulties of staffing them were immense, while parents were reluctant to send their sons as pupils, seeing in the schools a kind of conscription. The pupils were, in fact, regarded as government employees in embryo; besides being boarded and lodged, they were provided with clothes, and received pay on a graduated scale.

The phrase, 'the founder of modern Egypt', has become a cliché in referring to Muḥammad ʿAlī. His character and achievements have been excessively lauded by writers, both foreign and Egyptian, from his own times down to the fall of his house in 1952. Essentially, he was the last of the military adventurers who from time to time seized power in the Ottoman provinces, and gave their exploits a cloak of legitimacy. He was fortunate in the time and place of his emergence: Egypt after the French occupation was in a state of anarchy, while the feebleness of the central Ottoman government during the two decades between the deposition of Selim III and the massacre of the Janissaries gave him an invaluable opportunity to build up his strength. He had the ability to remodel his military forces and administration, adopting European models, in order to create a centralized despotism and steal a march on his suzerain. Here, too, he was fortunate, in that the collapse of the Napoleonic empire made available the services of talented soldiers and technicians, whose careers in Europe had been cut short. Admittedly, the changes which he introduced brought about radical alterations in the society, culture and political life of Egypt, but these were by-products of his immense ambitions for himself and his family. He may have identified Egypt with himself: he never identified himself with the Egyptians.

14

Egypt at the Crossroads

In the generation which followed the death of Muḥammad ʿAlī Pasha, the situation of Egypt underwent profound changes. Although the old viceroy had failed to keep his empire (apart from the Sudanese provinces, which were geographically remote and politically unimportant), he bequeathed to his successors an hereditary throne, a strong government, an effective army, and a country potentially the richest in the Near East. Within Egypt the Ottoman sultan's authority was nominal, while the European powers might influence but could not control his policy. He had acquired a genuine autonomy, partly through his own abilities, and partly because of the posture of international relations in his time. The great themes of Muḥammad ʿAlī's reign are taken up under his successors: relations with the sultan, relations with the great powers, internal reorganization, the development of an African empire. But the delicate balance of interests among the parties concerned, which had been maintained while Muḥammad ʿAlī lived, was to be shaken irreparably in the following decades. After a period of hectic brilliance in the days of Khedive Ismāʿīl, the hereditary viceroyalty was to approach its nadir with his deposition in 1879.

The firman of 1841 had conferred the right of succession to the viceroyalty on the eldest prince of Muḥammad ʿAlī's family. When he became too old to rule, therefore, he was succeeded by Ibrāhīm, who was formally invested in July 1848 but died in November of the same year. He was followed by ʿAbbās Ḥilmī I, the son of Aḥmad Tusun Pasha, who had died in 1816. When ʿAbbās was murdered, in July 1854, the viceroyalty passed to his uncle, Muḥammad Saʿīd, the fourth son of Muḥammad ʿAlī. He died in 1863 and was succeeded by Ismāʿīl, the son of Ibrāhīm.

The three successors of Ibrāhīm, whose reigns form the subject of this chapter, were men of very diverse characters. ʿAbbās I has usually been depicted as a morose reactionary, Saʿīd as frivolous and indolent, Ismāʿīl as an extravagant megalomaniac. While all of them undoubtedly had grave defects as rulers, there is an element of caricature in the textbook representations of them. Too much reliance has been placed on accounts written by contemporary European observers, who were interested partisans, for or against the viceroys. In later times, historical writing on the period had swung between the adulation common in the closing years of the dynasty and the denigration which has followed its fall. A balanced assessment of these men, as individuals and as rulers, has yet to be made.

Unsympathetic views of ʿAbbās I in particular have been common, partly because his reign in several respects runs counter to the main currents of Egyptian history between 1805 and 1882. He seems to have been a perfectly genuine traditionalist who disliked Europeans, resented their ubiquity in Egypt, and mistrusted his grandfather's westernizing innovations. This was an intelligible point of view, but it was not likely to commend itself either to the Europeans who found themselves deprived by ʿAbbās of lucrative employment, or to writers who regarded the westernization of traditional society as synonymous with progress. ʿAbbās's rejection of the West meant specifically the rejection of French technical advice and diplomatic support, which had played so large a part in the time of Muḥammad ʿAlī, and were to do so again under Saʿīd and Ismāʿīl. But rejection could not be absolute, and so ʿAbbās turned for support to Great Britain.

This diplomatic switch was necessitated by a crisis of relations between the viceroy and the sultan, which was the principal problem of ʿAbbās's reign. The Ottoman government had conceded, reluctantly and under pressure, the hereditary viceroyalty in 1841; it had never given up hope of resuming control over Egypt, and the course of events from 1848 seemed to offer a series of opportunities. The succession of Ibrāhīm, and then of ʿAbbās, threatened in each case a crisis, which was, however, averted. After his accession, ʿAbbās was at first demonstratively loyal to the sultan, an attitude which suggested to some observers that the autonomy won by Muḥammad ʿAlī was being relinquished. ʿAbbās's behaviour in these early months may be explained partly by his deference to tradition: not only was the sultan his legitimate suzerain, but the Ottoman connection was a safeguard, if a feeble one, against the intervention of the European powers and their nationals in the life of Egypt But ʿAbbās was a true member of his dynasty: he had no intention of abandoning the substance of his autonomy, which he sought to secure by evicting the French and turning to the sultan. It followed logically that if the Ottoman government tried to limit ʿAbbās's freedom of action within Egypt, a stubborn resistance might be expected from the viceroy

This indeed occurred. The leading Ottoman statesman at this juncture was Mustafa Reshid Pasha (1800–58), six times grand vezir and one o the principal initiators of the *Tanzimat* reforms. The antagonism which ʿAbbās had aroused among some of the leading men in Egypt, as well as within the viceregal family, seemed to Reshid to offer a favourable opportunity for intervention. If ʿAbbās could be weakened or removed, Ottoman control could be introduced over the internal affairs of Egypt, and the *Tanzimat* implemented as elsewhere in the empire. ʿAbbās, who was well aware that relations with the Ottoman government were deteriorating, sought in September 1850 the help of Britain; in return for which he was prepared to allow a railway to be built between Alexandria and Cairo to facilitate British communications with India. The crisis developed around two points: the right of ʿAbbās to sanction such a railway without reference to the sultan, and the requirement of the Ottoman government that the viceroy should receive into Egypt the new Ottoman penal code of 1851, which formed part of the *Tanzimat* regulations. Besides the matter of principle concerning the general applicability of the *Tanzimat* to Egypt, there was a specific point at issue, since the code of 1851 required that no murderer should be executed without the sultan's confirmation of the death sentence. For the viceroy to accept this restriction on his powers would seriously hamper the effectiveness of his administration.

The crisis was ultimately solved by negotiations, in which the British, who in different ways were committed to both the sultan and the viceroy, played an important part. The railway question was the first to be solved. ʿAbbās formally requested the sultan's permission to authorize the construction of the railway, and this was granted in October 1851. The settlement had three aspects, which were to be significant in the future. First, ʿAbbās had secured in practice his autonomy in internal matters. Secondly, the Ottoman government had asserted the principle that no major public works were to be undertaken without the sultan's consent. Thirdly, British mediation had been indispensable in bringing the parties to a settlement. Negotiations over the *Tanzimat* were next resumed, and, again with British mediation, brought to a successful conclusion. A compromise was reached over the death penalty, the right to confirm which was granted, subject to certain limitations, and for a period of seven years only, to the viceroy. A form of the *Tanzimat* code appropriate to Egypt was then devised, but seems not to have been implemented until the beginning of Saʿīd's reign.

ʿAbbās I thus succeeded in handing on the autonomous viceroyalty of Egypt intact to his successors. There was no attempt to infringe the viceregal powers under Saʿīd, although the cutting of the Suez Canal gave rise, as we shall see, to a situation resembling, in an aggravated form, that which had developed over ʿAbbās's railway project. On this occasion, however, the crisis was much more one between Britain and France than between the viceroy and the sultan.[1] The reign of Ismāʿīl (1863–79) was almost exactly contemporary with that of Sultan Abdülaziz (1861–76), and relations between the two rulers were usually friendly. Shortly after his accession, Ismāʿīl went to Istanbul to be invested by the sultan as viceroy. Later in 1863 Abdülaziz himself visited Egypt (the first sultan to do so since Selim I), and displayed much benevolence towards Ismāʿīl. This cordiality enabled the viceroy to acquire new privileges. The first of these concerned the succession. The provision in the firman of 1841 that it should pass to the eldest male, following current Ottoman practice,[2] had twice caused trouble at a change of ruler. Before Ibrāhīm died in 1848, he had tried to exclude ʿAbbās Ḥilmī from the succession, in favour of his own eldest son. When ʿAbbās was murdered, his death was concealed for twenty-four hours in order that his son might take the throne, instead of Saʿīd. Both these plots were defeated, however, and at Saʿīd's own death, Ismāʿīl succeeded without difficulty: he had, in fact, already acted as regent for Saʿīd on two occasions. After his accession, he sought legitimately to establish the succession by primogeniture in his own line. This he achieved, after a visit to Istanbul, by obtaining a firman from the sultan in May 1866. In return, the annual tribute paid by Egypt was almost doubled. All the subsequent rulers of Egypt were descended from Ismāʿīl, although the principle of strict primogeniture was twice abandoned.[3]

Ismāʿīl was further anxious to obtain a title which would indicate the superiority of his status to that of other Ottoman governors, who, like him, were entitled *vali* (Arabic, *wālī*). Unofficially, his predecessors had used the title of 'khedive' (Arabic, *khidīwī*; Turkish, *hidiv*; from the Persian *khidīv*, 'king'): the Department of the Interior under Muḥammad ʿAlī was called *Dīwān al-Khidīwī*. By a firman of 8 June 1867 the title was formally conferred upon Ismāʿīl.[4] Ismāʿīl obtained his new title partly by lavish gifts in Istanbul, partly by supplying the sultan with

[1] See below, pp. 198–201.

[2] See above, p. 62.

[3] Both Ḥusayn Kāmil (1914–17) and Fu'ād (1917–36) were sons of Ismāʿīl.

[4] Ismāʿīl would have liked the title of *ʿazīz*, for the significance of which, see above, p. 96. It is also a synonym for God, and formed part of the sultan's own name, ʿAbd al-ʿAzīz ('the slave of the Mighty One'), which might have acquired an undesirable significance if the title had been granted to Ismāʿīl.

troops to suppress a rising in Crete, partly by a blackmailing threat to withdraw them. After the conferment of the title, a period of tension developed between the viceroy and the sultan. The Suez Canal was steadily nearing completion, and in the summer of 1869, Ismāʿīl made a tour of Europe to invite the sovereigns to its opening festivities. His demeanour, as of an independent ruler, as well as the increase in his military forces, alarmed and annoyed the Ottoman government, which demanded a reduction of the Egyptian troops, war-vessels and armaments, and placed restrictions on the financial autonomy of the khedive. After an acute crisis, better relations were re-established, and a firman of 8 June 1873 consolidated and confirmed all the previous grants of privileges.[1]

Ismāʿīl had thus been notably successful in excluding Ottoman power from Egypt. In his dealings with the Europeans he was far less fortunate. Two principal questions of diplomatic significance occupied his reign; the Capitulations, and international communications. Both these matters had their origins before his accession, and to their past history we must first turn.

The Capitulations were commercial treaties by which the Ottoman sultans regulated the conditions of trade with Christian powers. As the empire declined, the privileges granted to foreign merchants became rights extravagantly and insolently asserted, and claimed not only by nations of European states but by people of local origin, who, by one means or another, had acquired consular protection. A problem to administrators throughout the Ottoman Empire, the Capitulations were a particularly serious one in nineteenth-century Egypt, with its rapidly growing foreign communities, its expanding economy, and the appetite of its rulers for political autonomy. There were seventeen different consular jurisdictions, each administering a different law. Conflicts of jurisdiction, when one party was an Ottoman subject, or where the two were nationals of different states, were of frequent occurrence. Arbitration was subject to diplomatic pressure. Since foreign nationals could not be brought before the local criminal courts, were virtually immune from domiciliary inspection by the local police, and were in practice able to escape much of the burden of local taxation, the foreign communities and their hangers-on constituted great enclaves of privilege within Egypt.

During the reign of Muḥammad ʿAlī, the status of the foreign communities under the Capitulations does not seem to have constituted a

[1] Text in Hurewitz, i, 174–7.

serious problem. By Saʿīd's time the situation had changed, and Ismāʿīl, while acting as regent in 1862, began to take the first tentative steps to modify the capitulatory régime. A circular was sent to the consulates, containing a draft regulation providing for the arrest and interrogation of foreign nationals, but the project met with no encouragement. Having become viceroy, Ismāʿīl renewed his efforts. The necessary plans were made and negotiations conducted, by his very able Armenian minister, Nubar Pasha (1825–99). The opening shot in the campaign was a memorandum, submitted by Nubar in August 1867, in which he proposed to unify the system of justice in Egypt by establishing Mixed Courts, staffed by both Egyptian and foreign judges, the latter being nominated by the khedivial government. The Mixed Courts would administer codes of law drawn up by an international commission on the basis of French law. The courts would deal with both civil and criminal cases, and the jurisdiction of the consuls would be restricted to their own nationals.

These proposals were wholly rejected by France. The other powers concerned accepted them with varying degrees of reserve. Negotiations dragged on over the next six years, but in 1873 the powers, with the exception of France, accepted Nubar's project in its final form, and also the six law-codes which the Mixed Courts would apply. France concurred in the following year, and the new courts were inaugurated in 1875. They did not represent the abrogation of the Capitulations, but rather a modification of the capitulatory régime in a limited but important field. In the event, the Capitulations were not abolished until 1937, when the Republic of Turkey and the Kingdom of Egypt had succeeded the Ottoman Empire and the Khedivate.

The first half of the nineteenth century witnessed the growing importance of Egypt as the channel of a vital route between Europe and the East—more specifically, between Great Britain and India. Although the potential importance of Egypt in this respect had been perceived in the eighteenth century by some observers, it did not become a matter of serious politics until after the French occupation of Egypt. At that time a preliminary survey of the isthmus of Suez was made, and a canal linking the Red Sea with the Nile was projected, but the French had neither time nor opportunity to proceed with this. British interest in communications passing through the Near East did not really develop until the reign of Muḥammad ʿAlī. The pioneer was Thomas Waghorn, who in 1829 went from London to Bombay in the record travelling time of forty and a half days. In 1837 regular steamship services began to link

Britain with Alexandria, and Suez with Bombay, and the British mails were sent by this means to India. The arrangements for their transit through Egypt by the 'Overland Route' were for some years in Waghorn's hands, before they were transferred to a company created by the viceroy. The transit-time from London to Bombay was reduced to thirty-one days, as against the three months taken by the journey round the Cape of Good Hope. At the same time, the possibilities of an alternative route, across northern Syria and down the Euphrates, were being considered, but this proved to be less effective than the Egyptian route.

Muḥammad ʿAlī favoured and assisted the British in developing the Overland Route, although when British proposals to build a railway were put to him, he temporized. Nor did he show any enthusiasm for the project of a Suez canal, which in France particularly continued to attract the interest of many. The value of the Overland Route was enhanced, and the grasp of the British on the international communications of Egypt was confirmed, when ʿAbbās I agreed to the construction of a railway from Alexandria to Cairo. The repercussions of this on the viceroy's relations with his suzerain have already been described. The contract was signed in July 1851, and Robert Stephenson was put in charge of the work. The line to Cairo was not completed until 1856, in the reign of Saʿīd, to be followed by a railway linking Cairo with Suez. But just at this point, the pre-eminence of the Overland Route was threatened by the viceroy's interest in the Suez Canal project.

The protagonist of the canal scheme was at this time Ferdinand de Lesseps, a former member of the French consular service, who, during Muḥammad ʿAlī's lifetime, had been a friend of Saʿīd. On Saʿīd's accession, the friendship was renewed, and de Lesseps was warmly welcomed to Egypt by the new viceroy, who, on 15 November 1854, granted him a concession for the construction of a canal from the Red Sea to the Mediterranean. This was, of course, only the first small step towards the realization of de Lesseps's dreams. The technical soundness of the scheme was far from established, while the project would meet with opposition, both from vested interests in the existing means of communications,[1] and from the British government, which in effect controlled both the Cape and Overland Routes to India. Finally, the concession would require the sultan's ratification. Hence the controversy

[1] Robert Stephenson's last speech in the House of Commons, as M.P. for Whitley, was a denunciation of the scheme: 'Honourable members talk about a canal. A canal is impossible—the thing would only be a ditch.' S. Smiles, *Lives of the engineers*, London 1862, iii, 463.

of the canal developed into a diplomatic struggle between France and Britain at Istanbul.

In the opening stages, however, the government of Napoleon III was by no means committed to the support of de Lesseps. This was the time of the Crimean War, when France and Britain were allied with the Ottoman Empire against Russia. De Lesseps therefore first proceeded on his own. He began, wisely, by organizing an international commission of experts who, after an examination of the project during which some of them visited Egypt, made a preliminary report in January 1856, stating that the construction of a waterway directly linking the Red Sea with the Mediterranean was feasible. Saʿīd forthwith, on 5 January 1856, issued a second and more detailed act of concession, which was followed by a regulation on 20 July 1856 concerning the employment of Egyptian labour.[1] Two matters assumed great importance in the subsequent controversy. First, the Suez Canal Company,[2] which was formed to implement the concession, was granted a strip of land linking the Nile with the canal site. Here a fresh-water canal (the Sweetwater Canal) was constructed, and the strip of land would be held free of taxation, while the company would enjoy all benefits from its cultivation. Secondly, the viceroy undertook to supply labour on demand for the construction of the canal.

In the autumn of 1858 a change took place in the attitude of Napoleon III and the French government towards the project. Hitherto, the French attitude had been chilly, and any appearance of a conflict with British interests had been avoided. The change which then appeared has been plausibly connected with the financial arrangements made by the Suez Canal Company about this time. Founder shares, entitling the holders to 10 per cent of the net profits of the company, were distributed to persons whose names were not divulged. De Lesseps now claimed to act, in the formation of the company, by virtue of an exclusive mandate and special instructions from the viceroy. He failed to indicate that the ratification of the sultan for the enterprise had yet to be obtained. He placed to the viceroy's account a large number of shares which had not been taken up by the public. Thus he gave to the company an appearance of greater political and financial backing than it in fact possessed. The

[1] The translated text of the two acts of concession of 1854 and 1856 may be found in H. J. Schonfield, *The Suez Canal in world affairs*, London 1952, 146–56. Another translation of the 1856 concession is in Hurewitz, i, 146–9. The text of the controversial first article of the regulation of 20 July 1856 is given by A. Sammarco in *Précis de l'histoire d'Égypte*, iv, Rome 1935, 146.

[2] The official title of the Company was *Compagnie universelle du Canal maritime de Suez*.

immediate consequence was a breach with Saʿīd, who disavowed his acts. This did not deter de Lesseps, who, on 25 April 1859, announced the opening of work on the canal. Both the viceroy and the sultan forbade him to proceed. De Lesseps brought fresh influence to bear on Napoleon III, and the ultimatum was quietly ignored.

The centre of intrigue was next transferred to Istanbul, where British influence supported the sultan's refusal to ratify the act of concession. A deadlock developed. Then in January 1863 Saʿīd died, to be succeeded by the more dynamic Ismāʿīl. In principle, the new viceroy was in favour of the canal, but he resented the very generous concessions which Saʿīd had made to de Lesseps, particularly on the two points of the Sweetwater Canal concession, and the unlimited provision of labour, which was adversely affecting the agricultural economy of Egypt. This later concession, which amounted in practice to a system of forced labour and which conflicted with Ottoman legislation abolishing slavery and forced labour, was also used by the British ambassador in Istanbul as a principal argument against ratification. Ismāʿīl was, however, prepared to compromise. He paid in full for the additional shares which de Lesseps had unscrupulously forced on Saʿīd, thus bringing his personal holding up to 177,642 out of 400,000 ordinary shares. He charged Nubar Pasha with the task of negotiating an agreement with the company over the two disputed concessions. Napoleon III, hardly a disinterested party, was invited to act as arbitrator. The commission which he set up found that the company was rightfully entitled both to its land and its labour. Since Nubar had already reached agreement with the company over the abolition of forced labour, and the retrocession of the disputed territory, the commission imposed an indemnity on the viceroy, totalling a little over £3,000,000, and payable over fifteen years.

This compromise did not immediately overcome the obstacle at Istanbul, but after renewed French pressure there, the sultan, on 19 March 1866, issued a firman authorizing the cutting of the canal. As we have seen, work had in fact begun seven years previously: but it had stagnated, owing to the political difficulties encountered by the company. It was now resumed, and three years later the canal was ready for its formal inauguration. This was the most brilliant state occasion of Ismāʿīl's reign. His tour of Europe in the summer of 1869 had attracted several royal guests to the opening, which was performed by the Empress of the French, Eugénie, on board her imperial yacht. The festivities of 17 November 1869 marked the zenith of Khedive Ismāʿīl. To him and to Egypt, however, the cutting of the Suez Canal left a legacy of troubles.

During the reigns of ʿAbbās I, Saʿīd and Ismāʿīl, important changes were taking place in the agrarian life of Egypt. The traditional village community, as it had survived down to the last years of Muḥammad ʿAlī, was breaking up. The influence of European social and legal ideas, and the spread of a new cash-crop, cotton, were working in the same direction, to substitute a differentiated rural society, and an individualistic economy, for the collective functions of the old village community. No important changes took place under ʿAbbās I, but legislation in Saʿīd's reign conferred on the peasantry rights of inheritance in their land and powers of disposal (falling short, however, of full proprietorship) such as they had never known before. This tendency continued under Ismāʿīl, whose *Muqābala* Law of 1871 granted full rights of ownership to peasants paying the due known as the *muqabāla*.[1] The increasing rights of the peasants in their land did not necessarily imply an improvement in their economic condition. On the contrary, flight from the land was a recurrent phenomenon in this period, as it had been under Muḥammad ʿAlī, and was the normal response to intolerable increases in taxation. An anomaly of the fiscal system in this period was that peasant land was heavily taxed, whereas the great estates, *jifliks* and *ibʿādiyyāt*, were free of tax until 1854, and thereafter subject to lower rates than peasant land. The military conscription and the *corvée*, or requirement of forced labour, also contributed to rural depopulation and impoverishment.

One section of the peasantry was, however, increasing in prosperity and importance in these decades. This was the class of village headmen (sing. *shaykh al-balad*).[2] Appointed under the old régime by the *multazims*, they had become agents of the government, in consequence of Muḥammad ʿAlī's resumption of the *iltizāms*. Although their functions changed with the substitution of individual for collective ownership of land, their social and economic status tended to rise, until they were at their height under Ismāʿīl. They became substantial landowners, with considerable political influence in their localities.[3] Only in the reign of Saʿīd had they suffered a setback, and one of the measures he directed against them had important consequences. On his accession, he ended

[1] See below, p. 208.

[2] The term *ʿumda* first appeared about the middle of the nineteenth century, and superseded the title *shaykh al-balad* towards the end of the century: cf. G. Baer, 'The Village Shaykh in Modern Egypt (1800–1950)', *Studies in Islamic history and civilization: Scripta Hierosolymitana*, ix, Jerusalem 1961, 121–3.

[3] The rising standard of living of the prosperous peasantry was shown, *inter alia* by the purchase of Circassian female slaves. The domestic and social consequences of acquiring this new status-symbol have been amusingly described by M. Rifaat, *The awakening of modern Egypt*, London 1947, 101–2.

the exemption of the headmen's sons from military conscription. Although the measure was resented, it resulted in the strengthening of the Egyptian rank-and-file of the army by men who had come from prosperous and locally influential homes. It was significant that Saʿīd also opened the higher ranks in the army to officers drawn from these peasant conscripts. Among them was a certain Aḥmad ʿUrābī, the son of a village headman in the Sharqiyya.

In quite a different category from these prosperous peasants were the great landowners, whose estates were *jifliks*, *ibʿādiyyāt* or converted *ʿuhdas*, swollen by lands abandoned by their cultivators. At the core of this class were members of the viceregal family, not least Ismāʿīl himself. The élite of the Turco-Circassian officers and officials profited greatly from the grants of land made by the viceroys. These estates were not completely stable: political vicissitudes and personal indebtedness worked against their perpetuation, as did the fragmentation resulting from the Muslim law of inheritance. Nevertheless, by the time of Ismāʿīl, there had developed in Egypt something very like a Turkish-speaking landed aristocracy, the creation of the Turkish-speaking dynasty.

An important contributory factor to social change in rural Egypt was the development of cotton-growing. Short-staple cotton was a traditional crop in Egypt, but the long-staple variety was introduced in 1821, and was eagerly developed as a profitable cash-crop and government monopoly by Muḥammad ʿAlī.[1] Although a decline in quality set in, more and more land was devoted to the new crop, and its cultivation continued in the years which followed his death. The American Civil War (1861–5) put a premium on Egyptian cotton. From about 350,000 cantars[2] in 1850, the amount exported had risen to 2,000,000 cantars in 1865, while the price per cantar increased during the war-years almost fourfold. Cultivators and land-owners at all levels of society hastened to profit from the new crop, but at the end of the Civil War the inflated prices suddenly collapsed. For the first time, there appeared in Egypt a serious problem of peasant indebtedness, with its inevitable concomitants of mortgages, foreclosures and usurious loans. The village headmen, however,

[1] There have been various accounts of the place of origin of the long-staple cotton introduced into Egypt, but the evidence cited by Richard Hill, *Egypt in the Sudan 1820–1881*, London 1959, 51–2, seems to confirm the belief that it was brought from the Abyssinian borders of the Egyptian Sudan. Maḥū Bey, who gave his name to the strain, was commander-in-chief in the Sudan in 1825–6. See also Helen Anne B. Rivlin, *The agricultural policy of Muḥammad ʿAlī in Egypt*, Cambridge, Mass., 1961, 335–6, n. 5.

[2] The cantar of cotton weighs just over 99 lbs.

profited from the financial crisis, since they were able to lend money to their bankrupt neighbours.

The prestige and political importance of the village headmen was enhanced by an important constitutional development introduced by Ismāʿīl. This was the creation of a quasi-parliamentary body, the Assembly of Delegates (*Majlis Shūrā al-Nuwwāb*), which was set up in November 1866. It consisted of seventy-five members, chosen (ostensibly at least) by indirect election. Only five represented the great towns of Cairo and Alexandria while the great majority of the members (from fifty-eight to sixty-four in different sessions) were village headmen. They were elected for a term of three years. Their powers were severely limited by the Organic Law of November 1866, which gave the khedive control over the Assembly. Nevertheless, as we shall see, a degree of independence of, and opposition to, the khedivial government developed as time went on.

Ismāʿīl's motives in setting up the Assembly of Delegates have been the subject of speculation, since in 1866 there were no very apparent reasons why he should voluntarily establish even so limited a check upon his despotism. It has been suggested that the Assembly was intended as a control over the village shaykhs, that it was deliberately constituted to counterbalance the power of the Turco-Circassian élite, and that it was a façade of constitutionalism designed to win sympathy and loans from France and Britain. There may well be something in all these explanations, but two other considerations should be borne in mind. There were two fairly recent Egyptian precedents for consultative assemblies working in association with an autocratic administration: Bonaparte's General *Divan* of October 1798 and, a closer parallel, the Advisory Council (*Majlis al-Mashwara*) set up by Muḥammad ʿAlī in 1829.[1] Moreover, the decade in which Ismāʿīl began his constitutional experiment was one in which parliamentary institutions had an obvious attraction for the Near Eastern statesmen and political thinkers. In 1861 the Bey of Tunis, whose position as an autonomous and autocratic vassal of the sultan resembled that of Ismāʿīl, granted a constitution including a consultative council. This and the Egyptian Assembly preceded any Ottoman parliamentary body, but a number of Turkish writers and politicians, stimulated into reaction against the increasing autocracy of Sultan Abdülaziz, were developing ideas of constitutional reform.

Under Ismāʿīl, Western influences on Egyptian education and culture

[1] See above, p. 190, n. 1.

became very marked. The educational developments of Muḥammad ʿAlī's time had been undone by ʿAbbās I. The change of atmosphere is symbolized in the career of al-Ṭahṭāwī.[1] In 1850 he was sent to virtual banishment in Khartoum, and the school of languages was closed. On Saʿīd's accession, al-Ṭahṭāwī returned to Egypt and resumed his work as a teacher and translator. It was not, however, until the reign of Ismāʿīl that the revival of education in Egypt really began. Education ceased to be a function of military organization. A Ministry of Education was set up, the most distinguished head of which was ʿAlī Pasha Mubārak (1824–93). The son of a village shaykh, he was a scholar whose monumental work, *al-Khiṭaṭ al-jadīda*, is a principal source of information on nineteenth-century Egypt. While ʿAlī Mubārak was minister, the important law of 1868 was passed which established the state system of education. Here a foundation had been laid by Muḥammad ʿAlī, but Ismāʿīl's reign saw a radical innovation in the opening of schools for girls, the first, in 1873, being founded by a wife of the khedive.

The reign of Ismāʿīl also saw the establishment of a group of learned institutions and societies, modelled on European and Ottoman prototypes. Among these was the Khedivial Library (now the Egyptian National Library), founded in 1870. ʿAlī Mubārak played an important part in building up its collection from the libraries of mosques and other sources. The foundation of the Egyptian Museum in 1863 indicated the development of Egyptology and the growing awareness among westernized Egyptians of their country's pre-Islamic past. The first of these learned societies, the *Institut Égyptien*, had already been founded in 1859, during the reign of Saʿīd. Its name evoked the *Institut d'Égypte*, which had flourished brilliantly and briefly during the French Occupation. The revived *Institut* had both European and Egyptian members. A purely Egyptian society was *Jamʿiyyat al-Maʿārif*, founded in 1868, which had as its principal function the publication of Arabic manuscripts.[2] The expansion of Ismāʿīl's African empire was reflected in the foundation in 1875 of the Khedivial Geographical Society, devoted to geographical research, and especially to African discovery.

The first Arabic newspaper was the official Egyptian gazette, *al-Waqāʾiʿ al-Miṣriyya*,[3] which began to appear, by Muḥammad ʿAlī's orders, in 1828. It did not become a daily until the reign of Ismāʿīl, when

[1] For al-Ṭahṭāwī's earlier career, see above, p. 191.

[2] The Ottoman learned societies, *Enjümen-i Danish* (an academy of letters and sciences), and *Jemiyet-i Ilmiye-i Osmaniye* (a scientific body), were founded in 1851 and 1861 respectively.

[3] Among the editors of *al-Waqāʾiʿ* were al-Ṭahṭāwī and Muḥammad ʿAbduh.

a number of other periodicals were started by private persons.[1] The first critical political paper was founded in 1866, and supressed in 1872. An important stage in the development of the Egyptian press was reached towards the end of Ismāʿīl's reign, when journalists of Lebanese origin, escaping from Ottoman autocracy, found greater freedom of expression under the khedive. Notable among these immigrants were the brothers Salīm and Bishāra Taqlā, who began in 1876 to publish *al-Ahrām*, in its heyday the greatest journal to appear in Arabic.

The reign of Ismāʿīl was also a period of imperial expansion into the heart of Africa. Here, as in other respects, he continued developments begun by Muḥammad ʿAlī, which had languished under ʿAbbās I and Saʿīd. The conquest of Nubia, Sennar and Kordofan had given Muḥammad ʿAlī the nucleus of an empire, which, however, proved far less useful and profitable than he had hoped. Later in his reign, his conquests had been rounded out by the occupation of the Tāka, the district around the present town of Kasala, and by the lease from the sultan of the ancient Ottoman Red Sea ports of Suakin and Massawa. The ports reverted to the sultan in 1846, and were not again granted to a ruler of Egypt until 1865. Saʿīd showed sufficient interest in his Sudanese provinces to visit them, although what he saw almost determined him to abandon them. In the administration of the Sudan, the reigns of ʿAbbās and Saʿīd were a time of feebleness and vacillation.

The expansion of Egyptian rule under Ismāʿil had been prepared in Muḥammad ʿAlī's reign by a series of voyages of discovery between 1839 and 1842, directed by an intrepid Turkish sailor, Salīm Qabūdān. Salīm's expeditions were the first to break through the hostile tribes and geographical obstacles that barred the way up the White Nile. They passed far south of the Arabic-speaking Sudanese peoples, whose territories were the limit of Muḥammad ʿAlī's conquests, and reached a point about 5°N of the Equator. Salīm and his crews made neither conquest nor settlement, but they opened the way to the penetration of the Upper Nile. For a few years the administration prevented general access to the south, but in 1851, as a result of a combined lobby of Catholic missionaries and European traders, the barriers were swept away. The impact of the ivory merchants on the tribal societies of the Upper Nile was disastrous. They were beyond the range of control from Khartoum or Cairo, and, in the course of a few years, slave-trading

[1] The most important Arabic newspaper of this period was, however, *al-Jawāʾib*. which was edited by a Lebanese, Aḥmad Fāris al-Shidyāq, and published in Istanbul. It circulated in Egypt as elsewhere in the Arab provinces of the Ottoman Empire.

grew up as an ancillary to the quest for ivory. At a slightly later date, the Baḥr al-Ghazāl, the great basin of the western tributaries of the Upper Nile, was also penetrated, and another predatory trading community established itself beyond the existing limits of the Egyptian Sudan. By the time that Ismāʿīl succeeded to the viceroyalty, the domination of the European traders on the Upper Nile was at an end. Both there and in the Baḥr al-Ghazāl the ivory and slave trade was controlled by merchant-princes of Egyptian, Sudanese or Syrian origin.

To bring these vast southern regions under his control was a project that appealed to Ismāʿīl. It would, moreover, commend itself to European opinion, since the suppression of the African slave-trade was a dominant aim of humanitarians, especially, perhaps, in Britain. The establishment of a new southern province, with its headquarters at Fashoda on the White Nile, marked the beginning of the expansion of khedivial rule. The obstructiveness of the Turco-Egyptian officials, as well as the complex ramifications of the slave-trade in the Sudan, led Ismāʿīl to recruit Europeans and Americans for his expansionist programme. An expedition commanded by Sir Samuel Baker carried the Ottoman flag to the equatorial lakes, and left a scattering of garrisons to represent khedivial authority on the Upper Nile. Baker's four years in the south (1869–73) did little towards either establishing an administration or suppressing the slave-trade. The Baḥr al-Ghazāl also was nominally attached to the khedive's dominions at this time, when, in 1873, Ismāʿīl appointed the Sudanese merchant-prince, al-Zubayr Raḥma, as governor of the region, in which he was already the dominant figure.

The immense task of organizing the territories of the Upper Nile fell to another Englishman, Charles George Gordon. While he was serving there between 1874 and 1876, the independent sultanate of Darfur, which the Defterdar had failed to conquer half a century before, was annexed by al-Zubayr. Shortly afterwards, al-Zubayr, while visiting the khedive, was detained in Cairo, and revolt flared out in the Baḥr al-Ghazāl. Gordon, appointed to govern the whole Sudan as *hükümdar*, strove with dynamic energy to overcome the host of administrative problems arising in the new province, as well as to suppress the slave-trade. He was assisted by a number of other Europeans: the Italians, Gessi in the Baḥr al-Ghazāl, and Messedaglia in Darfur; in the Equatorial Province, Emin, a German of Jewish descent, converted to Islam. But the task required resources of money and personnel which the khedive no longer possessed, and in 1880, shortly after Ismāʿīl's deposition, Gordon resigned.

Ismāʿīl's reign had also seen other attempts at imperial expansion. The cession of Suakin and Massawa to the viceroyalty in 1865 was followed by hostilities against Abyssinia. Their outcome was disastrous, two successive Egyptian expeditionary forces being defeated in 1875 and 1876. Elsewhere the khedive was more successful: in 1875 his troops occupied the Somali port of Zayla, and captured Harar, well within Abyssinian territory. This was not a haphazard adventure, but a bid for control of the approaches to the Red Sea, the western coast of which was almost wholly under khedivial rule.

These latest acquisitions were obtained at a time when the khedive's power was already on the wane. The real achievements, as well as the superficial magnificence, of his reign, had only been obtained at heavy financial cost. The situation was not entirely of his own making. Muḥammad ʿAlī was rarely free from financial difficulties, which led to excessive and abusive taxation and the introduction of such revenue-raising devices as the *ʿuhda*.[1] ʿAbbās, in spite of his numerous retrenchments, and his unadventurous policy, left the treasury in debt. Under Saʿīd the situation deteriorated. Not only did he leave, on his death, a debt of £7,000,000, but £3,000,000 of this was owing to a European banking house. Ismāʿīl was only too ready to follow his example, and by the end of his reign, the foreign financiers, backed by their governments, had a fast grip on the revenues of Egypt. By 1876 the Egyptian treasury, or the khedive (for there was then no substantial difference between Ismāʿīl's public and private liabilities), was in debt to nearly £100,000,000, of which £68,000,000 consisted of foreign loan.

By this time, Ismāʿīl was searching desperately for expedients to postpone bankruptcy. One such was the Law of the *Muqābala* in 1871, whereby the payment in advance of six years' land-tax would redeem half the tax in perpetuity, as well as confer rights of ownership on the holder of the land. The so-called *Rūznāmah* Loan of 1874 amounted in practice to a capital levy, since the loan was not returnable, and the interest was not regularly paid. Then in 1875 Ismāʿīl disposed of his last great asset, his shares in the Suez Canal Company. The story of their purchase by Disraeli for the British government, at a cost of £4,000,000, is well known. It was less of a bargain than Disraeli thought at first, since the shares did not give Britain control of the canal, although from the financial point of view it proved to be a profitable long-term investment.

During 1876 the autonomy of the khedive was limited by the increas-

[1]See above, pp. 188–9.

ing control of his international creditors. The crisis was precipitated by a report on Egyptian finance made, after a cursory enquiry, by Stephen Cave, an Englishman who was not, however, acting as a representative of the British government. In May 1876 Ismāʿīl set up an institution called the *Caisse de la Dette Publique*: its four members were British, French, Austrian and Italian respectively, and it was to organize the service of the debt.[1] Further pressure from the foreign bondholders led to the appointment in October of a British and a French controller, to supervise the revenue and expediture of Egypt: this system was known as the Dual Control. As yet the British government was not officially involved in these developments, but in March 1878 it joined with the French government to demand the setting up of an international commission of enquiry. This demanded that Ismāʿīl should accept the principle of ministerial responsibility for his acts of state, and should have a fixed civil list.

The khedive hastened to oblige. In August an international ministry was set up, headed by Nubar, and including a British minister of Finance and a French minister of Public Works. Franco-British control appeared to be effective, but Ismāʿīl was not yet at the end of his political resources. For several months he allowed the odium of financial retrenchment to attach itself to these aliens, while he himself played a waiting game. In February 1879 his opportunity came. Nubar and the minister of Finance, Sir Rivers Wilson, were mobbed in Cairo by army officers who had been put on half-pay, and were rescued from their predicament by the personal intervention of Ismāʿīl, who may well have instigated the incident. The next day he dismissed Nubar; and in April, supported by public opinion as expressed in the Assembly of Delegates, replaced the international ministry by one of his own choice under a man of constitutional views, Sharīf Pasha.

Ismāʿīl was now endeavouring to find support in Egypt against the danger of international control. On 17 May Sharīf submitted a fundamental law of his own drafting to the Assembly of Delegates. This was far more liberal than the laws of 1866 which had set up the Assembly, and would have given it control over the finances of Egypt. The project was popular, but the applause of the delegates could do nothing to strengthen Ismāʿīl's position externally. The French and British governments were determined that he must go. Since he would not abdicate

[1] The Ottoman treasury was facing a similar situation at about the same time. In October 1875 interest payments on the Ottoman debt were suspended, and in December 1881 a Council of the Public Debt was set up (after negotiation with the European bondholders), and certain revenues were reserved for the service of the debt.

he must be deposed. On 26 June 1879 he received a telegram from the grand vezir, addressed to 'the ex-Khedive Ismāʿīl Pasha'. His reign was at an end, and the viceregal throne passed to his son, Muḥammad Tawfīq (1852–92).

In the middle decades of the nineteenth century, Egypt was approaching a crossroads in her history. Of the three ways which opened before her, one led to full independence, another to reabsorption in the Ottoman Empire, the third to European control. By the time of the deposition of Khedive Ismāʿīl, the first two roads were already closed to her. During the decade that followed, she moved far along the path of European domination.

15

Egyptian Nationalism and the British Occupation

The deposition of Khedive Ismāʿīl by the Ottoman sultan under pressure from the European powers was a turning-point in the history of Egypt. Hitherto, in the three-quarters of a century during which Muḥammad ʿAlī and his dynasty had ruled, neither the sultan nor the powers had succeeded in placing any effective limitations on the internal autonomy of the viceroys. Muḥammad ʿAlī's incursions into foreign affairs and his attempts to build an empire in the Levant had been disastrously unsuccessful, but he and his successors had, stage by stage, imposed on their suzerain the recognition of their special position in Egypt and the Sudan. The last years of Ismāʿīl's reign had seen the ominous attempt at international control of the Egyptian finances, culminating in the experiment of an international ministry. In April 1879, however, the khedive still had the power to resume authority and defy his creditors. Only the act of deposition confirmed the effective and lasting infringement of khedivial autonomy, the extension of international control to the internal administration of Egypt.

International supervision was exercised through two instruments. The Dual Control of the Egyptian financial system was revived by the appointment of two controllers. The British nominee, Evelyn Baring (1841–1917), later Lord Cromer, was a newcomer to the Egyptian scene, which later he was to dominate for a quarter of a century. Secondly, an International Commission of Liquidation was appointed, with British, French, Austrian and Italian members. The outcome of their investigations was the promulgation, in July 1880, of a Law of Liquidation. This limited to about 50 per cent of the total revenue, the sum available to the Egyptian government for administrative expenses. The remainder was assigned to the *Caisse de la Dette* for service of the debt, while surplus revenue was paid into a sinking fund. The commissioners of the *Caisse de la Dette* had considerable powers over the administrative budget, which meant that representatives of the European powers could intervene in matters concerning the government and development of Egypt. Meanwhile the Assembly of Delegates had been dissolved in July 1879, and the constitutionalist prime minister, Sharīf Pasha, had been dismissed in the following month. Tawfīq appointed to the premiership a man of reactionary views, Riyāḍ Pasha. Thus the façade of khedivial autocracy was restored, while final authority in Egypt had passed to the great powers, especially France and Britain.

This was an inherently unstable situation. The force which was to upset it was one new in Egyptian history: the emergence of a nationalist movement. Its development had been fostered by several factors in Ismāʿīl's reign. By his constitutional experiments, Ismāʿīl had made possible the expression of the collective sentiments of the more prosperous peasantry. He himself had adroitly canalized their emotions to serve his own ends, but by so doing he had set in motion a force which his successor would be unable to control. At the same time, his policy had promoted discontent among the Egyptian army officers, who saw the khedive favouring the old Turco-Circassian élite to their own disadvantage. The last important military exploit of the reign had been the unsuccessful Abyssinian war, the failure of which was laid at the door o the Circassian general, Rātib Pasha. The resentment of the Egyptiar officers had been further provoked by financial economies made at thei expense in the last years of Ismāʿīl's rule: it flared out in the attack or Nubar and Rivers Wilson in February 1879. A third element in Egyptia nationalism was a militantly Islamic strain. This is a traditional ingredient in movements of opposition and protest in Muslim communities but at this period it was being particularly stimulated by the pan-Islami propagandist, Jamāl al-Dīn al-Afghānī, who was in Egypt from Marcl 1871 to September 1879, and had much influence on the students o al-Azhar in Cairo.

A secret society of army officers had come into existence in 1876 Among its members were three men who were to play a prominent par in the events of Tawfīq's reign: Aḥmad ʿUrābī, ʿAlī Fahmī and ʿAb al-ʿĀl Ḥilmī. Towards the end of Ismāʿīl's reign, in 1879, this secre society evolved into a nationalist organization, including religious leader and members of the Assembly of Delegates. Its members had links wit a prince of the viceregal family, Ḥalīm Pasha, the last surviving son c Muḥammad ʿAlī, who would have been Ismāʿīl's heir had the law c succession not been changed in 1866. The Patriotic Party (*al-Ḥizb a Waṭanī*) was not a political party in the Western sense, but a semi-secre semi-conspiratorial group, opportunist in its policy, and with a floatin membership around a permanent nucleus of Egyptian army officer At first, personal and group grievances rather than patriotic ain characterized the outlook of the members, whose target was originally the Turco-Circassian ruling élite. When hostility to the khedive and the foreigners developed, it was as a chain reaction.

The situation became critical in 1881, when it had become clear that Tawfīq was a man of straw, and when (as in 1879) members of the constitutional opposition combined with members of the military opposition. At the first stage, however, the revolt, which is associated with the name of ʿUrābī, was a struggle within the officer-corps of the army, culminating in a military mutiny. The minister for War in Riyāḍ's government was a Circassian, ʿUthmān Pasha Rifqī, whose policy alarmed and dissatisfied the Egyptian officers. In January 1881 the three colonels, Aḥmad ʿUrābī, ʿAlī Fahmī and ʿAbd al-ʿĀl Ḥilmī, addressed a petition to Riyād against Rifqī. On 1 February they were arrested and court-martialled, but the proceedings were interrupted by a mutiny which secured their release, and the capitulation of the government. Rifqī was dismissed, and the khedive appointed a new War minister, Maḥmūd Pasha Sāmī al-Bārūdī, who was known to be sympathetic to the ʿUrābī group.

In the months that followed, ʿUrābī and his friends became increasingly unsure of their victory and feared a counter-attack by their enemies. This seemed to be preparing, when, in August, al-Bārūdī was dismissed. To safeguard their position, they sought to widen the circle of their supporters by enlisting the support of the constitutionalist group. The critical event which ushered in the second stage of the revolt was a military demonstration outside the Abdin Palace in Cairo on 9 September 1881, when ʿUrābī confronted the khedive with three demands: the dismissal of Riyāḍ's ministry; the convocation of the Assembly of Delegates, which had not met for over two years; and the increase of the army to the limit of 18,000 men permitted by the sultan's firman. Once again, Tawfīq capitulated. Riyāḍ was dismissed, and Sharīf Pasha formed a new ministry, with al-Bārūdī back as minister for War.

The alliance between ʿUrabī and Sharīf was less solid than it appeared, and throughout the winter of 1881–2 a concealed struggle was taking place between the ministry and the Egyptian officers. The Assembly of Delegates met in December and contributed to the increasingly complex situation by attempting to increase its control over the government, especially in financial matters. In January 1882 the rising power of the military group was symbolized by ʿUrābī's entry into the ministry as under-secretary for War.

These developments were alarming to the European powers, especially to the British government, which feared for the security of the Suez Canal, and the French government, which was anxious for the foreign bondholders. While both were anxious to restore the authority of the khedive, and secure the system of international financial control, they did not wish to intervene forcibly in Egyptian affairs. On two occasions they sought to achieve their aims by bluff; each time the bluff went wrong, and in the end Egypt was occupied by British troops sent, ironically enough, by the Liberal and anti-imperialist government of Gladstone.

The first unsuccessful bluff was when the British and French governments, on 8 January 1882, sent a Joint Note declaring their support of the khedive.[1] This produced precisely the opposite effect to that intended. The position of the moderates, represented by Sharīf, became untenable. The mass of the Assembly of Delegates joined forces with the military group, and the way was opened to the development of anti-European nationalist feeling. In February the Assembly demanded Sharīf's resignation. For the third time the khedive capitulated. A new ministry was formed by al-Bārūdī, with ʿUrābī as minister for War.

The Joint Note marked the opening of the third stage of the ʿUrābī revolt, from which time it increasingly assumes the character of a genuine nationalist movement, directed against foreign control. Faced with what was, from their point of view, a deteriorating situation in Egypt, France and Britain sought a new means of breaking ʿUrābī's power without committing themselves to an invasion of Egypt. The British saw a way out in Ottoman intervention, for which the French showed no enthusiasm. At last the two powers agreed on a joint naval demonstration off Alexandria: another piece of bluff, intended to strengthen the hand of the khedive.

The Anglo-French fleet arrived off Alexandria on 19–20 May. A few days later the khedive dismissed al-Bārūdī, only to provoke so strong a popular reaction that, three days later, he was forced to reinstate ʿUrābī as minister for War. The bluff had failed and its failure had appalling consequences on 11 June, when murderous anti-European riots broke out in Alexandria, the prolonged tension of the time finding relief in xenophobia. Meanwhile a struggle was taking place within the Liberal Cabinet between those who were averse to direct intervention in Egypt and those who believed the national interests required forceful action. The riots at Alexandria, which were unjustly blamed on ʿUrābī, strengthened the hands of the latter group.

[1] Text in Hurewitz, i, 194–6.

Up to this point, the French had been the stronger and more determined partner, and the British government had acquiesced in such actions as the sending of the Joint Note, mainly to prevent unilateral French action in Egypt. During July the initiative passed to the British. An international conference which began to meet in Istanbul on 23 June was boycotted by the sultan, and the British failed to obtain either Ottoman intervention or any agreement among the powers on action. Once more a policy of bluff was adopted—this time by Britain alone. The British admiral off Alexandria was empowered to demand the cessation of work on forts commanding the harbour and to carry out a bombardment if this ultimatum were not complied with. Precisely what the British government hoped to achieve is not clear. The order seems to have been sent while the Cabinet was suffering from a fit of nerves over the security of the Suez Canal, even though ministers realized that action against Alexandria might itself precipitate reprisals on the canal. There was a vague hope that the bombardment would topple ʿUrābī, without necessitating a military invasion.

Of course it did no such thing. Alexandria was bombarded on 11 July and this immediately produced a violent anti-European reaction throughout Egypt. The incident completed the transformation of ʿUrābī from a disgruntled and mutinous army officer to a national hero. The ambiguous attitude of the nationalists towards the khedive was finally resolved when, as the Egyptian troops withdrew from Alexandria, Tawfīq sought the protection of the British fleet and on 22 July obligingly proclaimed ʿUrābī a rebel.

The bombardment of Alexandria was followed by another pause, during which the British government again sought in resumed co-operation from the French and authorization from the conference at Istanbul to avoid the logical implications of its unilateral action. By this time, however, the interventionists had got the upper hand in the Cabinet, and an expeditionary force under Sir Garnet Wolseley was prepared for action in Egypt. The French government would not commit itself so far, and in fact was heavily defeated in the Chamber of Deputies on this very question. In Britain, on the other hand, armed intervention was popular for a variety of reasons. Trading and shipping interests feared for the Canal. The Nonconformist conscience was appeased by Gladstone's evocation of atrocities in Egypt, and looked forward to a society pacified and advancing under British tutelage. The invasion of the Canal zone followed in August. The decisive battle took place at Tel el-Kebir (*al-Tall al-Kabīr*) on 13 September 1882. The forces of ʿUrābī were routed, and the capital was captured. The nominal authority of the khedive was restored, and the British occupation of Egypt which, in an attenuated form, was to subsist for seventy-two years, had begun.

The long duration of the British occupation was neither foreseen nor desired at the time of its inception. The declared aim of the Liberal government was to withdraw the British troops as soon as possible, but this could not be accomplished without the restoration of a khedivial administration. Since the circumstances of British intervention had completed the schism in Egyptian politics between Tawfīq and the nationalists, and since the khedivial office had lost what little prestige and dignity remained to it after the deposition of Ismāʿīl, the two purposes of the British were in fact incompatible. Moreover, Gladstone's government was not immune from the temptation to exploit the advantages accruing to Britain from her unilateral invasion of Egypt. Now, if ever, was the chance to supplant French influence in Cairo and thereby to secure control of the vital route to India. At this time, also, British influence in Istanbul was declining, as that of Germany increased: a consideration which further enhanced the value of Britain's position in Egypt. The slogan of early evacuation continued to be repeated for some time. In November 1882 Lord Dufferin was sent out to investigate the situation, and to report on the best means of attaining the British government's incompatible objects. Plans were made for the first phase of evacuation to begin in the autumn of 1883. Meanwhile, however, in October 1883, Sir Evelyn Baring (who in 1891 became Lord Cromer) arrived in Egypt as British agent and consul-general. A financier and administrator of ability, with a fair share of the unimaginative and unsympathetic qualities which tend to accompany financial and administrative skill, he recognized at once that solvency and political stability could not be reconciled with a speedy evacuation. During the following years his great and increasing authority was steadily thrown on the side of a continued British presence in Egypt, and by 1889 the British government had tacitly abandoned the idea of withdrawal.

The incoherence of the British government's Egyptian policy in the opening period of the occupation was reflected in an ambiguity of régime which subsisted until the declaration of the Protectorate in December 1914. The occupying power failed to define its status in regard to the khedivate, the Ottoman suzerain, or the other European powers which had a *locus standi* in Egypt. No formal machinery of control was set up. Tawfīq continued to reign, and on his death in 189[illegible] was succeeded by his son, ʿAbbās Ḥilmī II, in accordance with th firman of 1866. The façade of government by Egyptian ministries was preserved, the system of local administration and the judiciary continued as they had been before 1882. Nevertheless, the power of decision within Egypt had passed to the British agent and consul-general, whose liberty of action was, however, limited by the need to preserve the khedivial system, while, in a wider sense, the requirements of foreign policy dominated the attitude of the British government to Egyptian affairs.

The attitude of the occupying power towards the Ottoman suzerain was similar to that displayed towards the khedivate. Before the Occupation, as we have seen, the British government had hankered after Ottoman intervention in some form or other as a means of restoring the *status quo* in Egypt. The opposition of the French, and the reluctance, until the last minute, of the Ottoman government itself, had destroyed the feasibility of this scheme. After the occupation the British maintained the Ottoman suzerainty as they maintained the khedivial régime, but emptied it even more completely of reality. There was, however, a short period when the British once again entertained the idea of using the suzerain to enable them to maintain their influence in Egypt without the necessity of a military occupation. In August 1885 Lord Salisbury, the Conservative prime minister, sent Sir Henry Drummond Wolff to Istanbul to negotiate on the matter. In May 1887 a convention was signed providing for the evacuation of British troops within three years, but giving both the Ottoman and British governments the right of re-entry in certain specified circumstances.[1] But the convention was never ratified, and the only lasting trace it left was the residence until 1914 of an Ottoman commissioner in Cairo.

The Drummond Wolff convention broke on the opposition of France and Russia, and it is to the limitations which the European powers imposed on British control of Egypt that we must now turn. International rights in Egypt were of two principal kinds: the juridical privileges, derived from the Capitulations, now modified by the establishment of the Mixed Courts; and the financial claims of the bondholders, secured by the Law of Liquidation of 1880. Although the Capitulations and the Mixed Courts continued to be a nuisance and an obstacle to good administration, it was the situation arising from the claims of the bondholders which really caused serious and lasting difficulties to the British in Egypt. International hold over Egyptian finance was secured by the Franco-British Dual Control, and the *Caisse de la*

[1] Text in Hurewitz, i, 201–2.

Dette. Immediately after the occupation, the British abolished the Dual Control, and appointed a financial adviser (who was, of course, an Englishman) to supervise the Egyptian finances. This was one of the very few institutional changes made by the British, and it finally destroyed the understanding with France. Until 1904 French hostility to the British presence in Egypt was bitter and sustained. It made itself felt especially through the *Caisse de la Dette*.

When the occupation began, the *Caisse* had four members, who were respectively French, British, Austrian and Italian. In 1885 the British government negotiated a convention (the Convention of London) with the powers which gave the Egyptians a loan and a little more freedom in the disposal of its own revenues, while two further states, Germany and Russia, nominated members to the *Caisse*. From 1889 onwards there was a regular and increasing budget surplus and correspondingly greater freedom of action for the Egyptian government, or rather its British mentors. Nevertheless, it remained necessary for Britain to conciliate Germany in order to maintain a balance of support in her favour on the *Caisse de la Dette*.

The British occupation had taken place largely in order to safeguard the Suez Canal, but the presence of the British in Egypt aroused the apprehensions of other powers. When it became clear that the occupation would not quickly be terminated, negotiations over the status of the Canal were necessary. The Convention of Constantinople, which was their outcome, was signed by representatives of Britain, France, Germany, Austria-Hungary, Russia, the Ottoman Empire, Italy, Spain and the Netherlands on 29 October 1888.[1] The essential provision was that the Canal should 'always be free and open, in time of war as in time of peace, to every vessel of commerce or of war, without distinction of flag'. This was a satisfactory statement of principle: in practice, its implementation depended on Britain, which did not adhere to the Convention until after the Anglo-French settlement in the Entente Cordiale of 1904.

The necessity, which circumstances imposed on Cromer, of administering Egypt within the framework of the khedivial government, made the subservience of the khedive and the co-operation of his ministers highly desirable. Tawfīq's attitude could be taken for granted. He owed his throne to the British, and had no partisans in Egypt. The ministers were not quite so manageable. Deferential as they might be to the British, there were limits to their collaboration, and a succession of

[1] Text in Hurewitz, i, 202–5.

ministerial crises embarrassed, although it did not weaken, the British régime. The first of these occurred as early as December 1882. After the occupation, Tawfīq had appointed Sharīf Pasha as prime minister, and ʿUrābī was brought to trial with his associates. The Egyptian court sentenced ʿUrābī to death, but, through Dufferin's intervention, the sentence was commuted to banishment. ʿUrābī and his friends were taken to Ceylon. This intervention destroyed the fiction that Sharīf's government was independent of the occupying power, and Riyāḍ Pasha, the minister of the Interior, resigned.

Sharīf himself remained in office until January 1884, when his authority was still more seriously challenged by the occupying power. Since the deposition of Khedive Ismāʿīl, Egyptian power had crumbled in the Sudan, where a religious leader, the Mahdī Muḥammad Aḥmad, had arisen to lead a rebellion against the khedivial administration and to establish a Muslim theocracy. In November 1883 an Egyptian expeditionary force had been annihilated by the Mahdī. Sharīf realized that to abandon the Sudan would destroy what little popular standing his ministry had, while the British government were above all anxious not to add involvement in the Sudan to their involvement in Egypt. Although in form Baring could only advise the Egyptian government to evacuate the Sudanese provinces, he obtained instructions from the British government requiring such advice to be followed 'in important questions affecting the administration and safety of Egypt'. The establishment of this principle marked an important stage in the development of Baring's autocratic power, and its immediate result was the resignation of Sharīf.

Although the appointment of English ministers had been envisaged as a possibility, such an overt assumption of control proved unnecessary. The indestructible Nubar Pasha was appointed prime minister and held power for five years. Nubar's manner of proceeding was to establish a virtual division of government departments between himself and the British. While British advisers were allowed to reform the finances and reconstruct the army, Nubar was determined to exclude them from the Ministries of the Interior and of Justice. A clash developed in 1884, when the British under-secretary of the Interior endeavoured to transfer the provincial police from the control of the Egyptian governors to that of a European inspector-general. The time was not yet ripe for such an invasion of the routine administration. Nubar was indispensable; the British official was not, and had to resign. At the same time Nubar eliminated British control from the Ministry of Justice. In 1888, quite consistently, he seized the opportunity of the death of the British head of the police to attempt to establish his hold over this branch of the administration also. This time, however, he failed to gain his point, and in June 1880 he was dismissed.

His successor was another survivor of the old régime, Riyāḍ Pasha, who came to grief, much as Nubar had done, over the question of British control in the government departments. The Ministry of Justice had been free of British influence since 1885. In the meantime the ineffectiveness of the ordinary courts to suppress violent crime had led Nubar to appoint *ad hoc* administrative tribunals, called 'Commissions of Brigandage'. The arbitrary excesses of these led Baring to insist on their suppression in 1889. The incompetence of the ordinary courts was investigated by a British judge from India, who advocated a number of reforms and was appointed judicial adviser in 1891. Riyāḍ resisted the reforms and the appointment as long as he could, and then resigned in May 1891. His successor, Muṣṭafā Pasha Fahmī, was an ideal instrument with which Cromer could work. His suitability for office is summed up in Milner's encomium: 'Without being as strong a man as either of his predecessors, Mustafa Pasha is intelligent, loyal, well-meaning and well-beloved.'[1] Apart from an interval of a few months in 1893–5, he held office throughout the remainder of Cromer's proconsulate.

Shortly after his eulogy of Muṣṭafā Fahmī, Milner goes on to describe the blossoming of Khedive Tawfīq's talents as a ruler under the British occupation: 'Originality and initiative were not Tewfik's strong points. If they had been, he might have been less peculiarly suited to a situation, in which his cue was to fall in with and support a policy already traced for him by circumstances, rather than to make out a policy of his own. . . . He was growing more English in sympathy with every succeeding year.'[2] This happy situation, with a compliant khedive deferring to the occupying power, came to an abrupt end with the death of Tawfīq on 7 January 1892. A viceregal demise had always in the past been a time of some anxiety, and Cromer was perturbed to learn that the heir, ʿAbbās Ḥilmī II, was still under eighteen years of age and thus a minor according to the terms of the firman of succession. The appointment of a Council of Regency would have been necessary, but the British

[1] Alfred Milner, *England in Egypt*, London 1892, 163. Cromer himself alludes to 'the simplicity of Mustapha Pasha Fehmi's character', and asserts that he possessed 'all the qualities which Englishmen usually associate with the word gentleman': *Modern Egypt* London 1908, ii, 346.

[2] Milner, *op. cit.*, 165–7.

agent had recourse to the Muslim calendar. ʿAbbās's age was calculated in lunar years, and he attained his majority forthwith.

If the British authorities had wished to re-establish the authority and autonomy of the khedivate, the accession of ʿAbbās would have provided them with a favourable opportunity. Still little more than a boy, he was in no way implicated in the events which had humiliated Ismāʿīl and Tawfīq. He had the intelligence, as well as the arrogance, of his ancestors. But Cromer had been too long accustomed to the time-serving insincerity of Tawfīq to welcome ʿAbbās's attempts to assert his position. There was no room in Egypt for two masters, and Cromer, upheld by his sincere if narrow sense of mission as well as by his contempt for orientals, was not prepared to abdicate for the legitimate ruler. For two years an unrelenting struggle went on between the khedive and the domineering British agent.

Late in 1892 the stability of Cromer's political house of cards was threatened when the indispensable Muṣṭafā Fahmī fell seriously ill. In January 1893 the khedive dismissed him, and, without consulting Cromer, appointed a nominee of his own as prime minister. Cromer appealed to the British government, assuring the British Cabinet that 'if they permit the Khedive to win in this case, it will no longer be possible to continue the system which for the last ten years I have carried out'.[1] Armed with the full support of Britain, Cromer reached a compromise which left him the substance of victory. Muṣṭafā Fahmī remained out of office—for less than two years—but the khedive was not permitted to nominate his successor. Instead, Riyāḍ came back to power, to be followed the next year by Nubar. To emphasize the dependence of the khedive, Cromer dictated to ʿAbbās a formal declaration, by which the khedive professed himself 'most anxious to cultivate the most friendly relations with England', and declared that he would always most willingly adopt British advice.

ʿAbbās, however, was not quite finished yet, but in his next trial of strength he played directly into the hands of Cromer, as well as of Kitchener, a no less dangerous opponent. In January 1894 he made a tour of inspection of Egyptian army units stationed between Aswān and Wādī Ḥalfā. The reorganization of the Egyptian army, which had been completely reformed after the suppression of ʿUrābī, had been the work of British officers on secondment, and Kitchener had, since 1889, served as commander-in-chief. As the tour proceeded, ʿAbbās became increasingly critical of the British officers. Kitchener was finally

[1] Cromer, *Abbas II*, London 1915, 23–4.

nettled into offering his resignation, and although ʿAbbās attempted to make light of his previous criticisms and restore good relations, the damage had been done. Kitchener did not, in fact, resign, but Cromer seized on the incident to bring his heaviest guns to bear on the khedive. Once again he had recourse to the British government for backing, and, after he had threatened to place the army 'more directly under the control of the British Government',[1] ʿAbbās capitulated. He offered no more open opposition to Cromer. He acted in a manner far more dangerous to the maintenance of the British position in Egypt: he turned to the nationalists.

The first Egyptian nationalist movement had perished, discredited by failure, on the battlefield of Tel el-Kebir. The new Egyptian army, trained and controlled by British officers, was not a suitable milieu for revolutionary ideas, and did not become such until the Second World War. The second nationalist movement developed among civilians, members of the westernized and affluent middle class. The typical medium for the propagation of ideas was the political journal. Hence, the formulation of Egyptian nationalism was essentially a dialogue of the educated minority with themselves, since about 80 per cent of the population of Egypt was illiterate. It was perhaps for this reason that Cromer was content to leave the Egyptian press the freest in the Near East. Like other administrators of subject peoples, he was slow to realize that the nature and quality of the opposition is often more significant than its numerical extent.

The silence of the opposition during the first years of the British occupation did not imply content with foreign rule, but rather acquiescence in overwhelming power. The strength of subterranean resentment was indicated by the rapid development of nationalist feeling, when it was evoked at the turn of the century by a young journalist and lawyer, Muṣṭafā Kāmil (1874–1908). In his short career, Muṣṭafā Kāmil had neither time nor opportunity to grow to political maturity. His thought was superficial; his tactics, for all their conspiratorial trappings, were naïve; his talents were those of a brash demagogue. Yet his challenge to the entrenched occupying power roused the spirits of his politically conscious countrymen, and his almost mystical exaltation of Egypt rendered articulate their deepest emotions.

Muṣṭafā Kāmil had begun to express his opposition to British rule in Egypt when little more than a schoolboy. A decisive stage in his

[1] The phrase occurs in the communication of Lord Rosebery, the British prime minister, to Cromer, 21 January 1894. See Cromer, *Abbas II*, 57–8.

career was reached in 1895 when he went as a law-student to France. Here he fell among violently anglophobe French politicians and writers, and for the next eleven years looked to France as a means of delivering his country from British domination. At the end of 1894 he returned to Egypt, where he found a secret ally in the khedive. Muṣṭafā Kāmil in this way formed a personal link between the chief external and internal opponents of the British occupation. In 1900 he founded the newspaper *al-Liwā'*, which became the principal vehicle of his propaganda.

In 1896, on the instructions of the British government, Egyptian forces under the command of Kitchener advanced from Wādī Ḥalfā and occupied the province of Dongola. This was the first step in the reconquest of the former Egyptian Sudan from the Mahdist government, the organized resistance of which collapsed at the battle of Kararī (2 September 1898). The reconquest was undertaken purely on British initiative and to further the objectives of British foreign policy. Any advantages which might accrue to Egypt and the Sudan were a subordinate consideration.[1] The status and administration of the reconquered provinces had next to be decided. Cromer's great anxiety was 'to prevent the acquisition of rights and the recognition of privileges to Europeans, similar to the rights and privileges which exist in Egypt'.[2] To differentiate the Sudan from the rest of Egypt and the Ottoman Empire, therefore, a convention was concluded on 19 January 1899 between the British and Khedivial governments, in which the reconquered provinces were placed under their joint rule. The supreme military and civil command, as well as plenary legislative power in the new Anglo-Egyptian Condominium, was conferred on a governor-general, appointed by the khedive on the recommendation of the British government. Egyptian laws and decrees, the jurisdiction of the Mixed Courts, and consular representatives were specifically excluded from the Sudan.[3]

It should be noted that the object of all this was to exclude the European powers from the Sudan. From the first, however, Egyptians viewed the convention as an instrument designed to deprive them of any control over their former possessions. This, indeed, was how it

[1] Rather different interpretations of the British policy behind the reconquest are given by R. Robinson, J. Gallagher and A. Denny, *Africa and the Victorians*, London 1961, 346 ff.; and G. N. Sanderson, 'The European Powers and the Sudan in the later Nineteenth Century', *Sudan Notes and Records*, Khartoum, xi, 1959, 79–100.

[2] Cromer's memorandum of 10 November 1898. For the text of this and the two Condominium Agreements of 1899, see Hurewitz, i, 210–18.

[3] A second convention, on 10 July 1899, included Suakin in the Condominium régime, from which it had been partially excluded by the main convention.

worked. Every governor-general was British, as were the chief officials in the administration: the Egyptians were relegated to minor posts and to the garrisoning of the country. This denial to Egypt of a territory which her viceroys had ruled in the past, which she had been compelled by the British government to evacuate, and towards the reconquest of which she had made the major contribution in blood and treasure, was a fresh grievance to the nationalists, and one which became heavier with the passage of time.

Shortly after the reconquest, a clash between French and British at Fashoda, on the Upper Nile, was narrowly averted. Thereafter the two governments drew closer together, and in the Entente Cordiale of 1904 France recognized the special position of Britain in Egypt. This enormously eased the situation of the occupying power, since it was no longer necessary to conciliate a majority on the *Caisse de la Dette*, and since France no longer used her capitulatory privileges to embarrass Britain. The financial situation of Egypt was ameliorated through a new agreement on the service of the debt.

To Muṣṭafā Kāmil and the nationalists, on the other hand, the Entente Cordiale came as a disappointment. The welfare of Egypt was demonstrated to be no more an end in itself to the French government than to the British. The khedive also lost hope of ousting the British, and showed himself more willing to collaborate with them. In these circumstances, the alliance between Muṣṭafā Kāmil and ʿAbbās broke down. For a time the nationalist leader looked to the Ottomans as a support in his struggle against Britain. Yet, although the invocation of the sultan-caliph would stir the emotions of the great mass of orthodox Muslims in Egypt, there was no real compatibility between the Egyptian patriotism of Muṣṭafā Kāmil and the centralizing policy of Abdülhamid II.

Two incidents in 1906 stirred nationalist feeling. The first was a border dispute with the Ottoman government near the Gulf of ʿAqaba. The British refused to allow the incorporation of an area in Ottoman Syria. Their action was strongly opposed by Muṣṭafā Kāmil, who sought to enhance Ottoman suzerainty over Egypt in order to counterbalance the British presence. Opinion was, however, divided on the Ṭāba Incident, as this affair was called: not so on the Dinshawāy Incident, which followed in the same summer. An affray between a shooting-party of British officers and some Egyptian villagers was followed by the death of one officer. Cromer was in Britain, but the representatives of the occupying power determined to take an exemplary revenge. A special court was set up, which sentenced a number of the peasants to hanging, flogging and imprisonment. The executions were carried out publicly in the village of Dinshawāy, where the incident had occurred. These barbarous measures aroused indignation throughout Egypt, and contrasted grimly with British claims to enjoy the confidence and affection of the peasantry.

In May 1907 Cromer retired. His last years had been a time of increasing autocracy, and of growing detachment from both his British colleagues and the spokesmen of Egyptian opinion. His successor, Sir Eldon Gorst, had served in Egypt from 1886 to 1904, and brought a fresh and less autocratic mind to bear on the problems of its government. Gorst adopted a more flexible and conciliatory policy. He sought to restore good relations with the khedive; to diminish the predominance, both in numbers and influence, of British officials in the administration; and to give some practical functions to the consultative bodies set up shortly after the occupation.

Within limits, Gorst's policy was successful. ʿAbbas responded to his overtures, and a degree of personal friendship developed between the two men. This new situation resulted in the jettisoning of Muṣṭafā Fahmī, who resigned in November 1908. His successor as prime minister was, on Gorst's recommendation, Buṭrus Pasha Ghālī, a Copt who, as foreign minister, had signed the Condominium Convention and, as deputy minister of Justice, had presided over the special court which sentenced the peasants of Dinshawāy. The choice of a Christian with such a record indicated that Gorst, too, underestimated the strength of nationalist feeling.

Towards the end of Cromer's proconsulate, some moderate nationalists had, with his encouragement, begun to organize themselves. In March 1907 a newspaper, *al-Jarīda*, was founded to propagate their views,[1] which at that time were gradualist and co-operative with the occupying power. Gorst, concentrating his efforts on an understanding with the khedive, dissipated the goodwill of this group, which, forced to compete with the extreme nationalists, became more outspoken in its demand for independence. In the autumn of 1907 it was formed into a political party, known as *Ḥizb al-Umma*, the Party of the Nation.

At the same time, in October 1907, the extreme nationalists, led by

[1] The editor of *al-Jarīda*, Aḥmad Luṭfī al-Sayyid (1872–1963), was the leading theoretician and publicist of the liberal nationalists. Like ʿUrābī and Saʿd Zaghlūl, he came of a prosperous peasant family, the son of a village headman.

Muṣṭafā Kāmil, also formed themselves into a political party, called *al-Ḥizb al-Waṭanī*, the Patriotic Party.[1] The organization of the Patriotic Party was superior to that of its rival, and its uncompromising hostility to British rule gave it a greater popular appeal. Its chief asset was, however, the leadership of Muṣṭafā Kāmil himself, and his premature death, on 10 February 1908, was a blow from which it never fully recovered.

The close link between political journalism and party formation which can be seen in the origins of *Ḥizb al-Umma* and *al-Ḥizb al-Waṭanī* is also observable in a third instance. The journal *al-Mu'ayyad* was older than either *al-Liwā'* or *al-Jarīda*, having been founded in 1889 by Shaykh ʿAlī Yūsuf. From the outset it had expressed opposition to Cromer, but whereas Muṣṭafā Kāmil drew inspiration from Europe, ʿAlī Yūsuf's emotional drive came from feelings of Islamic solidarity. After the breach had occurred between ʿAbbās II and Muṣṭafā Kāmil, the khedive turned to ʿAlī Yūsuf as a means of influencing Egyptian opinion. Shortly after the foundation of the two previous parties, late in 1907, ʿAlī Yūsuf formed what was in effect the khedive's personal nationalist party, *Ḥizb al-Islāḥ ʿalā'l-Mabādi' al-Dustūriyya*, the Party of Constitutional Reform. It did not survive the death of its founder in 1911.

Gorst's conciliation of the khedive had done nothing to arrest the spread of nationalism, which thus crystallized out in political parties in the early months of his appointment. His attempts to increase the Egyptian share in the administration won him more opponents. In Cromer's later years the number of British officials had increased sharply, and not all the appointments made could be defended on the grounds of efficiency. Many of these men had influence far in excess of their formal rank, since the Egyptians clearly perceived that the British network and not the official administrative hierarchy, was the real power-élite of Egypt. The attempts of Gorst to reverse this development meant challenging powerful vested interests, and calling into existence a hostile group whose criticisms were amplified in the whispering-galleries of Cairo and London. As the prototype of the dismantler of imperial rule, Gorst had the misfortune to live forty years too soon.

The unsatisfactory illogicality of the dismantling process, which has

[1] *Al-Ḥizb al-Waṭanī* is usually called the National Party, and *Ḥizb al-Umma* the People's Party. I prefer the renderings given in the text, which bring out the force of the terms *umma* and *waṭanī* in modern Arabic. *Al-Ḥizb al-Waṭanī* of Muṣṭafā Kāmil was not connected with the group of the same name in ʿUrābī's time.

now become so familiar, was apparent in Gorst's constitutional experiments. While he was attempting to restore the functions of government to a timid Egyptian executive, he was also trying to confer powers of control and criticism on a quasi-parliamentary body. The Assembly of Delegates had ceased to exist on the British occupation, and on the advice of Lord Dufferin was superseded by two bodies, the Legislative Council and the General Assembly. They were essentially consultative bodies, whose advice was not binding on the government. In so far as they were representative, they represented mainly the more prosperous landowners. Gorst sought to give these bodies a definite rôle in the state by requiring their meetings to be held in public and by providing for the attendance of members of the government at debates and to answer questions.

On the whole, the results of this confrontation were discouraging, and in one instance the new rôle of the General Assembly contributed to a tragedy. In 1910 the Suez Canal Company sought an extension of its concession by forty years from 1968. The proposal, which offered a profitable consideration in return, was bitterly resented by the nationalists, who saw in it a British move to prolong foreign control over Egypt. With Gorst's approval, Buṭrus Ghālī, the prime minister, referred the matter to the General Assembly, which debated the project for nearly two months and then threw it out by an almost unanimous vote. This astonishing, if sporadic, demonstration of the new power of nationalism was not the end of the story. A few days later Buṭrus Ghālī was assassinated by a young Muslim nationalist.

The assassination was followed by a campaign of repression against the extreme nationalists and their press. Gorst did not long survive this setback to his policy. He died in July 1911 and was succeeded by the former commander-in-chief, Lord Kitchener, who returned to service in Egypt after eleven years' absence. The appointment indicated that Gorst's methods were to be abandoned, and strong, autocratic rule was to be restored. Conciliation of the khedive was at an end. By 1913 Kitchener was working to oust ʿAbbās. Using tactics not far removed from blackmail, he induced ʿAbbās to transfer the administration of *waqfs* from the Palace to a ministry, and also restricted the khedive's powers of conferring decorations. These were both desirable reforms, but the methods by which they were accomplished betray a personal animosity on Kitchener's part. At the same time he wrote to Cromer for advice on securing ʿAbbās's deposition, but Cromer pointed out the political unwisdom of such a step. The sole concession which Kitchener made to the politically conscious groups in Egypt was a reorganization of the consultative machinery. In 1913 a new Legislative Assembly was created, superseding the two former bodies and with somewhat wider powers. It was still mainly representative of the wealthier landed classes. Its most prominent member was a man already in his middle fifties, Saʿd Zaghlūl. Like ʿUrābī, Zaghlūl was the son of a village headman; like Muṣṭafā Kāmil, he had trained as a lawyer. In 1896 he married the daughter of Muṣṭafā Fahmī. His marriage assisted his entry into ruling circles; his abilities carried him forward. In 1906 Cromer appointed him minister of Education, and four years later he became minister of Justice. His election to the Legislative Assembly was the bridge by which he passed to his later and more celebrated career as leader of the Wafd, the successor of ʿUrābī and Muṣṭafā Kāmil as the embodiment of Egyptian nationalism.

To Kitchener and Cromer, perhaps to Gorst as well, the development of nationalism seemed an uncouth scrawl in the margin of Egyptian history. In their view the real importance of the British occupation lay in the reforms which they accomplished, in which they took legitimate pride and which have had a lasting effect on the structure of modern Egyptian society. The essential reform, on which all the others depended, was Cromer's restoration of financial stability. This was achieved in the difficult first five years during which he held office and was assisted by the Convention of London and the loan of 1885. A succession of British financial advisers administered the treasury. The budget surpluses obtained from 1889 onwards were used to keep taxation low, rather than to foster social development. To this principle there was one great exception. The maintenance and improvement of irrigation, on which the agrarian prosperity of Egypt depended, was a matter of primary importance to Cromer and his successors. The development of the irrigation system was largely the work of two British engineers who had had experience in India, Sir Colin Scott-Moncrieff and Sir William Garstin. The Nile Barrage, which had been built in Muḥammad ʿAlī's time to provide summer irrigation for the Delta, was restored after a long period of dilapidation and neglect. The original Aswān Dam was built between 1896 and 1903. Meanwhile, the corvée, the traditional recruitment of forced labour for the annual clearing of the irrigation canals, was shown by Scott-Moncrieff to be inefficient and liable to abuse. It was gradually abolished, not without French opposition to the raising of money by which labour could be hired.

The British record in promoting irrigation and agriculture and generally improving the condition of the peasantry, contrasts with the showing on education. The educational system, which had made considerable advances under Khedive Ismāʿīl, stagnated under Cromer. Here as elsewhere in the territories under their control, the British authorities were suspicious of the western-educated élite, who were in due course to inherit their power. Cromer sought to exculpate himself by alluding to the limited funds available under the international control of the finances. But the distribution of the funds as among the different departments was his responsibility. In contrast to the talented British advisers and officials who were connected with the finances, irrigation, the new army, the judicial system and the interior, the senior British official in the Ministry of Education was a Scottish pedagogue 'of limited ideas and rigid views'.[1] Life began to return to the Egyptian educational system only with the appointment of Saʿd Zaghlūl Pasha as minister at the end of Cromer's period of office. Because of this hesitant and grudging attitude towards the development of education, the matter became a political topic. One of Muṣṭafā Kāmil's principal charges against the occupying power was its neglect of education. In 1904 he demanded the establishment of a national university. When a university was founded in 1908 it owed nothing to the British, but was financed by the voluntary contributions of the Egyptians themselves.

Under Cromer the British occupation had been transformed from a temporary expedient to a 'veiled protectorate', which, after the Entente Cordiale of 1904, had no external challenge to fear. The outbreak of the First World War led to the logical conclusion of the process of events, with the incorporation of Egypt in the British Empire. When, in August 1914, war broke out between Britain and Germany, neither the khedive nor the British agent was in Egypt: ʿAbbās was in Istanbul, Kitchener in England. Neither was ever to return. For a time the future status of Egypt remained in the balance. Then, on 29 October 1914, the Ottoman Empire joined Germany as a belligerent. Martial law was declared in Egypt on 2 November. On 18 December the British government proclaimed a protectorate over Egypt, and, on the following day, ʿAbbās II was formally deposed.[2] To the headship of the state succeeded Ḥusayn Kāmil, a son of Khedive Ismāʿīl. His appointment had two interesting features. First, it marked a departure from the order of succession

[1] Humphrey Bowman, *Middle-East Window*, London 1942, 41. The whole of Bowman's account of his service in the Egyptian Ministry of Education from 1903 to 1911 is enlightening.

[2] For the texts of these instruments, see Hurewitz, ii, 4–7.

established by the firman of 1866: Ḥusayn succeeded as the eldest living prince. Secondly, he took the title of sultan, which had not been borne by a ruler of Egypt since the Ottoman conquest, and was intended to demonstrate the lapse of Ottoman suzerainty. Ironically, the form of independence was obtained at the moment when the autonomy of the dynasty was extinguished.

16

Syria and Lebanon during the Ottoman Revival

Bonaparte's invasion of Syria did not produce the cataclysmic effects which resulted in Egypt from the French occupation. His army came and went, leaving no permanent mark on the political landscape. In Aleppo, the factional rivalry of the Janissaries and the *Ashrāf* continued; and it is perhaps significant that Aleppo sent two separate contingents of troops to fight the French: the first consisting nominally of Janissaries, while the second was made up of *Ashrāf*, headed by Ibrāhīm Qaṭārāghāsī, and accompanied by the *naqīb al-Ashrāf*. Shortly after the return of Ibrāhīm from this campaign, in 1802, he was appointed governor of Aleppo, and it seemed possible that he might found a provincial dynasty in northern Syria. On the death of al-Jazzār, he was appointed governor of Damascus, and left his son to rule Aleppo in his place. Shortly after Ibrāhīm Pasha had left Aleppo, however, the people revolted and drove out his son.

The turbulence of the Aleppine Janissaries was never greater than in the first two decades of the nineteenth century. They dominated the city, and the governors were for the most part quite unable to assert their authority against them. Although Ibrāhīm Pasha Qaṭārāghāsī was appointed to Aleppo again in 1807–8, he did not succeed in re-establishing the power of his family there. Since there was a close link between the Qaṭārāghāsīs and the *Ashrāf*, the removal of Ibrāhīm Pasha marked the final decline of that faction. The ascendancy of the Janissaries was complete. In 1813, however, their turbulence was checked by a stratagem reminiscent of Muḥammad ʿAlī Pasha's massacre of the Mamluk chiefs two years previously. The governor, Jalāl al-Dīn Pasha,[1] invited the leaders of the Janissaries to a meeting at the convent of dervishes, outside Aleppo, where he was residing. On arrival they were put to death, and a wider proscription of the Janissaries followed. This action anticipated by several years the suppression of the Janissaries by Sultan Mahmud II, and it would seem that from the time of Jalāl al-Dīn Pasha the power of the faction in Aleppo was on the decline. There are,

[1] Jalāl al-Dīn Pasha belonged to the Chapanoghlu, a family of *derebeys*.

nevertheless, lingering traces of the Janissaries and the *Ashrāf* as organized groups even after the Egyptian occupation of Syria.

When the French invaded Syria in 1799, al-Jazzār remained ostentatiously loyal to the sultan, feeling, no doubt, that his autonomy would be more secure under the Ottomans than under Bonaparte. French propaganda was more attractive to other individuals and groups in the region—the son of Ẓāhir al-ʿUmar, recognized by Bonaparte as shaykh of the Tiberias district, the Matāwila (a Shīʿī minority of the hill-country south of Lebanon), and the Christian peasantry of Lebanon itself. These were, however, marginal groups, whose aid was of little significance. More important to the French was the attitude of Bashīr II. He did not respond to the overtures of Bonaparte, who wrote from the siege-lines of Acre, promising to render 'the Druze nation' independent, to lighten its tribute, and to facilitate its trade by the cession of Beirut and other towns. At the same time he temporized with al-Jazzār, but allowed Ottoman convoys to pass through his territory. He declared, with some truth, that the Lebanese feudatories were not under his control.

In spite of Bashīr's lukewarmness, the course of events in Syria tended on the whole to strengthen his position. Sir Sidney Smith, the British naval commander in the eastern Mediterranean, became his patron. When the Ottoman grand vezir, Yusuf Ziya Pasha, arrived in Syria to lead the sultan's forces against Egypt, Sir Sidney's sponsorship acquired for Bashīr a firman granting his authority over the Mountain and the surrounding territories, and empowering him to send their tribute directly to Istanbul without the mediation of the governor of Sidon. The grand vezir was obviously anxious to place a curb on al-Jazzār's great and increasing power in Syria, but his attempt to use Bashīr as a counter-weight was unsuccessful. The *amīr* found his position untenable and, in 1800, sought refuge on board the British ships, and spent a few months of exile in Cyprus.

Al-Jazzār was indeed irremovable. Bashīr in due course returned to Lebanon to resume his precarious vassaldom to the old pasha, who was again, for the last time, appointed governor of Damascus. He continued to reside in Acre, administering Damascus through a deputy who became notorious for his cruelty and extortions. Then, in 1804, al-Jazzār died; in the words of a chronicler, 'God commanded the death of al-Jazzār, and his transportation to the Gehenna of fire'.[1] As soon as the news reached Damascus, the populace rose and killed his deputy.

[1] Ḥaydar Aḥmad Shihāb, *Ta'rīkh Aḥmad Bāshā al-Jazzār*, Beirut 1955, 167.

After a period of uncertainty following al-Jazzār's death, he was succeeded as governor of Sidon by his former *mamlūk*, Sulaymān Pasha,[1] who is called by the contemporary writers, *al-ʿĀdil*, 'the Just'.

The death of al-Jazzār came at a time when Syria was being seriously threatened by the establishment of Wahhābī power in the Ḥijāz.[2] The great Wahhābī raid on Karbalāʾ in 1802 had shown their capability of ravaging the Fertile Crescent; their occupation of Mecca in 1803 and Medina in 1805 gave them power to hold the Pilgrimage caravans to ransom. This was an intolerable situation for the Ottoman sultan, and in 1807 Yūsuf Pasha had been appointed to Damascus to lead an expedition against the Wahhābīs. It was an utter failure, and the governor showed his zeal for the Faith by the easier means of regulations directed against the Christians and Jews. In 1810 the Wahhābīs raided as near Damascus as Ḥawrān and ʿAjlūn.

The raiders were driven off, but at this juncture Sulaymān Pasha received the appointment of governor of Damascus. He owed his installation to the armed levies of Bashīr Shihāb, a display of power which induced his reluctant predecessor to quit Damascus and seek refuge with Muḥammad ʿAlī Pasha in Egypt. The growing prestige of Bashīr, shown by this incident, was further demonstrated in the following year, when his intervention was sought by the persecuted Druzes of the Aleppo region. Four hundred families were escorted to the safety of the Mountain, where they settled in the Druze districts.

Once al-Jazzār was out of the way, Bashīr II pursued unflinchingly a single great purpose: to eliminate all rival powers within his territories and establish a centralized and autocratic government. He was thus undertaking on a small scale the same task that his contemporaries, Muḥammad ʿAli Pasha and Sultan Mahmud II, were attempting respectively in Egypt and in the Ottoman Empire as a whole. Among the first victims were the two sons of the Amīr Yūsuf, whom al-Jazzār had used as catspaws. They were blinded and put to death. The great families had their power diminished. But the execution of this policy depended on the maintenance of good relations with the governors of Acre, to avoid pretexts for Ottoman intervention. These, on the whole, Bashīr maintained, but the process cost money. His higher taxation and its rigorous enforcement produced in 1820 a revolt of the common people:

[1] He was the Sulaymān Pasha who, with Salīm Pasha, had headed the Mamluk revolt against al-Jazzār in 1789; see above, p. 131. Salīm died in Istanbul, but Sulaymān, after wanderings which brought him to Russia and to Baghdād, returned to Acre and made his peace with al-Jazzār.

[2] See above, pp. 153–4.

the first *ʿāmmiyya* (Arabic, *al-ʿāmm*, 'the common people'). For the second time, Bashīr withdrew from the Mountain; on this occasion to Ḥawrān, from which he was soon afterwards recalled.

Bashīr's policy of co-operation with the governor of Acre led him in the following year (1821) to intervene in a quarrel between ʿAbdallāh Pasha, who had succeeded to Acre on the death of Sulaymān in 1818, and Darwīsh Pasha, the governor of Damascus. Although Bashīr defeated Darwīsh Pasha, he found that he had backed the losing side, since the Ottoman government declared against ʿAbdallāh. Bashīr found himself abandoned by his closest ally among the Lebanese notables, Shaykh Bashīr Janbalāṭ,[1] and once more went into exile. This time he sought refuge in Egypt with Muḥammad ʿAlī Pasha, an event which was to have important results for both men. Muḥammad ʿAlī seized the opportunity to intervene in Syrian affairs, on the pretext of mediating between ʿAbdallāh Pasha and the sultan. ʿAbdallāh was amnestied, and confirmed in his tenure of Acre, which he had never quitted. Bashīr returned to Lebanon, but not before he had established a close understanding with the viceroy of Egypt. The condition of ʿAbdallāh Pasha's continuation in office was the payment of arrears of tribute to Istanbul. Bashīr demanded a heavy contribution from his former ally, Bashīr Janbalāṭ, who was driven into armed revolt. Janbalāṭ's forces were defeated in battle in 1825, and he himself was put to death by ʿAbdallāh Pasha. His removal marked a further success for Bashīr in destroying the power of the great families of Lebanon.

For reasons which we have discussed earlier,[2] the army of Muḥammad ʿAli Pasha invaded Syria in 1831, ostensibly because of a quarrel with ʿAbdallāh Pasha. After he had surrendered and Acre had been captured in May 1832, Ibrāhīm Pasha and the Egyptian troops went on to occupy the whole of Syria. Bashīr's attitude towards this new invader was in marked contrast to his behaviour towards Bonaparte. From the first he collaborated enthusiastically with Ibrāhīm, sending his troops to fight in company with the Egyptians, and his sons to administer the conquered towns. In return Ibrāhīm left to Bashīr a high degree of autonomy within Lebanon itself and used him as a principal instrument in administering the Syrian provinces. The two men had, indeed, much in common, since both were seeking to establish centralized autocracies in place of the lax, almost anarchic, traditional administrations of Syria and Lebanon. Had Bashīr been less submissive to the wider aims of

[1] For the origins of the Janbalāṭ clan, see above, p. 120.

[2] See above, pp. 184–5.

Ibrāhīm, a clash between the master and the vassal might well have occurred, but during the short period of Egyptian rule in Syria the two contrived to work in harmony.

At first the government of Ibrāhīm was acceptable. The clashes of rival provincial governors were at an end, taxes were moderate, the new régime was far more tolerant than the old towards the religious minorities. But in Syria, as in the Sudan, a brief honeymoon was followed by a period of growing disillusion, culminating in revolt. As in the Sudan also, the immediate cause of discontent was new taxation, rigorously applied. Muḥammad ʿAlī's system of monopolies was extended to cover the principal products of the region—silk, cotton and soap—while a corvée was established for mines and public works. These were disagreeable innovations, and revolt broke out in the traditionally insubordinate highlands of Nābulus in 1834. Thence it spread to other hill-communities, the Matāwila and the Nuṣayrīs, but these sporadic and unco-ordinated risings were suppressed piecemeal.

This first wave of insurrections was followed by still more unpopular measures. Ibrāhīm, assisted by Bashīr in Lebanon, endeavoured to disarm the population. Military conscription was next introduced: an act which particularly displeased the Lebanese, who as volunteers had already given good service to Ibrāhīm. Revolt now broke out among the Druzes in Ḥawrān, and several defeats were inflicted on the Egyptians before Sulaymān Pasha, the former Colonel Sèves, blockaded the rebels into submission.

It was at this point, with Syria and Lebanon resentfully submitting to the domination of Ibrāhīm and Bashīr, that Sultan Mahmud II judged the time ripe to intervene and regain his lost provinces. The first results of his intervention were calamitous. The Ottoman army was routed at Nezib in June 1839, and this defeat was followed by the death of Mahmud and the surrender of the Ottoman fleet to Muḥammad ʿAlī Pasha. In this desperate situation, the Ottoman Empire was saved by two things: the intervention of the European powers, who could not allow its total subversion, and the deterioration of the position of the Egyptians within Syria. It is the second factor that concerns us here.[1]

The final revolt against Ibrāhīm and Bashīr broke out in Lebanon. To suppress the Druze revolt in Ḥawrān, Ibrāhīm had armed seven thousand Maronites, and promised them that they might retain their weapons indefinitely. After the victory of Nezib, he sought to disarm

[1] For the international aspects of the Egyptian Question in 1840, see above, pp. 186–7.

them. This was bad enough in itself, but the Christians suspected that Ibrāhīm further intended to bring them under the conscription, from which they had hitherto been exempt. But when the revolt began on 8 June 1840 Muslims and Druzes joined the Christians in a popular movement, the second *ʿāmmiyya*, to oust the Egyptians. British and Ottoman agents had already been at work, fomenting the rising: and a British naval squadron, subsequently joined by Austrian and Ottoman warships, stationed itself off Beirut in August. In the following month the town was bombarded, and Ottoman troops landed near by. Under this pressure, both internal and external, the régime of Ibrāhīm and Bashīr quickly crumbled. On 10 October 1840 Bashīr surrendered to the British and went into exile. In November, Acre was bombarded, and during the winter months, Ibrāhīm evacuated Syria.

The deposition of Bashīr II opened two decades of internal conflict within Lebanon. The political instability which followed his downfall may be ascribed to three main factors. There was, first, the changing position of the great families, especially those of the Druze chiefs. Bashīr, as we have seen, steadily reduced their prestige and their importance. With his passing they had hopes of regaining their lost position, and indeed, from one point of view, the years from 1840 to 1861 are the last phase of Druze 'feudalism' in Lebanon. The great Christian families were also threatened by Bashīr's policy of reducing the Lebanese magnates, but not to the same degree, since the changing balance of power as between Christians and Druzes was characteristic of the period.

This shift of power was the second factor which promoted political instability. It was prepared by the southward expansion of the Maronites, from Kisrawān into the Druze districts of southern Lebanon, which, as we have seen, began as early as the time of Fakhr al-Dīn II.[1] This, however, was mainly a movement of peasants, who passed under the jurisdiction of Druze lords in the mixed districts. By itself it might have had no far-reaching political consequences. There was, however, an additional factor. As Christians and members of a Church which was being drawn into increasingly close connection with Rome, the Maronites were more aware of European cultural values than were the Druzes. Education was more widespread among them than among the other communities in the Mountain, and thus they played an important part in the local bureaucracy. Their growing pre-eminence was demonstrated by a development which is perhaps unparalleled in the Near

[1] See above, p. 119.

East: the ruling branch of the Shihābs, Muslims by origin, 'Princes of the Druzes' by title, was converted to Maronite Christianity; their allies and kin by marriage, the family of Abu'l-Lamʿ, following their example. These conversions both emphasized and promoted the predominance of the Christian element in the Lebanese polity.

Perhaps a conflict between the Druze and Maronite communities was sooner or later inevitable. It was undoubtedly accelerated by the course of events during Ibrāhīm Pasha's tenure of power in Syria. The tolerance of his régime, which gave the Christians social and political equality with the Muslims, was not, perhaps, very significant in the Mountain, where the Maronites had never been a depressed minority and where the other principal community was Druze, not Sunnī Muslim. More important was the close association of the Maronites with the collaborationist policy of Bashīr II, in the furtherance of which they had borne arms against the Druzes, notably in the suppression of the revolt of Ḥawrān in 1838. Although the Druzes and the Maronites had combined in 1840 against Ibrāhīm, their alliance was of short duration.

The third factor in the political situation was the diversity of aims of the various powers who had influence in Lebanon. There was, first, the Ottoman sultanate, which had as its policy the complete reintegration of the Syrian provinces in the Empire under the centralized régime of the *Tanzimat*. That the statesmen of Istanbul were seriously prepared to apply this policy to Mount Lebanon, which had never been under direct Ottoman control, is some measure of the hold which the new ideas of administration had taken. The European powers upheld in principle the integrity of the Ottoman Empire, but sought to further their own interests in the region. France was the power which had the strongest traditional links with Lebanon; although her recent support for Muḥammad ʿAlī had placed her in an embarrassing position, she could still assert her historical claim to protect the Maronites, the element in the population through which she chiefly worked. The attempt of Austria to take the place of France as protector of the Catholic communities had no lasting success.

Since Bonaparte's expedition in 1798, the British government had sought a paramount position in the affairs of the eastern Mediterranean. The maintenance of the Ottoman Empire, the restriction of Muḥammad ʿAlī to Egypt, and the establishment of influence in the Syrian provinces were three aspects of this policy. As France was the protector of the Catholics, so Britain endeavoured to establish a link with the Druze community, but her efforts were less thoroughgoing, and less effective in the long run.[1] The fourth great power which had interests in Syria was Russia, which claimed, by an abusive extension of rights under the Treaty of Küchük Kaynarja (1774), a protectorate over Greek Orthodox Christians of the Ottoman Empire.

The consequences of this complex system of internal and external pressures, resentments and rivalries appeared in the twelve months after the withdrawal of Bashīr II. The Ottomans, in accord with the British, nominated as his successor the descendant of another branch of the Shihābī family, Bashīr III. In the firman of appointment the sultan emphasized the dependence of the new prince on the Ottoman government, while the British seem to have assumed that a feeble ruler would best safeguard their influence in Lebanon. Bashīr III attempted to continue his predecessor's policy of reducing the power of the Druze chiefs, but neither his character nor the circumstances in which he attained power favoured his efforts. The fact that he was a Christian sharpened the antagonism of the Druzes, and when a plot to massacre their magnates miscarried it was only a matter of time before he was overthrown.

The Druze challenge was made in October 1841, when Bashīr III summoned a number of their chiefs to Dayr al-Qamar to discuss problems of taxation. The chiefs brought their armed retinues with them, and Bashīr found himself under siege. In January 1842 he was formally deposed by the sultan and went into exile. With him the rule of the Shihābī dynasty in Lebanon came to an end.

Since the Druzes were, at this time, feeling themselves pressed also by the growing power of the Maronites, it is not surprising that their triumph over Bashīr III was accompanied by an outburst against the Christians. A poacher's quarrel between a Maronite and a Druze at Dayr al-Qamar, at the very moment when the Druze chiefs were bringing in their armed men, led to hostilities in which the town was pillaged and burnt. Other places also suffered, and a fatal schism was opened between the two principal Lebanese communities. There was another alarming symptom. The Christians did not present a united front: the Greek Orthodox made common cause with the Druzes against the Maronites, while the Maronites themselves were on the point of splitting into two factions, the clergy joining with the common people against the great families.

[1] Shortly before the British established an understanding with Druze leaders, there had been some consideration of a project to re-establish a Jewish state in Palestine. See further, L. Stein, *The Balfour Declaration*, London 1961, 5–9. Of more real importance was the British policy of extending consular protection to Jews in Palestine.

The ending of the Shihābī amirate was followed by an attempt to place Lebanon under direct Ottoman administration. ʿUmar Pasha, a man of Croatian origin, was appointed as governor. He, too, attempted to limit the power of the magnates, who, after overthrowing Bashīr III, were disinclined to submit. Once again, Druzes and Christians combined against an alien ruler, but this time their alliance soon broke down. Meanwhile, the Ottoman government realized that its experiment in direct rule had failed. ʿUmar Pasha was removed after a few months of office, and the sultan accepted an administrative scheme backed by the great powers.

This was the device of the 'dual qaimaqamate'. Lebanon was to be partitioned administratively between two lieutenant-governors (sing. *qāʾim maqām*), a Druze and a Christian, each ruling over his own coreligionists. Had the two communities lived in geographically distinct areas, the scheme might have been feasible, but the existence of the mixed districts in the south indicated the likelihood of appalling conflicts of authority. In April 1843, over three months after the appointment of the *qāʾim maqāms*, their jurisdictions were geographically delimited by making the Beirut–Damascus road the frontier between them. This artificial line did not solve the administrative problems of the mixed districts. Since, moreover, the *qāʾim maqāms* were feeble in themselves and lacked sanctions to enforce their will, the real power in Lebanon passed to their immediate superior, the Ottoman governor of the coastal province, whose headquarters had been transferred from Acre to Beirut.

The Christians in the mixed districts continued to resent their submission to Druze magnates, and the Ottoman government sent the admiral, Halil Pasha, to investigate the problem. The solution he proposed was that Christian and Druze agents (sing. *wakīl*) should be appointed in the mixed districts, responsible to the *qāʾim maqāms* of their own confession, and empowered to try minor cases and serve as tax-collectors. The Christians objected to this scheme, and in May 1845 hostilities broke out again between the two communities in the mixed districts. The Ottoman government thereupon sent another commissioner to Lebanon, the foreign minister, Shekib Efendi, who in October 1845 promulgated a new administrative regulation, usually called the *Règlement Shekib Efendi*. While the dual qaimaqamate and the *wakīl* system were retained, a council (*majlis*) was created in each qaimaqamate consisting of representatives of the Muslims, Maronites, Druzes, Greek Orthodox and Greek Catholics. The council heard judicial appeals, apportioned taxes, and served as an advisory body. Its members were salaried full-time officials. Although the powers of the councils were severely limited, in favour of the *qā'im maqāms* and the Ottoman governor, their existence and functions marked a reduction of the traditional powers of the great families.

During the years that followed Shekib Efendi's regulation, Lebanon remained outwardly quiet, but fresh troubles were brewing—this time within the Maronite community. The difficulties centred around the great Maronite families of Kisrawān. Since this was a purely Christian region, the power of the magnates was not limited, like that of their Druze counterparts further south, by the appointment of *wakīls*. Hence, after 1845, there developed in Kisrawān a popular movement for peasant emancipation. In 1858 the peasants broke into open revolt, the third *ʿāmmiyya*, headed by a former blacksmith, Ṭaniyūs Shāhīn. At the beginning of 1859 the insurgents turned on the wealthy family of the Khawāzin, drove them out, and seized their property. Ṭāniyūs set up a short-lived peasant republic in Kisrawān, with himself at its head.

The success of the peasant *ʿāmmiyya* was partly due to another intestine conflict in the Maronite community at this time. The Khawāzin were not only at odds with their peasantry but also with the Maronite hierarchy and with the Christian *qā'im maqām*. In 1854 the death of the first *qā'im maqām* was followed by the appointment of another from the same family, that of Abu'l-Lamʿ, to which the Khawāzin resented their subordination. Later in the same year the Maronite patriarch, a member of the Khawāzin, died. His successor was a man of plebeian descent who disliked the great families. Although he and his clergy were chiefly opposed to the new Abu'l-Lamʿ *qā'im maqām*, they stood to gain from the weakening of the Khawāzin, who, until the time of Bashīr II, had exercised enormous influence within the Maronite Church. Hence, the *ʿāmmiyya* was not unwelcome to the Church, although the attitude of the patriarch and clergy to the movement remained ambiguous. Meanwhile, the governor of Beirut avoided effective intervention against the *ʿāmmiyya*, which, by overthrowing the northern magnates, was doing the Ottomans' work for them.

The collapse of the traditional authorities in the north, and the struggle of rival groups among the Christians, encouraged the Druzes in southern Lebanon and outside the limits of the Mountain to strike a blow for the restoration of their own supremacy. In doing this they received advice, if not material support, from the Ottoman governor. The climate of opinion among the Muslims of Syria also favoured measures against the Christians. From the time of Ibrāhīm Pasha onwards, the emancipation of the Christians had been going forward: in 1856 it had been formally proclaimed by the sultan in the *Hatt-i Hümayun*. With their traditional authority and prestige visibly crumbling, the exasperated Muslims were prepared to make common cause with Druze heretics against the Christians.

After some anticipatory clashes in 1859, the Druzes took the offensive in the mixed districts in April 1860. Massacres of the Christians followed, both in the villages and in the towns. Kisrawān, under Ṭāniyūs Shāhīn, lay outside the zone of conflict, but sent no effective help to the southern Christians. The massacres spread to the Druze districts outside the Mountain, and in July the Muslims of Damascus attacked the Christians of the city. The sympathies of the Ottoman authorities, both in Lebanon and in Damascus, were clearly on the side of those committing the massacres. Among the Muslims, the only effective protector of the Christians was the exiled hero of the Algerian resistance to France, the Amīr ʿAbd al-Qādir al-Jazāʾirī.

These events inevitably produced European intervention, the initiative being taken by France, which in August 1860 landed troops at Beirut. Meanwhile the Ottoman government had sent its foreign minister, Fuad Pasha, to repress the disorder. In Damascus, from which he wished to avert a European occupation, he set up summary tribunals which tried and executed, among others, the governor. In October 1860 an international commission began its sessions, at first in Beirut, subsequently at Istanbul. Under the adroit presidency of Fuad Pasha, supported by the British representative, the attempts of Napoleon III to strengthen French influence in Lebanon and Syria were thwarted. In June 1861 the French troops were withdrawn.

The same month witnessed the signature by the powers of an agreement establishing a new administrative régime in Lebanon. This was the Organic Regulation (*Règlement organique*) of 9 June 1861,[1] which, as modified three years later, formed the constitution of Lebanon until the First World War. The double qaimaqamate was superseded by a unified régime, which, however, had authority only over the Mountain proper. At the head of the administration was a Christian administrator (*mutaṣarrif*) directly responsible to the sultan. The interests of the constituent communities of Lebanon were represented by agents appointed by the communal chiefs and notables. There was also a Central Administrative Council of twelve members, representing the six religious

[1] For the text of the Organic Regulation, see Hurewitz, i, 165–8.

communities, which assessed the taxes, controlled the finances, and advised the administrator. Among other important provisions of the Organic Regulation were the declaration of equality before the law and the formal abolition of feudal privileges. Of the seven administrators who governed the Mountain between 1861 and 1914, the first was outstanding. Da'ūd Pasha (1861–8) was an Armenian Catholic. He had to overcome opposition from the magnates and from a nationalist leader, Yūsuf Bey Karam, who, as Christian *qā'im maqām* in 1860–1, had suppressed Ṭāniyūs Shāhīn's *ʿāmmiyya* in Kisrawān. Yūsuf Karam, who had hoped to head the new administration himself, was expelled from Lebanon in 1861, and, when he returned in 1864 hoping to regain power, was permanently banished.

The settlement of 1861 was a turning-point in the history of Lebanon. The predominance of the Christian element had been tacitly recognized and formally safeguarded. The long struggle of Bashīr II and his successors against the magnates had been brought, ostensibly at least, to a satisfactory conclusion by the abolition of their privileges and the establishment of administrative machinery which was independent of them. Under the *Mutaṣarrifiyya*, Lebanon had over fifty years of quiet development in which the foundations of her modern prosperity were laid. But there were other, less favourable, aspects of the situation. The long preceding period of tension between Druzes and Maronites, culminating in the massacres of 1860, had created a deep division between the two communities, which was not easily healed and which has left traces to this day. Furthermore, the anarchy of 1860 was only overcome by international intervention, and it was to the sanction of the powers, rather than to its inherent virtues or acceptability, that the settlement of 1861 owed its success. Finally, the influence of the great families, based on their estates, their wealth and their hereditary standing, could not be legislated out of existence by a clause in the Organic Regulation. Their alliances and their rivalries have, over the past century, been a continuing force in Lebanese politics.

The troubles in Lebanon and Syria made the Ottoman reformers acutely conscious of the provincial maladministration in the Empire. In 1864 Fuad Pasha, as grand vezir, promulgated a new provincial code, the Law of Vilayets, which substituted for the traditional *eyalets* large administrative units, the *vilayets*, whose governors (sing. *vali*) had considerable discretionary powers. The *vilayets* were divided into subprovinces called *sanjaks*, administered by *mutaṣarrifs*, and these were still further subdivided. With the exception of Lebanon, which as an autonomous *sanjak* stood outside the provincial structure, geographical Syria was at first divided into two *vilayets*, with their capitals at Aleppo and Damascus respectively. The old coastal province, which had been governed from Sidon, Acre and Beirut in turn, thus disappeared, but something like it was restored in 1888 with the creation of the *vilayet* of Beirut. This consisted of three distinct portions: a strip of coastal territory north of Tripoli, the city of Beirut itself (forming an enclave in Lebanon), and a block of northern Palestinian territory, stretching inland to the River Jordan. About the same time a second autonomous *sanjak* was created in the south of Palestine, the *sanjak* of Jerusalem.

The nineteenth century witnessed two developments, initiated from outside geographical Syria, which had important political, social and cultural results for the region. The first of these was the growth of Protestant missionary activity; the second was the opening of the modern phase of Jewish immigration into Palestine.

Organized Protestant missionary work did not exist in Syria before the nineteenth century, although there are earlier traces of sporadic individual efforts. Thus, Robert Huntington, the Anglican chaplain to the merchants of the Levant Company at Aleppo, made some attempts at the evangelization of the local population from 1671 onwards, using chiefly apologetic and liturgical material translated by Edward Pococke, the professor of Arabic at Oxford.[1] Roman Catholic missionary work, by contrast, was sustained, organized and (within limits) successful. Since conversion of Muslims was virtually impossible, the Catholic missionaries devoted their attention chiefly to the various Oriental Christian confessions, which they sought to bring into communion with Rome. With the Maronites they were in the end completely successful, since at the Synod of al-Luwayza (1736) these Lebanese Christians finally accepted the status of a Uniate Church, acknowledging the papal supremacy. Elsewhere, the effect of Catholic intervention was to produce schisms among the Oriental Christians, so that only some of each confession formed Uniate Churches. In this way the so-called Chaldaean Church seceded in the seventeenth century from the Nestorians, as did the Greek Catholics from the Orthodox, and the Armenian Catholics from the Gregorian Church in the eighteenth century.

Proselytization in the nineteenth century by Protestant organizations was of necessity still virtually confined to the non-Muslim communities. Two contrasting patterns of missionary activity may be seen in the American Presbyterians, who had their headquarters at Beirut, and the

[1] Pococke had himself been chaplain at Aleppo from 1630 to 1636.

Anglicans, centred at Jerusalem. The Americans started work in 1823, and their activities among the old Christian communities, especially the Greek Orthodox, aroused local resentment. In 1848 their converts, organized into the Syrian Evangelical Church, added another to the numerous Christian denominations of the Near East. The significance of the American mission should, however, rather be gauged by its cultural contribution. In 1834 it brought to Beirut an Arabic press (originally set up in Malta), which played an important rôle in the cultural revival of the western Fertile Crescent.[1] Educational work by the missionaries culminated in the foundation in 1866 of the Syrian Protestant College, now the American University of Beirut, which has long been a distinguished centre of higher studies for all the Arab lands. These institutions were paralleled on the Catholic side by the establishment of the Imprimerie Catholique in 1853 and the Université de St. Joseph in 1875. Both were founded under Jesuit auspices and both have made notable contributions to Arabic studies.

The Anglican mission, centred at Jerusalem, was aimed originally at a different community, the Jewish population of Palestine. Proselytization in this direction was linked with the fundamentalist Evangelicalism which was so prominent a religious trend in nineteenth-century England, and which expected the ingathering and conversion of the Jews as heralding the Millennium. Early attempts, in the 1820s, had little success, but the missionaries succeeded in establishing a foothold in Jerusalem under the régime of Ibrāhīm Pasha. Unlike the American Presbyterians, the Anglicans enjoyed a measure of protection from their government. The establishment of a British vice-consulate at Jerusalem in 1838 promoted the influence of the missionaries, and in 1841 Britain and Prussia combined to set up a Protestant see in the city.[2] The first bishop, Michael Solomon Alexander, was himself a converted Polish Jew. The Anglican missionaries, like the Presbyterians, aroused the animosity of the communities they sought to convert: in this case, primarily, the Jews of Jerusalem. Their contributions to education and culture were negligible by comparison with those of the Presbyterians and Jesuits in Beirut.

A small Jewish community had existed in Palestine and other parts

[1] The American press was not the first in Syria. As early as 1610 a Lebanese monastic press printed the Arabic psalms in Syriac characters, while the first oriental press to use Arabic characters was established at Aleppo (again under Christian auspices) in 1702. Two other monastic presses were established in the eighteenth century. The first director of the Būlāq press was a Lebanese.

[2] In 1886 the see of Jerusalem became purely Anglican.

of geographical Syria continuously since Biblical times. Like the Jewries in other parts of the Ottoman Empire, it had been greatly augmented by the talented Sephardic refugees, expelled from Spain and Portugal in the last decade of the fifteenth century. Some of these immigrants and their descendants obtained positions of importance, particularly in the financial administrations of their provinces. During the eighteenth century the Farḥī family acquired great influence in the financial administration of Damascus. Ḥayyim Farḥī became the chief minister of Aḥmad Pasha al-Jazzār. He served al-Jazzār's successors, Sulaymān Pasha al-ʿĀdil and ʿAbdallāh Pasha, in a similar capacity, but was finally put to death by ʿAbdallāh's orders.

In Palestine proper, the Sephardic immigrants chiefly settled in the four towns of Jerusalem, Hebron, Tiberias and Ṣafad, the last of which became, in the sixteenth century, a centre of Jewish mysticism. At about the same time a Jewish refugee from Portugal, Joseph Nasi, had become a trusted adviser of Süleyman the Magnificent and of his son and successor, Selim II. He obtained the grant of Tiberias, where he hoped to develop a small, autonomous Jewish principality. The town was rebuilt and attempts were made to establish the manufacture of textiles. The experiment did not long outlive Joseph's death in 1579. The sixteenth century was, nevertheless, in general a time of some intellectual and economic revival for the Palestinian Jewry. By the nineteenth century conditions had changed, and, on the whole, the Jews of Palestine lived in great poverty. Many of them devoted their lives to rabbinical or mystical studies, others were aged immigrants, who had come to end their lives in the Holy Land. For its maintenance the Palestinian community depended largely on the *ḥalūqāh*, the alms collected in the Jewries of the Diaspora.

The nineteenth century saw three important changes in the situation of Ottoman (and more especially Palestinian) Jewry. With the passing of the traditional society and administration of the Ottoman Empire, the old Sephardic patrician families, which had formed part of that society and had served that administration, found their position deteriorating. The Farḥīs are a case in point: about the middle of the century it was stated that of the sixteen adult males of the family in Damascus 'only seven are tolerably well off, the others can with difficulty earn a scanty living'.[1] Unlike the Greeks and Armenians under Ottoman rule, the Jews experienced no national, cultural or educational revival. Thus they lost ground to rivals who were better equipped and could count on

[1] L. Loewe (ed.), *Diaries of Sir Moses and Lady Montefiore*, London 1890, ii, 358.

firmer support from Europe. The emancipation of the Jews in wester Europe did, however, lead to the emergence there of influential spokes men and protectors of the Oriental communities. Among these was th patriarchal Sir Moses Montefiore, who made seven visits to Palestin and intervened to protect the Jews of Damascus after an accusation c ritual murder in 1840. The third and ultimately the most importar development was the beginning of Zionist immigration in the last tw decades of the century. This movement was essentially the combina tion of two factors: the rise of Zionism, a secular Jewish nationalism bearing obvious marks of kinship with contemporary and Europea nationalisms;[1] and the various forms of pressure, rising at times t persecution, exerted upon the Jews living under Russian rule. Th pogroms of 1881 started a wave of immigration, the First *ʿAliyāh* which in the course of little over twenty years brought between twent and thirty thousand Jews into Palestine. The new immigrants differe on almost every point from the old community. They were drawn fro the north European group of Jews, the Ashkenazim, while their pre decessors were predominantly Sephardic and Oriental. The immigrant were increasingly secular in outlook, strongly imbued with Europea political and social ideas. As time went on, the aim of settlement wa transformed into the dynamic purpose of building up a Jewish stat They broke deliberately with the old restricted ways of life of th traditional Jewish communities, and turned to agriculture as the bas of their livelihood. At the outbreak of the First World War, there we still only about 85,000 Jews in Palestine, but their presence was both challenge and an omen.

[1] The development of Zionism is analysed in his introduction to an anthology selections from Zionist literature by Arthur Hertzberg, *The Zionist idea*, New Yo and Philadelphia 1960.

17

The Iraqi Provinces during the Ottoman Revival

The history of the Iraqi provinces during the period of the Ottoman revival provides a useful measure of both the success and the failure of the reforming policies in the Arab lands. Egypt is untypical, since the hereditary viceroys, Muḥammad ʿAlī Pasha and his successors, themselves initiated innovations and westernization, and since from 1882 the country was under British control. In Syria, the interlude of Egyptian rule and the inroads of Western influence affected the introduction and impact of the Ottoman reforms. The Iraqi provinces, by contrast, were fully reintegrated in the empire, were never brought under alien domination until the cataclysm of the First World War, and were only to a very moderate degree exposed directly to European influences. In this region we can see most clearly the problems encountered by the Ottoman reformers and the limitations which circumstances imposed on their works, as well as the changes which the innovations brought about in traditional, and especially tribal, society.

At the beginning of the nineteenth century Baghdād was ruled by Büyük Sulaymān, the greatest of the Mamluk pashas.[1] Although his attempts to curb the growth of Wahhābī power were a complete failure, his personal position was unshaken until his death in 1802, and the pashalic duly passed to members of his household. The fundamental political instability of the Mamluk régime is shown by the circumstances in which Büyük Sulaymān's successors acquired power, and the short duration of their reigns. A factional struggle between ʿAlī Kâhya, the late pasha's deputy, and the *agha* of the local Janissaries ended in ʿAlī's victory. He was, however, assassinated in 1807 and succeeded by his nephew, Küchük Sulaymān Pasha. In 1810 Sultan Mahmud II made a first attempt to establish his authority in Iraq, and Sulaymān was deposed, defeated in battle, and killed. The overthrow of the Mamluk régime as such was, however, still beyond the sultan's powers, and a former retainer of Büyük Sulaymān, Tütünjü ʿAbdallāh, was installed as pasha. Factional fighting broke out again, and ʿAbdallāh found himself

[1] See above, pp. 147–8.

opposed to Saʿīd, the son of Büyük Sulaymān, who was supported by the tribal levies of the Muntafiq. Defeated and deserted, ʿAbdallāh Pasha was captured and killed by his enemies. Saʿīd entered Baghdād as pasha in 1813, but his feebleness led to his supersession three years later, and the appointment to the governorship of another former *mamlūk* of Büyük Sulaymān.

This was Da'ūd Pasha, the last of the Mamluk governors, who was to rule Baghdād for the exceptionally long period of fifteen years. He was already about fifty years old at the time of his appointment; he had shown an inclination to traditional literary scholarship, and had held high office as *defterdar* and *kâhya* (i.e. deputy governor) under his immediate predecessors. During his governorship there took place the last of the wars between Persia and the Ottoman Empire which had been a recurrent theme in the history of the Iraqi provinces. Its outbreak was due to the action of ʿAbbās Mīrzā, the governor of Āẕarbāyjān, who was induced by Russia to commence hostilities across the Ottoman frontier in 1821. At the same time Muḥammad ʿAlī Mīrzā, the governor of Kirmānshāh, and, like ʿAbbās Mīrzā, a son of the ruling shah, began an invasion of Shahrizor, where he could count on Kurdish disaffection. An army sent by Da'ūd Pasha was defeated, and Muḥammad ʿAlī Mīrzā led his forces on towards Baghdād. An outbreak of cholera stopped the Persian advance, and, after negotiations, Muḥammad ʿAlī Mīrzā withdrew. This was not, indeed, the end of the war, which went on until 1823. Like earlier conflicts on the Iraqi frontier it resulted in no change of any significance, and the Treaty of Erzurum which concluded it reaffirmed the old, undelimited boundary, going back ultimately to the time of Murad IV.[1]

While the Persian war linked the reign of Da'ūd Pasha with the earlier history of the Iraqi provinces, another event was indicative of developments to come. The destruction of the Janissaries of Istanbul by Mahmud II in 1826 was followed by measures to break Janissary power in the provincial garrison towns. The Janissaries of Baghdād, as elsewhere in the provinces, had long ago become a locally recruited body and as a military force they were far inferior to the personal Mamluk troops of the governor. In 1826 their corps was dissolved, and they were formally enrolled as new regular forces of the sultan. Da'ūd Pasha arranged for their training by a French officer, and workshops were set up to provide their clothing and equipment.

The creation of this new-model army at Baghdād, although carried

[1] Text in Hurewitz, i, 90–2. See above, p. 138.

ut in accordance with the sultan's wishes, augmented the power of a'ūd Pasha, and increased his autonomy. Rapid action by the sultan as clearly necessary if the Iraqi provinces were not to follow Egypt into irtual independence. The first envoy sent by Mahmud to demand a'ūd Pasha's submission was assassinated by the governor's retainers October 1830. The Mamluk régime, in Iraq as in Egypt, could only e ended by superior force. An army was placed under the command of certain ʿAlī Riḍā Pasha, who was nominated governor of Aleppo and he Iraqi provinces except Mosul. In January 1831 he began his march rom Syria against Baghdād. The outcome of his expedition might have een very different had not a serious epidemic of plague broken out in aghdād, which ruined the prosperity of the city, wrought havoc among he governor's Mamluk officers and troops, and endangered for a time he life of Da'ūd Pasha himself. In June the advanced forces of ʿAlī Riḍā ntered Baghdād, and the deposition of Da'ūd was proclaimed, but a ising in favour of the old governor enabled him to resist the Ottomans ntil September. ʿAlī Riḍā, whose army was unpaid and on the verge of utiny, succeeded in negotiating for entry into the city, and at last ffected Da'ūd Pasha's deposition. Da'ūd was taken to Istanbul, but his fe was spared, and he survived to serve in high office for another twenty ears. He died in 1851 at Medina.

The fall of Da'ūd Pasha meant the end of the Mamluk régime, already ebilitated by the plague of 1831. The new governor, ʿAlī Riḍā Pasha, assacred and proscribed the remaining officers and men of Da'ūd's ousehold. The full reintegration of the Iraqi provinces in the Ottoman mpire was not, however, at once attained. Mosul still remained under he rule of the Jalīlī family, who had been its hereditary governors since 726.[1] Their hold had been shaken in 1831, and the last Jalīlī pasha fell hree years later. He was succeeded by a client of ʿAlī Riḍā, Inje Bay-aktar Muḥammad Pasha, who not only reorganized the administration f Mosul, but played a leading part in the reduction of the autonomous urdish principalities in the hill-country to the north and east. One of he chief of these, the principality of Shahrizor, survived for a few more ears, to be extinguished finally in 1850.

Although the more obvious obstacles to Ottoman rule were thus liminated, the governors who succeeded Da'ūd Pasha had little success n dealing with the inveterate problem of tribal control and administra-ion. Faced with the powerful groupings and influential chiefs of central nd southern Iraq, the new régime at first could not go beyond the old

See above, p. 148.

policy of setting tribe against tribe, kinsman against kinsman, and demonstrating the limits of Ottoman authority by ineffective punitive expeditions. It was not until the appointment of Midhat Pasha as governor in 1869 that a more positive and constructive policy was attempted.

Midhat's short governorship, from 1869 to 1872, was a turning point in Iraqi history. Midhat, who was born in 1822, was already known as an able administrator and was closely associated with the reformers in high government circles. In 1864 the reforming grand vezir, Fuad Pasha, promulgated a new plan for the administration of the provinces, known as the Law of Vilayets.[1] Midhat was chosen to apply it as a pilot scheme in the province of the Danube. His subsequent appointment to Baghdād enabled him to attempt reforms in a region less sensitive to international pressures. Following the scheme laid down in the Law of Vilayets, the province was divided into sub-provinces, and these into districts. Councils were set up at district and sub-province level, while, for the province, Midhat set up an Administrative Council and a General Council with financial functions. With variations in detail this system of administrative subdivisions survived Ottoman rule.

Of more far-reaching importance were Midhat Pasha's agrarian reforms. Early in his governorship he was confronted with a serious triba rising in the district of Ḥilla, south of Baghdād. A tax-collecting expedition was annihilated, and the rebels were only defeated after large-scale military operations in the Euphrates marshes. Midhat realized tha suppression was not enough: an attempt must be made to settle the tribes and to win their support by making them beneficiaries of the government. He decided to apply to his province (which included the Baṣra region as well as Baghdād) the provisions of the Ottoman Lan Law of 1858. Basically, this law sought to assure the rights in land of it actual possessors. Although the state retained the final ownership, individual freehold rights could be secured by title-deeds (sing. *tapu* o *tapu senedi*) issued by the responsible ministry in return for a fee. Land Commission was duly set up in Baghdād to survey the agricultura land and grant the title-deeds. As inducements to the semi-nomadi tribesmen, Midhat reduced tax-demands and promised further reductions to individuals who became settled tenants under the Land Law.

In practice these reforms did not work out as Midhat had intendec It was unfortunate that he himself was not able to see them throug to their conclusion. When he left Baghdād in 1872 the survey of lan and issue of title-deeds had been completed only in some parts of hi

[1] See above, p. 242.

rovince. Although the process continued under his successors, the drive ehind it had gone. Apart from this, the agrarian changes were faulty oth in their conception and their execution. The Land Law was itself specimen of westernizing legislation, the implications of which had not een thought out fully. It had been drafted with the conditions of the Turkish provinces in view, and hence was doubly unsuitable to local onditions in Iraq. Here its concepts conflicted with tribal custom, ccording to which land was held by the tribe as a whole, and holdings lepended not on formal grants by the government but on the continued bility of the tribesmen to defend what they held against other tribal roups. From their point of view the operations of the Land Commission vere a gratuitous intervention by a third party. Had the Commission een more efficient, the agrarian settlement might have been more uccessful. As it was, incompetence and corruption were common.

The consequences of all this were grave. Generally speaking, in Iraq as elsewhere in the empire) the new system worked against the interests f the actual cultivators of the land, who mistrusted the *tapus*, and were nwilling to accept them. The title-deeds were bought up by others— ity merchants or members of the great tribal families, who in this way vere transformed from chiefs into landlords. A notable example of this vas among the Muntafiq, who had dominated the south-west of Iraq ntil well into the nineteenth century. The leader of the confederacy, Shaykh Nāṣir of the Saʿdūn family, co-operated with Midhat from the utset. He acquiesced in the conversion of the tribal lands into a *sanjak*, r sub-province, with himself as *mutaṣarrif*, or sub-governor. In 1876 he vas appointed governor of Baṣra, which was made into a distinct *vilayet*. During his period of office the bulk of the Muntafiq lands were brought nder the new agrarian régime, and most of the title-deeds were acquired y Nāṣir and other members of the Saʿdūn family. In 1881 Nāṣir was emoved from Baṣra and the Muntafiq made their last great revolt under Saʿdūn leadership. They were defeated and the Saʿdūn were temporarily anished from the region.

The last twenty years of the nineteenth century were a period of rowing tribal confusion and anarchy in southern Iraq. Among the Muntafiq the transformation and withdrawal of the traditional authority f the Saʿdūn were not followed by the imposition of an effective Otto- nan administration. Further to the north, in the Ḥilla region of the niddle Euphrates, the situation was chaotic for another reason. Here the ld policy of playing off one tribe against another was resumed, but nore was now at stake. By withdrawing and regranting the *tapus*, the administration could intervene to promote hostility between, and even within, tribal groups. The old loyalties of the tribes were visibly dissolving, while the resultant anarchy reduced the actual control of the government to a very limited sphere.

These conditions of tribal chaos and agrarian decline were not found everywhere. It was the policy of Sultan Abdülhamid II to take over, for the service of his privy purse, profitable sources of revenue throughout the empire. Hence, for example, much of the fertile agricultural land of ʿAmāra, lying on the lower Tigris, was brought under the sultan's private *Seniye* administration, as were also estates in Baṣra and Mosul. The control of the *Seniye* properties was resumed by the state after the Young Turk revolution of 1908, but they continued to be separately administered.

Throughout this period the Iraqi provinces aroused remarkably little sustained interest in Europe. Unlike the western Fertile Crescent, they possessed no holy places to incite Christian dissension, nor did their minorities attract to any significant extent European patronage. There were old-established Catholic missions, followed by Protestant missionary enterprise in the nineteenth century: both of these succeeded in promoting schisms among the native Christians. Their activities were lacking, however, in the intense political overtones associated with the Christian missions in the Syrian provinces. Under both the later Mamluk pashas and the revived Ottoman régime, the dominant Western influence was that of Britain, represented by a resident (at first a servant of the East India Company) at Baghdād from 1798 onward. This appointment was originally made to counteract the threat of French power in the Near East, but, once the Revolutionary and Napoleonic wars were over, there was no prolonged local rivalry between France and Britain, such as occurred in Syria and Egypt.

On two occasions, at the beginning and end of this period, international communications through Iraq aroused British interest. After the Napoleonic wars the problem of developing quicker means of communication between India and Britain was receiving attention from servants of the East India Company. Two routes seemed possible: one up the Red Sea to Suez and thence overland to Alexandria; the other by the Persian Gulf to Baṣra, then by way of the Euphrates and across country to the Syrian coast. The pioneer surveys of the Euphrates route were made in 1830–1, and in 1836 Captain Chesney, who had taken part in the original survey, brought a river-steamer down the river and out to the Persian Gulf. It was clear, however, that the Euphrates route was not satisfactory for regular communication between the Indian Ocean and the Mediterranean. The Overland Route across Egypt was shorter and passed through territory under firm and effective administration.[1]

Chesney's expedition, however, marked the beginning of modern river-transport in Iraq. A flotilla of four iron steamers navigated the waters, under the command of Lieutenant Lynch, from 1839. In 1861 the Lynch family established the Euphrates and Tigris Steam Navigation Company,[2] which survived Ottoman rule and went into voluntary liquidation only in 1951. In its early days it met with competition from a company sponsored by the provincial administration. Originally founded by one governor in 1855 and reorganized by another in 1867, the Oman-Ottoman Administration, as the enterprise was called, was taken over in 1904 by the *Seniye* administration. After the fall of Sultan Abdülhamid, it reverted, like other *Seniye* properties, to state control.

The use of river-steamers long preceded the development of modern means of land-transport in the Iraqi provinces. The building of a railway, in the interest of communications between Britain and India, was proposed to the East India Company as early as 1843, and other plans were put forward in the decades that followed. The advantages of the Overland Route across Egypt, which were enhanced by the construction of a railway and the subsequent opening of the Suez Canal, prevented any of these schemes from being carried out, although one of them obtained the support of the British government. British interests promoted a more successful project: the establishment of a telegraphic link with India through Iraq. The line was constructed by British engineers on behalf of the Ottoman government. Istanbul was connected with Baghdād in 1861, and the line was, in the next few years, extended to link up with India through the Persian Gulf, and with Persia by way of Khāniqīn. Here as elsewhere in the Ottoman Empire, telegraphic communication subserved a policy of administrative centralization.

The project of a railway through the Iraqi provinces was revived at the end of the nineteenth century, in consequence of the growth of German influence over the government of Abdülhamid II. A German syndicate, the Anatolian Railway Company, surveyed the route from Konya to Aleppo, Mosul, Baghdād and the Persian Gulf. A convention between the Ottoman government and the company was concluded in

[1] See above, pp. 198–9.

[2] The company acted under a firman of 1834, originally issued to sanction Chesney's expedition. For the text, see Hurewitz, i, 109–10.

March 1903,[1] and British co-operation was sought. After some hesitation, the British government refused participation. There were fears for the British position in the Persian Gulf, control of which, as an approach to India, was a vital object of British policy. In 1907 the British government agreed to cease opposition to the railway if the final section of the line, from Baghdād to Baṣra, were constructed solely by the British. Six years of negotiations over this and related questions followed, and on the eve of the First World War an Anglo-German convention regulated the interests of the two powers in Iraq, and removed the diplomatic obstacles to the completion of the railway.[2] The outbreak of the war, however, prevented the implementing of this agreement, and only eighty miles of line, between Baghdād and Sāmarrā, were in fact constructed under the Ottoman régime.

[2] Text in Hurewitz, i, 252–62.

[1] Text in Hurewitz, i, 281–6.

18

The Emergence of Arab Nationalism

The modern Arab nationalist movement, like other nationalisms in Europe and elsewhere, looks back to early history and links itself with the heroic episodes of the remote past. A protonationalist tendency can indeed be discerned at an early period, in the Arabs' pride of descent and pride in language, their sense of superiority which was enhanced and confirmed at the coming of Islam, when an Arab Prophet transmitted the Word of God in an Arabic Qur'ān. But such emotions do not in themselves amount to the particular political attitude which we call nationalism. The social loyalties of the early Arabs were primarily directed towards the kinship group: the family first, then the clan, then the tribe. Among the members of such a group existed the sentiment of solidarity, *ʿaṣabiyya*,[1] and the obligation of blood-vengeance.

While familial and tribal bonds continued to be, and indeed still are, important in Arab society, it would be demonstrably untrue to deny the existence of a powerful sentiment of unity and brotherhood in the Islamic community. This had important political implications, but again it was not equivalent to Arab nationalism, since only for a very short space of time in the seventh century was Islam a religion of the Arabs only. From traditional Arab *ʿaṣabiyya*, and from membership of the Muslim community, the Arab peoples of today have inherited attitudes and emotions which characterize and distinguish Arab nationalism, but that nationalism is, in its developed form, a phenomenon of the twentieth century.

Ottoman rule, until the twentieth century, did not affect Arab national feeling, because no such feeling then existed. The enclaves of Arab autonomy within the empire, such as the amirate of Mecca, or that of the Maʿnids and Shihābs in Mount Lebanon, or the transient shaykhdom of Ẓāhir al-ʿUmar in Galilee, were personal or dynastic dominions, innocent of any nationalist implications. They were paralleled by other autonomies set up in the same period by rulers who were not of Arab origin, and were essentially a phenomenon of the Ottoman decline.

[1] *ʿAṣabiyya* means, in the first place, the sense of unity derived from blood-relationship, but already in pre-Islamic times the tribal group could be extended to include clients (*mawālī*). Ibn Khaldūn used the term in the wider sense of group-solidarity and group-assertion, and saw in *ʿaṣabiyya* the fundamental factor in Arab and Islamic history.

Linked in a common loyalty, as Muslim subjects of a Muslim sultan, the Turks and Arabs existed in a symbiosis which paid little attention to linguistic and ethnic distinctions. While Turkish was the language of administration, Arabic was that of the state religion. The circles of powerful officials and influential notables which surrounded the Ottoman governors of Arab provinces, included both those who were linguistically Turks and those who were linguistically Arabs. It is modern nationalist legend rather than historical fact which asserts that the Ottoman period was a time of unrelieved misery and oppression for the Arabs: a tyrannous régime imposed on a resentful people. This legend was a late by-product of developments within the Ottoman Empire during the nineteenth and early twentieth centuries. It owes most, perhaps, to the final phase of Ottoman rule in Syria, under Jemal Pasha during the First World War.[1]

The way was prepared for Arab nationalism by precursors who in various respects had formed the climate of opinion in which nationalist ideas could find understanding and acceptance. Among these was the writer and agitator, Jamāl al-Dīn al-Afghānī, who, between 1869 and his death in 1887, had attracted disciples and fomented conspiracies in the Ottoman Empire, Egypt and Persia. His great and unrealized political aim was Pan-Islam, a union of the Muslim states to withstand the impact of Christian Europe. His principal achievement was to stimulate Muslim self-consciousness in the countries he visited and to propagate resentment at the weakness and dissensions of the Islamic world. Precursors in another sense were the *littérateurs*, of Christian Lebanese origin, Nāṣīf al-Yāzijī and Buṭrus al-Bustānī, who set on foot an Arabic revival, and also Jurjī Zaydān, whose historical writings and novels played a large part in creating the modern Arab image of the Arab past.

Arab nationalism began as the expression of a sense of alienation from the Ottoman régime in its latest phases. It bears witness to the breakdown of the traditional Turco-Arab symbiosis. At first, this sense of alienation was felt only by scattered individuals or minority groups. It is significant that the first recorded secret society which had, ostensibly at least, Arab nationalist aims, was formed by young Lebanese, who were mostly Christians, in about the year 1875. The real purpose of their organization was the liberation of Christian Lebanon from Muslim Ottoman rule: the appeal to Arab national pride was a tactic to gain local Muslim Arab support. This was not, therefore, in any real sense a manifestation of Arab nationalism, but a disguised Lebanese separatist

[1] See below, p. 276.

movement. It completely failed in its political aims and came to an end in 1882 or 1883.

The real history of Arab nationalism begins with the writings and activities of two individuals, both of Syrian origin, ʿAbd al-Raḥmān al-Kawākibī and Najīb ʿAzūrī (Negib Azoury). Although both had links with the traditional Ottoman establishment, they became alienated from it and passed the later part of their lives in exile. Al-Kawākibī, who was born in 1849, spent some time in government service, was imprisoned, and in 1898 went into exile in Egypt. In Cairo he published two political works, and there he died in 1903.

It has been pointed out that al-Kawākibī's political ideas are unoriginal, and were largely derived from the Italian, Alfieri, and the Arabophile Englishman, W. S. Blunt.[1] However this may be, al-Kawākibī's two books, *Tabāʾiʿ al-istibdād* ('The characteristics of tyranny') and *Umm al-qurā* are important because they mark the point at which a definitely Arab nationalist ideology begins to differentiate itself from the general complex of movements for Islamic revival and reform. The preaching of Pan-Islam by al-Afghānī coincided with the assertion by the Ottoman sultans (especially Abdülhamid II) of their claim to the universal caliphate of Islam. While this claim was a device of some political value, it suffered from a serious technical defect. Muslim law, and the practice of the historical caliphate down to the extinction of the ʿAbbasids, required the caliph to be an Arab of Quraysh, the tribe of the Prophet. This genealogical qualification was notably lacking in the Turkish sultans of the House of Osman. Al-Kawākibī, at odds with the Hamidian régime, rejected the theory of the Ottoman caliphate. Instead, he advocated the return of the caliphate to the Arabs, believing that through the Arabs latter-day Islam would be regenerated. Breaking away from traditional Muslim concepts, however, al-Kawākibī envisaged that the caliph would be merely a spiritual head of the Muslim community, without political power.

Behind al-Kawākibī's writings and their ostensible purport lies an obscure background of personal and political relations. His animus against the Ottoman caliphate is at least partly to be explained on familial grounds: Abdülhamid's court astrologer and religious adviser, Abu'l-Hudā al-Sayyādī, belonged to an Aleppine family which challenged the Kawākibīs for the post of *naqīb al-Ashrāf*. During his residence in Egypt, al-Kawākibī seems to have become a propagandist for Khedive

[1] By S. G. Haim in 'Alfieri and al-Kawakibi', *Oriente Moderno*, xxxiv, 1954, 321–334, and 'Blunt and al-Kawakibi', *Oriente Moderno*, xxxv, 1955, 132–43.

ʿAbbās Ḥilmī II and to have undertaken on his behalf a journey in Muslim East Africa and Arabia. The khedive was secretly competing with the sultan for the hegemony of the Muslims (a recurrent phenomenon in the history of Muḥammad ʿAlī's dynasty), and al-Kawākibī's figment of a spiritual Arab caliph may have been deliberately designed to leave room for a temporal Egyptian head of Islam.

The career of Najīb ʿAzūrī has certain resemblances to that of al-Kawākibī. Both of them quitted the service of the Ottoman government in unsatisfactory circumstances and went to live in exile. But, whereas al-Kawākibī was a Muslim of traditional upbringing, ʿAzūrī was a French-educated Christian, and spent part of his years of exile, which lasted from 1904 until his death in 1916, in Paris. While there, he claimed to have established a nationalist organization, *La Ligue de la Patrie arabe*, which may have been merely a cover for his personal activities. In 1905 he published a political manifesto, *Le réveil de la nation arabe*, and during 1907–8 issued a periodical entitled *L'indépendance arabe*. ʿAzūrī had French collaborators, and may have received money from the French government.

ʿAzūrī's doctrine was more radical than that of al-Kawākibī. In this, his Christian background is significant. A Muslim Arab might reject the Ottoman claim to the caliphate, while yet seeking to keep the empire in being as a defence against European Christendom. ʿAzūrī had no such inhibitions, but visualized an Arab empire consisting of the Arabian Peninsula and the Fertile Crescent. He specifically excluded Egypt from the Arab empire, because the Egyptians did not belong to the Arab race, but at the same time he proposed a prince of the khedivial family as ruler of the empire. Al-Kawākibī's scheme of an Arab caliphate was taken up by ʿAzūrī, who allotted to the caliph political sovereignty over the Ḥijāz, and moral authority over all Muslims. As a Christian, however, ʿAzūrī was concerned to emphasize religious freedom and the equality of all citizens, and he envisaged an Arab Christianity delivered from the current hostility of the sects.

The Young Turk revolution of 1908 was a turning-point in the history of Arab as well as of Turkish nationalism. Down to that time there had been no evidence of widespread support for the doctrines of al-Kawākibī and ʿAzūrī. Like the Turks, the Arabs were divided into supporters and opponents of Sultan Abdülhamid and his régime. There was, indeed, a very influential group of Arabs in the inner circle of the sultan's retinue, while the physical links between the Arab provinces and the heart of the empire were strengthened by the construction of the Ḥijāz railway, which ran from Damascus to Medina, and was completed in 1908.

On the other hand, the Young Turk movement was supported by Arabs as well as Turks, and served to channel off Arab opposition to Ottoman rule. Mahmud Shevket (Shawqat) Pasha, who commanded the army which crushed the counter-revolution of 1909 and was subsequently grand vezir, came from an Iraqi family.[1] Immediately after the revolution of 1908, the Arabs in Istanbul founded a society called *al-Ikhāʾ al-ʿArabī al-ʿUthmānī* (the Arab-Ottoman Brotherhood), devoted to the maintenance of the constitution, the promotion of loyalty to the sultan, and the welfare of the Arab provinces. It published a newspaper, and branches of the society were founded in the Fertile Crescent.

This harmonious relationship did not long endure. The deposition of Sultan Abdülhamid in 1909 involved the fall of his personal clique, including his Arab advisers. The odium which they had incurred was not without effect in promoting Turkish animosity against the Arabs, who were deprived of advocates at the centre of power. Arab politicians resented the fact that their provinces were under-represented in the Ottoman parliament, which met in 1908 after an intermission of thirty years. Moreover, once the Young Turk régime was firmly in the saddle, it pursued a policy which had disastrous implications. Conscious of the threatened disintegration of the empire, the Young Turks sought to coerce its heterogeneous peoples into political unity, by centralization and by the imposition of Ottoman Turkish culture. The Arabs, who were perhaps rather more numerous than the Turks themselves, found this policy odious. The suppression of the Arab-Ottoman Brotherhood by the government marked the opening of a breach between the Young Turk régime and the Arab nationalists.

The result of this was a proliferation of nationalist societies in the Fertile Crescent and Istanbul, as well as in Cairo and Paris—the principal refuges of Arab exiles. They ranged from associations such as *al-Muntadā al-ʿArabī* (the Literary Club) founded in Istanbul in 1909, which moved on the fringe between literary and political activities, to secret conspiratorial groups such as *al-Qaḥṭāniyya*,[2] also founded in 1909, which had a particular appeal to Arab officers in the Ottoman army. Its leader was the only Egyptian who played a leading part in the politics of early Arab nationalism—ʿAzīz ʿAlī al-Miṣrī, himself an Ottoman officer. Of more importance were *al-Fatāt* (the Young Arab

[1] The remoter origins of his family were Georgian.

[2] The name is derived from Qaḥṭān, one of the legendary ancestors of the Arabs.

Society), a secret group founded by Arab students in Paris in 1911, and *Ḥizb al-Lāmarkaziyya al-Idāriyya al-ʿUthmānī* (the Ottoman Party of Administrative Decentralization), established by Syrian *émigrés* in Cairo in 1912. In spite of the diversity of their membership and methods, these and the numerous other political societies had broadly the same object: to resist the centralization and turkification imposed by the Ottoman government and to obtain a measure of autonomy for the Arab provinces. The scheme which appealed to some nationalists, such as *al-Qaḥṭāniyya*, was a dual monarchy of the sultan over Turks and Arabs, on the contemporary model of Austria-Hungary.

The most successful publicity operation staged by the nationalists was the holding of an Arab Congress in Paris during June 1913. The Young Arab Society was the initiator of the project, which was supported by the Party of Administrative Decentralization, and by a Syrian autonomist organization, the Committee of Reform, which had been established by some notables of Beirut. The Congress was attended by twenty-five persons, two of whom were Iraqis, the rest of Syrian provenance or origin. The purpose of the Congress was to publicize the current aims of the nationalists—the autonomy of the Arab provinces, Arab participation in the central administration, and the recognition of Arabic, along with Turkish, as an official language of the Ottoman Empire. Although the Ottoman government sent a delegate to the Congress to confer with the nationalist leaders, only limited concessions were made to their demands. The Congress failed to coerce the government, and behind the façade of nationalist unity a serious rift existed between at least some of the Beirutis, whose objective was a Christian Lebanon, possibly under French protection, and the other delegates.

In this early phase of the development of nationalist ideology and organizations, a leading part was played by men from the western Fertile Crescent; it would hardly be an exaggeration to say that Arab nationalism began as the ideological response of the Syrian intelligentsia to late Ottoman rule. The Iraqi provinces had, however, a contribution to make. Officers of Iraqi origin formed an important element in the Ottoman army. They had taken part in *al-Qaḥṭāniyya*, but this society was allowed to lapse by its members, who suspected a spy in their midst. The failure of the moderate nationalists in the 1913 Congress was the opportunity of the extremists. In 1914 ʿAzīz ʿAlī al-Miṣrī organized a new secret society called *al-ʿAhd* (the Covenant), on the lines of *al-Qaḥṭāniyya* but recruited almost entirely from army officers. ʿAzīz ʿAlī was, shortly afterwards, arrested, tried *in camera*, and sentenced to death. The sentence was not carried out, and he returned to Egypt. The Covenant society meanwhile grew and flourished. Branches were formed in Baghdād and Mosul, and the Covenant became in effect a military counterpart to the civilian Young Arab Society, although the two did not join forces until 1915.

Apart from the army officers, the leading exponent of Arab nationalism in the Iraqi provinces was Sayyid Ṭālib ibn Rajab, a member of the family which provided the *naqīb al-Ashrāf* of Baṣra. He was a man of great influence and ambition, the head of a powerful faction in the Baṣra region. He had sought to use in turn both Abdülhamid and the Young Turk régime to further his own schemes for local autonomy. Having failed in both attempts, he turned to nationalism. During the years immediately before the outbreak of the First World War he was playing a double game, keeping in both with the authorities in Istanbul and with the British, who had a long-standing interest in the coastlands of the Persian Gulf, while at the same time presenting himself as a champion of Arab national rights. The later phases of his career will be discussed subsequently.[1]

At the outbreak of the First World War there was much discontent in the Arab provinces with the Young Turk régime. This discontent was mainly felt and expressed by the élite of army officers and Western-educated civilians. It did not in itself constitute a serious threat to the Ottoman Empire: the nationalists did not overtly propose secession from the empire, and their forces were divided among a handful of ineffective conspiratorial groups. That, four years later, Ottoman rule over the Arab provinces had ended, and the nationalists were in expectation of immediate independence, was only to a very limited extent due to their own achievements.

[1] See below, pp. 287, 290–1.

19

The First World War

When, on 29 October 1914, the Ottoman Empire entered the First World War on the side of the Central Powers, the event had long been expected by Britain, and measures were at once taken to secure British interests threatened by this development. As we have seen, the Ottoman suzerainty over Egypt was terminated by the declaration of the British protectorate on 18 December, while, on the following day, ʿAbbās Ḥilmī II was deposed *in absentia*. Concern over communications with India, which led to the annexation of Egypt to the British Empire, accounted also for action in the Persian Gulf. During the first months of the war, consultations were taking place between the British government and the government of India over the advisability of sending an expeditionary force to secure the head of the Gulf and the important oil installations at Abadan. On 3 November the ruler of Kuwayt was recognized as independent under British protection, and urged to co-operate with the expeditionary force from India. Before the end of the month, Ottoman resistance around the Shaṭṭ al-ʿArab had been overcome, and Baṣra occupied. There, for a time, the matter rested.

At this point the British had no general plan for the future disposal of Ottoman territory. Suggestions for an advance on Baghdād began, indeed, to be made shortly after the fall of Baṣra, while the commander-in-chief in Egypt proposed, in December 1914, an expedition to Alexandretta to divert the Ottomans from an attack on Egypt. These, however, were merely schemes for military action, and the second of them was never in fact implemented. Unlike the British, the French from the outset saw in the war an opportunity for the realization of an ancient dream—the establishment of their control over Syria, the restoration of Frankish Outremer by the Third Republic. The French government had, moreover, reason to believe that its aspirations in this region would be regarded sympathetically by Britain, since a declaration made by Sir Edward Grey, the foreign secretary, on 5 December 1912, was interpreted in France as a concession of the French claims.

A clarification of British and French policy in regard to the Ottoman territories became urgently necessary early in 1915, when the Russian government put forward a claim to Constantinople and the Straits. This was reluctantly accepted both by France and Britain, who were therefore induced to consider their own demands for compensation in the event of a partition of Ottoman territory. The French claims, enunciated on 14 March 1915, were clear and comprehensive: the annexation of 'Syria together with the region of the Gulf of Alexandretta and Cilicia up to the Taurus'. Enquiries elicited that, in the French view, Syria included Palestine, an interpretation which caused the Russians to demur, in view of the interests of the Orthodox Church in the Christian Holy Places. At this stage the British government reserved its position over territorial claims, while pointing out the necessity of consultation with the French government, but made the point that it had 'stipulated that the Mussulman Holy Places and Arabia should under all circumstances remain under independent Mussulman dominion'.[1]

The status of the holy cities of Mecca and Medina was indeed a consideration of great importance to Britain. War against the Ottoman sultan-caliph would, it was feared, imperil British control of the millions of Muslims in Egypt, the Sudan, India and elsewhere, to say nothing of those under French and Russian rule. On 7 November 1914 a *fatwā* of the *shaykh al-Islām* of Istanbul declared it to be the duty of all Muslims to unite in arms against Britain, France and Russia as enemies of Islam. Although the evidence of Allied military power was so obvious that few Muslims would be so naïve as to answer the call of the puppet caliph to the *jihād*, the Ottoman propaganda was a potential danger. A Muslim figurehead, to counteract the prestige of the sultan, was therefore needed by the Allies, and the British in particular.

The *amīr* of Mecca, the Hashimite Sharīf Ḥusayn, was an obvious candidate for this role. As the actual and hereditary lord of the holy city, as a descendant of the Prophet (which the Ottoman sultan was not), and as an Arab chief with great personal influence among the tribes of the Ḥijāz, Ḥusayn would be a valuable ally—if he could be persuaded to declare himself openly. The Sharīf Ḥusayn had, for his part, reasons for working with the British. As an ambitious but insecure vassal of the Ottomans, he was anxious to reinforce his dynastic position in the Ḥijāz. Although the *amīrs* of Mecca possessed a good deal of autonomy, they were dependent on the sultan, who appointed and could depose them, and Ottoman intervention in their affairs was facilitated by the division of the Hashimites into two rival clans competing for the amirate. Ḥusayn himself, after fifteen years of detention in Istanbul, had been appointed

[1] For the text of these exchanges, known comprehensively as the Constantinople Agreement, see Hurewitz, ii, 7–11.

to the amirate in 1908 by the Committee of Union and Progress.[1] During the following years he had quietly strengthened his position in the Ḥijāz. In February 1914, a few months before the outbreak of the First World War, he became apprehensive of Ottoman attempts to reduce his power. He therefore sent his son, ʿAbdallāh, later the first king of Jordan, to Cairo, to sound Kitchener as to the attitude of the British government in the event of a revolt in the Ḥijāz. The official reply was discouraging at that time, but Kitchener renewed contact with Ḥusayn in September and again in October 1914.

Kitchener's overtures were followed up in the next year by more specific negotiations between Ḥusayn and Sir Henry McMahon, the British high commissioner in Egypt.[2] In the meantime, Ḥusayn had begun to move from the purely dynastic position which had been his in 1914. He was becoming aware, at first through ʿAbdallāh, of the Arab nationalists in Syria, and was preparing to make their territorial aspirations his own demands in negotiations with the British. A hint by Kitchener of the possibility of a revived Arab caliphate had also worked on his ambition.[3] Hence, in the Ḥusayn–McMahon correspondence[4] which passed between July 1915 and March 1916, the *sharīf* was no longer anxious merely to consolidate his principality in the Ḥijāz, but to emerge as king of the Arabs, a potential caliph, the spokesman of an Arab nationalist movement which had developed independently of him in centres far outside his control.

Ḥusayn's new standpoint is made clear in his first note to Sir Henry McMahon, dated 2 Ramaḍān 1333/14 July 1915. In it, he speaks throughout of 'the Arab nation', which offers terms to Britain and

[1] See above, p. 174.

[2] The title of 'high commissioner' had superseded that of 'British agent and consul-general' on the declaration of the protectorate in 1914.

[3] This was not, of course, a new idea. Al-Kawākibī had proposed the revival of the Arab caliphate, as a spiritual office. Najīb ʿAzūrī had proposed that 'the universal religious caliphate' should be held by a *sharīf* and combined with the political rule over the Ḥijāz. In 1911 thirty-five Arab members of the Ottoman parliament had sent a letter to the Sharīf Ḥusayn (through Sayyid Tālib of Baṣra) offering to follow him as the leader of an Arab revolt, and to recognize him as caliph. See above, pp. 257–8, and also Albert Hourani, *Arabic thought in the liberal age, 1798–1939*, London 1962, 284.

[4] An English translation of the Ḥusayn–McMahon Correspondence was first published by George Antonius, *The Arab awakening*, London 1938, 413–27. Another translation (including two further letters) was officially published by the British government as a White Paper, Miscellaneous No. 3 (1939), *Correspondence between Sir Henry McMahon . . . and the Sherif Hussein of Mecca, July 1915–March 1916* (Cmd. 5957). Except where otherwise indicated, I have quoted from the White Paper translation. A selection from the Correspondence is printed in Hurewitz, ii, 13–17. Photographic reproductions of the Arabic text of two of the letters are given in Z. N. Zeine, *The struggle for Arab independence*, Beirut 1960, Plates 1 and 2.

requests an answer to its proposals. His own status in regard to this 'Arab nation' is never made explicit, although in one clause the phrase 'the Arab government of the Sherif' is used in a context which clearly implies that this will be the government of 'the Arab countries'. The particular interest of this letter is that it specifies the prospective frontiers of the independent 'Arab countries'. The terms in which it does so reproduce a document, the Damascus Protocol, drawn up in Damascus by nationalists of the Young Arab and Covenant societies, and transmitted to Ḥusayn in May 1915 by Fayṣal, the third of his sons.

The essential clause in Ḥusayn's letter is as follows: 'Great Britain recognizes the independence of the Arab countries which are bounded on the north by the line Mersin–Adana to parallel 37°N and thence along the line Birejik–Urfa–Mardin–Midiat–Jazirat (ibn ʿUmar)–Amadia to the Persian frontier; on the east, by the Persian frontier down to the Persian Gulf; on the south, by the Indian Ocean (with the exclusion of Aden whose status will remain as at present); on the west, by the Red Sea and the Mediterranean Sea back to Mersin.' The letter also, and in this it did not follow the Damascus Protocol, demanded, as one of the terms offered by 'the Arab nation', that 'Great Britain should agree to the proclamation of an Arab Caliphate for Islam'.[1]

In his reply, dated 30 August 1915, McMahon confirmed that Britain 'would welcome the resumption of the Khalifate by an Arab of true race'. This, as we have seen, had been suggested in the first place by Kitchener, and was consonant with the British policy of building up the *sharīf* as a figurehead for Islamic loyalties in opposition to the Ottoman sultan-caliph. Over the question of future Arab frontiers, McMahon and the British government were bound to demur, since the territory specified in the Damascus Protocol and Ḥusayn's letter included the 'Syria' to which a claim had been advanced by France in March 1915. Since, furthermore, in Palestine the French claims had not been conceded by Russia, Ḥusayn's demand placed the British in a quandary. McMahon therefore temporized, asserting that detailed negotiations on frontiers appeared to be premature. Ḥusayn, whose position as a nationalist leader as well as a dynastic claimant was now in the balance, could not let the matter rest there. In a second note to McMahon, dated 29 Shawwāl 1333/9 September 1915, he therefore insisted urgently and at length on the clarification of Britain's attitude towards the proposed frontiers.

In the circumstances, the British government did two things: it

[1] In the quotations in this paragraph, I have used Antonius's translation, which is clearer than that in the White Paper.

authorized McMahon to make a declaration on the frontiers; and simultaneously it opened negotiations with France, as the ally immediately affected by the territorial claims of the Arab nationalists. The declaration was made in McMahon's second note, dated 24 October 1915. Since it concerned areas the future disposal of which had not been negotiated among the Allies, it was to some extent vague and tentative. It did however indicate the existence of French and British claims and interests in the region, which would have to be borne in mind in any future settlement. The crucial passages are as follows:

'The two districts of Mersina and Alexandretta and portions of Syria lying to the west of the districts of Damascus, Homs, Hama and Aleppo cannot be said to be purely Arab, and should be excluded from the limits demanded.

With the above modification, and without prejudice to our existing treaties with Arab chiefs, we accept those limits.

As for those regions lying within those frontiers wherein Great Britain is free to act without detriment to the interests of her ally, France, I am empowered in the name of the Government of Great Britain to give the following assurances and make the following reply to your letter:

1. Subject to the above modifications, Great Britain is prepared to recognize and support the independence of the Arabs in all the regions within the limits demanded by the Sherif of Mecca.
2. [Britain guarantees the Holy Places against aggression.]
3. When the situation admits, Great Britain will give to the Arabs her advice and will assist them to establish what may appear to be the most suitable forms of government in the various territories.
4. [Britain to have exclusive rights of advice, and of providing administrative advisers and officials.]
5. With regard to the *vilayets* of Bagdad and Basra, the Arabs will recognize that the established position and interests of Great Britain necessitate special administrative arrangements in order to secure these territories from foreign aggression, to promote the welfare of the local populations, and to safeguard our mutual economic interests.'

The scope of the pledges given in this letter, the sincerity of the British government and its servants in tendering them, and the degree of their compatibility with other and subsequent British commitments in the Sykes–Picot Agreement and the Balfour Declaration, have been topics of bitter controversy since the end of the First World War. It is therefore important to consider both the terms of McMahon's note, and the historical context in which it was written.

It will be noted that two specific blocks of territory are singled out for special mention. 'The *vilayets* of Bagdad and Basra', while not excluded from the area of Arab independence, are to be placed under 'special administrative arrangements', amounting to a British protectorate. This assertion of a particular status for Britain in Lower Iraq was the logical corollary of the action which had been taken there at the outbreak of war with the Ottoman Empire.

Explicitly excluded from the projected area of Arab independence are 'the two districts of Mersina and Alexandretta and portions of Syria lying to the west of the districts of Damascus, Homs, Hama and Aleppo'. This, in its most reasonable and obvious interpretation, would mean the northern Syrian littoral and its westward continuation to the foot of the Taurus. It would thus correspond to a part of 'Syria together with the region of the Gulf of Alexandretta and Cilicia up to the Taurus', which France had claimed in March 1915. It was, however, smaller in extent than the territory demanded by France, since the northern Syrian interior ('the districts of Damascus, Homs, Hama and Aleppo') is explicitly placed within the sphere of Arab independence. Palestine, as such, is not mentioned, and cannot, on any reasonable reading of this clause, be regarded as part of the excluded territory. After the First World War, with the emergence of the Palestine problem, the supposed ambiguity of McMahon's letter concerning Palestine aroused much controversy. The Arab nationalists argued that Palestine was included in the area in which the independence of the Arabs would be recognized. Winston Churchill, as British colonial secretary in 1922, rejected this interpretation, and asserted that McMahon's reservation of 'the portions of Syria lying to the west of the district of Damascus' excluded 'the whole of Palestine west of the Jordan'.[1] This is indeed a straining of the text. Presumably it would be defended on the grounds that the term *wilāya*, rendered in the English versions of McMahon's letter as 'district', is the equivalent of *vilayet*. Since the *vilayet* of Damascus extended south to the Gulf of ʿAqaba, this interpretation would indeed place Palestine in the excluded territory. But McMahon's text speaks of 'the districts of Damascus, Homs, Hama and Aleppo', although Ḥimṣ and Ḥamāh formed part of the *vilayet* of Damascus. It would seem to follow from this incongruity that Churchill was using this passage for a purpose for which it was not originally intended.

Nevertheless, this does not mean that McMahon in 1915 believed himself to have conceded Palestine as part of the area of independence.

[1] Hurewitz, ii, 105–6.

Indeed, in a letter to *The Times* of 23 July 1937, he explicitly denied that he had done so. It is significant, however, that in this letter he makes no allusion to the clause excluding 'portions of Syria lying to the west of the districts of Damascus, Homs, Hama and Aleppo'. We are therefore justified in looking elsewhere for an indication of McMahon's intentions regarding Palestine. It must here be emphasized that in October 1915 Britain was restrained by the claims of two of her allies in regard to Palestine, the future of which was an issue between France and Russia, as advocates respectively of the Latin and Orthodox Churches. The *locus standi* of Britain in this delicate question, in which she was not yet one of the major parties, was safeguarded by the proviso which limits the pledges to 'those regions lying within those frontiers wherein Great Britain is free to act without detriment to the interests of her ally, France'. In other words, by this letter Palestine was neither promised as part of the area of Arab independence nor yet specifically excluded, as was the northern Syrian littoral. The significance of this absence of commitment on Palestine will become apparent when we consider the Sykes–Picot negotiations.

Apart from the question of the inclusion or otherwise of Palestine, the territories excepted by McMahon from the area of Arab independence are very oddly defined. 'The two districts of Mersina and Alexandretta' might justifiably be described as 'not purely Arab', but (granting the inevitable confusion of linguistic and ethnic categories) this could hardly be said of the northern Syrian littoral. An interesting clue to the background of McMahon's phraseology has been provided by a recent investigator, who suggests that the phrase 'Damascus, Homs, Hama and Aleppo' may have been the contribution of Sir Mark Sykes, and may contain an echo of his reading of the history of the Crusades, these being the four cities of the Syrian interior which remained to the Muslims when the power of the Crusaders was at its height.[1] Thus it would seem that the phrase which was to evoke such legalistic controversy in the outcome owed its origin to the sentimental romanticism of an amateur in the history of the Orient and the diplomacy of the Levant.

Some other matters arising from McMahon's second note may now be considered. First, while the Damascus Protocol, followed by Ḥusayn's first note, had tactfully excluded Aden from the area of Arab independence, McMahon made a more comprehensive proviso when he accepted

[1] Emile Marmorstein, 'A note on "Damascus, Homs, Hama and Aleppo"', in *St Antony's Papers, Number 11* (*Middle Eastern Affairs, Number 2*), London 1961, 161–5.

the delimitation 'without prejudice to our existing treaties with Arab chiefs'. This safeguarded Britain's position on the coast of the Persian Gulf, as well as in ʿUmān and Ḥaḍramawt. Secondly, by giving a British pledge to assist the Arabs 'to establish . . . forms of government in those various territories', McMahon indicated that Britain was not committed to the installation of a single Arab government within the area of Arab independence—still less to uphold the sole sovereignty of Ḥusayn. This was made brutally clear when Ḥusayn, on 2 November 1916, assumed the title of 'king of the Arab Countries', and Britain and France refused to recognize this title. He was accorded by them only the style of 'king of the Ḥijāz'.

While the British government regarded with some misgivings the growing ambitions of Sharīf Ḥusayn, its own aspirations were becoming more extensive and definite than they had been in the spring of 1915. Vague as the provisions of McMahon's second note are, they bear witness to an intention to whittle down French claims in Syria to the northern littoral, while leaving the future of Palestine in suspense: at the same time, they safeguard all Britain's existing rights in Arab territories, foreshadow a protectorate of Lower Iraq, and assert a monopoly of providing advice and assistance to future Arab governments. In order to translate these general claims in specific diplomatic terms, Sir Edward Grey, as foreign secretary, proposed negotiations with France about the frontiers of Syria. The proposal was made on 21 October 1915, three days before the writing of McMahon's second note to Ḥusayn.

The concluding and decisive negotiations were handled on the British side by Sir Mark Sykes, a man who combined an intelligent and hard-headed appreciation of British interests in the Near East with a sentimental streak which led him to sympathize concurrently with Arab nationalism and with Zionism. This sentimentality was, however, more apparent than real, being rooted in no genuine feeling for the peoples behind the national causes he espoused. His romantic view of the Arabs was a reaction against the contempt in which he held the 'Levantines', the westernized Arabs of the Fertile Crescent. His advocacy of Zionism arose similarly from his dislike of the assimilated Jews of Europe, and was not far from being a mirror-image of anti-Semitism. Sykes's counterpart in the negotiations, Charles François Georges Picot, was a professional diplomat who had served as French consul-general in Damascus before the war. He fought stubbornly for the fullest recognition of French claims in Syria, but was steadily forced to retreat. The so-called 'Sykes–Picot Agreement', which was embodied in Grey's note of 16 May

1916 to the French ambassador in London, represented the substantial embodiment of those British claims which had been foreshadowed in McMahon's second note to Ḥusayn.[1]

The territorial provisions of the Sykes–Picot Agreement, so far as they concerned Arab territories, were as follows. Two areas were delimited in which France and Britain respectively would 'be allowed to establish such direct or indirect administration or control as they desire'. The French 'blue area' included the northern Syrian littoral from a point south of Sidon, and inland to a line excluding Damascus, Ḥimṣ, Hamāh and Aleppo. The British 'red area' consisted of the Baghdād–Baṣra region of Lower Iraq, and also of a small enclave of the Palestinian coast including Haifa and Acre. The rest of Palestine, lying west of the Jordan and southwards as far as Gaza, was designated as the 'brown area'. In it was to 'be established an international administration, the form of which is to be decided upon after consultation with Russia, and subsequently in consultation with the other allies, and the representatives of the Shereef of Mecca'. The remainder of the Fertile Crescent and the Syrian Desert, lying north of the Arabian Peninsula proper, was divided into two areas. The more northerly 'area (A)', stretched eastwards from the Damascus–Ḥimṣ–Ḥamāh–Aleppo line and including Upper Iraq with Mosul. To the south of this lay 'area (B)'. In these two areas, it was agreed 'That France and Great Britain were prepared to recognize and protect[2] an independent Arab State or a Confederation of Arab States.' The two areas were to be spheres of influence respectively for France and Britain in the matters of 'right of enterprise and local loans' and the sole right of supplying advisers and foreign officials.

Arab nationalists and others have unsparingly denounced the Sykes–Picot Agreement. Much of the criticism which may be levelled at it arises from the anomalies of its origin. Essentially, it was a last essay in the old diplomacy of the nineteenth century, where territorial changes were negotiated by the great powers, where annexation had to be compensated by annexation, sphere of influence by sphere of influence. In this international system, the independence of a minor state (still more, that of a state which existed only in prospect) was contingent and limited. Since, moreover, the provisions of the agreement could be implemented only in the event of an Allied victory, considerable secrecy had necessarily to be maintained over its terms. But in 1916 these assumptions of the

[1] The exchanges constituting the so-called Sykes–Picot Agreement are given in Hurewitz, ii, 18–22. The essential document concerning the Arab territories is also printed in Antonius, 428–30.

[2] In August 1916, 'uphold' was substituted for 'protect'.

old diplomacy were already challenged, and were soon to be popularly discredited. The concept of secret great power diplomacy as the determinant of territorial settlements was to give way to the Wilsonian concepts of national self-determination and open diplomacy. This was not yet the case, but already McMahon, in his negotiations with Ḥusayn, had spoken of 'independence' in a context which remains ambiguous, and to that extent had invoked a principle which could hardly be reconciled with the Sykes–Picot Agreement.[1]

The McMahon pledges and the Sykes–Picot Agreement were incompatible in principle rather than in substance. The blue, red and brown areas were identical with those which had been excluded from the area of Arab independence, or in regard to which Britain had safeguarded her position. The provision for 'an independent Arab State or a Confederation of Arab States' in areas (A) and (B) was compatible with the phraseology of McMahon's note, although the concession of area (A) as a French sphere of influence derogated from the British monopoly envisaged by McMahon. The Sykes–Picot Agreement did indeed mark a new stage in the assertion of British claims in the Arab lands, but it was an assertion at the expense of French, rather than of Arab, interests as they had been presented up to that time. By the agreement the French accepted the limitation of their direct control to the northern Syrian littoral. In the Syrian interior they had a sphere of influence; in Palestine they could at best expect a share in an international régime. The charge that the incompatibility of the McMahon pledges and the Sykes–Picot Agreement was dishonestly concealed by the British from the Sharīf Ḥusayn and the French alike, has now been shown to be misconceived.[2] Through an Arab ex-officer of the Ottoman army, and a member of the Covenant society, named Muḥammad Sharīf al-Fārūqī, the British authorities in Cairo informed Ḥusayn of the negotiations, and secured agreement to the Damascus–Ḥimṣ–Ḥamāh–Aleppo line. At the same time, the French were informed of the *sharīf*'s demands, on the basis of which, as limited in McMahon's second note, the British negotiated.[3]

[1] The crucial passage occurs in McMahon's letter of 30 August 1915. This is translated in the White Paper as '. . . we confirm to you the terms of Lord Kitchener's message, . . . in which was stated clearly our desire for the independence of Arabia and its inhabitants'. Antonius translates the last phrase as 'the independence of the Arab countries and their inhabitants'.

[2] See Elie Kedourie, *England and the Middle East*, London 1956, 38 ff.

[3] The provisions of the Sykes–Picot Agreement respecting Anatolia were supplemented in favour of Italy by the Tripartite Agreement (St Jean de Maurienne) of 18 August 1917. This did not affect the territorial settlement envisaged in the Sykes–Picot Agreement for the Arab lands. See Hurewitz, ii, 23–5.

The Sykes–Picot Agreement represented, then, a considerable success for the British. The future of Palestine remained, however, a matter of some anxiety. The British government had been unwilling to see it brought under French domination, since this would have brought French power up to the frontiers of Egypt; and, in spite of the Entente Cordiale and the wartime alliance, ancient mistrust remained. International control of Palestine, combined with British rule in the Haifa–Acre enclave, seemed a preferable solution, although other ideas about Palestine were already in the air.

During 1917 the military situation in the Near East changed to the Allies' advantage. In Iraq, the occupation of the Baṣra district had been followed in 1915 by an advance up the Tigris. An attempt to capture Baghdād in the autumn was ordered with inadequate preparations, and this phase of the campaign ended with the surrender of the British striking-force at Kūt al-Amāra in April 1916. During the rest of the year the British forces in the south were built up, and preparations were made for a new offensive. A new commander, General Maude, took over, and in December 1916 the British advance up the Tigris was resumed. Baghdād was entered on 11 March 1917, and its tenure was ensured by the occupation of the surrounding territory. Britain was thus established in military control of Lower Iraq, the region in which she had declared a special interest in both the Ḥusayn–McMahon Correspondence and the Sykes–Picot Agreement.

The British forces in Egypt were, at the start of the war, on the defensive, seeking to secure the safety of the Suez Canal against an Ottoman attack across Sinai. Such an attack was delivered and repulsed in February 1915. The British position in Egypt and on the Canal was never subsequently threatened, and in 1916 the British assumed the offensive. The Egyptian Expeditionary Force advanced across Sinai, and in March 1917 attacked the Ottoman positions in the south of Palestine at the first battle of Gaza. In this, and in the second battle of Gaza in April, the Expeditionary Force suffered reverses. During the summer a new British commander, General Allenby, went out, and under him the Expeditionary Force outflanked the Ottomans and broke through into Palestine at the third battle of Gaza in October–November 1917. The Ottomans were pursued to the north, and Allenby made his official entry into Jerusalem on 11 December.

Meanwhile, in June 1916, the Sharīf Ḥusayn had proclaimed his revolt in the Ḥijāz. The Ottoman garrison in Mecca surrendered after some fighting, and Jedda as well as other towns capitulated during the first few weeks of the revolt. Medina alone remained under Ottoman control, and the garrison maintained its stubborn resistance to the end of the war. On the outbreak of the revolt the Ottoman government nominated as *amīr* of Mecca a prince belonging to the rival Hashimite clan, the Sharīf ʿAlī Ḥaydar, then living in Istanbul. He went to Medina, where he remained as a legitimist figurehead until 1917. Medina lay at the end of the Pilgrimage railway from Syria, and as long as this remained open, supplies and reinforcements could be sent to the beleaguered garrison. The cutting of the line, the isolation of Medina, and the elimination of the smaller pockets of Ottoman power in the Ḥijāz were the principal objectives of the early stages of the Arab campaign. Although the bulk of Sharīf Ḥusayn's forces were tribal levies, a body of regular troops and officers was being built up from Arab prisoners of war captured in the Allied operations against the Ottomans. Their first commander was ʿAzīz ʿAlī al-Miṣrī, the founder of the Covenant society, but he was soon succeeded by an Iraqi officer, Jaʿfar Pasha al-ʿAskarī.[1] The Iraqi Arab officers were a distinctive and important element in the supporters of the revolt: one of them, Nūrī al-Saʿīd, also a member of the Covenant society, was subsequently to play a political rôle of great significance in his country of origin. Among the Hashimites, the most distinguished military service to the revolt was given by the Amīr Fayṣal, who, in January 1917, occupied the port of al-Wajh, in northern Ḥijāz. By his capture of al-ʿAqaba in the following July he brought the advanced Arab forces out of the Ḥijāz, into a position where they could operate on the flank of Allenby's forces as they advanced into Palestine. Besides the Hashimite princes, the Arab chiefs and the ex-Ottoman regular officers, the forces of the revolt were advised, organized and assisted by a handful of British officers, one of whom, T. E. Lawrence, acquired a celebrity to which his unusual personality and his literary ability contributed no less than his military exploits.

While these events were taking place in the field there was an important development in British policy regarding Palestine. The provisions of the Sykes–Picot Agreement for the internationalization of the territory no longer seemed adequate. The occupation of Palestine by British forces was about to be realized; while the impending withdrawal of Russia from the war meant the defection of one of the main participants in the proposed international régime. The future of Palestine was

[1] This episode is investigated in a recent study of the career of ʿAzīz ʿAlī, see Majid Khadduri, 'ʿAzīz ʿAlī Al-Miṣrī and the Arab Nationalist Movement', in *St Antony's Papers, Number 17* (*Middle Eastern Affairs, Number 4*), London 1965, 140–63.

an open question, and in these circumstances the British government, on 2 November 1917, authorized a statement of policy which has become known as the Balfour Declaration.[1]

The Balfour Declaration, which announced that the British government '[viewed] with favour the establishment in Palestine of a national home for the Jewish people, and [would] use their best endeavours to facilitate the achievement of this object', represented a hesitant and partial commitment to the support of Zionist aspirations. It was the culmination of a struggle which had been going on since the early days of the war, waged by Zionists and their sympathizers in Britain, to obtain government sponsorship of their aims. The considerations which led to the publication of the Balfour Declaration are not, perhaps, as obvious as they might appear. The link between support for Zionism and a claim to British control over Palestine had been important at a rather earlier stage, but does not seem to have been significantly in the minds of Cabinet ministers in the weeks immediately preceding the Declaration. The future of Palestine was a far less important factor than the attitudes of the Russian and American Jewries towards the Allied war effort. It was naïvely hoped that Jewish influence would arrest the withdrawal of Russia from the war, just as it was hoped, with rather more realism, that the Declaration would stimulate the enthusiasm of American Jewry for the Allied cause.

Down to this point the British government had been working essentially within the framework of traditional diplomacy, and had constructed a scheme for the partition of the Ottoman Arabian territories which took into account the demands of other interested parties—the Hashimites, the French and the Zionists. The success of the scheme depended essentially on the acceptance by all the parties of their shares under the scheme—shares which were in all cases less than their maximum demands. Thus, the Hashimites were promised the independence of Arab territories subject to limitations indicated in the Ḥusayn–McMahon Correspondence, and more precisely specified in the Sykes–Picot Agreement. The French, by this same agreement, were excluded from the Syrian interior and from Palestine. The Zionists were promised support for a national home, but not for a Jewish state.

In the winter of 1917 this scheme, based on partition, compromise and secret agreements among the interested parties, broke down. The publication of the Balfour Declaration was the first stage in its disintegration, since this, for all its tentativeness, was a public statement of

[1] For the Balfour Declaration, see Hurewitz, ii, 25–6.

policy—the first of its kind—and an open appeal to an organized body of opinion. A few weeks later, early in December 1917, the contents of the Sykes–Picot Agreement, which had been communicated by the Bolsheviks to the Ottoman government, were announced by Jemal Pasha, the governor of Damascus, at a public banquet in Beirut. Although Ḥusayn had undoubtedly been informed by the British of the tenor of the Sykes–Picot Agreement, the publication of its terms, and of the Balfour Declaration, could not fail to damage his standing in the eyes of the Arab public. From this time to the end of the war and afterwards, the scheme for the post-war settlement of the Arab lands disintegrated, and the various parties to the diplomacy of 1914–17, lacking any common plan, fought confusedly for their own interests.

At the outset, the British endeavoured to bolster up the position of Ḥusayn, who, for his part, professed ignorance of the terms of the Anglo-French Agreement. On three occasions, reassurances were sent to him by the British government.[1] The Hogarth Message, delivered on 4 January 1918, sought to diminish the impact of the Balfour Declaration and envisaged 'a special régime' for the Muslim, Christian and Jewish holy places in Palestine. On 8 February, in response to Ḥusayn's disclosure that Jemal Pasha had attempted to open negotiations with the Hashimites, a second message denounced Ottoman intrigues to create dissension. Finally, on 8 June, after Ḥusayn had protested his ignorance of the Sykes–Picot Agreement and had asked for particulars, Sir Reginald Wingate (who had succeeded McMahon as high commissioner in Egypt) declared that the published documents '[did] not constitute an actually concluded agreement', and went on to say that 'the subsequent outbreak and the striking success of the Arab Revolt, as well as the withdrawal of Russia, had long ago created an altogether different situation'. The real significance of Wingate's message lies in this indication that the British government was now prepared to abandon the Sykes–Picot Agreement as the draft of a post-war territorial settlement.

While Ḥusayn was still prepared to work with the British, Fayṣal endeavoured during the summer of 1918 to reinsure himself by negotiations with the Ottomans. Jemal Pasha had contacted Fayṣal as early as January 1917, and had made fresh overtures, on 26 November 1917, to

[1] The Hogarth Message of 4 January 1918 was published in a British White Paper, *Miscellaneous No. 4 (1939), Statements . . . in regard to the future status of certain parts of the Ottoman Empire* (Cmd. 5964), 35. The Message (without accompanying material) is reproduced in Hurewitz, ii, 28–9. The message of 8 February was published in an English translation by Antonius, 431–2. Wingate's message of 8 June was also published by Antonius, 257, where the message is wrongly dated: cf. Elie Kedourie, *England and the Middle East*, 112, n. 2.

Fayṣal and Jaʿfar al-ʿAskarī. This was the correspondence that Ḥusayn had disclosed to the British. During the summer of 1918, Fayṣal was in touch with both Jemal Pasha and Mustafa Kemal, soon to emerge as the Turkish national leader, and indicated his willingness to transfer his support from the British to the Ottomans. The negotiations became known to Lawrence, under whose tutelage Fayṣal appears to have continued them for a time, ostensibly as bluff. The whole incident remains obscure, and the defeats inflicted on the Ottomans in the autumn rendered the negotiations pointless.

Meanwhile the situation of the Hashimites was further weakened in the summer of 1918 by the emergence of Arab nationalist spokesmen who were not committed to Ḥusayn. The *sharīf*'s relations with the nationalists had, from the outset, been equivocal; his assumption in 1916 of the title of 'king of the Arab countries' had been no more acceptable to them than to the Allies. In the Arab nationalism of the Syrians there was from the start a strong element of localism, which had asserted itsel in the past against the centralizing policy of the C.U.P., as now agains Ḥusayn's dream of a Hashimite monarchy. Under the military rule o Jemal Pasha, the nationalists within Syria had been reduced to silence A treason-trial, followed by twenty-two executions in Damascus anc Beirut during April and May of 1916, provided the cause with it martyrs, but drove nationalism underground. However, in June 1918 seven Syrians domiciled in Egypt addressed a memorial to the Britisl government expressing their point of view. The British reply, known a the Declaration to the Seven, was delivered on 16 June 1918.[1] It divide the Arab territories into four categories. In the first two, 'territorie which were free and independent before the outbreak of the War' an those 'liberated from Turkish rule by the action of the Arabs themselves' the British government recognized 'the complete and sovereign inde pendence of the Arabs'. In the third category, of 'territories liberate from Turkish rule by the action of the Allied armies', the British polic was 'that the future government of those territories should be based upo the principle of the consent of the governed'. With regard to the fourt category, of 'territories still under Turkish rule', the British governmer desired 'that the oppressed peoples . . . should obtain their freedom an independence'.

Thus, the Declaration to the Seven invoked a new principle for th

[1] For the Declaration to the Seven, see Cmd. 5964 of 1939, 5–6; also Antonius, 433– The White Paper version is reproduced in Hurewitz, ii, 29–30. The Antonius renderir is cited in the text.

future territorial settlement. Independence, actual or potential, was to be fostered: the reservations of the Ḥusayn–McMahon Correspondence, like the balancing interests of the Sykes–Picot Agreement, were totally ignored. The euphoria induced by these assurances stimulated the co-operation of the Arab forces in the field with Allenby's troops in the final stage of the campaign against the Ottomans. In the middle of September, Fayṣal, who was now operating in Transjordan, cut the railway communications to the south, west and north of Darʿā in the upper valley of the Yarmūk, thus preventing quick and easy reinforcement of the Ottoman forces in Palestine. On 19 September Allenby launched his attack against the Ottoman Eighth Army in the north of the Palestinian coastal plain. The Ottomans fell back, and the British troops broke through into Galilee, trapping the enemy between their own forces and those of the Arabs across the Jordan. The great push to the north had begun.

With the Ottoman forces in rout, the four cities of the Damascus–Ḥimṣ–Ḥamāh–Aleppo line became vital political objectives to the Arabs, since to secure them would ensure as independent territory the Syrian hinterland, under the terms of the Declaration to the Seven. To facilitate this, Allied forces were held back from Damascus until the Hashimite troops entered on 1 October.[1] Among them was Lawrence, who dismissed a provisional government, headed by two descendants of the Amīr ʿAbd al-Qādir al-Jazāʾirī, and substituted an administration of his own choice. Allenby and Fayṣal arrived in Damascus two days later. Meanwhile the advance to the north continued. Aleppo fell on 26 October, and four days later, with the signing of the Armistice of Mudros, the Ottoman Empire withdrew from the war.

[1] The first Allied troops to enter Damascus were actually the Third Australian Light Horse Brigade, who passed through in pursuit of the enemy. See Elie Kedourie, 'The Capture of Damascus, 1 October 1918', in *Middle Eastern Studies*, i/1, 1964, 66–83.

20

The Post-War Settlement in the Fertile Crescent and Egypt

The Western Fertile Crescent

The First World War ended four centuries of Ottoman sovereignty i the Arab lands. As to what should take its place, opinions were numerou and conflicting. For the time being, Britain was the dominant powe In the western Fertile Crescent, supreme authority lay in the hands of British soldier, the Allied commander-in-chief, General Allenby. Apa from her military predominance in the region, Britain had, betwee 1915 and the end of the war, undertaken a series of diplomatic initiative which were to affect the subsequent settlement. These had resulted i the McMahon pledges to Sharīf Ḥusayn, the Sykes–Picot Agreeme with France, and the Balfour Declaration to the Zionists. It has bee suggested in the previous chapter that there was perhaps less form incompatibility between the McMahon pledges and the Sykes–Pic Agreement than has generally been believed, and that even the Balfo Declaration represented a development of the policy implied or expresse in these earlier negotiations. At the end of the war, however, the make of the settlement in the Near East were not solving an academic proble in pure diplomacy. They were hard-bitten politicians, subject pressures from their partisans and their opponents, concerned to obta the interpretations which most favoured their own interests.

While the settlement envisaged in the wartime statements w threatened on the one hand by the incompatible aims of the parti thereto, it was menaced on the other by the enunciation of new politic principles. British propaganda had from the start spoken of 'the freei of the Arab peoples from the Turkish yoke, which for so many yea has pressed heavily upon them'.[1] These trite and dubious platitud came to be taken increasingly seriously by the Arabs themselves, by t Arabophile British officers who worked with them, and even by respo sible statesmen. They prepared the way for the publication, ostensibly serious statements of policy, of such rhetorical communications as th to King Ḥusayn on 8 February 1918, which asserted that the Briti

[1] McMahon to Ḥusayn, 24 October 1915.

government and the Allies were 'determined to stand by the Arab peoples in their struggle for the establishment of an Arab world in which law shall replace Ottoman injustice, and in which unity shall prevail over the rivalries artificially provoked by the policy of Turkish officials'.[1] From this, it was a short step to the full acceptance of the Wilsonian doctrine of self-determination. But in spite of appearances, this was a step never taken by the British government. Hence, the settlement as it was finally made seemed to the Arab leaders a treacherous betrayal. They felt that they had been deceived, as indeed they had, but the deception began after the Sykes–Picot Agreement, and was the result of opportunism and inconsistency rather than of deliberation and malevolence.

In the evolution of the post-war settlement in the Fertile Crescent, two, and only two, powers were ultimately of importance. These were the two parties to the Sykes–Picot Agreement, France and Britain, and to both of them the Near East was but one of a number of fields in which their aims and policies had to be harmonized and regulated. When this had been achieved, as was the case in the Near East by the end of October 1919, the settlement followed as a matter of course, and what in fact emerged was something curiously like the old, disavowed scheme of the Sykes–Picot Agreement.

At the outset, however, in October and November of 1918, the lines of future development were by no means obvious. The French military presence in the western Fertile Crescent was insignificant. Britain was in physical control, and associated with the British were the Arab forces under the command of Amīr Fayṣal. Although Allenby himself strove to act with impartiality, much of British opinion (and not only in the Near East) was as sympathetic to Arab aspirations as it was hostile to French claims. Furthermore, the pre-eminence of President Wilson at the Peace Conference of Paris suggested that the political principles he sponsored would predominate in the settlement, and that the United States would assume an active rôle in the politics of the Near East. In the event, the importance of Fayṣal was to prove illusory, and the influence of Wilson transient.

The establishment of an Arab administration, dependent on Fayṣal, in Damascus on 1 October 1918, synchronized with the recognition of Hashimite authority in Beirut by an administration which had been formed on the Ottoman withdrawal on the previous day. This extension of Fayṣal's power was, however, short-lived. Allenby insisted on his instructions, which were to allow the French to occupy the blue area

[1] See above, p. 275.

of the Sykes–Picot Agreement. Fayṣal, as representing King Ḥusayn, was restricted to the Syrian interior and Transjordan. On 5 October he appointed a government at Damascus under a former Arab officer of the Ottoman army, ʿAlī Riḍā Pasha al-Rikābī. Three days later the authority of the Hashimites in Beirut came to an end. On 23 October Allenby set up three zones of Occupied Enemy Territory Administration. The southern zone (O.E.T.S.) consisted of Palestine west of the River Jordan; the western zone (O.E.T.W.)[1] was formed from Lebanon and the coastal districts north of Palestine; while the interior of Syria and Transjordan composed the eastern zone (O.E.T.E.). British, French and Arab administrators respectively controlled the three zones.

The limitations on the sphere of authority allotted to Fayṣal, and the assignment of O.E.T.W. to France, were ominous indications to the Arab nationalists that the complete independence of the western Fertile Crescent was not a foregone conclusion. The dilemma—or the inconsistency—of British policy was now evident. The situation was not improved, although Arab suspicions may have been temporarily alleviated, by an Anglo-French Declaration which was published on 7 November. This pronouncement stated that the object of the two powers was 'the complete and definite emancipation of the peoples so long oppressed by the Turks and the establishment of national governments and administrations drawing their authority from the initiative and free choice of the indigenous populations'.[2] Apparently the British and French governments were prepared to commit themselves to the principle of self-determination. This was, however, by no means the fact.

In an atmosphere very different from that engendered by this heady manifesto, the British and French prime ministers met in London during the first days of December 1918 to discuss their policy at the coming Peace Conference. Although Lloyd George wished to modify the Sykes–Picot Agreement in the British interest, there was no question of abandoning it as the basis of the territorial settlement in the Fertile Crescent. Since the making of the Agreement British forces had occupied the Iraqi provinces, while the circumstances in which an internationa régime had been envisaged for Palestine had ceased to exist. Lloyc George therefore demanded and obtained the abandonment of th French claim to Mosul (which lay within area (A) of the Agreement) anc

[1] This was at first known as O.E.T. North, a designation which in December 1918 wa transferred to French-occupied Cilicia.

[2] The British White Paper version (followed above) is given in Hurewitz, ii, 30. A independent translation from the French text is given in Antonius, 435–6.

the acceptance of British control over Palestine. This represented a serious modification of the Agreement in favour of Britain, although in practice it only sanctioned the actual position of Britain in the Fertile Crescent. In return, Clemenceau obtained certain concessions, of which the most important was the confirmation of French rights in Syria and Cilicia (i.e. the blue area and the rump of area (A) of the Agreement).

By the Sykes–Picot Agreement, and again by the verbal agreement of December 1918, the British reduced to comparatively small proportions the vast Levantine empire of which the French had dreamed before 1914. As they did so, the British appetite had grown. Their originally vague and unformulated territorial aims had steadily become more precise as the war went on and the British conquest of the Fertile Crescent proceeded. But although in 1918 the British wanted far more than they had done even at the time of the Sykes–Picot negotiations, their demands were definite and, in December 1918, final. Given the control of Iraq and Palestine, they had neither the desire nor the intention of retaining responsibility for the territory administered by Fayṣal.

It was, therefore, the future of this territory, O.E.T.E., which was to be the principal issue among the British, the French and Fayṣal during 1919. The struggle took place against the background of the Peace Conference of Paris, which began in January of that year. Almost from the start one matter was clear, and it was a matter highly discouraging to Fayṣal and the Arab nationalists. The former Arab provinces of the Fertile Crescent would receive at best only a limited degree of autonomy under European tutelage, by the application to them of the so-called mandate system. Although expressed in a Wilsonian idiom, the mandates were recognized by the Arabs for what they were in fact—the fulfilment of the process which had been in train since 1798, whereby an Anglo-French ascendancy was extended and legitimized in the Near East. The clause establishing the mandate system was approved by the Peace Conference on 28 April 1919.

The full implications of this were not at first obvious. Fayṣal still retained some political importance. In November 1918 he left for Europe, where he was received coolly in France, and warmly in Britain. When the Peace Conference opened he acted as the representative of King Ḥusayn, first submitting a memorandum[1] which stated the case of the nationalists for the independence and ultimate unity of Arab Asia. This he reaffirmed in a second statement. Subsequently he appeared in person, supported by Lawrence, and emphasized his demand for Arab self-determination,

[1] Text in Hurewitz, ii, 38–9, and Zeine, 248–51.

citing particularly the Anglo-French Declaration of the previous November. A curious and abortive side-issue of Fayṣal's diplomacy at this period was an agreement with Dr Chaim Weizmann, the Zionist leader, for 'the closest possible collaboration in the development of the Arab State and Palestine'. Born of a common mistrust of the nature and scope of French aims in the western Fertile Crescent, the agreement had no practical consequences.[1]

A more valuable ally to Fayṣal and the Arab nationalists was President Wilson. The American leader had no sympathy with either the French or the British attempts to safeguard their positions in the Fertile Crescent. When, at a conference on 20 March,[2] a dispute arose between Lloyd George and the French foreign minister over French claims in Syria, Wilson demanded that an inter-allied commission should be sent out 'to discover the desires of the population of these regions'. Thus, it appeared, the relics of the Sykes–Picot Agreement were to be swept aside and the mechanism of self-determination to be set up. But Wilson's project soon ran into difficulties. Clemenceau had conceded all he was prepared to concede, and at the end of May he refused to allow French participation in the commission while the British military forces remained in Syria (i.e. O.E.T.E. and O.E.T.W.). The British had up to this point supported the project, but did not relish the possibility that the commission would extend its enquiries to Iraq, and Lloyd George seized the opportunity of Clemenceau's boycott to dissociate himself from the scheme. In the end, a purely American commission, composed of Dr Henry Churchill King and Mr Charles R. Crane, went out to Syria, made their enquiries, and in due course presented their findings. The King–Crane Report was overtaken by events, and had no effect whatsoever on the ultimate settlement.[3]

The abortive King–Crane Commission marked the end of American political intervention in the affairs of the Fertile Crescent. Its lack of political significance was not, however, clear to Fayṣal or the Arab nationalists, or, indeed, to the British military and political officers in Syria. Fayṣal returned to Syria at the end of April, and forthwith began to stimulate the nationalist demand for complete independence. He convoked a Syrian National Congress, which included delegates from O.E.T.W. and O.E.T.S. as well as from his own territory. The Congress

[1] Text of the Fayṣal–Weizmann Agreement in Antonius, 437–9.

[2] For the record of this conference, see Hurewitz, ii, 50–9.

[3] The recommendations of the King–Crane Commission are printed in Antonius, 443–58; and, less fully, in Hurewitz, ii, 66–74.

claimed to speak for the whole of the western Fertile Crescent. It met in June 1919 and shortly afterwards proceeded to pass a series of resolutions which embodied the nationalist programme. Syria (i.e. the whole of the western Fertile Crescent) should be completely independent as a constitutional monarchy under Fayṣal. The necessity for a mandate was rejected; but should one be imposed, the preferred mandatory power would be the United States or, failing America, Britain. The validity of French claims in Syria was totally rejected, as were Zionist pretensions in Palestine.[1]

Already, in June, Britain had made it clear that she would not accept a mandate for any part of the western Fertile Crescent other than Palestine. Although, for some months yet, Fayṣal continued to cherish hopes that the United States or Britain would in extremity intervene on his behalf, these were illusory. America was out of the running, even before Wilson left Europe at the end of 1919. As between France and Britain, it was simply a matter of time before they reached agreement over Syria. This was delayed a few weeks longer, because of a residual feeling of responsibility towards Fayṣal, which caused the British government to endeavour to secure by negotiation what it was unwilling to maintain by a military occupation. On 13 September, however, Lloyd George and Clemenceau came to terms.[2] The British forces were to commence the evacuation of Syria (i.e. O.E.T.W. and O.E.T.E.) by 1 November. The French were to take over the garrisons in O.E.T.W., while those of Damascus, Ḥimṣ, Ḥamāh and Aleppo were to be taken over by Fayṣal's troops. Fayṣal, who reached London on 18 September, denounced this partition of Syrian territory, but his influence had now diminished to vanishing-point. Apart from a final advocacy of Fayṣal's claims to Clemenceau on 18 October, Lloyd George took no further action on his behalf. The evacuation of British forces proceeded, and was completed by the first week in December.

Thus, by the end of 1919 it was clear that all Fayṣal could hope to do was to safeguard the autonomy of the truncated Syria east of the Sykes–Picot line. Two possibilities were open to him: to conciliate the French, or to defy them. He first turned towards conciliation. While in Europe he negotiated a provisional agreement with Clemenceau conceding to France a primacy in Syria which amounted to a protectorate, and recognizing the independence of Lebanon under French mandate.

[1] For the text of the resolutions, see Antonius, 440–2; Zeine, 265–9, and Hurewitz, ii, 62–4.

[2] For the *aide-memoire* of 13 September 1919, see Zeine, 260–2.

Meanwhile the situation in Fayṣal's territory was deteriorating, and the country was seething with unrest. As the British shield against the French was withdrawn, the nationalists sought other allies. These were the Turks, so recently execrated as the oppressors of the Arab nation. An understanding with the Syrians was also useful to Mustafa Kemal, the leader of the Turkish national resistance. Co-operation between the two groups began in the autumn of 1919 and continued into the following summer. But the Kemalists were too heavily committed in Anatolia to lend much help to the Arab nationalists, and their mutual co-operation, although an interesting political phenomenon, was of marginal importance. Meanwhile there were sporadic hostilities between the Syrian nationalists and the French. Raids were launched into French-occupied territory, while the French for their part encouraged the Lebanese to undertake guerrilla warfare in Syria, and pressed on with the occupation of the Biqāʿ. In December 1919 conscription was introduced and urban committees of defence were instituted.

It was to this disturbed and militant country that Fayṣal returned in January 1920. There had already been demonstrations against him, and the news of his draft agreement with Clemenceau had damaged his standing with the nationalists. In an attempt to safeguard his own position and to exert a moderating influence on the national movement, he jettisoned his policy of conciliation. The National Congress, which had been dissolved in December 1919, was reconvened in February 1920. Henceforward it dominated the situation, and Fayṣal was little more than its instrument. On 7 March it passed a resolution claiming complete independence for Syria within its natural boundaries (thereby including Palestine and Lebanon), and electing Fayṣal as constitutional monarch. A political and economic union between Syria and Iraq was declared, and a so-called 'Iraqi Congress' in Damascus proclaimed the Amīr ʿAbdallāh, Fayṣal's brother, ruler of Iraq. ʿAlī Riḍā Pasha al-Rikābī, who had headed Fayṣal's administration since the capture of Damascus, became the prime minister of the Syrian kingdom.

These gestures were irrelevant to the territorial settlement which was about to be made by the European powers. In April the Allied Supreme Council, dominated by Britain and France, since the United States had by now withdrawn from the work of peace-making, met at San Remo to draft the treaty with Turkey. On 25 April the mandates for the former Arab provinces were assigned. Great Britain obtained Iraq and Palestine, France was given Syria, including Lebanon.[1] When the news became

[1] These dispositions were incorporated in the Treaty of Sèvres (10 August 1920): see

known, nationalist opinion in Fayṣal's kingdom reacted violently. Al-Rikābī fell from power, and a new ministry was formed to defend Syrian independence. On 8 May the National Congress passed another resolution, demanding full independence and rejecting both the imposition of the mandate and the amputation of Palestine.

Neither the physical resources nor the military organization of the Syrian kingdom were adequate to maintain the independence which the National Congress so jealously asserted. Since November 1919 the French high commissioner in the former O.E.T.W. had been a soldier, General Gouraud, who, with the backing of public opinion in France, was anxious to assert his country's claims and end the pretensions of Hashimite Syria. Until the end of May he was preoccupied with hostilities against the Kemalists in Cilicia, but the conclusion then of a Franco-Turkish armistice left him free to prepare a reckoning with Fayṣal.

In July Fayṣal determined to return to Europe to state his case to the Peace Conference. He sent his envoy, Nūrī Pasha al-Saʿīd, to Gouraud to announce his intention, but Nūrī was warned that important demands were about to be sent to Fayṣal. These amounted to an ultimatum which reached Fayṣal on 14 July. Their gist was that Syria should accept the mandate and should carry out measures to end the harassing of the French. Already, before the ultimatum was delivered, premonitions of its contents had produced mob-risings and war-fever in Damascus. On 19 July the National Congress, with a total disregard of the military capacity of Syria, declared that it would regard as null and void any act by the government which did not maintain the full independence of the country. Fayṣal asserted his authority by dissolving the Congress, but his kingdom was crumbling into anarchy. Conscious of weakness, he and his government sought to gain time, and on 20 July he sent a telegram to Gouraud, accepting the terms of the ultimatum. Owing to the destruction of telegraph lines in the growing disorder, the telegram failed to arrive in time and the French troops began to advance towards Damascus.

Although there were further desperate negotiations, Gouraud was determined to continue his advance. A final note from King Fayṣal, written on 23 July, rejecting the latest French demands, was of little significance. Ill-armed volunteer reinforcements from Damascus, headed by the minister for War, went out to support the regular troops at Khān

---

Hurewitz, ii, 84–5. For Article 22 of the Covenant of the League of Nations (28 June 1919), which established the mandate system, see Hurewitz, ii, 61–2.

Maysalūn, at the approach to the capital. They were overwhelmed on 24 July and the French entered Damascus. Fayṣal, who had at first withdrawn to the outskirts of the city and then returned, was compelled by Gouraud to leave both his capital and his kingdom. On 1 August he reached Haifa. The Syrian kingdom was at an end, and the French had imposed their mandate.

The Iraqi Provinces

The developments in the Ḥijāz and the western Fertile Crescent, which we have chiefly followed so far, have a spectacular and dramatic quality which is hardly matched in the Iraqi provinces. The course of events, from Sharīf Ḥusayn's proclamation of revolt in June 1916 to the expulsion of his son, Fayṣal, from Damascus four years later, reflected the rise and fall of a British policy in Arab affairs that was the product of wartime conditions. The object of this policy was to seek the military co-operation of the Arabs against the Ottomans, its chosen instrument was the Hashimite family, it sympathized with Arab nationalism, and it professed to envisage Arab independence. The centre of this policy during and immediately after the war was the group of British officers who constituted the Arab Bureau in Cairo.[1]

There was, however, another policy-making institution, which could assert a longer tradition of handling Arab affairs, and which had a standpoint very different from that of the Arab Bureau and the so-called 'Western school'. This was the government of India, which had inherited the East India Company's strategic and commercial interests in the Persian Gulf and the peripheral territories. On almost every point the 'Eastern school' of Arab policy differed from the 'western school'. The campaign in the Iraqi provinces was mounted from India: it was British and Indian in personnel and it made virtually no attempt to secure Arab collaboration. The protégé of the government of India was the Wahhābī *amīr*, ʿAbd al-ʿAzīz ibn Saʿūd, who had, since the beginning of the century, re-established the hegemony of his family in Najd and eastern Arabia and was the rival and enemy of the Hashimites. The 'Eastern school' viewed Arab nationalism with mistrust, and, in the tradition of British rule in India, rated efficient administration far above self-

[1] The Arab Bureau, officially established in February 1916, with the geographer D. G. Hogarth as director, developed out of a group of experts who advised McMahon on Arab affairs. Its members included G. F. Clayton, the Sudan agent and director of Military Intelligence in Cairo; two other members of the Sudan Political Service, Kinahan Cornwallis (who later played an important rôle in Iraq) and Stewart Symes (subsequently governor-general of the Sudan), and also T. E. Lawrence.

government. Thus, the occupation and administration of the Iraqi provinces were accomplished by persons whose outlook was widely different from that of their counterparts in the western Fertile Crescent. British policy towards the Arabs at the end of the war was not monolithic: a schism existed between Cairo and Baghdād, and this dualism was reflected even at Cabinet level in London.

Baṣra fell in November 1914, Baghdād in March 1917, Mosul was not surrendered until November 1918—a week after the Armistice of Mudros. The administration set up as the occupation proceeded was largely Indian in its concepts and methods, while its personnel was mainly composed of British and Indian officials. Although deference was paid to Arab notables, such as the *naqīb* of Baghdād, ʿAbd al-Raḥmān al-Jaylānī, and the Shīʿī *mujtahids*[1] of the holy cities, only the tribal chiefs had any portion of recognized authority. This denial of power to the Arabs was initially easy to achieve, since there was virtually no nationalist leadership in the country. The Iraqi officers of the Covenant society were serving with Fayṣal, while the powerful and notorious Sayyid Ṭālib of Baṣra was excluded from the country from 1915 to 1920.[2] Since, in both the Ḥusayn–McMahon Correspondence and the Sykes–Picot Agreement, the British had insisted on a special status in the Baṣra–Baghdād region, and since Clemenceau had abandoned the French claim to Mosul in December 1918, the future administration of the Iraqi provinces as a dependency of Britain seemed to be assured.

At the head of the civil administration, under the general officer commanding, was the chief political officer, whose title was changed in September 1917 to civil commissioner. The first to hold this office was Sir Percy Cox, who had previously been foreign secretary in India, and had had long experience in the Persian Gulf. During 1918 Cox was transferred to Tehran, and A. T. (later Sir Arnold) Wilson became acting civil commissioner. Wilson was a dedicated believer in the 'Eastern school' of Arab policy. He was, therefore, horrified at the Anglo-French Declaration of 7 November 1918, which promised 'national governments and administrations' in Syria and Mesopotamia. Twelve days later the India Office asked for his views on a proposal, emanating from Lawrence, that three states should be constituted in Lower Mesopotamia, Upper Mesopotamia and Syria, under the sons of King

[1] The *mujtahids* are Shīʿī religious leaders, whose status and influence approximates to that of the chief *'ulamā'* among the Sunnīs. As the name shows, they assert a claim to *ijtihād*, i.e. individual and authoritative interpretation of the *Sharīʿa*. Among Sunnī Muslims generally, *ijtihād* is held to have ceased since the third century of Islam.

[2] See above, p. 261.

Ḥusayn, ʿAbdallāh, Zayd and Fayṣal respectively. Ḥusayn would himself remain king of the Ḥijāz, and, beyond the insertion of his name in the *khuṭba*, would have no status in the Fertile Crescent.

These indications of the influence of the 'Western school' in London were alarming and distasteful to Wilson. He was reassured by the India Office that the intention of the Declaration 'was primarily to clear up the existing situation in Syria', and he was informed that a régime was envisaged in Iraq analogous 'to the position of Egypt before the war, exclusive of the capitulations'. Taking up a suggestion by Wilson himself, the India Office asked him to give 'an authoritative statement of the views held by the local population' on three points:

1. Do they favour a single Arab state under British tutelage stretching from the Northern boundary of the Mosul wilayat to the Persian Gulf?
2. In this event, do they consider that a titular Arab head should be placed over this new State?
3. In that case, whom would they prefer as head?[1]

Fortified by these instructions, Wilson proceeded to hold a plebiscite. As might have been expected, in a country unused to such ostensibly democratic procedures, one lying moreover under British occupation and administration, the responses were favourable to Wilson's own views. The inclusion of Mosul in the new state was generally desired; the continuation of British control was widely welcomed; there was no clear indication as to whom the Iraqis desired as the Arab head of state.

At the beginning of 1919, therefore, Wilson and the 'Eastern school' were still firmly in control of Iraq. The situation was to change to their disadvantage in the next eighteen months. Iraq could not be sealed off from the western Fertile Crescent, where Fayṣal, with British support, was establishing himself in Damascus. The Iraqi officers, who formed an important section of his supporters and entourage, were anxious for the future of their own homeland, and were in a position to revive and subsidize nationalist agitation in Iraq itself. An incident during the summer of 1919 demonstrated the incompatibility between Wilson and the nationalists. After a conversation in Damascus, he invited the Iraqi officers to send a representative to advise him in Baghdād. Their nominee, a lawyer named Nājī Bey al-Suwaydī, arrived in June but soon found that he was no more than a cipher and returned to Damascus. This event sharpened the mistrust of the nationalists and pointed the

[1] A. T. Wilson, *Loyalties: Mesopotamia, 1914–17*, London 1930, ii, 111.

contrast between Iraq, administered by British and Indian officials, and Fayṣal's Syria, apparently on the verge of independence.

Events in the western Fertile Crescent continued to have their repercussions in Iraq. The Iraqi officers with Fayṣal were themselves an alien group in Syria, and their consciousness of this fact increased their desire for an independent Iraqi state in which they would be assured of a place. Throughout the summer their agents stimulated anti-British feeling in Iraq, and in December 1919 a base for infiltration was established at Dayr al-Zūr, on the upper Euphrates, which was taken over from the Iraqi administration. As the final confrontation between Fayṣal and the French approached, the rising excitement in Syria communicated itself to Iraq. When, on 8 March 1920, Iraqi nationalists in Damascus proclaimed ʿAbdallāh ibn Ḥusayn king of Iraq, this was not an isolated gesture of defiance but an episode in a mounting campaign against the British. The assignment to Britain of the mandate for Iraq, in April, further inflamed public opinion.

Although Wilson, faced with the threat from the Hashimites and the Iraqi nationalists, was moving towards the establishment of an Arab government, he was full of reluctance and misgivings. Finally, on 9 June, he expressed in a telegram to London his mistrust of what he called 'a policy of conciliation of extremists'. He set before the British government two alternatives: 'to maintain continuity of control for years to come', or to evacuate the country. But the government remained unconvinced, and enunciated its policy in an announcement made in Baghdād on 20 June. Wilson and his policy of direct British control were both jettisoned. Sir Percy Cox was to return in the autumn, and would 'be authorized to call into being, as provisional bodies, a Council of State under an Arab President and a General Elective Assembly, representative of and freely elected by the population of Mesopotamia. And it [would] be his duty to prepare in consultation with the General Elective Assembly, the permanent organic law'.[1]

Before Cox could return, however, and indeed within a fortnight of this announcement, revolt had flared out in Iraq. The rebellious elements were for the most part the Shīʿī Arab tribes of the lower and middle Euphrates, but there was also trouble north of Baghdād, and in the Kurdish areas. The insurrection thus stood in the long line of tribal revolts against governmental authority which had been recurrent in the Ottoman period, but it possessed certain distinguishing features. In the first place, it was a revolt against an authority which was more alien

[1] Wilson, ii, 263.

than that of the former Ottoman and Mamluk pashas: it was at least partly fomented and directed by the Shīʿī religious leaders in the holy cities, and hence it assumed the aspect of a *jihād*. Secondly, this religious resentment against British domination went hand in hand with nationalist resentment: as we have seen, nationalist agents had been at work in the tribes since 1919, and Baghdād was a centre of underground nationalist activities in the weeks preceding the insurrection. Thus, the revolt took on the appearance of a war of independence in the eyes of the nationalists.

Its immediate effect was, however, limited. The insurrection was crushed, although not without difficulty, and British control was not fully re-established until the early part of 1921. The rebels did not succeed in evicting the British, nor did they accelerate the transfer of power to an Iraqi government. In this matter the vital decisions had been made in Britain before the rising and proclaimed in the announcement of 20 June.

When Cox returned, on 1 October, he was indeed impeded in the execution of the new policy by the loss of confidence, the material destruction, and the continuing disorder which had resulted from the insurrection. Nevertheless, he proceeded with his programme, working in close co-operation with Arabophile British officials. The aged *naqīb* of Baghdād was persuaded to head the provisional Council of State, which included Sayyid Ṭālib as minister of the Interior, Jaʿfar Pasha al-ʿAskarī as minister for Defence, and Sāsūn Efendi Haskayl, a member of a prominent Jewish family, as minister of Finance. The new government came into being on 11 November 1920.

In the meantime Fayṣal's Syrian kingdom had been overthrown and he himself was in exile. The prominent Iraqis of his entourage were gradually repatriated—first among them, Jaʿfar al-ʿAskarī. The bulk of the Iraqis, including Nūrī Pasha al-Saʿīd and Nājī al-Suwaydī, returned in February 1921. The eviction of Fayṣal from Syria had important bearings on another aspect of Iraqi politics—the selection of a permanent head of state for the new country. The acclamation of ʿAbdallāh in Damascus had never been accepted by the British, although it gave him a body of followers and a species of claim which he was loth to concede, even to his brother. The candidature of an Ottoman prince was briefly canvassed by the Sunnī interest. The *naqīb* of Baghdād seemed a possible choice, but his great age and poor health, as well as his popularity with the British, worked against his acceptability to the nationalists. A far more vigorous and influential local candidate was Sayyid Ṭālib, but his talents and achievements were too obviously those of the political boss and gang-leader to render him congenial either to many Iraqis or to the British. In April 1921 Cox took advantage of some indiscreet remarks uttered by Ṭālib to have him arrested and deported.

Meanwhile the prospects of Fayṣal were improving. He had some supporters among his former Iraqi officers, although others would have preferred ʿAbdallāh. Of more importance was the existence of an influential pressure-group of British, both inside and outside Iraq. As presented by them, Fayṣal's character showed no tinge of politic deviousness or vacillation. Loyal and moderate throughout his career, the former ruler of Syria merited compensation from his British allies for his lost kingdom. This was the picture of Fayṣal which finally commended him to the British government. The affairs of Iraq were at that time under the oversight of Winston Churchill, as secretary of state for the colonies, and it was Churchill who presided over the Cairo Conference of March 1921, which worked out the schedule for the presentation of Fayṣal to his future subjects. With such backing it was obvious that the coolness or hostility with which many Iraqis regarded Fayṣal would be ineffectual. On a hint from Sir Percy Cox, the Council of State, on 11 July 1921, passed a unanimous resolution declaring Fayṣal to be the constitutional king of Iraq. Thus did Fayṣal accede to the doomed throne which he was to bequeath to his unfortunate descendants.

Palestine, Transjordan and the Ḥijāz

As Occupied Enemy Territory South, Palestine remained under British military administration during the months which immediately followed the end of the war. The demands which were put forward in Fayṣal's Syria for a Hashimite monarchy over the whole of the western Fertile Crescent were echoed in Palestine. Apprehensions of the consequences of Jewish immigration and settlement, which had already been voiced before the First World War, contributed to Arab unrest, which flared out on Easter Sunday of 1920 in an attack on the Jewish quarter of Jerusalem.

The mandate, which was assigned at San Remo in 1920 and confirmed as to its text in July 1922, incorporated in its preamble the terms of the Balfour Declaration to establish a National Home for the Jewish people, while safeguarding the rights of the non-Jewish communities in Palestine. The attempt to reconcile these two undertakings was to prove futile, and mandatory Palestine existed in a perpetual state of schism between the Arab and the Jewish communities. At the outset, however, there still seemed a possibility of reconciling the provisions of the mandate. A civil administration was established on 1 July 1920, headed by the British high commissioner, Sir Herbert (later Lord) Samuel.

From the Cairo Conference, Churchill went on to Jerusalem where he disposed of another legacy of the British wartime negotiations with the Hashimites. The territory east of Jordan had been part of Fayṣal's Syrian kingdom, but it was assigned to Britain under the Palestine mandate, and thus had not been occupied by the French in the summer of 1920. In February 1921 the Amīr ʿAbdallāh ibn Ḥusayn had arrived with an armed force at Maʿān, near its southern frontier, intending to raise a rebellion against the French in Syria. Entering Transjordan, he assumed control of the administration. Churchill accepted the *fait accompli* by recognizing him as ruler under the British mandate, on condition that he abandoned his agressive intentions against the French. In this way was founded the amirate of Transjordan, the nucleus of the subsequent Hashimite Kingdom of Jordan. Although Transjordan was included in the mandated territory of Palestine, the British government excluded it from the area designated for the Jewish National Home. It was regarded as coming within the scope of the independent Arab territories promised in the Ḥusayn–McMahon Correspondence.

The Ḥijāz, from which the Hashimite expansion had begun, sank back at the end of the war into obscurity. It formed a kingdom for Ḥusayn whose dreams of 1914 were thus ironically realized. Irritated and petulant at the frustration of his wider aims, Ḥusayn became increasingly embittered against Britain, and espoused the cause of Arab rights in Palestine. Across his eastern border was the growing power of ʿAbd al-ʿAzīz ibn Saʿūd, whose forces had already inflicted a heavy defeat on the Hashimites at the battle of Turaba in May 1919, and who had only been restrained on that occasion by British intervention. By 1924 Ḥusayn had so far alienated the British government that he was left unsupported to face the new Wahhābī threat. Ibn Saʿūd began his invasion of the Ḥijāz in August 1924. Ḥusayn abdicated in favour of his son ʿAlī, but the Wahhābī advance continued. Mecca fell in October. ʿAlī remained in Jedda until December 1925, but with his surrender and flight to Baghdād, Hashimite rule in the peninsula came to an end. Ḥusayn had already gone into exile, and he died in Transjordan in 1931. He was a pathetic rather than a tragic figure: in his maturity a shrewd operator within the ambience of Ottoman politics, he failed to develop the higher qualities of statesmanship.

Egypt under the Protectorate

Although the proclamation of the British protectorate over Egypt on 18 December 1914 made little practical difference, since it merely formalized and legitimized a régime which had existed in fact for over thirty years, it was an act of great symbolic significance. Egypt was now finally amputated from the Ottoman sultanate, which even in its decline was the last of the Muslim great powers. This transition from the suzerainty of the Padishah to the domination of a Frankish and Christian power could not fail to be offensive to the Muslims of Egypt, and especially to the poor and ignorant masses, whose religion was their highest ideal and their strongest social bond.

The Egyptians, and the peasantry in particular, had more practical grievances. Although the British government 'accepted exclusive responsibility for the defence of Egypt',[1] this did not mean that the country could be shielded from the onerous incidents of warfare. The cost of living rose, and the real wages of the unskilled labourers did not rise proportionately. Egypt was an important base for the operations of the British forces. The grain and animals of the peasantry were requisitioned, and their owners were inadequately compensated. Money was extorted as contributions for the Red Cross—a peculiarly tactless demand in a Muslim country, where public opinion was inflamed and anxious. Manpower was needed to serve in the Camel Corps and Labour Corps—not only in Palestine, as the British army advanced, but also in France. Conscription would have been bad enough, but this comparatively straightforward means was not adopted. Instead, the recruitment remained, in theory, voluntary, and was organized in the provinces by the local government authorities. When, in May 1918, the supply fell below the army's requirements, the prime minister, Ḥusayn Rushdī Pasha, was caused to issue a circular to the provincial governors urging them to 'intensify [their] effort for the encouragement of recruiting', and threatening to deal with those 'of whose neglect the Military Authorities complain'.[2] The Egyptian peasant, so recently the chief object of care and attention under the Cromerian régime, was delivered into the hands of the venal and subservient agents of government.

The westernized middle and upper classes did not suffer in their property and persons as did the peasantry, but they also had their

[1] Note from the acting British high commissioner to Sultan Ḥusayn Kāmil, 19 December 1914: Hurewitz, ii, 6.

[2] Translation of the circular in R. Wingate, *Wingate of the Sudan*, London 1955, 216–17.

reasons for disliking the protectorate. The Legislative Assembly, set up by the Organic Law of 1913 under Kitchener's auspices, had quickly developed into an institution for the expression of their opposition to the occupation. It had thus provided a safety-valve for Zaghlūl and the mass of the more cautious nationalists. On 18 October 1914 it was prorogued, never to meet again. This constitutional retrogression manifested its consequences at the end of the war, when the westernized nationalists joined forces with the Egyptian masses, and Zaghlūl, the former moderate and protégé of Cromer, emerged as a demagogic leader.

Another governmental change which had accompanied the establishment of the protectorate was the deposition of Khedive ʿAbbās Ḥilmī, and the installation of Sultan Ḥusayn Kāmil. Although the khedive had proved a broken reed to the nationalists, he was a man of ambition and resource, well able to harass a domination that he could not overthrow. He was thus not without value as an irritant, serving to remind the British authorities that they should not take their position in Egypt too much for granted. His elderly uncle and successor, by contrast, caused them no anxiety, but in October 1917 he died. Once again the principle of primogeniture was set aside to ensure the succession of a candidate agreeable to the British government. Ḥusayn Kāmil was thus followed as sultan by his younger half-brother, Aḥmad Fu'ād.

Fu'ād was, however, by no means reconciled to the status of a deferential puppet ruler. He had ambitious and autocratic proclivities, and a mastery of the devious means needed to accomplish his purposes. Moreover, he had succeeded to an equivocal position: the nominee, like Ḥusayn Kāmil, of the British government, while ʿAbbās Ḥilmī was yet alive and still maintaining his claim. In these circumstances, to establish his standing in Egypt, as well as to circumvent the British, Fu'ād began to consult Zaghlūl and the nationalists. The same motives that impelled the sultan to these tactics affected his ministers. Ḥusayn Rushdī and the rest could only purge their long subservience to the British and safeguard their position in the event of political changes by keeping open at least the channels of communication with Zaghlūl. Thus, at the end of the war, Zaghlūl had become an essential piece in the jigsaw of Egyptian politics. He was acquiring power while excluded from responsibility—a situation dangerous to the Egyptians, the British, and himself.

Impending political changes seemed likely in November 1918. The Wilsonian doctrine of self-determination was in the air; and the Anglo-French Declaration of 7 November 1918, while not mentioning Egypt might be taken to imply, *a fortiori*, a recognition of the Egyptian claim to national self-government. What was being conceded to the backward Arabs of the Ḥijāz, and the newly emancipated territories of the Fertile Crescent, could hardly be refused to Egypt, which, under its present ruling house alone, had known over a century of autonomy. But, in the eyes of the British government, the maintenance of control over Egypt was essential. While there might be some scope for negotiation over the form of that control, there could be no idea of abandoning it.

This uncompromising position was not, however, clear at the start, when, on 13 November 1918, Zaghlūl and two of his associates obtained an interview with the high commissioner, Sir Reginald Wingate. This was a friendly meeting, but during it Zaghlūl demanded complete autonomy for Egypt. Over this he was to be as uncompromising as was the British government in the opposite sense. A conflict that was to last for nearly forty years was in the making. While demanding autonomy, Zaghlūl offered a treaty of alliance with Britain. He further announced the intention of going with a group of his associates to England in order to state the nationalist case. This delegation (in Arabic, *wafd*) of nationalists to Wingate was the starting-point both of the third phase of Egyptian nationalism, and of the Wafd, the largest and most important political organization in Egypt down to the Revolution of 1952.

At this time, although Balfour was British foreign secretary, the day-to-day work of the Foreign Office in London was controlled by Lord Curzon. As a former viceroy of India, Curzon was unlikely to be sympathetic to Egyptian nationalism, which might endanger control of the Suez route. While Wingate was aware of the strength of nationalist feeling and the alarming situation that might develop if it were frustrated, he was unable to convince the British government of the need for conciliation. On 27 November he was informed that, while the Egyptian prime minister, Ḥusayn Rushdī Pasha, and his colleague, ʿAdlī Yegen Pasha, would in due course be received in London, no nationalists would be permitted to leave Egypt. Ḥusayn and ʿAdlī realized that they were being placed in an impossible position, and sought to resign.

In January 1919 Wingate left Cairo to arrange for the reception of an official ministerial and an unofficial nationalist delegation in London. On 17 February his proposals were completely rejected by Curzon, who was supported by Balfour. On 26 February a telegram was sent to Cairo, renewing the invitation to the ministers but deprecating any delegation, either official or unofficial, from the nationalists. The Egyptian ministers at once resigned and the situation began to deteriorate. On

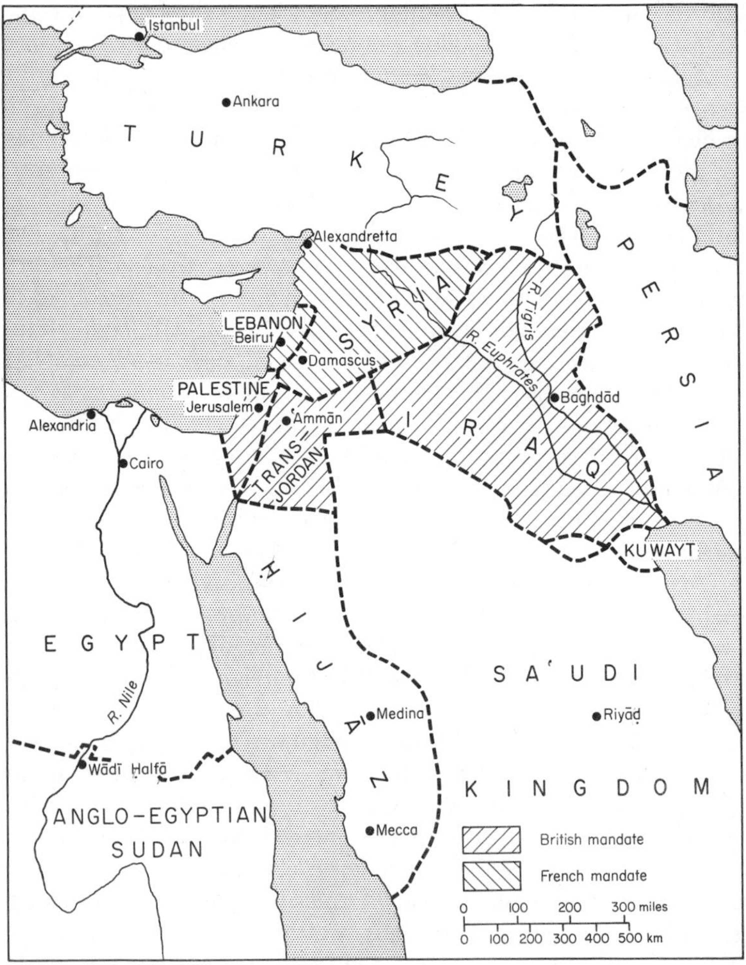

MAP 6: The Near East in 1922

8 March Zaghlūl and three of his associates were arrested and deported to Malta. At once revolt broke out in Egypt, taking the British authorities by surprise. Order was restored by the end of the month, but Wingate was superseded by General Allenby, who was sent to Egypt, at first with the title of 'special high commissioner'. Whatever had been expected of Allenby by the British government, he soon showed himself not less ready to make concessions to the nationalists than Wingate had been. Zaghlūl and his colleagues were released on 7 April, and forthwith set out for Paris, where the Peace Conference was in session.

Zaghlūl and the Wafd were now quite clearly the pacemakers in Egyptian politics, and no settlement devised by the British government could hope to succeed without at least their acquiescence. This became clear when a commission headed by Lord Milner was sent out, its principal object being to report 'on the form of Constitution which, under the Protectorate, [would] be best calculated to promote [Egyptian] peace and prosperity, the progressive development of self-governing institutions, and the protection of foreign interests'. The commission was appointed in May 1919, but for a variety of reasons deferred its arrival in Egypt to the more salubrious month of December. Meanwhile, nationalist opposition had grown and become organized in reply to the expressed intention of maintaining the protectorate. The commission found its enquiries almost completely boycotted: no public contact with the nationalists was possible, and it left Egypt in March 1920 having virtually failed in its purpose. Milner realized that a direct approach to Zaghlūl was necessary, and in the summer of 1920 private talks between the two men took place in London. From these there emerged what came to be known, somewhat inaccurately, as the Milner–Zaghlūl Agreement, in which, for the first time, the possibility of Egyptian independence was envisaged. Zaghlūl, however, now felt that he had the initiative and that further concessions could be obtained. In this he was, at the time, mistaken, and negotiations ceased in December 1920.

Nevertheless, the British government had conceded far more than had seemed possible a year earlier. Zaghlūl published the so-called Agreement, thereby making clear to all that Britain would no longer seek to maintain the protectorate. This was formally announced in February 1921, when the British government stated that it would accept the abolition of the protectorate as the basis for negotiations over a treaty with Egypt. In March, ʿAdlī Yegen became prime minister. During the summer he led a delegation to London to negotiate the projected treaty. But ʿAdlī in London was powerless as long as Zaghlūl headed the nationalist opposition in Egypt. ʿAdlī broke off the negotiations in November, returned home, and shortly afterwards offered his resignation. Zaghlūl had, once again, displayed his mastery.

During the next four months Allenby ostensibly played the leading part. His policy had two aspects: to break the political power of Zaghlūl, and to build up a pro-British group to whom the independence of Egypt might safely be committed. This led him to commit his government to a gamble: the concession of independence without the preliminary negotiation of a treaty guaranteeing British interests. On 23 December 1921 Zaghlūl and his leading colleagues were again arrested and deported. Allenby was in touch with Zaghlūl's chief opponents: ʿAdlī himself, ʿAbd al-Khāliq Tharwat Pasha, who had served as deputy prime minister in the previous summer, and Ismāʿīl Ṣidqī Pasha, a former associate of Zaghlūl. Terms were worked out on which Tharwat was prepared to form a ministry. Failing to obtain the agreement of the Foreign Office to these stipulations, Allenby himself went to London in February 1922, and, overriding the opposition of Curzon (now foreign secretary) and the reluctance of the prime minister, Lloyd George, obtained the acquiescence of the Cabinet. On his return to Egypt he published on 28 February the Declaration of Egyptian Independence.[1]

The Declaration announced the end of the protectorate and recognition of Egypt as an independent sovereign state. Martial law, which had been in force since 2 November 1914, was to be terminated on the passing of an Act of Indemnity. Four matters were 'absolutely reserved to the discretion' of the British government until agreements concerning them could be negotiated. These were:

(*a*) The security of the communications of the British Empire in Egypt;
(*b*) The defence of Egypt against all foreign aggression or interference, direc or indirect;
(*c*) The protection of foreign interests in Egypt and the protection o minorities;
(*d*) The Sudan.

The first, second and last of these 'reserved matters' were to be th subject of repeated and frustrating negotiations throughout the followin thirty years.

[1] For the text of the Declaration, see Hurewitz, ii, 102.

Postscript: The Anglo-French Paramountcy and its Passing

The political settlement which was devised, primarily between France and Great Britain, in the four years succeeding the end of the First World War, substituted a European for an Ottoman domination of the Fertile Crescent and Egypt. In Iraq, Palestine and Transjordan the British, in Syria and Lebanon the French, received international recognition as mandatory powers, and became thereby the effective administrators of those countries. To Egypt, Britain formally conceded independence, but the powers of the Egyptian government were substantially limited both by the 'reserved matters' of the 1922 Declaration, as well as by the influence of the British embassy, backed as it was by the presence of British troops.

The Anglo-French paramountcy, for all its impressive appearance, rested on deep internal contradictions, and was to prove impermanent. Unlike the Ottomans, the new suzerains lacked the bond of a common religious and cultural inheritance with the Arab peoples. Even at their feeblest, the Ottoman sultans could evoke a residual loyalty from their Muslim subjects, and the continuance of this sentiment is attested by the divided counsels and hesitations of the Arab nationalists in the early years of the war. The British and French had little to offer in the place of this. Essentially, their hold over the mandated territories and Egypt, while backed by military power, depended upon clients who would collaborate in maintaining the post-war régimes. The most eminent of these were the new monarchs: the Hashimites who ruled briefly in the Ḥijāz, and more durably in Iraq and Transjordan, and the former khedivial dynasty of Egypt. There were also the nationalist politicians, whose prestige had been enhanced by the Allied appeal to nationalism as a counter to traditional loyalty to the sultan-caliph, and who had become indispensable in the post-war régimes. But both the rulers and the politicians were at heart uncommitted to their Franco-British suzerains. Personal interests as well as nationalist ideology inevitably led them to thwart and circumvent, when they could not openly challenge or ignore, the authority of the British and French governments.

The Anglo-French paramountcy, for its part, was not monolithic.

Even during the war, the British had displayed caution and reserve towards the aspirations of their French allies in the Near East, and it was ironical that France, with her long tradition of military, cultural and commercial interests in the region, should acquire territory in consequence of a campaign which was predominantly British. After the war, personal and political mistrust continued, and divergencies of policy became increasingly apparent as time went on. The British adopted in Iraq the procedure which had been used in Egypt, of conceding to the territorial government formal independence and much of the substance of power, while receiving a special position for Britain in defence of imperial interests. The French moved more slowly in this direction. Whether in the long run one policy can be regarded as more meritorious or successful than the other may be doubted: both were conceived in the interests of the mandatory powers rather than of the mandated territories; the one failed to suppress, as the other failed to conciliate, nationalist opinion.

The development of Arab nationalism in the Fertile Crescent proceeded during the post-war period. It was stimulated by the tension between the mandatory powers and the Arab peoples under their control, by the partition of the Fertile Crescent into five separate territories, and by Jewish immigration into Palestine. Although there were recurrent clashes between Arabs and Jews from 1920 onward, these did not have wide repercussions until the following decade. The sharp rise in immigration, accompanying the establishment and spread of Nazi power in Germany and Central Europe, rendered acute the question of Arab–Jewish relations in Palestine. The serious disturbances of 1936, which evoked efforts at mediation by the Arab states, marked the point at which the Palestine problem became a matter of general Arab concern, and hence a theme in the repertory of Arab nationalism.

Between 1939, when the Second World War broke out, and 1956, when the Suez crisis occurred, Anglo-French paramountcy in Egypt and the Fertile Crescent came to an end. The French position in Syria and Lebanon could not be maintained after the collapse of France in 1940. At the end of the war, Britain lacked both the material strength and the will to hold on, while the United States emerged as the predominant Western power in the region. Britain abandoned the mandate for Palestine in May 1948. The establishment of the State of Israel, and the Arab–Israeli war, had momentous consequences for the whole region. The war was the last act of the old generation of Arab nationalists. Their failure to defeat the Israelis, or even to agree upon a concerted strategy, discredited them and the governments in which they predominated. A revolutionary situation was created.

The most important outcome of this was in Egypt, where the revolution began with the *coup d'état* of July 1952. The nationalist leadership passed to a new generation, whose strength lay in the control of the armed forces and whose outlook was totalitarian. The Hashimite monarchy in Iraq was swept away six years later, that of Jordan retained a precarious authority, while Syria and Lebanon entered a long period of political instability. It was with the new republican régime in Egypt that the British government, in July 1954, signed an agreement for the evacuation of British troops from the Suez Canal Zone. The unhappy Suez incident, two years later, was, in the circumstances, an aberration which accomplished nothing. The surviving British interests in the region are primarily the freedom of communications, especially through the Suez Canal, and the unimpeded supply of oil from the Persian Gulf area. These, it is clear, cannot now be secured by the military and political expedients of the years between the wars.

Seen in retrospect, the Anglo-French paramountcy was a period of transition, in which the Arab peoples of Egypt and the Fertile Crescent severed the links with their Ottoman past and were exposed to the full force of westernizing influences in politics, society and culture. Ottoman sovereignty over four centuries, and Anglo-French rule over less than forty years, have both made important contributions to the modern Arab states, but the time has not yet come in which these diverse elements will be reconciled and accepted by those who inherit them.

Appendix 1

Chronological Table

1512–20: Reign of Sultan Selim I

1514: Battle of Chaldirān

1516: Ottoman conquest of Syria

1517: Ottoman conquest of Egypt

1520–66: Reign of Sultan Süleyman I

1520–21: Revolt of Jānbardī al-Ghazālī

1522: Death of Khā'ir Bey

1524: Revolt of Aḥmad Pasha al-Khā'in

1525: Promulgation of the *Qānūn-name* of Egypt

1529: First Ottoman siege of Vienna

1534: Ottoman conquest of Baghdād

1538: Sulaymān Pasha's expedition to Diu

c. 1559: Death of Özdemir Pasha

1566–74: Reign of Sultan Selim II

1569: Sinān Pasha's expedition to the Yaman

1574–95: Reign of Sultan Murad III

1584: Raid on the tribute-convoy at Jūn ʿAkkār

1586: First military revolt in Egypt

1587–1629: Shah ʿAbbās I in Persia

1590: Emergence of Fakhr al-Dīn II Maʿn

1595–1603: Reign of Sultan Mehmed III

c. 1596: Afrāsiyāb acquires Baṣra

1603–17: Reign of Sultan Ahmed I

c. 1604: Emergence of Muḥammad al-Ṭawīl in Baghdād

1604–5: Ḥusayn Pasha Jānbulād governor of Aleppo

1605: Assassination of Ibrāhīm Pasha, viceroy of Egypt

1608: Fakhr al-Dīn II's treaty with Tuscany

1609: Military revolt in Egypt against Muḥammad Pasha

1613–18: Exile of Fakhr al-Dīn II

1617–18: First reign of Sultan Mustafa I

1618–22: Reign of Sultan Osman II

1619: Emergence of Bakr Ṣūbāshī in Baghdād

1622–23: Second reign of Sultan Mustafa I

1623–40: Reign of Sultan Murad IV

1623: Conquest of Baghdād by Shah ʿAbbās I

1625: Victory of Fakhr al-Dīn II at ʿAnjarr

1630: Settlement of Jānbulād in Lebanon

1631: Suspension of the viceroy of Egypt, Mūsā Pasha, by the grandees

1635: Capture of Fakhr al-Dīn II

1639: Treaty of Zuhāb

1640–48: Reign of Sultan Ibrahim I

1648–87: Reign of Sultan Mehmed IV

1656: Death of Riḍwān Bey al-Faqārī

1659: Assassination of Abaza Ḥasan Pasha

1660: Proscription of the Faqāriyya

1662: Assassination of Aḥmad Bey the Bosniak

1668: Overthrow of the family of Afrāsiyāb

1676: Emergence of Küchük Muḥammad

1683: Second Ottoman siege of Vienna

1687–91: Reign of Sultan Süleyman II

1691–95: Reign of Sultan Ahmed II

1694: Assassination of Küchük Muḥammad

1695–1703: Reign of Sultan Mustafa II

1696: Peter the Great's conquest of Azov

1697: Assembly of al-Samqāniyya in Lebanon

1699: Treaty of Carlowitz

1703–30: Reign of Sultan Ahmed III

1704–11: Ḥasan Pasha governor of Baghdād

1711: Victory of Ḥaydar Shihāb at ʿAndārā
The Great Insurrection in Cairo

1722: Battle of Gulnābād

1723–47: Aḥmad Pasha governor of Baghdād

1725–30: Ismāʿīl Pasha al-ʿAẓm governor of Damascus

1726: Establishment of the Jalīlī pashalic at Mosul

1729: First Turkish printing press

1730–54: Reign of Sultan Mahmud I

1730: Establishment of the Faqāriyya ascendancy

1733–38: Sulaymān Pasha al-ʿAẓm governor of Damascus

1736–47: Nādir Shāh in Persia

1736: Synod of al-Luwayza in Lebanon

1741–43: Second governorship of Sulaymān Pasha al-ʿAẓm in Damascus

1743–57: As‘ad Pasha al-ʿAẓm governor of Damascus

1745: Muḥammad ibn ʿAbd al-Wahhāb at Darʿiyya

1746: Ẓāhir al-ʿUmar obtains Acre

1747: Establishment of the Mamluk pashalic of Baghdād

1748–54: Duumvirate of Ibrāhīm Kâhya and Riḍwān Kâhya in Egypt

1754–57: Reign of Sultan Osman III

1757–73: Reign of Sultan Mustafa III

1760: Emergence of Bulut Kapan ʿAlī Bey

1768–74: Russo-Ottoman War

1770–89: Yūsuf Shihāb *amīr* of Lebanon

1770: ʿAlī Bey's campaign in Arabia

1771: ʿAlī Bey's campaign in Syria

1772: Flight of ʿAlī Bey to Ẓāhir al-ʿUmar

1773: Death of ʿAlī Bey

1773–89: Reign of Sultan Abdülhamid I

1774: Treaty of Küchük Kaynarja

1775: Abu'l-Dhahab's campaign in Syria
Death of Ẓāhir al-ʿUmar
Aḥmad Pasha al-Jazzār governor of Sidon

1780–1802: Büyük Sulaymān Pasha governor of Baghdād

1786–87: Expedition of Ḥasan Pasha to Egypt

1789–1807: Reign of Sultan Selim III

1789–1840: Bashīr II Shihāb *amīr* of Lebanon

1798: Bonaparte's occupation of Egypt

1799: Bonaparte's invasion of Syria

1801: French evacuation of Egypt

1802: Wahhābī raid on Karbalāʾ

1803: Wahhābī occupation of Mecca

1804: Death of Aḥmad Pasha al-Jazzār

1805–48: Muḥammad ʿAlī viceroy of Egypt

1807–8: Reign of Sultan Mustafa IV

1808–39: Reign of Sultan Mahmud II

1811: Massacre of the Mamluks in Cairo

1811–18: Muḥammad ʿAlī's campaign against the Wahhābīs

1815: Massacre of the Janissaries of Aleppo

1816–31: Da'ūd Pasha governor of Baghdād

1820–21: Muḥammad ʿAlī's Sudanese campaigns

c. 1822: Establishment of the Būlāq press

1824–27: Muḥammad ʿAlī's campaign in the Morea

1826: Massacre of the Janissaries in Istanbul

1827: Foundation of schools of medicine in Istanbul and Cairo

1831: End of the Mamluk pashalic of Baghdād
Muḥammad ʿAlī's invasion of Syria

1833: Convention of Kütahya

1834: Establishment of Arabic press in Beirut
End of the Jalīlī pashalic of Mosul

1836: Chesney's Euphrates expedition

1839: Battle of Nezib

1839–61: Reign of Sultan Abdülmejid

1839: Promulgation of *Hatt-i Sherif* of Gülhane

1840: End of Egyptian occupation of Syria

1841: Hereditary viceroyalty of Egypt granted to Muḥammad ʿAlī

1842: End of the Shihābī amirate in Lebanon

1843: Establishment of the Dual Qaimaqamate in Lebanon

1848–54: ʿAbbās Ḥilmī I viceroy of Egypt

1851: Beginning of railway construction in Egypt

1854–63: Muḥammad Saʿīd viceroy of Egypt

1856: Promulgation of *Hatt-i Hümayun*

1860: Massacres of Christians in Lebanon and Syria

1861: The Organic Regulation of Lebanon

1861–76: Reign of Sultan Abdülaziz

1863–79: Ismāʿīl khedive of Egypt

1864: Ottoman Law of Vilayets

1866: Succession by primogeniture in the ruling house of Egypt

1869: Opening of the Suez Canal

1869–72: Midhat Pasha governor of Baghdād

1875: Establishment of Mixed Courts in Egypt

1876: Establishment of *Caisse de la Dette* and Dual Control in Egypt

1876: Reign of Sultan Murad V

1876–1909: Reign of Sultan Abdülhamid II

1876: Promulgation of the Ottoman Constitution

1879–92: Muḥammad Tawfīq khedive of Egypt

1881: The First *ʿAliyāh*
Outbreak of the Sudanese Mahdia

1881–82: ʿUrābī revolution

1882: British occupation of Egypt

1883–1907: Cromer British agent and consul-general in Egypt

1887: Death of Jamāl al-Dīn al-Afghānī

1888: Convention of Constantinople

1892–1914: ʿAbbās Ḥilmī II khedive of Egypt

1899: Establishment of Anglo-Egyptian Condominium in the Sudan

1900: Foundation of *al-Liwāʾ* by Muṣṭafā Kāmil

1904: The Entente Cordiale

1906: Dinshawāy Incident

1907–11: Gorst British agent and consul-general in Egypt

1908: The Young Turk Revolution

1909–18: Reign of Sultan Mehmed V	
	1910: Assassination of Buṭrus Ghālī Pasha
	1911–14: Kitchener British agent and consul-general in Egypt
	1913: Arab Congress in Paris
	1914: Formation of *al-ʿAhd* nationalist society
1914–18: First World War	1914–17: Ḥusayn Kāmil sultan of Egypt
	1915: Ḥusayn–McMahon Correspondence
	1916: Sykes–Picot Agreement
	1917: Capture of Baghdād by British Accession of Aḥmad Fu'ād as sultan of Egypt Balfour Declaration
1918–22: Reign of Sultan Mehmed VI	
	1918: Allied capture of Damascus
	1919: Revolt in Egypt
	1920: Fayṣal declared king of Syria San Remo Conference Overthrow of kingdom of Syria Revolt in Iraq
	1921: Fayṣal declared king of Iraq
1922: End of the Ottoman sultanate	1922: Egypt declared independent; Fu'ād I king of Egypt

Appendix 2

Genealogical Tables

I: OTTOMAN SULTANS: 1512–1922

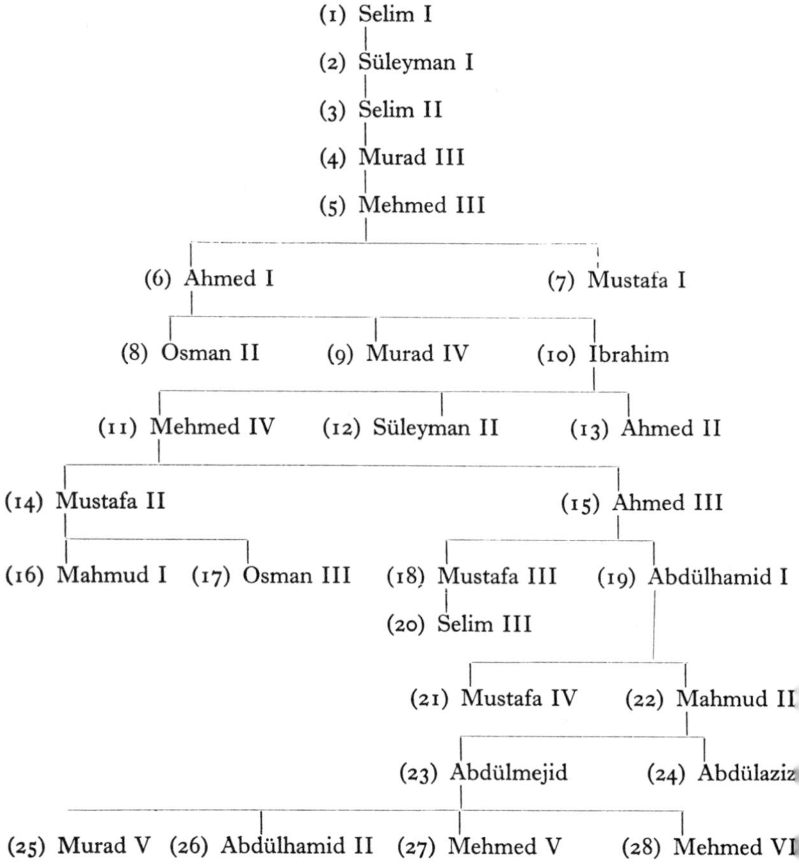

II: THE JĀNBULĀD FAMILY

- Jānbulād
  - Aḥmad
    - ʿAlī
  - Ḥusayn
    - Muṣṭafā
      - Saʿīd
        - Jānbulād
          - ↓ Janbalāṭ clan in Lebanon

III: THE ʿAẒM FAMILY

Governors of Damascus are underlined.

- Ibrāhīm
  - Ismāʿīl
    - Asʿad
      - daughter = Muḥammad
        - ʿAbdallāh
    - daughter = Muṣṭafā
      - Muḥammad
  - Sulaymān
  - Fāris
    - Muṣṭafā

IV: THE MAʿNID DYNASTY

- (1) Fakhr al-Dīn I
  - (2) Korkmaz
    - (3) Fakhr al-Dīn II
      - ʿAlī
    - Yūnus
      - (4) Mulḥim
        - (5) Aḥmad

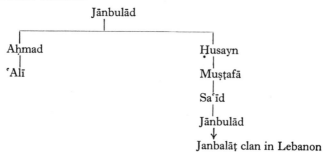

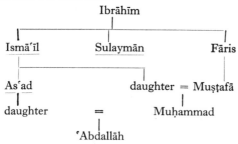

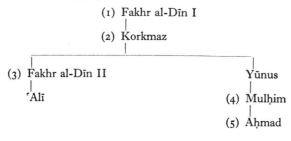

V: THE SHIHĀBĪ DYNASTY

- (1) Bashīr I
- (2) Ḥaydar
  - (3) Mulḥim
    - (5) Yūsuf
    - Qāsim
      - (7) Bashīr III
  - (4a) Aḥmad
  - (4b) Manṣūr
  - ʿUmar
    - Qāsim
      - (6) Bashīr II

VI: THE DYNASTY OF MUḤAMMAD ʿALĪ

- (1) Muḥammad ʿAlī
  - (2) Ibrāhīm
    - (5) Ismāʿīl
      - (6) Muḥammad Tawfīq
        - (7) ʿAbbās Ḥilmī II
      - (8) Husayn Kāmil
      - (9) Aḥmad Fu'ād I
        - (10) Fārūq
          - (11) Aḥmad Fu'ād II
  - Tusun
    - (3) ʿAbbās Ḥilmī I
  - (4) Muḥammad Saʿīd

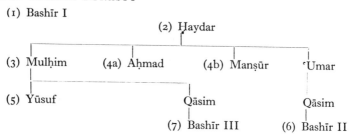

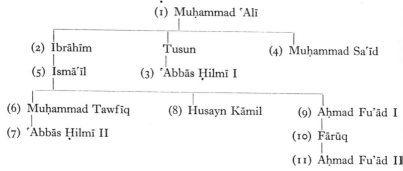

Bibliography

A. WORKS OF REFERENCE

The standard introduction and bibliography to Islamic history is the revised edition by Cl. Cahen of J. Sauvaget, *Introduction à l'histoire de l'orient musulman: éléments de bibliographie*, Paris 1961; English translation, *Introduction to the history of the Muslim East*, Berkeley 1965. A comprehensive survey of Islamic culture, history and religion is to be found in *The encyclopaedia of Islam*, 1st edn., Leiden 1913–38; 2nd edn., Leiden 1960 (in progress).

Historical atlases are of limited value for the region in this period, but some useful maps may be found in H. W. Hazard, *Atlas of Islamic history*, Princeton 1954, and in R. Roolvink, *Historical atlas of the Muslim peoples*, Amsterdam 1957. The former is mainly composed of a series of maps (with accompanying notes) showing at century intervals political changes in the Muslim lands as far east as Afghanistan. The latter consists of maps illustrating developments in specific areas at various periods. A good contemporary regional atlas remains necessary. Such are the Macmillan *Atlas of the Arab world and the Middle East*, London 1960, and the Oxford University Press *Oxford regional economic atlas: the Middle East and North Africa*, London 1960. A useful collection of documents, mainly diplomatic, is J. C. Hurewitz, *Diplomacy in the Near and Middle East*, Princeton 1956.

B. THE GEOGRAPHICAL, SOCIAL AND HISTORICAL BACKGROUND

A contemporary geographical survey is W. B. Fisher, *The Middle East*, 3rd edn., London 1961. An older work, interesting because it was written in the last years of Ottoman rule, is D. G. Hogarth, *The nearer East*, London 1902. Xavier de Planhol, *Le monde islamique*, Paris 1957, is a short but brilliant monograph on the geography of Islamic society: the English translation, *The world of Islam*, Ithaca (N.Y.) 1959, is not always accurate. Over a more limited area, Jacques Weulersse, *Paysans de Syrie et du Proche-orient*, Paris 1946, is an important detailed study: Ch. II, 'Les conditions historiques', is a most useful survey of historical geography.

Amongst numerous studies of Islam, one which is both scholarly and sympathetic is H. A. R. Gibb, *Mohammedanism*, London 1953. H. A. R. Gibb and Harold Bowen, *Islamic society and the West*, Vol. I, *Islamic society in the eighteenth century* (2 parts), London 1950, 1957, ranges widely but unevenly over the history, institutions and society of the Ottoman Empire. A classical and highly readable description of traditional society in Egypt before the impact of westernization is E. W. Lane, *The manners and customs of the modern Egyptians*, London, first published in 1836 and many times reprinted. A study of contemporary society is Gabriel Baer, *Population and society in the Arab East*, London 1964.

An illuminating historical sketch, mainly concerned with the pre-Ottoman period of Arab history, is Bernard Lewis, *The Arabs in history*, revised edn., London 1964. The later period is dealt with at more length in George E. Kirk, *A short history of the Middle East*, 7th edn., London 1964, but the emphasis is on relations with the West. The pedestrian but careful work by Carl Brockelmann, *Geschichte der Islamischen Völker und Staaten:* English translation, *History of the Islamic peoples*, London 1949, remains a sound and useful guide. For the general Ottoman background, see the relevant chapters in *The new Cambridge modern history*, Cambridge 1957 (in progress), and also two books by Bernard Lewis, *The emergence of modern Turkey*, London 1961, and *Istanbul and the civilization of the Ottoman Empire*, Norman (Oklahoma) 1963.

C. EGYPT

There is no detailed study of the history of Egypt during the period covered by the present work. General accounts, of varying quality, are given by the contributors to *Précis de l'histoire d'Egypte*, Vols. III, IV, Cairo 1933, 1935; and to Gabriel Hanotaux (ed.), *Histoire de la nation égyptienne*, Vols. V–VII, Paris 1931 ff.

For the period 1517–1798, one must mainly depend on the chronicles, still largely unpublished and unexploited. The fall of the Mamluk sultanate and the early years of Ottoman rule are described in Muḥammad ibn Aḥmad ibn Īyās, *Badāʾiʿ al-zuhūr fī waqāʾiʿ al-duhūr*, Vol. V (ed. Muḥammad Muṣṭafā), 2nd edn., Cairo 1380/1961. This has been translated into French by Gaston Wiet, *Journal d'un bourgeois du Caire*, Vol. II, Paris 1960. The English translation of a shorter excerpt covering Selim's campaign to the taking of Cairo, by W. H. Salmon, *An account of the Ottoman conquest of Egypt*, London 1921, is made from an inferior text, and is of mediocre quality. The only seventeenth-century chronicle to have been published, Muḥammad ibn ʿAbd al-Muʿṭī al-Isḥāqī, *Kitāb akhbār al-uwal fī man taṣarrafa fī Miṣr min arbāb al-duwal*, Cairo (several editions in the later nineteenth century), is of inferior value. The eighteenth century and part of the reign of Muḥammad ʿAlī Pasha are covered by the great chronicle of ʿAbd al-Raḥmān ibn Ḥasan al-Jabartī, *ʿAjāʾib al-āthār fiʾl-tarājim waʾl-akhbār*, Būlāq 1297/1879–80, and other editions, but a critical edition and an established text are still wanting. The French translation of al-Jabartī, Chefik Mansour *et al.*, *Merveilles biographiques et historiques ou chronique du Cheikh Abd-El-Rahman El-Djabarti*, Cairo 1888–96, is of poor quality and unreliable. See further, David Ayalon,

'The historian al-Jabartī and his background', *BSOAS*, xxiii/2, 1960, 217–49, and P. M. Holt, 'Ottoman Egypt (1517–1798): a study of Arabic historical sources' (forthcoming). A detailed investigation of the administration of Ottoman Egypt has been made on the basis of archival material by Stanford J. Shaw, *The financial and administrative organization and development of Ottoman Egypt, 1517–1798*, Princeton 1958. Dr Shaw has also published two long documents relating to the period: *Ottoman Egypt in the eighteenth century*, Cambridge (Mass.) 1962, and *Ottoman Egypt in the age of the French Revolution*, Cambridge (Mass.) 1964. The former is the text and translation of a Turkish report by Aḥmad al-Jazzār, and the latter the translation only of an Arabic memorandum by Ḥusayn Efendi, a financial official at the time of the French occupation. Both have introductions and copious notes.

Much more work has been done on Egyptian history from 1798 onwards, although many aspects have only been superficially investigated. Two accounts of the French occupation, based mainly on Western sources, are F. Charles-Roux, *Bonaparte, gouverneur d'Egypte*; English translation, *Bonaparte: governor of Egypt*, London 1937; and P. G. Elgood, *Bonaparte's adventure in Egypt*, London 1936. For the nineteenth century there is a wealth of archival material, some of which has been published: one may note especially the series of volumes of documents relating to the reign of Muḥammad ʿAlī Pasha, published under the auspices of King Fu'ād by the Société Royale de Géographie d'Egypte. The Egyptian writer, ʿAbd al Raḥmān al-Rāfiʿi, has over many years published a long series of volumes covering the political history of Egypt from the French occupation down to the eve of the revolution of 1952. Adolf Hasenclever, *Geschichte Aegyptens im 19. Jahrhundert*, Halle 1917, has not yet been superseded. The standard English biography of Muḥammad ʿAlī Pasha, H. H. Dodwell, *The founder of modern Egypt*, Cambridge 1931, is still of use, but no longer really adequate. It may be supplemented by Shafik Ghorbal, *The beginnings of the Egyptian question and the rise of Mehemet Ali*, London 1928, and by Helen Anne B. Rivlin, *The agricultural policy of Muḥammad ʿAlī in Egypt*, Cambridge (Mass.) 1961, which covers a wider range than the title suggests. For Khedive Ismāʿīl, there is the voluminous and detailed (but nevertheless unfinished) study by G. Douin, *Histoire du règne du Khédive Ismail*, Rome 1933 ff. For the period of the British occupation, the classic account by Lord Cromer, *Modern Egypt*, London 1908, is still valuable, although its character as a subtle apologia for the author's career must be kept in mind. Kitchener's periods of service in Egypt are described in the official biography, Sir George Arthur, *Life of Lord Kitchener*, London 1920, and by a more detached writer, Philip Magnus, *Kitchener, portrait of an imperialist*, London 1958. Some light is thrown on the course of events leading to the 1922 Declaration of Independence by the biographies of two successive British high commissioners in Egypt; Sir Ronald Wingate, *Wingate of the Sudan*, London 1955, and Lord Wavell,

Allenby, Soldier and statesman, London 1944. A general study of the link between Egypt and Britain is provided by John Marlowe, *Anglo-Egyptian relations, 1800–1953*, which is useful, although written only from European sources. Two important works on special aspects of Egyptian history are Jacob M. Landau, *Parliaments and parties in Egypt*, Tel Aviv 1953, New York 1954, and Gabriel Baer, *A history of landownership in modern Egypt, 1800–1950*, London 1962. Turco-Egyptian rule in the Sudan is studied in Richard Hill, *Egypt in the Sudan, 1820–1881*, London 1959.

D. THE WESTERN FERTILE CRESCENT

A fair amount of source material has been published. This includes two selections of Ottoman documents published in translation: Robert Mantran and Jean Sauvaget, *Règlements fiscaux ottomans*, Beirut 1951 (in French), and Uriel Heyd, *Ottoman documents on Palestine, 1552–1615*, Oxford 1960 (in English). The period of the Ottoman conquest is covered by the chronicle of Shams al-Dīn Muḥammad ibn Ṭūlūn, *Mufākahat al-khillān fī ḥawādith al-zamān*. This has been published in two volumes (ed. Muḥammad Muṣṭafā, Cairo 1381/1962 and 1384/1964), of which the second covers the years 922–6/1516–20. A portion of the later part was published by Richard Hartmann, 'Das Tübinger Fragment der Chronik des Ibn Ṭūlūn', *Schriften der Königsberger Gelehrten Gesellschaft*, 3. Jahr, Heft 2, Berlin 1926. Another chronicle of Ibn Ṭūlūn and that of Ibn Jumʿa are published in translation by Henri Laoust, *Les gouverneurs de Damas sous les Mamlouks et les premiers Ottomans (658–1156/1260–1744)*, Damascus 1952. The Arabic text of Ibn Jumʿa and that of Ibn al-Qārī were published by Ṣalāḥ al-Dīn al-Munajjid, *Wulāt Dimashq fi'l-ʿahd al-ʿuthmānī*, Damascus 1949. For the eighteenth century, there is the chronicle of Mikhā'īl Burayk (Michel Breik) ed. Quṣṭanṭīn al-Bāshā (Constantin Bacha), *Ta'rīkh al-Shām (1720–1782)*, Harissa 1930. Lebanon during the Shihābī paramountcy is chronicled in the two parts of the annals of Ḥaydar Aḥmad al-Shihābī, originally entitled *al-Ghurar al-ḥisān fī akhbār abnā' al-zamān*, edited by Asad Rustum and Fu'ād Afrām al-Bustānī (Fouad E. Boustany), *Lubnān fī ʿahd al-umarā' al-shihābiyyīn*, Beirut 1933. Two important memoirs are: *al-Ḥarakāt fī Lubnān ilā ʿahd al-mutaṣarrafiyya*, Beirut n.d., recorded by Yūsuf Abū Shaqrā (Abu-Shacra) from the account of Ḥusayn Abū Shaqrā, and edited by ʿĀrif Abū Shaqrā; and Mīkhā'īl Mishāqa, *Muntakhabāt min al-jawāb ʿalā iqtirāḥ al-aḥbāb* (ed. Asad Rustum and Subḥī Abū Shaqrā), Beirut 1955. A third memoir, Anṭūn Ḍāhir al-ʿAqīqī, *Thawra wa-fitna fī Lubnān* (ed. Yūsuf Ibrāhīm Yazbak), Beirut n.d., has been translated with a very useful introduction by Malcolm H. Kerr, *Lebanon in the last years of feudalism, 1840–1868*, Beirut 1959. For Aleppo, there are the three volumes of ecclesiastical documents published by Fardīnān Tawtal (Ferdinand Taoutel), *Wathā'iq taʾrīkhiyya ʿan Ḥalab*, Beirut n.d. Biographical material includes the great biographical dictionaries of this period: for the tenth/sixteenth century, Najm al-Dīn al-Ghazzī, *al-Kawākib al-sāʾira* (ed. Jibrāʾīl Sulaymān Jabbūr), Vols. I and II, Beirut 1945, 1949, Vol. III, Harissa 1959; for the eleventh/seventeenth century, Muḥammad al-Muḥibbī, *Khulāṣat al-athar*, Cairo 1868; for the twelfth/eigththeenth century, Muḥammad Khalīl al-Murādī, *Silk al-durar*, Būlāq 1301/1883–4. There is also the seventeenth-century biographical dictionary of al-Hasan ibn Muḥammad al-Burīnī, *Tarājim al-aʿyan min abnāʾ al-zamān* (ed. Ṣalāḥ al-Dīn al-Munajjid), Vol. I, Damascus 1959; the rest has not yet been published. A modern biographical dictionary, covering the thirteenth/nineteenth century, is ʿAbd al-Razzāq al-Bīṭār, *Ḥilyat al-bashar* (ed. Muḥammad Bahjat al-Bīṭār), Vol. I, Damascus 1380/1961, Vols. II and III, Damascus 1382–3/1963. A compilation mainly of Lebanese biographical and familial material is Ṭannūs ibn Yūsuf al-Shidyāq, *Akhbār al-aʿyān fī jabal Lubnān*, Beirut 1954. A published biography of Shaykh Ẓāhir al-ʿUmar is Mikhāʾīl Niqūlā al-Ṣabbāgh, *Taʾrīkh al-Shaykh Ẓāhir al-ʿUmar al-Zaydānī* (ed. Qusṭanṭīn al-Bāshā), Harissa [1935]. For al-Jazzār, there is the biography, reputedly by Ḥaydar Aḥmad Shihāb (al-Shihābī), *Taʾrīkh Aḥmad Bāshā al-Jazzār* (ed. Anṭūniyūs Shiblī and Ighnātiyūs ʿAbduh Khalīfa), Beirut 1955. Another biographical work, Ibrāhīm al-ʿAwra, *Taʾrīkh wilāyat Sulaymān Bāshā al-ʿādil* (ed. Qusṭanṭīn al-Bāshā), Sidon 1936, covers important aspects of Syrian history after the death of al-Jazzār.

There is no detailed general history of the western Fertile Crescent in this period. The relevant chapters of Henri Lammens, *La Syrie, précis historique*, Beirut 1921, although opinionated, remain a valuable outline. Lebanese history in the Ottoman and post-Ottoman period is sketched in the later chapters of Philip K. Hitti, *Lebanon in history*, London 1957, and a very full treatment is promised by Adel Ismail, *Histoire du Liban*, of which two volumes have so far appeared; Vol. I, *Le Liban au temps de Fakhr-ed-Din II*, Paris 1955, and Vol. IV, *Redressement et déclin du féodalisme libanais*, Beirut 1958. The period from 1788 onwards is treated in detail in Kamal S. Salibi, *The modern history of Lebanon*, London 1965. William R. Polk, *The opening of south Lebanon, 1788–1840* Cambridge (Mass.) 1963, is a socio-historic study of the effect on Lebanon of the domination of the area by Muḥammad ʿAlī Pasha. For the history of Aleppo, one must have recourse to two modern representatives of a traditional genre of historiography; Kāmil al-Ghazzī, *Nahr al-dhahab fī taʾrīkh Ḥalab*, Aleppo 1342–5/1923–6, and Muḥammad Rāghib al-Ṭabbākh, *Iʿlām al-nubalāʾ bi-taʾrīkh Ḥalab al-shahbāʾ*, Aleppo 1923–6. A monograph on the political situation in Aleppo in the late eighteenth and early nineteenth centuries is Herbert L. Bodman, Jr., *Political factions in Aleppo, 1760–1826*, Chapel Hill 1963. For the political history of Damascus, there is material in Muḥammad Kurd ʿAlī, *Khiṭaṭ al-Shām*, Vols. II, III, Damascus 1925. Studies of Damascus under the ʿAzm Pashas, based on independent researches by Abdul Karim Rafeq and Shimon Shamir, are shortly expected. European trade with the western Fertile Crescent is dealt with in P. Masson's two works, *Histoire du commerce français dans le Levant au 17e siècle*, Paris 1896, and *Histoire du commerce français dans le Levant au 18e siècle*, Paris 1911, and also in Alfred C. Wood, *A history of the Levant Company*, London 1935. A. L. Tibawi, *British interests in Palestine, 1800–1901*, London 1961, is largely a study of Anglican missionary activities in Jerusalem. The most accessible account in English of the Wahhābī movement and the rise of the Saʿūdī dynasty is in the early chapters of H. St John Philby, *Saʿudi Arabia*, London 1955.

E. THE EASTERN FERTILE CRESCENT

The amount of published source material remains small. There is a recent Arabic translation of the Turkish chronicle of Rasūl al-Kirkūklī, *Dawḥat al-wuzarāʾ fī taʾrīkh Baghdād al-zawrāʾ* (tr. Mūsā Kāẓim Nūrus), Beirut n.d. Part of the chronicle of ʿAbd al-Raḥmān ibn ʿAbdallāh ibn al-Ḥusayn al-Suwaydī, *Ḥadīqat al-zawrāʾ fī sīrat al-wuzarāʾ*, covering the governorship of Ḥasan Pasha (1704–23), has been published under the title of *Taʾrīkh al-Baghdād liʾbn-Suwaydī* (ed. Ṣafā Khulūṣī), Vol. I, Baghdād 1962. Ibrāhīm Faṣīḥ ibn Sibghatallāh ibn al-Ḥaydarī al-Baghdādī, *ʿUnwān al-majd fī bayān aḥwāl Baghdād waʾl-Baṣra wa-Najd*, Baghdād 1962, is an early nineteenth-century work.

The fullest recent account of the eastern Fertile Crescent in the Ottoman period is contained in the later volumes of ʿAbbās al-ʿAzzāwī, *Taʾrīkh al-ʿIrāq bayn iḥtilālayn*, Baghdād 1949 ff., but this is essentially a compilation in the traditional manner. Clément Huart, *Histoire de Bagdad dans les temps modernes*, Paris 1901, has not been wholly superseded by S. H. Longrigg, *Four centuries of modern Iraq*, Oxford 1925, although the latter is wider both in its range and in its use of source material. A study of European impact on the Persian Gulf area is provided by Sir Arnold T. Wilson, *The Persian Gulf*, London 1928.

F. THE FIRST WORLD WAR AND ITS SEQUEL

The Arab nationalist thesis of the diplomacy of the First World War and its aftermath forms the principal subject of George Antonius, *The Arab awakening*, London 1938. A critical and more fully documented study is Elie Kedourie, *England and the Middle East*, London 1956. A fuller examination of the relationship of Arab nationalism to the Ottoman background is provided in a book by Zeine N. Zeine, entitled *The emergence of Arab nationalism*, Beirut 1966. Leonard Stein, *The Balfour Declaration* London 1961, and H. F. Frischwasser-Ra'anan, *Frontiers of a nation*, London

1955, are both relevant to the development of the Palestine problem. For the post-war period, Arnold J. Toynbee, *Survey of international affairs 1925*, Vol. I, *The Islamic world*, London 1927, is still important. Developments in Syria are dealt with in Zeine N. Zeine, *The struggle for Arab independence*, Beirut 1960, and S. H. Longrigg, *Syria and Lebanon under French mandate*, London 1958. The history of Iraq forms the subject of S. H. Longrigg, *Iraq, 1900 to 1950*, London 1953, and P. W. Ireland, *Iraq, a study in political development*, London 1937.

G. CULTURAL CONSEQUENCES OF THE IMPACT OF THE WEST

The cultural aspects of the impact of European power on the Ottoman Empire and its Arab territories have recently been investigated by several writers. The whole field is surveyed by Bernard Lewis, *The Middle East and the West*, London 1964. The development of Western-type education in Egypt is described in detail by J. Heyworth-Dunne, *An introduction to the history of education in Egypt*, London 1939. The reaction of Islam to the culture of the West is examined by H. A. R. Gibb, *Modern trends in Islam*, Chicago 1947; an earlier and more limited, but useful, work is C. C. Adams, *Islam and modernism in Egypt*, London 1933. A general study of the development of political thought is provided by Albert Hourani, *Arabic thought in the liberal age, 1798–1939*, London 1962. For the history of political ideas in Egypt, see J. M. Ahmed, *The intellectual origins of Egyptian nationalism*, London 1960, and Nadav Safran, *Egypt in search of political community*, Cambridge (Mass.) 1961. Early accounts of the development of nationalism appear in two books by Hans Kohn, *A history of nationalism in the east*, London 1929, and *Nationalism and imperialism in the Hither East*, London 1932. A selection of documents with a critical and historical introduction is provided by Sylvia G. Haim (ed.), *Arab nationalism, an anthology*, Berkeley and Los Angeles 1962. There are some important studies in two works by G. E. Von Grunebaum, *Islam: essays in the nature and growth of a cultural tradition*, London 1955, and *Modern Islam: the search for cultural identity*, Berkeley and Los Angeles 1962.

H. PERIODICALS

A close acquaintance with the periodical literature is indispensable to the study of this period of Arab history. The use of such material has been immensely facilitated by the publication of J. D. Pearson, *Index Islamicus, 1906–1955*, Cambridge 1958, and its *Supplement, 1956–1960*, Cambridge 1962. Further supplementary volumes are expected in due course. The work forms a comprehensive guide to articles in learned journals, contributions to *Festschriften* and similar collective publications. While there is no periodical specifically devoted to the historical field surveyed in the present book, relevant articles may be found from time to time in the following among others: *Bulletin of the School of Oriental and African Studies*, London; *Journal of the Economic and Social History of the Orient*, Leiden; *Journal of the Royal Asiatic Society*, London; *Middle East Journal*, Washington (D.C.); *Middle Eastern Studies*, London; *Orient*, Paris. Many of the European works listed earlier in this bibliography are the subjects of critical reviews in these periodicals. There are also some important articles in the series of *St Antony's Papers: Middle Eastern Affairs*, London, of which four issues have so far appeared, in 1958, 1961, 1963 and 1965.

Index

Abadan, 262
Abaza Ḥasan Pasha, 105
ʿAbbās I, Shah, 57, 118, 137–8, 145
ʿAbbās Ḥilmī I, 190, 193–6, 199, 202, 205–6, 208
ʿAbbās Ḥilmī II, Khedive, 216, 220–2, 224–7, 229, 258, 262, 294
ʿAbbās Mīrzā, 248
ʿAbbasids, 2, 12–16, 18–19, 40, 49, 56, 70, 257
ʿAbd al-ʿĀl Ḥilmī, 212–13
ʿAbd al-ʿAzīz I, Amīr, 152–3
ʿAbd al-ʿAzīz II ibn Saʿūd, King, 286, 292
ʿAbd al-Dā'im ibn Baqar, 50
ʿAbd al-Jalīl, 148
ʿAbd al-Khāliq Tharwat Pasha, *see* Tharwat, ʿAbd al-Khāliq, Pasha
ʿAbd al-Malik, Caliph, 12
ʿAbd al-Qādir al-Jazā'irī, Amīr, 241, 277
ʿAbd al-Raḥmān III, Caliph, 14
ʿAbd al-Raḥmān al-Jaylānī, Naqīb, 287
ʿAbd al-Raḥmān al-Kawākibī, *see* al-Kawākibī, ʿAbd al-Raḥmān
ʿAbd al-Raḥmān al-Qāzdughlī, Kâhya, 93–4
ʿAbd al-Raḥmān al-Rashīd, Sultan, 181 n.
ʿAbdallāb, 53
ʿAbdallāh Pasha, 184–5, 234, 245
ʿAbdallāh al-ʿAẓm, Pasha, 103 n., 154
ʿAbdallāh ibn Ḥusayn, King, 264, 284, 288–92
ʿAbdallāh Jammāʿ, 53
ʿAbdallāh ibn Muḥammad Qanbar, 137
ʿAbdallāh ibn Saʿūd, Amīr, 180
ʿAbduh, Muḥammad, Shaykh, 155, 205n.
Abdülaziz, Sultan, 173, 196, 204
Abdülhamid II, Sultan, 171–4, 224, 252–3, 257–9, 261
Abdülmejid, Sultan, 171, 186–7
Abū Bakr al-Ṣiddīq, Caliph, 9–10, 108
Abu'l-Dhahab, *see* Muḥammad Abu'l-Dhahab, Bey.
Abū Ḥanīfa, 56
Abu'l-Hudā al-Sayyādī, 257
Abu'l-Lamʿ family, 121–3, 237, 240
Abū Qīr, 157–9, 177
Abyssinia, 53–4, 203 n., 208; *see also* Ḥabesh
Abyssinian war (1875–6), 212
Acre, 6, 97, 99, 124–9, 131, 158, 184–5, 187, 232–4, 236, 239, 243, 270, 272
Adana, 105, 110, 186, 265
Aden, 52, 55, 265, 268
ʿĀdila, 146
ʿAdlī Yegen Pasha, 295, 297–8
Administrative Council (Baghdād), 250
Adrianople, *see* Edirne
Advisory Council (Egypt), 190n., 204
al-Afghānī, Jamāl al-Dīn, 212, 256–7
Afghans, 143–44
Afranj Aḥmad, 88–9
Afrāsiyāb, 134, 138, 140, 142
Africa, 9, 11, 53, 67, 181 n., 187, 193, 205–7, 258; North Africa, 10, 13–14, 170, 173
Afshārs, 144
al-ʿAhd, *see* Covenant society
Aḥmad Pasha, 144–6
Aḥmad ibn Afrāsiyāb, 141
Aḥmad al-Badawī, 75, 95
Aḥmad the Bosniak, Bey, 82–5
Aḥmad al-Dinkizlī, 126–8
Aḥmad Fu'ād, *see* Fu'ād I, King
Aḥmad al-Jazzār, Pasha, 95, 123–4, 127, 129–32, 157–8, 231–3, 245